# THE SENATE SYNDROME

THE JULIAN J. ROTHBAUM DISTINGUISHED LECTURE SERIES

# THE SENATE SYNDROME

## The Evolution of Procedural Warfare in the Modern U.S. Senate

STEVEN S. SMITH

UNIVERSITY OF OKLAHOMA PRESS : NORMAN

**Library of Congress Cataloging-in-Publication Data**

Smith, Steven S., 1953–
The Senate syndrome : the evolution of procedural warfare in the modern U.S. Senate / Steven S. Smith.
pages cm — (Julian J. Rothbaum distinguished lecture series ; v. 12)
Includes bibliographical references and index.
ISBN 978-0-8061-4439-9 (hardcover : alk. paper) 1. United States. Congress. Senate—History. 2. United States. Congress. Senate—Reform. 3. Legislation—United States. 4. Political parties—United States. 5. United States—Politics and government. I. Title.
JK1161.S65 2014
328.73'077—dc23

2013038472

*The Senate Syndrome: The Evolution of Procedural Warfare in the Modern U.S. Senate* is Volume 12 in The Julian J. Rothbaum Distinguished Lecture Series.

The paper in this book meets the guidelines for permanence and durability of the Committee on Production Guidelines for Book Longevity of the Council on Library Resources, Inc. ∞



1 2 3 4 5 6 7 8 9 10

# CONTENTS


List of Figures vii
List of Tables ix
Foreword, by Carl B. Albert xi
Acknowledgments xiii

Introduction 1
1. The Senate Syndrome 15

Part I. Emergence of the Senate Syndrome
2. The Procedural Condition of the Senate in the 1950s 49
3. The Rise of Individualism, 1961–1976 77
4. The Intensification of Individualism and Obstructionism, 1977–1988 120
5. Rising Partisanship, 1989–2004 163
6. The Emergence of the Senate Syndrome, 2005–2012 209
7. Reform by Ruling, 2013 251

Part II. Implications of the Senate Syndrome
8. Controversies about Senate Practice 269
9. The Media, the Public, and Accountability 289
10. The Implications of Reform-by-Ruling 312
11. The Senate Syndrome and Reform 332

Notes 363
References 373
Index 391

# FIGURES


1.1. Number of Cloture Petitions, by Disposition, 1961–2010 19
1.2. Percentage of Key-Vote Measures Subject to Cloture Petitions, 1961–2010 20
1.3. Number of Actual and Predicted Cloture Motions Filed, 1917–2010 36
1.4. Workload Indicators, 1961–2010 38
2.1. Percentage of All Votes on Which the Conservative Coalition Appeared, 1925–2010 51
3.1. Party Sizes as Percentage of Senate, 1951–2012 79
3.2. Number of Southern Senators, 1951–2012 79
3.3. Percentage of Senators' Votes Correctly Predicted Using One or Two Dimensions, 1947–2010 81
3.4. Distribution of Senators on Liberal-Conservative and Civil Rights Dimensions, by Party and Region, 89th Congress (1965–1966) 82
3.5. Distribution of Senators on the Liberal-Conservative Dimension, by Party and Region, 100th Congress (1987–1988) 84
3.6. Number of Cloture Petitions, 1961–2010 98
3.7. Number of Motions to Table Amendments That Received Roll-Call Votes, 1949–2010 103
3.8. Distribution of Vote Margins for Amendment Votes and Motions to Table Amendment Votes, 1969–1976 106
5.1. Liberal-Conservative Distribution, by Party, Selected Congresses, 1961–2010 165
5.2. Number of Hold Requests Received by Republican Leader Bob Dole, by Type, 1985–1996 172

5.3. Example of a Senate Amendment Tree 181
5.4. Number of Amendments to Budget Resolutions, by Disposition, 1982–2010 195
5.5. Mean Number of Days between Nomination and Confirmation, Federal Court Nominees, 1947–2010 197
5.6. Number of Public Laws Enacted and Measures in Conference, 1963–2010 204
6.1. Liberal-Conservative Scores, by Party, 1951–2010 214
6.2. Number of Appropriations Bills, by Disposition, 1961–2009 232
6.3. House and Senate Action on Appropriations Bills by Beginning of Fiscal Year, 2001–2011 234
8.1. Party and Senate Means, Liberal-Conservative Dimension, 1961–2010 273
8.2. Decision Thresholds and Party Size, 1961–2009 275
9.1. Responses to Majority Pass and Minority Block Questions (Group 1), in Percentages 303

# TABLES


I.1 Major Developments in Senate Procedure, 1949–2013, by Chapter 10–13
1.1. Estimates of the Effects of Partisan Alignments, Party Size, Time Constraints, and Sessions on the Number of Filibusters and Cloture Petitions (Poisson regression) 35
2.1. Provisions of Senate Unanimous Consent Agreements (UCAs), 1935–2000 62–63
8.1. Disposition of Cloture Petitions, 1961–2010 (in percentages) 276
8.2. Vote Outcomes on Cloture Petitions, 1961–2010 (in percentages) 277
8.3. Estimates of the Effects of Reform, Majority Party Size, and Majority Party Cohesiveness on Cloture Motion Adoption, 1961–2010 278
9.1. Public Knowledge of Senate Procedure, 2009 (in percentages) 294
9.2. Public Knowledge of Senate Procedure, 2012 (in percentages) 296
9.3. Group Treatments in Survey Experiment, 2012 300
9.4. Mean Responses to Majority Rule and Minority Rights Questions, by Treatment Group (5-point scale) 301
9.5. Mean Responses to Majority Rule and Minority Rights Questions, by House-Senate Treatment Groups (5-point scale) 304
9.6. Percentage of Votes in Interest Group Scales That Are Cloture Votes, 2007–2009 310

11.1. Cloture Reform Proposals, 112th Congress (2011–2012) 342–344

# FOREWORD

AMONG THE MANY GOOD THINGS that have happened to me in my life, there is none in which I take more pride than the establishment of the Carl Albert Congressional Research and Studies Center at the University of Oklahoma, and none in which I take more satisfaction than the Center's presentation of the Julian J. Rothbaum Distinguished Lecture Series. The series is a perpetually endowed program of the University of Oklahoma, created in honor of Julian J. Rothbaum by his wife, Irene, and son, Joel Jankowsky.

Julian J. Rothbaum, my close friend since our childhood days in southeastern Oklahoma, has long been a leader in Oklahoma in civic affairs. He served as a Regent of the University of Oklahoma for two terms and as a State Regent for Higher Education. In 1974 he was awarded the University's highest honor, the Distinguished Service Citation, and in 1986 he was inducted into the Oklahoma Hall of Fame.

The Rothbaum Lecture Series is devoted to the themes of representative government, democracy and education, and citizen participation in public affairs, values to which Julian J. Rothbaum was committed throughout his life. His lifelong dedication to the University of Oklahoma, the state, and his country is a tribute to the ideals to which the Rothbaum Lecture Series is dedicated. The books in the series make an enduring contribution to an understanding of American democracy.

Carl B. Albert
*Forty-sixth Speaker of the*
*United States House of Representatives*

# ACKNOWLEDGMENTS

THIS BOOK FOLLOWS MY 2011 Julian J. Rothbaum Distinguished Lecture in Representative Government, which is sponsored by the Carl Albert Center of the University of Oklahoma. My friends at the center—Cindy Rosenthal, Ron Peters, Glen Krutz, and LaDonna Sullivan—provide a service to the political science profession, to the university, and to the nation that is unmatched. Joel Jankowsky's friendship—for me, for the Carl Albert Center, and for the University of Oklahoma—deserves special mention. His commitment to public service is a model for us all. Byron Price, Chuck Rankin, and Jay Dew at the University of Oklahoma Press have been amazing partners in moving this manuscript to publication.

Sarah Binder and Gerald Gamm have been my long-term collaborators in thinking and writing about the Senate and continue to motivate my work. Rick Beth, Forrest Maltzman, Tony Madonna, Ian Ostrander, Hong Min Park, Christopher Pope, Jason Roberts, Elizabeth Rybicki, and Ryan Vander Wielen encouraged, informed, and assisted me in many ways. My colleagues at the Weidenbaum Center—Murray Weidenbaum, Steve Fazzari, Dick Mahoney, Melinda Warren, Gloria Lucy, Chris Moseley, and Alana Bame—made everything related to this project possible. Patrick Tucker, Stephanie Budrus, Adam Caplan, Chelsey Erway, Austin Kim, Mark Plattner, and Michele Shapiro provided superb research assistance. My colleagues Larry Evans, Burdette Loomis, and Barbara Sinclair, along with anonymous reviewers, offered very useful advice on the project and helped me improve the manuscript in many ways.

My children, Tyler and Shannon, inspire me with their passion for life, brilliance, and good humor. I will be forever grateful for their love.

I thank all of you.

# INTRODUCTION

ON NOVEMBER 21, 2013, the United States Senate changed. Using a procedure called the "nuclear option," Democratic majority leader Harry Reid (D-NV) made a point of order that the Senate can close debate on the consideration of a presidential nomination, other than to the Supreme Court, by a simple majority vote. Because Reid's point of order was inconsistent with Senate Rule XXII, the cloture rule that requires a three-fifths majority of all senators to close debate, the presiding officer ruled against Reid's point of order. Then, by a 48–52 vote, the Senate failed to sustain the ruling, thereby adopting the precedent that Reid requested. In a few minutes, the Senate had overturned a practice, over two hundred years old, that allowed a minority of senators to prevent a vote on nominations.

Republicans, and one prominent Democrat, Carl Levin (D-MI), protested that the Senate had changed in fundamental ways. An important minority right, the ability to block or delay action on presidential nominations, had been swept away. Moreover, the reform-by-ruling procedure used to establish the new precedent improperly circumvented the standing rule of the Senate that requires a two-thirds majority to close debate on a measure to change the rules. The Democratic leader, they argued, had turned the Senate into a second House of Representatives; in the House a majority can freely alter the rules governing debate to suit its convenience. The procedure would surely be used again and again. The Senate would never be the same.

Reid and most Democrats insisted that they were responding to unrelenting and unprecedented obstruction of presidential nominations by the minority Republicans. They pointed to Republicans' repeated violation of promises to reduce partisan obstructionism, which, they contended, had already altered the character of Senate decision making. Forcing a change in Senate procedure through a majority-backed precedent, they argued, would restore normalcy to Senate action on nominations. It would send a message that there was a limit to the majority's tolerance of the all-out minority obstructionism that the Democrats had endured for years.

My purpose in this book is to explain how the Senate arrived at this point and what it means for the Senate as a policy-making body. Senators of both parties believe that the Senate is broken and dysfunctional; many outsiders do as well. What they mean is that senators' use of inherited parliamentary rules and practices has undermined their role as senators and harmed the role of the Senate as a national policy-making institution. This is an important story—about how an important institution has evolved in recent decades and about how America is governed.

The U.S. Senate has a special place in American policy making. Its members embody the federal character of American governance by representing states, have a role in the appointment of judges and executive branch officials and in ratifying treaties, serve terms longer than those of representatives and presidents, and enjoy visibility in the nation and their home states that is unmatched by most representatives and judges. Along with the Senate's relatively small size and the continuity associated with its staggered terms of office, these features facilitate creativity, collaboration, and risk-taking. During much of its history, the Senate has achieved distinction for promoting new policy ideas, striking key compromises among competing interests, and generating presidential candidates.

The Senate of the last quarter century does not look much like that. The institution's characteristic individualism, long enabled by its informal, accommodative, civil, and flexible procedural environment, has given way to ill-mannered outbursts, policy stalemate, and procedural warfare motivated by deep partisan divisions. Senators recognize that their institution has changed and complain about it with some frequency. Many of them blame the other party's policy extremism and procedural abuses for the institution's problems. While the partisanship originates outside the Senate and is brought into the institution by elected senators, the Senate's procedural heritage makes that partisanship debilitating.

The procedural warfare of the modern Senate has taken the form of minority obstructionism and a majority response to control floor proceedings. Obstruction comes in the form of filibusters, threatened filibusters, or simple objections to the common unanimous consent requests to move legislation and nominations to a vote. A filibuster is a refusal to allow a matter to come to a vote, often by demonstrating a willingness to endlessly debate the issue. Obstruction, once uncommon and newsworthy, has become a standard feature of minority party parliamentary strategy and is so routine that it seldom warrants journalistic attention. The majority party has responded by looking for procedural shortcuts, limiting minority amendments, and more carefully managing time, all of which has changed the way the Senate does business.

The combination of minority-motivated obstruction and majority-imposed restrictions has created a pattern of behavior that I call the Senate syndrome. This syndrome has blossomed in the last two decades, but it has origins deeper in Senate history. Explaining its emergence and consequences is my challenge in this book.

## VETO PLAYERS IN AMERICAN GOVERNANCE

Constitutions, laws, institutional rules, and informal norms create sources of positive and negative power for political actors. Sources of positive power involve the assignment of authority to act and resources that make someone or a group capable of acting. Sources of negative power involve the ability to block action that others want to pursue. To political scientists, an actor who can block action is known as a veto player. American national government, with three branches and a bicameral legislature, is notable for the way positive power is shared and for the large number of veto players. Positive power is shared among several institutions. To enact legislation, a simple majority of the House and Senate, along with the president, must approve the legislation, unless, in the event of a presidential veto, a two-thirds majority can be mustered in both houses of Congress. The House and Senate can effectively veto legislation by withholding majority support. And the Supreme Court can veto legislation on constitutional or other grounds as it deems necessary. Every student of American government knows that much.

The Senate has added a potentially important complication. Due to the absence in its rules of a limit on debate for most legislation, the Senate allows a senator to speak without a time limit on most matters. By taking turns, a team of senators can hold the floor indefinitely. Typically, the Senate manages to deal with the uncertainties of unlimited debate through unanimous consent agreements that lend some order to floor proceedings. In fact, a central function of the majority leader, working with bill managers, is to negotiate such agreements. An individual senator may refuse consent to a request to limit debate. Ending debate without unanimous consent requires the adoption of a cloture motion. Under the Senate's Rule XXII, a three-fifths majority of all elected senators is required to pass a cloture motion, except on a measure to amend the rules, which requires a two-thirds majority of voting senators. The effect of these cloture thresholds is to make it more difficult for a majority to exercise positive power and easier for the minority to exercise negative power. In fact, with a few exceptions, a minority of at least 41 senators can withhold permission for the Senate to conclude debate and vote on a matter.

A long debate conducted for the purpose of preventing a vote is called a "filibuster" in Senate parlance. The term was first used in Congress in the mid-nineteenth century to describe protracted debate intended to prevent voting on a motion or measure. The term was used at the time to describe military adventurers and pirates operating in the Caribbean and other places. It came to be used more generally to describe efforts to obstruct legislative action on legislation, nominations, and treaties, although the term is most commonly associated with marathon speeches by a minority of senators that are intended to delay or prevent a vote that they would likely lose.

The Framers of the Constitution did not create the filibuster. The Constitution requires a two-thirds majority for taking a few specified actions (the override of a presidential veto, ratification of treaties, impeachment, expulsion of a senator, or approval of a constitutional amendment or convention), which gives a sizable minority the ability to prevent the Senate (and, in some cases, the House) from acting. On other matters, including the passage of legislation and confirmation of presidential nominations to executive and judicial positions, the Constitution is silent on the number of votes required and is taken to imply that decisions are made by simple-majority vote. How the House and Senate structure the decision-making process to get a measure to a vote is subject to the rules adopted by each house. The ability of a Senate minority to block action on legislation or nomination with a filibuster and the "supermajority" threshold for cloture are products of rules adopted by the Senate. Effectively, through its own rulemaking power, the Senate has made it possible for a large minority to block a majority by preventing a vote, in essence granting a veto power to the minority.

A central theme of this book is the large and unanticipated increase in the Senate minority's use of extraconstitutional veto power in recent decades. The minority party leadership even refers to the institution as the "60-vote Senate," which reflects the new behavior and expectations that have emerged in the last quarter century. The majority party has been deeply frustrated by these developments and has made countermoves of its own, setting off cycles of procedural maneuvers that have escalated the use and abuse of the Senate's parliamentary rules.

## GRAPPLING WITH THE SENATE SYNDROME

I am writing this introduction in late 2013, just after the majority party Democrats acted to limit filibusters on presidential nominations. At the start of 2013, as the 113th Congress opened for business, the Senate adopted modest procedural reforms to mitigate the effects of minority obstructionism and the majority's response. The reforms adopted in early 2013 would seem quite modest to most Americans: limiting the number of times that any one bill can be filibustered without eliminating the opportunity to filibuster, and limiting the time to debate a motion to take up a bill or to debate a minor nomination. The minority Republicans went along with the reforms because they were guaranteed opportunities to offer amendments in return. The most important changes were temporary, good only for the 113th Congress (2013–2014), unless renewed by the Senate.

If the Senate observed the terms of Rule XXII, which requires a two-thirds majority for closing debate on a measure to amend the standing rules, a minority party could easily block a majority party's reform proposals. In 2013, Democrats anticipated this and seemed prepared to proceed in a different way. In a manner consistent with an opinion offered by Vice President Richard Nixon in 1957 and reinforced by reformers' arguments since then, leading reformers planned to make a point of order that the Constitution's Article I, Section 5, implies that a simple majority is empowered to acquire a vote on the rules at the beginning of a Congress. If adopted by a simple majority, this point of order would create a path that would allow a simple majority to act on reform. The reference to constitutional authority led reformers to use the term "constitutional option," which was invented a decade earlier by Republicans upset with an obstructive Democratic minority.

Two factors that encouraged Democratic reformers as the new Congress convened deserve emphasis. First, Harry Reid, the Senate majority leader, seemed to come around to the procedural strategy that reformers advocated. Like many floor leaders, Reid had taken a very cautious approach to reform. He resisted demands for a reform-by-ruling move at the start of the 212th Congress in 2011 and instead negotiated an agreement with Republican leader Mitch McConnell to reduce partisan tensions over floor procedure. By the fall of 2011, Reid declared the agreement a dead letter and in mid-2012 indicated sympathy for the approach advocated by reformers within his party.

Second, the surprising outcome of the 2012 Senate elections, which increased the Democrats' majority from 53 to 55 seats, and the reelection of Democratic president Barack Obama encouraged the majority party to act on its agenda in the 113th Congress. To be sure, the Senate Democrats would confront a Republican majority in the House of Representatives, but the Democrats expected to lose seats in the 2014 elections and to suffer a loss of presidential influence in Obama's last two years in office during the next Congress. Liberals wanted to maximize their leverage in the 113th Congress, and 55 votes would not get them very far under the inherited rules and practices of the Senate.

The reformers were disappointed with the outcome. Reid backed away from his commitment to the full range of proposals that reformers in his party had developed and negotiated a more modest set of changes that were acceptable to McConnell and most Republicans. Contrary to Reid's and the reformers' public claims, they may not have had a majority for the constitutional option even if they had majority support for their reform proposals. Moreover, Reid indicated that he was not keen to take steps that might lead to simple-majority rule in the Senate, which was considered a reversal of position by many liberals. With the adoption of a compromise endorsed by Reid and McConnell, the issue was defused for the time being.

In a few months, Reid was threatening stronger reforms. In the summer of 2013, Republicans blocked action on seven presidential nominations to executive branch posts. Reid charged that McConnell and the Republicans had reneged on a commitment to reserve the filibuster of nominations for extraordinary cases. With what appeared to be the backing of most Democrats, Reid threatened to use the reform-by-ruling approach—the nuclear option—to force action on executive branch nominations if the Republicans did not back down. McConnell, pushed by some of his party colleagues to avoid a showdown with Reid, relented. The nominations were allowed to come to a vote.

Although a crisis was averted on executive branch nominations in midsummer, Republicans immediately showed signs that they would block action on nominations to the U.S. Court of Appeals for the District of Columbia circuit, usually considered the second most important court. The D.C. circuit, a court with eleven judges, had three open judgeships, and the other eight were evenly divided between appointees of Democratic and Republican presidents. By mid-November, Republicans were refusing to allow votes on three nominations to the D.C. circuit court. Reid had reissued his threats of forcing approval of a new precedent on cloture for nominations, but Republicans did not back down.

After cloture motions on all three nominations failed, Reid took just two days to bring a motion to reconsider the first of the three cloture votes, an action that gave him the opportunity to make his point of order that a simple majority can invoke cloture on executive and judicial branch nominations, except for nomination to the Supreme Court. He had managed to persuade a handful of Democrats who had previously been reluctant to use the reform-by-ruling approach and mustered a 52-vote majority for his position.

The new precedent of 2013 was one of the most important procedural developments in Senate history. The new threshold reshaped the strategic calculations of presidents and senators involved in the nomination and confirmation process. The reform-by-ruling approach to establishing a new procedure had been used before, but the approach had never been used to directly and explicitly undermine Rule XXII.

The Senate changed itself in a significant way. At this writing, senators and outsiders are still speculating about the implications of the 2013 precedent. Would the minority be tamed by the experience, or would it retaliate with more obstructionism on other matters? Would future Senate majorities use the reform-by-ruling technique to circumvent Rule XXII and acquire other changes in the rules that sizable minorities oppose?

This book is designed to set these developments in proper historical context. The procedural tendencies of the Senate are being taken now to greater extremes than at any time in the institution's history. I call them a syndrome because they involve the emergence of several behaviors that combine to make the Senate's decision-making process much different from what it has been during most of its history. These behaviors include the greater frequency of minority obstruction, more concerted efforts by the majority to limit amending activity and circumvent the floor, the invention of new parliamentary strategies, quicker resort to last-resort tactics, and an enhanced role for party leaders in coordinating and implementing these strategies. An "obstruct and restrict" pattern has dominated the Senate in recent Congresses—obstructive strategies by the minority are met by majority strategies to limit debate and amendment. "Regular order" evaporates and the Senate, known historically for its informality, is tied up in parliamentary procedure.

## ORGANIZATION OF THE BOOK

The book has two parts. Part I details the Senate's path of procedural warfare and development. For some readers, Part I will be tedious history. I hope that most readers recognize the importance of getting the Senate's modern history right. Senators often misuse that history in their arguments about their institution, so an independent view of the historical record is essential. More important, only by appreciating the path that Senate procedural warfare has taken over recent decades can we understand the procedural warfare in which senators have been engaged in recent years. Step by step, senators, while pursuing their individual, factional, and partisan interests in the context of inherited parliamentary practices, have brought the Senate syndrome to its full manifestation in recent years.

The major developments outlined in Part I are listed in table I.1. Senate rules are not adjusted to suit the needs of the majority party every two years, as they are in the House. Typically, many years pass before a significant change in the Senate's cloture rule takes place. Nevertheless, tensions over the way the Senate conducts its business yield a regular flow of procedural innovations, most of which take the form of tactical changes by senators in the midst of legislative battles without changes in

**Table I.1.** Major Developments in Senate Procedure, 1949–2013, by Chapter

| | | | |
|---|---|---|---|
| Introduction | 1890–1910s | floor leaders | emergence of modern floor leadership positions |
| | 1914 | Rule XII amended | modern use of unanimous consent agreements established |
| | 1917 | Rule XXII adopted | cloture rule adopted: two-thirds of senators present and voting may invoke cloture |
| | 1937 | ruling on first recognition | vice president announces practice of recognizing the majority leader to speak or make a motion whenever the leader and another senator seek recognition simultaneously |
| Chapter 1 | 1948 | ruling on procedural motions | presiding officer offers opinion that cloture does not apply to procedural motions |
| | 1949 | overturning ruling on procedural motions | Senate overturns vice president's ruling and votes to prohibit the application of cloture to procedural motions |
| | 1949 | Rule XXII amended | cloture threshold raised to two-thirds of elected senators<br>cloture applied to procedural motions, except for motions to consider a change in Senate rules |
| | 1957 | vice president's opinion on simple-majority cloture on the rules | Vice President Nixon offers opinion that a simple majority may invoke cloture on a change in the rules, at least at the start of a Congress |
| | 1959 | Rule XXII amended | cloture threshold lowered to two-thirds of senators voting<br>cloture may be applied to motions to consider a change in Senate rules |

| | | | |
|---|---|---|---|
| Chapter 2 | 1970s | expanded use of the filibuster | more frequent use of holds, invention of tracking, new provisions in unanimous consent agreements |
| | 1974 | Budget Act enacted | budget and reconciliation measures created<br>debate limits for budget and reconciliation imposed |
| | 1975 | Rule XXII amended | cloture threshold lowered to three-fifths of elected senators<br>cloture threshold of two-thirds of senators voting retained for motions related to measures on Senate rules |
| Chapter 3 | 1977 | ruling on dilatory motions in post-cloture debate | Senate upholds vice president's ruling that the presiding officer must take the initiative to rule out of order dilatory amendments and motions |
| | 1979 | Rule XXII amended | limits post-cloture debate to 100 hours, including time on votes and quorum calls<br>allows three-fifths of senators to extend the 100-hour period of post-cloture debate<br>prohibits a senator from offering two amendments until every senator has had an opportunity to offer one<br>guarantees 10 minutes of debate for every senator who has not spoken before the debate limit is reached<br>clarifies that amendments must be submitted by a certain hour after cloture motion is filed |
| | 1985 | Byrd rule | rule barring extraneous matter in reconciliation bills first adopted |
| | 1986 | Rule XXII amended | post-cloture debate limited to 30 hours<br>motion to approve the Senate *Journal* is made nondebatable |

*(continued)*

**Table I.1.** Major Developments in Senate Procedure, 1949–2013, by Chapter, *conintued*

| | | | |
|---|---|---|---|
| Chapter 4 | 1992–1994 | Joint Committee on the Organization of Congress | no change in Senate rules adopted |
| | 1990s | new and expanded use of procedural tactics | side-by-side amendments<br>filling the amendment tree<br>reconciliation process for tax measures<br>omnibus appropriations<br>avoiding conference<br>the nuclear option |
| Chapter 5 | 2005 | nuclear option threat | Gang of 14 acts to prevent the nuclear option from being pursued |
| | 2005 | 60-vote threshold | the 60-vote threshold for amendments and motions becomes common in unanimous consent agreements |
| | 2007, 2011 | rules on holds adopted | rules requiring the disclosure of senator placing a hold |
| | 2007–2012 | more explicit use of the "Thurmond Rule" | obstruction to confirmation of judicial nominees late in a presidential term |
| | 2011 | informal Reid-McConnell agreement | the minority leader would only rarely filibuster a motion to proceed<br>the minority leader would support a rule to ban secret holds<br>the majority leader would protect the minority's opportunities to offer amendments<br>both leaders agree to avoid the nuclear option in the 112th and 113th Congresses |

| | | | |
|---|---|---|---|
| Chapter 5 *continued* | 2011 | precedent on use of suspension motion in post-cloture debate | Senate sustains a point of order that use of a motion to suspend the rules to consider a nongermane amendment in post-cloture debate is dilatory |
| | 2013 | Rule XXII and other rules amended | bars debate on a motion to proceed if the associated cloture motion is signed by the two floor leaders and seven senators of each party<br>combines the three motions to go to conference with the House (to disagree or insist, to request a conference, and to authorize the appointment of conferees) into one motion |
| | 2013 | standing order adopted for 113th Congress | limits debate to four hours on the motion to proceed<br>limits post-cloture debate to eight hours on lower-level executive branch positions and two hours on district court nominations |
| Chapter 6 | 2013 | precedent on cloture threshold for nominations | Senate supports a point of order that a simple majority is required to invoke cloture on executive and judicial branch nominations, except for nominations to the Supreme Court |

the standing rules. Part I details how these procedural fights, formal reforms, and informal adjustments have played out in recent decades.

Part II addresses important issues about Senate policy making and history. Does the cloture threshold matter? Which party has contributed most to the procedural entanglements of today's Senate? How do the media and the public contribute to the Senate's predicament? Does the filibuster undermine accountability? Does the existence of the reform-by-ruling strategy mean that Senate majorities, at least until late 2013, really have wanted supermajority rule for their institution? What reforms have been proposed? Who supports those reforms, and why? What are the conditions under which reform is most likely?

My answers to these questions flow from the observation that the Senate syndrome has changed the character of the Senate in fundamental ways. An institution that once encouraged creativity, cross-party collaboration, individual expression, and the incubation of new policy ideas has become gridlocked on legislation of modest importance. Not only has the role of individual senators in American policy making been sharply restrained, but the Senate as an institution has defaulted on much of its responsibility to pass necessary legislation and address the challenges facing the nation.

CHAPTER 1

# THE SENATE SYNDROME

CONDITIONS SEEMED RIPE FOR Senate filibuster reform in January 2013. As noted in the introduction, Democrats were as agitated as ever about Republican obstructionism. After increasing their numbers from 53 to 55 in the 2012 elections, reform-oriented Democrats thought that the start of the new Congress would be the ideal time to change the Senate's rules to reduce the ability of a minority to block votes on legislation and presidential nominations favored by the majority. Knowing that the minority would filibuster any change in the rules, the reformers plotted a procedural strategy—one considered revolutionary by the minority Republicans—to get a majority vote on a rules package. Known as the "nuclear option," or more tamely as the "constitutional option," the strategy involved persuading a majority of senators to back a point of order that the Constitution implies that a simple majority can get a vote on the rules at the start of a new Congress. Liberal groups organized lobbying efforts to pressure Democrats to pursue the strategy.

The minority party Republicans were frustrated, too. They complained about Democrats closing opportunities for senators to offer amendments, a move that, they claimed, encouraged them to obstruct the majority with more vigor. Republicans promised even more obstruction if Democrats pursued the nuclear option. They could refuse consent to every minor unanimous consent request, obstruct with demands for a quorum, conduct extended debate wherever allowed, and, in principle, make it very difficult to accomplish anything. This is "going nuclear" in a parliamentary body.

Over the previous few years, a handful of Democrats had developed a package of reform proposals that long-term reformers considered quite modest. The proposals included a limit on debate for the motion to take up a bill, a requirement that filibustering senators conduct debate or risk that debate would be ended by a simple majority, and a limit on debate for sending a bill to conference with the House of Representatives.[1] Related proposals included a requirement that 41 senators vote to continue debate (a change from the requirement that 60 senators vote to close debate) and that senators be barred from having objections to unanimous consent requests registered by another senator. The package was considered modest because it did not limit the ability of a large minority to block action on a bill, nomination, or amendment. The limited scope of the proposals seemed to reflect the authors' genuine preferences, but it also may have been necessary to acquire majority support.

The reform proposal appeared to have the backing of a sufficient number of Democrats to gain majority support, but the effort failed. At least a few Democrats refused to endorse the constitutional point of order required to get to a simple-majority vote over the objections of Republicans. They feared that the minority would follow through on threats to retaliate and make Senate life even worse. Critically, Majority Leader Harry Reid (D-NV) indicated that he did not support some of the reforms that his party's leading reformers advocated and preferred to negotiate a package with Minority Leader Mitch McConnell (R-KY).

The Reid-McConnell negotiations produced changes that a large majority of senators supported. The most important provisions—limiting debate to four hours on the motion to take up a bill and guaranteeing each party two amendments on a bill—applied only to the 113th Congress (2013–2014) and so became an experiment that is under way as this book is going to press. In addition, changes to the standing rules included ending post-cloture debate on a motion to proceed if cloture is endorsed by leaders of both parties and at least seven senators of each party, and reducing the opportunities to filibuster motions to go to conference with the House.[2] The reforms left untouched the minority's power to block action on a bill, nomination, House amendment, or conference report.

Reformers were disheartened that more fundamental and lasting changes were not made. Perhaps to gain leverage with Republicans, Reid claimed that he had a majority for exercising the constitutional option, and at least some reformers believed that he missed an opportunity to make more meaningful changes in the rules. But more than a few senators of both parties expressed a sense of relief that the Senate had avoided the abyss they predicted would follow exercise of the constitutional option. In the end, without Reid and a handful of other Democrats who followed his lead, reformers clearly lacked even a simple majority for the point of order required to pursue their strategy.

Predictably, Democrats' interest in reform did not end with the Reid-McConnell reforms. By May, Reid expressed frustration with Republicans' unwillingness to allow several presidential nominations to be considered on the floor and with their continued insistence on 60 votes to take up important legislation. Discussion of the nuclear option was renewed and, at this writing, remained a live possibility for many Democrats, including Reid.

## THE SENATE SYNDROME

The United States Senate is known for the stability of its rules, but the Senate exposed its procedural fragility in the early twenty-first century. The parliamentary arms race between the parties that unfolded in the previous two decades eventually brought the Senate to the brink of chaos in 2005. Tensions had been building for years—minority obstructionism motivated majority countermoves, generated partisan incrimination, and led to more obstruction and preemptive action. In the spring of 2005, the majority leader promised to change the application of the Senate's most distinctive rule, Rule XXII, by a ruling of the presiding officer, rather than suffer more delay in acting on several judicial nominations. The minority promised to retaliate by going nuclear—making the Senate ungovernable by obstructing nearly all Senate action—but a small group of senators negotiated an arrangement that allowed neither party to follow through on its threats.

While it did not go "nuclear" in 2005, the Senate spiraled into all-out "conventional" parliamentary warfare in the following years, which motivated the negotiated changes in the rules in 2013 (chapter 6). Over that period, minority obstruction intensified and majority leaders frequently took steps to restrict debate and amending activity. The result is a Senate, an institution historically distinguished for the flexibility and informality of its floor proceedings, that is more bound by formal rules and precedent and more frequently tied into parliamentary knots than at any time in its history. In today's Senate, each party assumes that the other party will fully exploit its procedural options: the majority party assumes that the minority party will obstruct legislation, and the minority assumes that the majority will restrict its opportunities to offer amendments. Leaders are expected to fully exploit the rules. Senators of both parties are frustrated by what has happened to their institution.

I call this "obstruct and restrict" pattern the Senate syndrome. It is not simply a matter of experiencing more filibusters or suffering under an irritable majority leader who is quick to file for cloture or block amendments. It is a combination of symptoms that have changed senators' expectations about how their colleagues will behave. It has changed the character of the Senate.

My purpose is to describe and explain the Senate syndrome. While some features of the Senate syndrome have appeared only in recent years, the syndrome did not emerge in an instant. It has a history, an important history, that stretches over many decades. In spite of pleas from senators for self-restraint, it is not likely to fade away soon.

I begin this chapter by addressing the fundamentals of how senators govern themselves. As with many legislative or parliamentary bodies, the Senate has a decision-making process that is guided by constitutional requirements but is given essential detail in rules, precedents, and practices of the senators' own making. These rules and practices affect policy outcomes, the role that senators and the Senate play in American governance, and the accountability of senators and their parties to the American people.

## THE LANDSCAPE

In recent decades, senators' strategies have changed in fundamental ways. I will detail these in the next few chapters, but we can start with figure 1.1, which provides an overview of the frequency with which cloture motions have been filed. Cloture motions are usually filed by the majority leader in response to a minority threat to prevent a vote on a bill or nomination. They have other purposes, such as barring nongermane amendments, but there is little doubt that a large increase in minority obstruction has driven the general pattern evident in the figure.

The pattern is reconfirmed when we look at major legislation, as in figure 1.2. In this figure, I take advantage of Congressional Quarterly's annual listing of "key votes," which are

**Figure 1.1.** Number of Cloture Petitions, by Disposition, 1961–2010

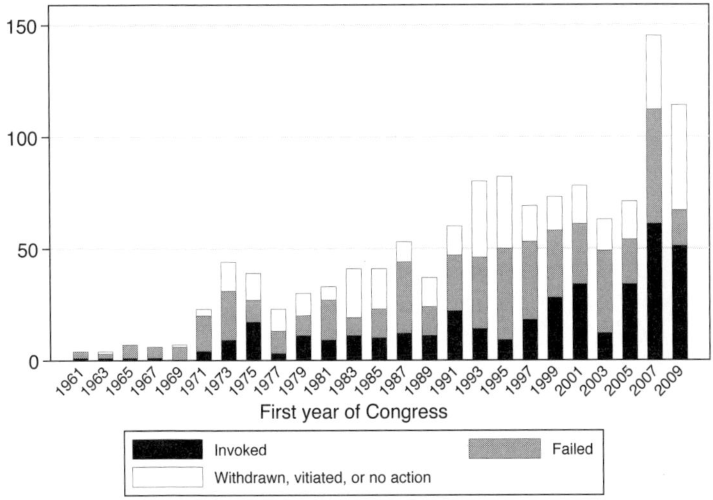

*Source:* www.senate.gov.

**Figure 1.2.** Percentage of Key-Vote Measures Subject to Cloture Petitions, 1961–2010

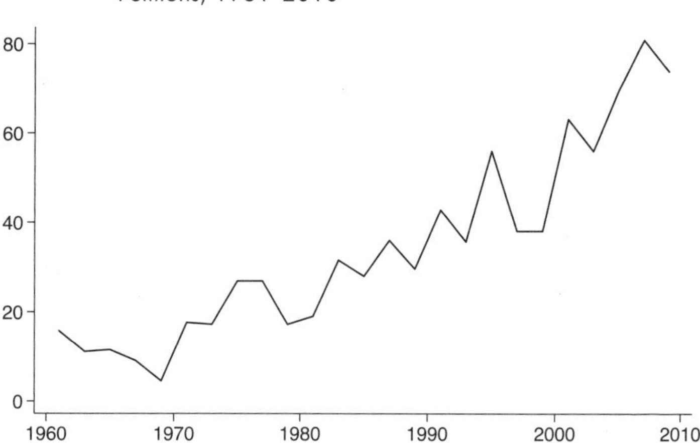


*Source:* www.senate.gov, Congressional Quarterly.

the 20 or so votes that are judged to be the most critical on the most important legislation, nominations, and treaties in each Congress. The figure shows that most major legislation in recent Congresses has been subject to a cloture motion (and some form of minority obstruction).

The pattern in figure 1.1 shows a step increase in cloture motions in the early 1970s, another in the 1990s, and yet another at the end of the first decade of the twenty-first century, after the Republicans lost majority control in the 2006 elections. The pattern of increasing obstruction is smoother for major measures, but the same general trend is evident.

The character of Senate policy making has changed in a fundamental way in recent decades. The trend in these figures is only the most conspicuous feature of the political record of obstruction and response that has created a Senate that is often tied into parliamentary knots, bound by the application of formal rules and precedents, impermeable to public scrutiny, and unable to meet the expectations of the vast majority of Americans.

## GOVERNING THE SENATE

How senators govern themselves is already an important subject to political scientists who study political institutions. Americans rarely give the subject much attention, but we should give it our attention now. To begin, we must understand where the Senate's procedural rules originate.

Senators determine most of the formal rules, precedents, and informal practices that govern their institution's policy-making process. At the start of any two-year Congress, senators inherit rules, precedents, and practices from previous Congresses, but they are empowered to accept or change features of their inheritance, subject to a few requirements of the U.S. Constitution. Remarkably, after 225 years, there remains genuine and deep disagreement among senators about how they can exercise their power to determine their own rules.

The Constitution provides only limited guidance to senators about how they should run their institution. The Constitution, of course, assigns two senators to each state, requires senators to be thirty years of age and citizens for at least nine years, and gives senators staggered, six-year terms. State-based representation, equal representation of states, and long, staggered terms have influenced the Senate's behavior in fundamental ways (Fenno 1982; Lee and Oppenheimer 1999).

The Constitution provides for a presiding officer. It makes the vice president of the United States the president of the Senate, who may vote only when the Senate is equally divided. As a result, the president of the Senate is not a senator and, in practice, is more closely connected with the president of the United States than to senators and their parties. The political separation of the Senate from its presiding officer has had a significant effect on the procedural development of the institution (Gamm and Smith 2000). In the House of Representatives, the speaker is both presiding officer and leader of the majority party, which has allowed the position to become powerful. The president of the Senate has only ministerial and ceremonial duties as presiding officer, although, on a few occasions, parliamentary rulings of the presiding officer have proven important.

The Constitution also provides that "the Senate shall chuse [*sic*] their other Officers, and also a President pro tempore, in the Absence of the Vice President, or when he shall exercise the Office of President of the United States." The informal norm of electing the most senior member of the majority party to be president pro tempore did not emerge until the mid-twentieth century. Previously, the Senate had often elected a president pro tempore who had proven skills in presiding without regard to seniority (Gamm and Smith 2000).

On procedural matters, the Constitution says little. It gives each senator one vote and requires the Senate to keep a journal of its proceedings. It provides that a two-thirds majority of voting senators is required to expel senators, ratify a treaty, convict an impeached federal official, override a presidential veto, or approve an amendment to the Constitution. Otherwise, the Constitution is silent on the decision rule, but both the House and Senate assume that a simple majority is implied to be the standard decision rule. As we will see, the implied decision rule remains a central feature of today's debates about reform of the Senate's rules.

Otherwise, senators are left to devise important details of their institution's formal rules. Nothing in the Constitution dictates how senators are to prepare legislation or other matters for a vote. Instead, Article I, Section 5, provides that "each house may determine the rules of its proceedings." Over the decades, the Senate has acquired forty-four standing rules, many of which have been amended several times.

## CHOOSING RULES

Most of the Senate's typical policy-making process is structured by the rules it has adopted. Senators set the rules that govern the Senate's agenda, parliamentary procedures, committee system, party privileges, relations with the House of Representatives, and the procedures by which they consider presidential nominations and treaties. The absence of detail in the Constitution about these aspects of Senate procedure created the opportunity for the Senate to adopt Rule XXII, which currently provides for a three-fifths majority to end debate on legislation and is central to the Senate syndrome.

The Senate's procedural rules do not start and end with the Constitution and its standing rules. As I outline in chapter 11, the Senate has allowed, even encouraged, limitations on floor debate and amendments in statutes. Many of these statutory rules were central features of major legislation. Moreover, points of order decided by the presiding officer or by a Senate majority added important interpretations to the standing rules. For example, the right of first recognition accorded to the majority leader, which gives the majority leader the opportunity to make a motion before other senators do, is a precedent that dates only to the 1930s and is now an essential feature of everyday Senate proceedings. The large body of precedents is reported in *Riddick's Senate Procedure: Precedents and Practices.*

As a matter of social science, explaining senators' choice of rules is a complicated matter (Binder 1997, 2006; Binder and Smith 1997, 1998; Schickler 2000). We might like to think that the "public interest" and abstract principles about good and fair rules guide these choices, but the public has diverse interests, and democratic rules come in many forms. In fact, a wide range of political considerations influence senators' choices about rules, including senators' personal and state interests, partisan and factional interests, and the Senate's institutional interests, all of which evolve over time.

The trade-off between majority rule and minority rights is a central feature of rules in all legislative bodies. Most legislative bodies achieve some balance between allowing a simple majority to decide a question and allowing the minority a right to participate in policy making in a meaningful way. Minority interests may be preserved in a variety of ways—a right to offer amendments, an opportunity to persuade legislators and win majority support through debate, a requirement for more than a simple majority to adopt important motions, or an election system that gives the minority a chance to become a majority. In many settings, charters or constitutions determine the mix of majority and minority advantages, but in some, like the houses of Congress, rules and laws put in place by legislators themselves shape majority rule and minority rights in vital ways.

In the Senate, the balance between majority rule and minority rights leans toward minority rights, but it is not a settled matter. Today's Senate has both a simple-majority decision rule for passing legislation and confirming nominees to executive and judicial posts, and a supermajority decision rule (cloture) to force an end to debate on legislation and nominations. On most matters, closing debate requires at least a three-fifths majority of all elected senators (whether they vote or not) on a cloture motion. Therefore, a minority of more than two-fifths of senators (whether they vote or not) can prevent an end to debate and prevent the Senate from moving to a vote.

A cohesive minority party able to block action has become the norm in the modern Senate. Since 1980, when the Republicans won a Senate majority for the first time since the early 1950s, the mean size of the minority party has been nearly 46. Only for half a year in 2009, after the seating of Senator Al Franken (D-MN) in July and before the special election of Republican Scott Brown (R-MA) in January 2010, did the majority party hold 60 seats—a three-fifths majority—in the Senate. Thus, for today's generation of senators, the ability of a minority party, if it is fairly cohesive, to obstruct a majority party is the normal state of affairs.

The current balance between majority rule and minority rights is the foundation of the Senate syndrome. It is controversial among senators and outsiders and has motivated a flurry of new reform proposals in recent years.

## EMERGENCE OF THE MODERN SENATE

The modern Senate has been molded by all of the salient features of American politics—the rise of political parties and their changing role in electing senators, the expanding role of the federal government in American life, hundreds of political battles, decades of rulemaking, and the natural emergence of informal practices among senators. The full story of Senate development is beyond the scope of this book, but several chapters of that story require a brief summary to place into perspective the developments of recent decades.

### *No Rule to Limit Debate until 1917*

In *Robert's Rules of Order,* the manual that guides the procedure for the business meetings of many organizations, adopting a motion on the previous question ("I move the previous question") closes debate and leads to a vote on the matter at hand. *Robert's Rules* was first published in 1876 as the *Pocket Manual of Rules of Order for Deliberative Assemblies* and was loosely modeled on the rules of the House of Representatives. The wide use of *Robert's Rules* made the previous-question motion the standard way to close debate on an issue in most American decision-making bodies. The motion on the previous question, or something similar to it, is essential to a majority that seeks to act on legislation.

The Senate was different and became a model for few other American organizations or national parliaments. The Senate adopted a variety of rules in the first Congress, between 1789 and 1806, when it codified its rules in a single document. The committee that consolidated the rules left out the motion on the previous question, but as far as we can determine, this omission was not deliberate. The senators most involved did not debate or argue it, and it may have been accidental (Binder 1997).

The absence of a motion on the previous question proved important. In the House, the previous-question motion acquired its modern use as a way for a majority to stop debate and get a vote in 1816 (Binder 1995). In the Senate, dropping the motion on the previous question meant that senators were without a motion to limit debate, even on a resolution to change the rules (Binder 1997). They could agree by unanimous consent to bring a matter to a vote, but, as a technical matter, debate would continue as long as a senator wanted to be recognized to speak. This allowed for the emergence of the practice of filibustering—conducting extended debate to prevent a vote on an issue—which proved important on anti-slavery and many other measures over the next century (Burdette 1940; Binder and Smith 1997). And the absence of a rule to limit debate meant that a filibuster could prevent a vote on a resolution to change the rules, including a resolution to create a rule to limit debate.

In 1917, in response to a filibuster by eleven senators of a bill to allow American merchant ships to be armed against German U-boats, President Woodrow Wilson advocated and the Senate adopted a cloture rule, Rule XXII(2). The new rule provided that cloture could be invoked on "any pending measure" by "two-thirds of those voting." Under the rule, an additional hour of debate for each senator was allowed once cloture was invoked, and only germane amendments could be considered during post-cloture debate. Intended to be airtight, the rule provided that after cloture is invoked, "no dilatory motion, or dilatory amendment" shall be in order, and points of order are to be decided without debate (*Congressional Record,* March 8, 1917, 19). It appears that a majority of senators favored simple-majority cloture, but there were objections that could not be readily overcome (in the absence of a cloture rule), and the compromise at two-thirds was readily approved (Binder and Smith 1997).

The rule was used to limit debate on the Treaty of Versailles in 1919 but was not used much in the following decades. Between 1917 and 1949, a period that included the New Deal and World War II, nineteen cloture motions were filed and only four were adopted. The other three times that cloture was invoked were in 1926 and 1927, when a Republican-controlled Senate wanted to gain action on prohibition, banking, and world court legislation. On eight occasions before 1949, a majority voted for cloture but fell short of the two-thirds majority required. I will pick up this story in chapter 2.

### *The Emergence of Floor Leaders at the Turn of the Twentieth Century*

In today's Senate, each party has more than a half dozen leadership positions. The two top leaders—majority leader and minority leader—are known as floor leaders. Each of them assumes the responsibility for overseeing the party organization, managing floor activity, handling public relations, finding the votes to support or oppose legislation, and serving as an intermediary with the House and president.

Remarkably, the Senate operated without the floor leadership positions for more than a century (Gamm and Smith 2009). The Democrats came to view Arthur Pue Gorman, who was their formally elected caucus chairman, as their floor leader in the 1890s, when the party was in the minority and successfully blocked action on several important Republican bills. When the Democrats became a majority party after the 1912 elections, their leader became known as the majority leader, and the minority Republicans soon copied their model.

Even after floor leaders were widely recognized, the modern role of a floor leader took time to develop. In 1927, the Democratic (minority) leader took the front-center desk on his party's side; the Republican leader finally took the complementary seat in 1937. More important, not until the 1930s did the Senate's presiding officer acknowledge the majority leader's right to be recognized if he and another senator seek recognition at the same time. The "right of first recognition," as it is known, gives the modern majority leader the opportunity to attempt to set the floor agenda by making motions, including the motion to proceed to the consideration of a measure, before any other senator can do so.

### *Unanimous Consent Agreements as Orders of the Senate in 1914*

On almost a daily basis, the modern majority leader uses the right of first recognition to request unanimous consent for the Senate to consider legislation and to structure debate and amendments. By unanimous consent, senators supplement or supplant the standing rules and precedents to order floor activity to their convenience. These "unanimous consent agreements," or "time agreements," are essential to the smooth functioning of the Senate but, because they require unanimous consent, are often difficult to negotiate. Arranging unanimous consent agreements, which can be very elaborate, is a central part of the majority leader's responsibilities.

The modern treatment of unanimous consent agreements did not become established until 1914 (Roberts and Smith 2007). In the nineteenth century, presiding officers ruled that unanimous consent agreements were informal arrangements among senators that could neither be enforced by the presiding officer nor changed by a subsequent unanimous consent agreement. This treatment of unanimous consent agreements made them ineffective as a means to give order to the Senate's proceedings.

An event in 1913 led the Senate to adopt a new rule, Rule XII(4), which made unanimous consent agreements orders of the Senate that were enforced by the presiding officer and could be modified by unanimous consent (Roberts and Smith 2007). In January 1913, prohibitionist Newell Sanders (R-TN) asked for unanimous consent for consideration of and a vote upon his bill concerning interstate movement of liquor. In the hubbub of senators' chatter following a vote on another matter, many senators could not hear Sanders speak, and the presiding officer, hearing no objection, granted the request. When another senator inquired about what just happened and objected, the presiding officer observed that "it is beyond the power of the Senate to change or interfere with a unanimous consent agreement after it is made." They managed to reverse the situation the next day, when the Senate voted to have the request resubmitted and an objection killed the request.

The Sanders experience motivated senators to adopt a rule to govern unanimous consent agreements. In early 1914, the Senate accepted a committee's recommendation with an amendment to require a one-day advance notice of a proposed agreement (*Congressional Record*, January 16, 1914, 1716–1759). As adopted, the rule provides:

> No request by a Senator for unanimous consent for the taking of a final vote on a specified date upon the passage of a bill or joint resolution shall be submitted to the Senate for agreement thereto until after a quorum call ordered for the purpose by the Presiding Officer, it shall be disclosed that a quorum of the Senate is present; and when a unanimous consent is thus given the same shall operate as the order of the Senate, but any unanimous consent may be revoked by another unanimous consent granted in the manner prescribed above upon one day's notice.

The one-day rule can be, and usually is, waived by unanimous consent. Very quickly, the Senate came to view all unanimous consent agreements as orders of the Senate to be enforced by the presiding officer.

Rule XII(4) gave the modern majority leader a tool for attempting to bring legislation to the floor, order floor proceedings, and expedite business without lengthy debate and formal votes. However, because unanimous consent is required, the majority leader must often accommodate a wide range of demands from his colleagues. They often expect unanimous consent agreement to allow their amendments, provide time for debate, and adjust the floor schedule to their personal needs. With important exceptions, which are discussed in later chapters, the inability to acquire unanimous consent to bring up or arrange for a vote on a measure forces the majority leader to seek cloture.

### *Setting the Stage*

The floor leadership posts, unanimous consent agreements, cloture, and the majority leader's right of first recognition are features of the modern Senate that emerged in different ways. Internal party practices led to the emergence of floor leaders whose formal roles are now recognized in a variety of party and Senate rules. The adoption of standing rules was required for cloture and enforceable unanimous consent agreements. Later, a ruling of the presiding officer, creating an important procedural precedent, served as the basis for the right of first recognition. These developments produced valuable tools for the modern majority party.

It is important to keep in mind that these features were not planned or intended by the framers of the Constitution but rather crystallized in the early twentieth century. Senators often defend their institution's practices by referring to the intentional design of the Senate as a body that honors deliberation and preserves minority rights. The actual path of Senate procedural development is more complicated than that. No right to unlimited debate was placed in the Constitution, and only over time did senators begin to articulate one. In due course, senators created leadership posts and rules to gain some ability to lend order to Senate business. Without the right of first recognition, floor proceedings would have remained far more disorderly than they are today.

Even with the tools created in the early twentieth century, the Senate majority party and its floor leader, in setting the agenda and gaining Senate approval of measures, face obstacles that their counterparts in few other legislatures confront. The Senate majority does not always have a sympathetic or even a neutral presiding officer and may face a minority large enough to prevent action on its legislation. It has the advantage of being a majority and having some procedural tools that work to its advantage, but there remains a gap between the expectations of majority rule and the reality that a large minority can block action on much of the majority's agenda.

## EXPLAINING THE SENATE SYNDROME

Explaining the emergence of the Senate syndrome is a matter of explaining senators' procedural strategies. Minority obstruction and the majority reaction are matters of deliberate choice. Senators can allow a bill or nomination to come to a vote, which is decided by a simple majority, or even a small minority can insist on cloture, which is decided by a supermajority, as a step toward a vote on the matter. The majority, confronted by the prospect of minority obstruction, can try to wear down the minority by forcing long sessions, compromising to acquire more votes, clamping down on the dilatory actions of the minority as best it can, or setting aside the legislation or nomination. These choices are strategic in character. That is, they anticipate the response by the other side, the reactions of other political actors who matter to senators (the president, the House, the public, and perhaps others), and the backlog of other legislation (the opportunity costs) created by obstruction and responses to it.

We would like to have a viable theory about minority obstruction and the majority response. In fact, just as for the choice of rules, these are subjects for which developing good theory and adequate tests has proven difficult. We might model the forces at work on a bill-by-bill basis, in which case we would characterize the circumstances surrounding the consideration of each bill, perhaps even accounting for bills that fail to get introduced because of anticipated obstruction. Political science has not taken on this gargantuan task. Instead, for the few studies on the subject, political scientists have sought to characterize obstruction and the related forces at work by using each Congress as a whole as the unit of analysis.

### *Previous Studies*

Scholars seeking to model the frequency of filibusters struggle with a fundamental problem. With so many political forces potentially involved and so few Congresses over which we can measure senatorial behavior, it is difficult to draw reliable inferences about the relative importance of the forces at work. Only the strongest relationships reach statistical significance. Thus, we must be a little forgiving about the ability of our analytical tools to identify relationships with confidence.

Binder, Lawrence, and Smith (2002) were the first to provide an overview of the forces that may drive the frequency of filibusters and other obstructive tactics. I describe many of these in greater detail, along with relevant literature, in the following chapters, so I merely list them here:

- *Individualism.* In the last half of the twentieth century, stronger incentives for senators to appeal to organized interests and a national audience produced greater individualism, including individual efforts to obstruct Senate action.
- *Party strength.* Each party's strength—its size and cohesiveness—has varied widely. A strong majority party may leave the minority party with little hope of forcing compromise and so the minority resorts to obstructionism, but its ability to successfully obstruct depends on its own strength.
- *Time constraints.* As time for enacting the majority's agenda became scarce, a product of the expanding federal government and congressional workload, obstruction and delay became more serious problems for the majority party, which made minority obstruction more effective in killing bills or forcing compromise.
- *Congressional calendar.* Until the mid-1930s, each Congress was forced to adjourn sine die on March 4 of each

odd-numbered year, which allowed the minority to filibuster important measures until sessions expired. The Twentieth Amendment to the Constitution did away with a fixed expiration date for Congress and, so reformers hoped, weakened the hand of the minority in the last session of Congress.

- *Tracking.* In response to the difficulty of managing an agenda with more filibustering, majority leadership adopted a system of scheduling debate on filibustered bills during limited hours of the day to allow other business to be conducted. This may have made filibusters less painful to the minority and encouraged more filibustering.
- *Cloture threshold.* In 1917, the Senate adopted a cloture threshold of two-thirds of senators present and voting, raised the threshold to two-thirds of senators duly elected and sworn in 1949, lowered the threshold to two-thirds of senators present and voting in 1959, and lowered the threshold to more than three-fifths of senators duly elected and sworn in 1975. Lower thresholds for cloture may reduce the number of successful filibusters and the incentive to filibuster in the first place.

Examining the filibusters between 1917 and 1996, Binder, Lawrence, and Smith (2002) found that filibusters are more frequent in the last session of a Congress, when the majority party is strong, after tracking became a regular practice, and as the minority party's strength exceeds the cloture threshold (controlling for the time trend in the data).

Koger (2010) extended the analysis to the 1901–2004 period and confirmed that time constraints (days in session, the concentration of work into the Tuesday–Thursday period, last sessions before the Twentieth Amendment) were related as predicted to the frequency of filibusters. He also tested two important hypotheses:

- *Policy distance between the parties.* We would expect that greater policy distance between the parties, measured by the scaled roll-call votes of senators, is associated with more filibusters.
- *Cloture threshold.* The 1975 change in the cloture threshold was associated with an *increase* in the number of filibusters.

With his longer time series, Koger found that, contrary to expectation, filibusters increased with the size of the mean difference in policy positions for senators in the two parties and that more filibustering occurred after the 1975 reform (controlling for the time trend). This latter finding is inconsistent with the expectation that a lower cloture threshold would make filibustering less frequently effective and reduce the number of filibusters. Of course, it may attest to the strength of the forces in recent decades that have created incentives to filibuster. I will return to this topic in later chapters.

### *Another Look*

These efforts exhibit an unfortunate credulity in counting the number of filibusters. Binder, Lawrence, and Smith relied on secondary accounts of Senate floor activity to identify filibusters, while Koger searched major periodicals for references to "filibuster." When obstructionism was rare, these methods may have been reasonable, but, as I emphasize in chapter 9, the sheer volume of obstructionism in the last two decades has overwhelmed journalists and produced little or no mention of many instances of obstructionism. Any attempt to use the same methods to extend the counts through the more recent Congresses would be foolhardy.

Instead, to see the distinctiveness of the Senate in recent Congresses, I have reworked the models developed by Binder, Lawrence, and Smith and by Koger to predict the number of filibusters.[3] This new model takes the variables that the previous researchers found were related to the number of filibusters and reconstructs several of them. I apply the model to the pre-2005 Congresses, as Koger did, for both the number of filibusters and the number of cloture petitions, which can be counted reliably. I include a trend variable and a trend-squared variable to determine whether there is a change in behavior, as figures 1.1 and 1.2 suggest, once I control for the political considerations discussed in previous studies. Trend-squared indicates whether the rate of increase is rising. I then use the estimates to predict the expected number of filibusters and cloture petitions for the three Congresses since 2005 that were complete at the time of this writing.

The variables and multivariate estimates for the statistical models are reported in table 1.1. Not surprisingly, the estimates for the number of filibusters and number of cloture petitions are similar.

The estimates show these relationships:

- the distance between the parties is unrelated to the number of filibusters and the number of cloture petitions;
- more heterogeneous parties are correlated with a larger number of filibusters and petitions;
- the size of the parties is unrelated to the number of filibusters and petitions;[4]
- time demands (the number of days in which the Senate is casting votes and the concentration of voting in the Tuesday–Thursday period) are associated with more filibusters and petitions;
- pre–Twentieth Amendment Senates and second sessions of post–Twentieth Amendment Senates exhibit more filibusters and petitions, all things being equal.

Critically, and hardly surprising, the trend effects are large and statistically significant for filibusters and petitions. The significant trend coefficients imply that the party alignment, party size, time constraint, and session variables have not captured the dynamics in senatorial behavior, particularly for the last two decades. Senatorial behavior has changed in ways beyond what the measured political forces predict based on previous experience.

The statistical estimates for the pre-2005 period provide a basis for appreciating the distinctiveness of the Senate in recent years. Largely powered by the trend, the equations predict an increase in the number of cloture motions in the most recent Congresses. Using the pre-2005 estimates for cloture petitions, figure 1.3 shows the predicted and actual number of cloture petitions for the entire period from 1917 through 2009–2010 (111th Congress). Plainly, the number of cloture petitions in the

**Table 1.1.** Estimates of the Effects of Partisan Alignments, Party Size, Time Constraints, and Sessions on the Number of Filibusters and Cloture Petitions (Poisson regression)

| | Number of filibusters (1901–2004) ß (s.e.) | Number of cloture petitions (1917–2004) ß (s.e.) |
|---|---|---|
| *Party Alignment* | | |
| Difference between party means | −1.05 (1.08) | .976 (2.07) |
| Majority party standard deviation | −5.20* (1.24) | −5.53* (2.61) |
| Minority party standard deviation | −2.33* (.743) | −1.97 (1.54) |
| *Party Size* | | |
| Majority party larger than cloture threshold | .116 (.106) | .249 (.151) |
| *Time Constraints* | | |
| Number of days when voting occurred | .005* (.002) | .014* (.002) |
| Concentration of votes in Tuesday–Thursday period | .997* (.477) | 3.47* (.806) |
| *Sessions* | | |
| Pre–20th Amendment | .557* (.282) | 2.82* (.719) |
| Last session | .336* (.058) | .361* (.073) |
| *Trend* | | |
| Trend | .050* (.016) | .170* (.047) |
| $\text{Trend}^2$ | −.0002* (.0001) | −.001* (.0003) |
| Constant | −.765 (.727) | −10.74* (2.04) |

Robust standard errors clustered on Congress.
Dependent variable for second column: Koger count of number of filibusters per session (Koger 2010). Pseudo $R^2$ = .47; $N$ = 115; log likelihood = −312.14. *$p < .05$.
Dependent variable for third column: Number of cloture motions filed per session. Pseudo $R^2$ = .77; $N$ = 93; log likelihood = −214.30. *$p < .05$.

**Figure 1.3.** Number of Actual and Predicted Cloture Motions Filed, 1917–2010

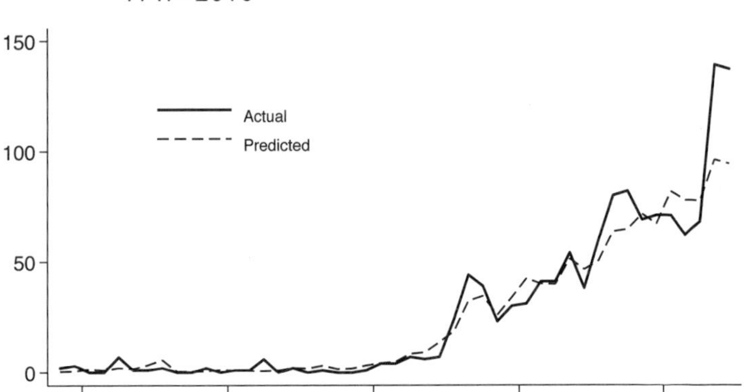


*Source:* www.senate.gov, and estimates in table 1.1.

2007–2010 period far exceeded the trend line, and at the time of this writing, the incomplete 112th Congress (not shown) was on track to continue the pattern. Senators in the most recent Congresses have behaved very differently from their predecessors.

### *The Limits of Previous Models*

There is no simple explanation for recent developments. It is tempting to say that we have witnessed more extreme values of those factors that investigators in previous studies hypothesized to have long driven filibustering. For several reasons, however, that is not what we have witnessed.

First, most analysts quite reasonably associate the minority obstructionism and majority response in today's Senate with sharply polarized Senate parties. From the above estimates, we would be led to believe that the policy distance between the parties is irrelevant and the heterogeneity, not homogeneity, within the majority party drives an increase in filibustering. Those estimates are strongly influenced by the step up in filibustering in the 1970s, when both parties were not as different and were quite heterogeneous, relative to the previous decades.

As we will see in chapters 4, 5, and 6, the parties have become more polarized since the 1970s and it is reasonable to assume that senators' strategies reflect that development. This is a Senate version of "conditional party government," a political science term developed for the House of Representatives (Rohde 1991). The key proposition is that polarized parties produce a policy-making process that is centralized in majority party leaders. On matters of public policy, polarized legislative parties are internally cohesive and quite distant from each other. The cohesiveness implies that nearly all members of the party would trust strong central leaders to act on their behalf; distant parties have few policies on which they are willing to cooperate with each other. For the House, it is argued, polarized parties empower assertive central leaders who, in the case of the majority party, control the agenda and exercise influence over party members whose votes may be needed, particularly if the majority is small. The empowerment involves, at least in part, the adoption of House and party rules that give the majority party and its leader greater control over the agenda and outcomes.

The conditional party government thesis fits the House better than the Senate (Gamm and Smith 2009). In the Senate, the ability of a minority to block changes in the rules and the constitutional designation of the vice president as the presiding officer have limited the powers assigned to the majority party leadership. As a result, variation in the polarization of the parties is not readily translated into rules that enhance the procedural advantages of the majority party and its leader.

Nevertheless, the same line of argument would dictate that with polarized parties, each Senate party generates more collective action with fewer detractors from within its ranks. More legislative activity is subject to party strategy. Elected party leaders are expected to direct the process of finding votes and building coalitions, implementing public relations strategies, and devising parliamentary tactics. Thus, while the Senate's policy-making process does not become very centralized with polarized parties, party conflict and strategies become more common and party leaders more regularly organize the party effort.

Second, the Senate workload and associated time constraints, judged any number of ways, have not increased much, if at all, since the 1970s. Figure 1.4 shows Koger's measures of workload, which are based on the volume and concentration of roll-call votes. In recent years, the total number of votes has dipped, which has allowed a slightly higher proportion of votes to take place in the Tuesday–Thursday period. Alternative measures of workload, such as bills considered, hours in session, or the number of floor amendments, do not show any upward trend (data not shown). Unfortunately, standard measures of Senate workload are not independent of senators' floor strategies. In fact, filibusters may suppress the number of votes, amendments, or hours in session. But the inference that the Senate workload is larger in recent years does not comport with any observations about trends in congressional activity.

While we cannot attribute recent developments to any significant *change* in the severity of time constraints, it is reasonable

**Figure 1.4.** Workload Indicators, 1961–2010

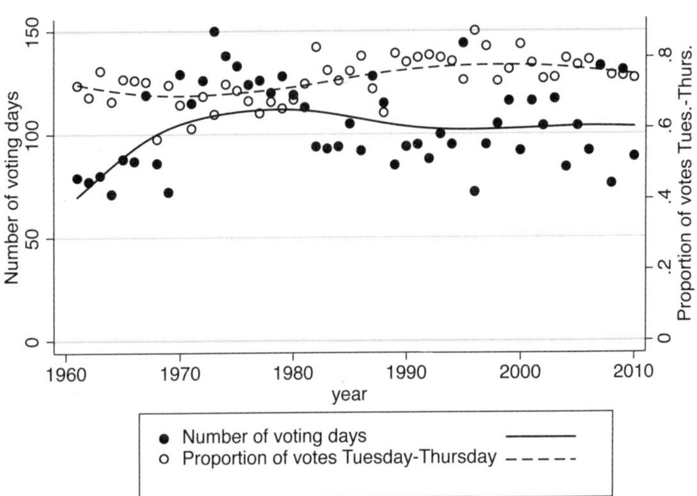


*Source:* Koger (2010). Lines are lowess regression lines.

to argue that the Senate's work schedule has been full throughout the period since the 1970s. By several measures (for example, see voting days in figure 1.4), there was an increase in the workload in the 1960s and 1970s as the many new programs of the Johnson and Nixon administrations were enacted and reauthorized. Oppenheimer (1985) persuasively argued that this created time constraints to be exploited by an obstructionist minority eager to squeeze the majority party agenda-setting ability. In this view, time constraints have been severe throughout recent decades, a condition that has been more fully exploited by the minority party in recent Congresses.

Third, in recent Congresses, the distinction between first and second sessions has become less useful in predicting a filibuster, as minority obstructionism has become so common. Deadlines abound in the modern Congress, so running out the clock is no longer a uniquely end-of-Congress source of leverage for the minority. Moreover, minority strategies have changed. Orchestrated, repetitive, all-season delay may have become a minority party strategy in recent Congresses, which has the effect of distributing minority obstruction and filibuster episodes throughout a two-year Congress.

Fourth, it bears notice that an active, "talking" filibuster, the kind that a C-SPAN viewer would recognize as unending debate orchestrated by a minority, has been an uncommon form of obstruction in recent decades. Not counted are the many other forms of obstruction, only some of which are reflected in filed cloture motions. Holds, dilatory amendments and motions, and the simple refusal to agree to limited debate, at least temporarily, are reflected in only a few of the cloture motions that are filed or the stories about obstructionism reported in the press.

Finally, previous studies have not taken into account majority behavior that may prompt minority obstruction. Uncompromising behavior by majority party members in committee, denying opportunities for minority amendments, and other majority party actions may prompt minority responses, at least if the minority's complaints are taken seriously. Unfortunately, the majority's behavior is not readily documented beyond the filing of cloture motions and so is not taken into account in systematic studies.

### *What Is New?*

The syndrome of behaviors that has emerged in recent years is not readily predicted on the basis of previous systematic studies. The essence of a syndrome is that symptoms or behaviors feed on each other in a nonlinear way. This condition of a mutually reinforcing set of symptoms is different in kind from isolated efforts by one minority and then another to block specific bills. It is a partisan process that involves a succession of moves and countermoves—a parliamentary arms race—that creates new strategic premises for the contending parties and their leaders.

How do we explain this pattern of senatorial behavior? Unfortunately, the beyond-past-experience nature of recent developments and the very small number of Congresses involved in the most recent period make it unlikely that systematic statistical evidence can be employed to test any new account. Too many forces are likely to be at work and too few Congresses are involved in the new period to be able to draw firm inferences about the relative importance of those forces.

Instead, I offer analysis throughout Part I that provides circumstantial evidence for several propositions about the dynamics of Senate policy making in recent years. Some are controversial among scholars and I address those issues in Part II.

*Inherited Rules.* We must begin with inherited rules. Supermajority cloture enables minority obstruction and limits the effectiveness of majority responses. As long as the minority can successfully prevent cloture, most of the majority party responses—holding long sessions, limiting opportunities for amendments to be considered, packaging proposals into larger bills—are of limited value. To be sure, these can be useful for a majority leader who seeks to affect the costs and benefits of minority obstruction, but a dedicated, large minority is difficult to overcome. For most legislation—and the Senate has created important exceptions—the supermajority threshold becomes relevant whenever a senator refuses to grant unanimous consent to bring up a measure or limit debate in some way.

A significant issue in senators' understanding of their institution and in scholarly theories about Senate development is whether a current majority could readily change the inherited rules if it wanted to do so. As we will see, there are ways for a majority to force a change in the rules, but there also are costs that the minority can impose if the majority does so. In the context of most legislating, a fight over the rules is too costly for the majority, even if it wants to change the rules, so a minority can force the majority to muster a supermajority to proceed with a bill, nomination, or treaty.

*Distribution of Policy Positions.* There is often some incentive for Senate minorities to avail themselves of the cloture rule and to force the majority to acquire a supermajority to proceed to the consideration and disposition of a legislative measure. Senators who are part of a minority large enough to prevent cloture—since 1975, a minority of more than two-fifths—would be capable of blocking action and perhaps forcing concessions. And yet there are times when a large minority chooses not to block action. Since 1975, more than 6 percent of final passage votes on bills have produced a "large" minority of more than two-fifths of the Senate. Of course, bills that are blocked by a successful filibuster never receive a final passage vote.

With polarized coalitions, both sides may favor no bill over any version favored by the other side. If so, and if the minority is large, the bill is doomed whenever the minority refuses to limit debate and force cloture votes. A recurring, polarized minority is likely to develop leadership and skill in using the rules to obstruct and stimulate similar developments on the other side.

The Senate's parties might be viewed as an overlay on the distribution of senators' policy positions. When the *parties* are polarized across most important issues, their elected leaders become the chief strategists for the opposing coalitions. Partisan interests beyond the immediate issues influence legislative strategies (Smith 2007). With less resistance from within the party, each party has an incentive to score political points against the opposition. Parliamentary procedure becomes a tool in a larger battle over control of the federal government.

In chapters 5 and 6, the deepening polarization of the parties will be discussed. The partisan polarization we have witnessed is deeper than at any time since the start of the last century, and even then there were more important intraparty factions than there are today. It is not surprising that analyses based only on the twentieth century do not capture the current dynamics between the parties.

Polarization of the congressional parties, of course, is closely associated with partisan polarization in the electorate.[5] The relationship between the two is complicated, but it does appear that congressional polarization preceded the polarization in the general electorate. Party activists and well-organized groups, particularly in the Republican party, have promoted the nomination of more extreme candidates for Congress, a process that has been supported and sometimes led by legislators themselves. The activist community and a polarized electorate reward minority obstruction and strong majority responses.

*Party Size.* Previous studies show, and I confirm, little relationship between party size and the frequency of filibusters. That finding is surprising only if we theorize that obstructionism is a partisan matter and motivated solely by desire to kill a bill. Before the 1970s, whatever the sizes of the parties, filibusters were rare. When filibusters occurred, they were likely to concern race and civil rights, an issue that divided both parties and generated factional strategies that were not immediately a matter of relative party sizes. In recent years, filibusters have become so common that Congress-to-Congress variation in party sizes has made little difference.

Nevertheless, the effects of party size on filibustering behavior, even if significant, may be difficult to measure because of the strategic behavior of the parties. A majority party expecting successful obstruction by the minority may keep a bill from the floor, which yields no observable filibuster or cloture vote. Similarly, a minority that recognizes that the majority party has a coalition that can easily invoke cloture may not bother to filibuster and provoke a cloture motion, also yielding no observable filibuster or cloture vote. In this way, strategic behavior can dampen the observable relationship between party sizes and filibustering.

*Competition for Majority Control.* Missing from previous studies is an account of the effect of electoral competition on senatorial behavior. While we have plenty of evidence that individual legislators adjust their behavior to their electoral circumstances, we usually ignore how congressional parties and their leaders adjust their agenda and procedural strategies to the next election.

The frequency of change in party control appears to have led Senate parties to give more weight to gaining and retaining majority party status in setting legislative strategies. In the seventeen congressional elections held after 1978, party control switched seven times, equal to the seven times in the forty elections between 1900 and 1978. Since 1978, the Senate has gone no more than eight years without a change in party control. Nearly all senators have experienced a change in party control and are sensitized to its consequences. They have gained and lost control of committee chairmanships, hearings, and agendas. Their committee staffs have expanded and contracted. Their party's floor leader has gained and lost the right of first recognition, important to setting the floor agenda.

This experience may have consequences for both the policy and electoral calculations of the parties. From the point of view of accomplishing policy objectives, the prospect of a change in party control encourages the minority to withhold support for legislation in the hope of having a stronger hand after the next election. It also may encourage the majority to push a larger agenda for fear of losing seats in the next election. Either way, obstructionism is encouraged.

As I observe in chapter 9, the minority recognizes that it may not be held accountable for outcomes in a Senate "controlled" by the other party and can hope that frustration with Washington will cost electoral support for majority party senators. The sheer volume of obstructionism reduces the per-episode cost to the minority, if there is any. Moreover, attentive outsiders come to expect that senators will exploit new tools, senators witness how their colleagues get credit with outside audiences for their creative dedication to the cause, the media take obstructionism for granted, and little blame for obstruction is attributed to the minority.

*Procedural Innovation.* The Senate syndrome is only partly a matter of the more extensive use of parliamentary tactics that have been used for decades. It also involves learning new tactics and repeating what works. As we will see in chapters 4, 5, and 6, senators have proven to be quite creative in devising legislative tactics that, once learned, tend to be used again and again. Leaders are urged to use the new tactics and, if they hesitate, sometimes find their colleagues proceeding on their own.

A switch in party control inevitably leads to pleas within the losing party to learn from the innovations of the other side. Retribution sometimes motivates invention—giving them a dose of their own medicine—but surely more important is the learning of what works. Improving on the other side's successful tactics then intensifies the parliamentary warfare.

The development of more polarized, competitive, innovative parties seems to account for much of what the Senate has experienced in recent years. Parties and their leaders still had to make procedural choices, and they did. Step by step, over a period of twenty-five years, the Senate parties *radicalized political strategy.* They were not alone—important changes were occurring in the way House parties were conducting business, too. But in the Senate, with the obstructionist capacity of a minority, a very different parliamentary dynamic developed. It changed the character of the Senate.

## CONCLUSION

In introducing the Senate syndrome in this chapter, I have just scratched the surface. It is obvious that the Senate has become a very different policy-making body from what it was a generation ago. It also is obvious that the pattern of obstruct and restrict behavior that we have witnessed in recent years goes beyond the behavior that is predicted by models generated from behavior in previous eras. Less obvious is the political and procedural path that the Senate took to get to this point. That is the subject of Part I.

You may have noticed that I have yet to use the word "dysfunctional" to describe today's Senate. It is a term used only a few times in this book and then only to describe the views of senators and other observers. It is the adjective most frequently applied to the United States Senate in the last decade. Most senators and close observers agree that the Senate of the early twenty-first century behaves in ways that are new to the institution. Most of them would agree that something is wrong with the Senate, but there is no consensus about what is wrong, how severe the problem is, what should be done about it, or even how changes should be accomplished. Nor is there much agreement about what the basic facts are. Is the majority party unfair, unnecessarily restrictive, uncompromising, and incompetent? Or is the minority obstructionist, radical, and inflexible? Are the rules the problem, or are senators the problem? Are senators stuck with a Senate they dislike, or have senators chosen the Senate they want?

I provide answers to many of these questions, but I am not motivated by a need to assign blame or credit to senators and their parties. This book is about the way senators govern themselves. I describe the procedural path taken by the Senate over recent decades in order to demonstrate that today's Senate is, in major part, the by-product of procedural battles fought by past generations of senators. I argue that the ability of a minority to block the majority, the Senate's most distinctive parliamentary feature, is central to the Senate's procedural development and senators' everyday legislative strategies. Senators make tactical adaptations to changes in their political circumstances and they continue to exploit new tactics until the formal rules governing the process are reformed. Over the last fifty years, the political conditions that produced some self-restraint in exploitation of the rules have given way—first under pressure from forces that motivated individual senators and factions to fully exploit the rules and then under partisan pressures that have created a parliamentary arms race between the two Senate parties.

In Part I, I report how the Senate, a body of legislators who have long taken pride in the informality and civility of their deliberations, has become so obsessed with parliamentary procedure. This story is more complicated than even most close observers of the Senate appreciate. In fact, senators themselves often repeat incorrect or misleading versions of their institution's history as they offer commentary on how the Senate does and should operate. Getting the history right is essential to explaining how the Senate syndrome emerged.

In Part II of this book, I evaluate key arguments about the Senate to clarify what has transpired, assess the consequences, and evaluate senatorial and scholarly arguments about reform. Senators' own accounts of recent developments are filled with competing interpretations and sprinkled with misconceptions of Senate history. These interpretations reflect both political biases and political science theories about how the Senate behaves.

The setting is much larger than the Senate—most important developments in America and the world are registered in the Senate. The policy challenges confronting government, the changing contours of the two parties' electoral coalitions, and the distribution of power across the institutions of government are reflected in the changing nature of the Senate. Space constraints require that I treat these developments in a very limited way. My focus must be on what is so poorly reported and understood—how the Senate has changed.

# PART I

# EMERGENCE OF THE SENATE SYNDROME

CHAPTER 2

# THE PROCEDURAL CONDITION OF THE SENATE IN THE 1950s

ALTHOUGH ITS CHARACTERIZATION is exaggerated, William S. White's *Citadel* (1957) describes the mid-twentieth-century Senate as "the world's most exclusive club." The Senate was an insular institution composed of senators who specialized in the work of their committees and attended to their states' affairs. For most issues, senators observed self-conscious norms that limited active participation in policy making to the non-junior members of the committees with relevant jurisdiction. An inner club of senior senators, mainly committee chairmen, dominated the Senate. The Senate was not without partisanship and contentious issues, but the normal mode of operation was informal and deferential to senior legislators.

Nevertheless, the 1950s were not years of procedural harmony in the Senate. Conflict among senators over their institution's fundamental procedure surfaced several times. At stake were the issues of race and civil rights. Liberals advocating action on civil rights legislation found themselves stymied by southern Democrats who could easily block floor action. Cloture reform became a high priority for the civil rights movement and its Senate champions, but the decade ended with most liberals frustrated with the modest reforms that had been adopted and pessimistic about the chances for reform in the near future.

## THE RED CARPET SENATE

This was a "red carpet" Senate—literally. Extensive renovations to the Senate Chamber were completed in 1950. Badly needed improvements in ventilation and lighting were made, along with an upgrade of furnishings. A worn green carpet with a black pattern was replaced by a red-and-black-patterned carpet, a general color and design that was used into the 1970s.

The 1950s warrant a close look. The decade is sometimes heralded as the time in which the Senate reached its ideal form as a deliberative body. The Senate appeared to be a fully mature, well adapted, and powerful institution. Its slow pace, informality, and tranquility seemed to match the relative calm of American domestic life. Senators enjoyed great national prestige, and many were icons of their home states.

The Senate of the 1950s was not without its detractors. It was a conservative place—tied to traditional ways of doing things and greatly influenced by the conservative elite of committee chairmen (Finley 2008; Foley 1980; Hinckley 1971; Huitt 1961; Patterson 1967; Ripley 1969). After southern Democrats revolted against President Franklin Roosevelt's court-packing plan in 1937, they continued to oppose important elements of the legislative program and frequently joined forces with Republicans in a "conservative coalition" that often constituted a majority of the Senate in the following decades (Manley 1973; Margolis 1973; Patterson 1967; Shelley 1983). Conservatives dominated Congress in the 1940s and 1950s, and on most issues, liberals did not effectively challenge them until after the 1958 elections, when a cohort of northern liberals was elected to both houses. As figure 2.1 shows, the conservative coalition emerged in the 1930s and survived as a force in Senate politics until Republicans began to win a significant number of southern Senate seats at the expense of Democrats in the 1970s and 1980s.

The split among Democrats, who were in the majority during most of the 1950s, preserved the basic form of Rule XXII as written back in 1917. By the 1950s, southern Democrats, who were anxious about the rising support for civil rights legislation, had developed a rationale for opposing cloture, and certainly cloture reform, as a matter of principle. Serving in the minority party during most of this period, Republican leaders and most of their party opposed significant changes in the

**Figure 2.1.** Percentage of All Votes on Which the Conservative Coalition Appeared, 1925–2010

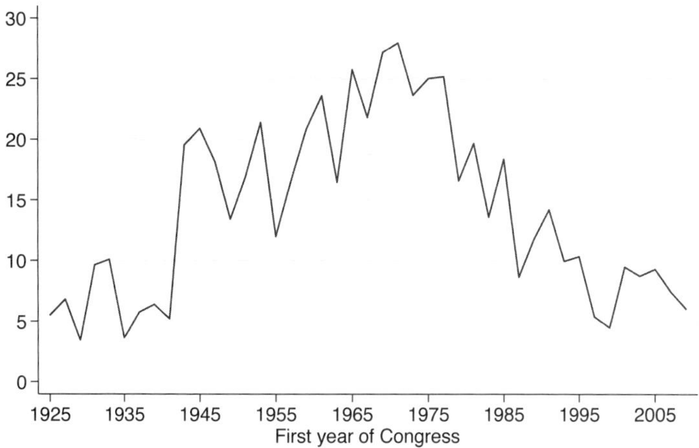


*Source:* Senate roll-call votes, by Congress.

rule. That left only liberal Democrats and the few liberal Republicans, a clear minority in the Senate, in favor of significant change in Rule XXII.

The Senate of the 1950s set the stage for the procedural developments to follow. The formal rules and the use of those rules in the 1950s are the subjects of this chapter. Repeated efforts to reform Rule XXII yielded only the most modest changes. Nevertheless, by the time of the elections of 1960, a rising liberal tide showed signs of changing the balance of power on civil rights legislation and forever changing the exclusive club.

## CLOTURE REFORM, 1949

By the 1950s, the connection between the civil rights issue and Senate rules, especially the cloture rule, was well established in the public's mind. In the 1930s and 1940s, legislative battles over anti-lynching legislation, which would have made lynching a federal crime, the Fair Employment Practices

Commission, anti–poll tax measures, and other matters were subject to conspicuous delays at the hands of southern senators (Berman 1970; Brinkley 1995; Burdette 1940; Finley 2008; Friedel 1965; Garson 1974; Sitkoff 1978). With increasing intensity, civil rights advocates demanded changes in the Senate's Rule XXII, the cloture rule, which they viewed to be the major obstacle to enacting strong legislation.

The 1949 fight over cloture reform set the rules of the game for the Senate of the 1950s and reflected the factionalism and gamesmanship of the mid-twentieth century. The immediate goal of the reformers was to reverse a 1948 interpretation of Rule XXII. Republican Arthur Vandenberg (MI), presiding over the Senate when his party was in the majority, ruled in August 1948 that the original rule's reference to ending debate on "any pending measure" did not apply to procedural motions (*Congressional Record,* August 2, 1948, 9598–604).[1] He made the ruling in response to a point of order raised against an effort to invoke cloture on a procedural motion—the motion to proceed to the consideration of a civil rights bill (a bill banning poll taxes). While the ruling was a reasonable interpretation of the rule and comported with a report of the Committee on Rules and Administration, which recommended that the rule be changed to explicitly cover procedural motions, it was disheartening to both Democratic and Republican advocates of civil rights legislation.

With Vandenberg's ruling that motions are not measures, there was no way to close debate on a motion to proceed. Opponents of legislation could easily prevent the consideration of a bill even if the supporters had the two-thirds majority required to invoke cloture for a measure. Liberal Democrats were spurred to push for reform of Rule XXII after the 1948 elections, when their party regained a Senate majority. Their president, Harry Truman, who had just been elected in his own right and was eager to see a sizable legislative agenda enacted, urged that the Senate adopt simple-majority cloture.

Carl Hayden, an Arizona liberal and Democratic chairman of the Committee on Rules and Administration, and William

Knowland (R-CA), the Republican leader, supported a resolution to apply cloture to "any motion, measure, or other matter." Knowland, who knew that the reform issue divided Democrats, pushed for rapid action. Richard Russell (D-GA), the leader of the southern Democrats, threatened to filibuster and interfere with Senate business by objecting to the usual unanimous consent requests to allow committees to meet while the Senate was in session. While he supported cloture reform, President Truman worried that southerners' response would sidetrack other legislation he sought, a view shared by a few other liberals. This would not be the last time that filibuster reform opponents sought to intimidate reform sympathizers with a promise to generally disrupt legislative business.

Southerners made plain that they would exploit the 1948 ruling to prevent a vote on a motion to proceed to the reform resolution. In response, reformers sought the cooperation of the presiding officer, Vice President (and former Senate Democratic leader) Alben Barkley, whom they wanted to reverse Vandenberg's ruling by upholding a point of order rule that Rule XXII applied to a motion to proceed. The twisted logic of the situation was not lost on senators—reformers wanted a ruling that cloture applied to motions so that a resolution making the rule explicitly apply to motions could receive a vote.

Barkley ruled as wished, but when the opposition appealed the ruling to the Senate and a motion to table the appeal failed, 41–46, the ruling was overturned by the same vote. At least some minority party Republicans, led by Vandenberg, said they favored the reform resolution but opposed Barkley's ruling on the grounds that the "reform by ruling" approach—a favorable ruling backed by a successful motion to table the appeal—would allow a future majority and presiding officer to get any ruling (or rule) they desired. Democrats saw the Republicans' argument as camouflage for their real motive—to block filibuster reform so they would not have to vote on civil rights measures (Andrews 1949; Albright 1949).

After the path to a vote on the reform resolution was blocked by the appeal, southern Democrats banded with Republicans to amend the reform resolution. Their revision included a provision to extend Rule XXII to all motions, as the liberal Democrats wanted, but it included two additional features that the conservative coalition desired. First, it changed the threshold for cloture from two-thirds of senators voting to two-thirds of all senators ("duly elected and sworn"), which meant that absent senators would count against cloture. Second, it prohibited cloture on a change in the rules, which would allow a small group of senators to block future changes in the rules. These changes were opposed by liberal and civil rights advocates, but this version was adopted by the Senate with the votes of the conservative coalition. Most liberals voted against the amended resolution, but they did not filibuster it. They may have thought that applying cloture to motions was important enough to suffer the other two changes. The result was a somewhat higher threshold for cloture on regular measures and an insuperable threshold for future reform of the cloture rule.

The 1948–49 episode had features in common with subsequent filibuster reform efforts. First, Rule XXII was a self-protecting rule—it created a serious obstacle to changing it. Second, the obstacles to getting a vote on a reform resolution led reformers to seek parliamentary rulings that would pave the way for a vote on reform. Third, the minority party worried about the implications of a presiding officer making rulings of convenience for the current majority. Fourth, the parties and factions took into account a mix of short-term partisan advantage and longer-term policy implications in generating and evaluating reform proposals. And fifth, the outcome did not settle the matter for long.

## CLOTURE REFORM, 1953

Civil rights issues continued to motivate liberals to seek cloture reform. The conservative coalition, led by strategists Robert Taft (R-OH) and Richard Russell, successfully blocked a 1953 effort to reform Rule XXII. The reform resolution died when a motion to table was adopted 70–21, with liberal Democrats and five Republicans in the minority. The 1953 debate over reform was noteworthy for the development of arguments about the nature of the Senate and its rules that have been repeated by reformers since then.

The reformers' central argument was that the Constitution gives the Senate the right to consider its rules at the start of each new Congress. They noted that Article I, Section 5, provides that "each house may determine the rules of its proceedings." "Each house," they inferred, must be a simple majority of each house, and a majority must be allowed to consider the rules at the start of a Congress. That "each house" implies that a simple majority has the right to act is inferred from the whole of the Constitution. The Constitution is silent on the voting rule for passing legislation or resolutions, but both houses interpret the Constitution as implying a simple-majority threshold. The Senate, in fact, does not have a rule that requires a simple majority and has always operated on the implicit majority threshold. In contrast, the Constitution explicitly sets a two-thirds threshold for certain matters (veto override, treaty ratification, approval of a constitutional amendment, removal from office, and Senate conviction of an impeached official). If a two-thirds threshold applies to a few matters and a simple-majority threshold to all other matters, then "each house" must mean a simple majority. This certainly must be true, reformers insisted, at the start of each new Congress. Rule XXII allows a minority to prevent a majority from acting on the rules and therefore violates the constitutional principle that a majority of senators may determine the rules.

Reform opponents insisted that the Senate, as a continuing body, must honor the rules that carry over from the previous Congress. The Senate's status as a continuing body is a by-product of staggered six-year terms, with two-thirds of senators' terms continuing from one Congress to the next. They have the right to have the rules continue from one Congress to the next, including the provisions of Rule XXII. The rules can be changed at any time, but any change in the rules must be considered under the terms of those rules. The rules include Rule XXII, which provides no means for limiting debate on a change in the rules. Thus, as long as any senator seeks recognition to speak on a resolution to amend the rules, it is not possible to force a vote on the resolution.

In response, reformers insisted that the Senate's adopted principle of the continuity of the rules is subordinate to the constitutional principle that the Senate—any Senate—may determine its rules. Applying Rule XXII as reform opponents demanded meant that a Senate could effectively bind the Senate of future Congresses to its rules as long as even a small minority of senators wanted to retain the inherited rules. At least at the start of a Congress, the reformers insisted, the Senate's majority must be allowed to consider and vote on the rules. Some reformers, most notably Clinton Anderson (D-NM) and Paul Douglas (D-IL), insisted that the Senate operate without formal rules until they were adopted at the start of a Congress, just as the House did.

Reformers also noted that the Senate behaves as if it is not a continuing body in some important ways. There are two constitutional responsibilities that the Senate times with the transition between Congresses: The Senate's administrative officers are elected at the start of each Congress, and presidential nominations to executive and judicial positions expire at the end of a Congress and must be resubmitted. The Senate also requires that all bills and resolutions be reintroduced at the start of a new Congress. Thus, although the Senate has traditionally treated itself as a continuing body for the purpose of adopting rules, it has always accepted discontinuity between Congresses in key functions.

In 1953, defenders of Rule XXII did not mount a detailed response to reformers' arguments. With 71 votes to table the reform resolution, they did not have to persuade anyone of the justice of their cause. The nondebatable motion to table disposed of the matter expeditiously.

## 1954: LIBERAL DEMOCRATS FILIBUSTER

In July 1954, just weeks before majority party Republicans hoped to adjourn the Congress and return home to campaign, the Senate considered legislation to spur the development of a private nuclear energy industry and encourage international cooperation in the development of the technology. The Atomic Energy Commission (AEC) controlled the process and generated a multifaceted debate about private and public responsibilities in acquiring and licensing fissionable materials and technology. On a related front, Democrats were upset with an AEC contract with a private company to provide power to Memphis in place of the Tennessee Valley Authority and wanted the bill to include a provision on the matter. The bill eventually passed with the support of nearly all majority party Republicans and a few Democrats, but only after two weeks of debate and a failed cloture motion.

Republican leaders knew from the start that they had a majority to pass the bill, although they were uncertain about what amendments would be proposed and adopted. After just a few days of debate, it was clear that the Democrats would not agree to a time limit for the bill and were prepared to debate amendments and the bill at great length. With some Republicans observing that a filibuster was underway, Republican majority leader William Knowland (CA) complained that, with the end of the Congress approaching, the entire program of President Dwight Eisenhower was threatened by the delay in acting on the bill.

Knowland kept the Senate in several all-night sessions in an effort to wear down the opposition. Large crowds arrived on the Senate side of the Capitol to take turns watching an uncommon, live filibuster that was the product of stubbornness on both sides. On the last night of the debate, Wayne Morse, who had resigned from the Republican conference earlier in the Congress, kept the floor for twelve hours and twenty-two minutes, sipping orange juice and hot tea brought to his desk. After giving up the floor, Morse gladly posed for a photo that appeared in many newspapers the next day—with the Capitol dome in the background, Morse held a handkerchief to his forehead but managed to have a big smile on his face.

Once the Democrats' tactics had become obvious, Knowland began to use the motion to table to quickly dispose of amendments. The motion to table is not debatable under Senate rules, so it yields an immediate vote and, with a simple majority, stops further consideration of an amendment. This approach to disposing of amendments is common today but was unusual in the early 1950s. Liberals complained about the Republican leader for "his bull-dozing tactics," "applying the parliamentary buggy whip," and "parliamentary bludgeoning." They even insisted that their extended debate on the bill was a response to Knowland's extraordinary use of the motion to table to end debate on individual amendments.

A cloture motion, initiated by Knowland, failed with only 42 votes in favor—far short of the two-thirds of all senators (64) that was required. The tactics of southern Democrats proved interesting. Most southern Democrats actually supported the bill, but they voted against cloture because, as a *New York Times* correspondent noted, they wanted to remain consistent in their public position in opposition to cloture as a matter of principle. Blocking civil rights bills, which southerners took as their highest legislative priority, required that they defend unlimited debate. Under the tutelage of Richard Russell, they had turned opposition to cloture into a matter of fundamental principle. Still, it was reported, southerners were concerned about the possibility that the liberals' filibuster would push Republicans into becoming more supportive of filibuster reform, as liberal Democrats had long been.

Lyndon Johnson, in his second year as Democratic leader, showed his mettle by finding a path that reflected the delicate situation of the southern faction. He voted against cloture along with fellow southerners, intervened with Knowland to allow lengthy debate on a few amendments, and successfully appealed to his liberal colleagues to allow a vote on the bill after their amendments were considered. This arrangement allowed a final vote to occur without cloture and resulted in a majority of 57 votes for the bill.

Several aspects of the 1954 episode are noteworthy. First, the liberal-conservative divide among Democrats shaped the outcome and parliamentary strategies. As was typical of the decade, Democratic leader Johnson worked to manage this divide and reduce the chances that views of filibusters and cloture would deepen it. Second, both minority and majority senators exploited their parliamentary tools. Each side blamed the other for obstruction and upsetting the normal process for disposing of amendments and the bill. And both sides argued that their parliamentary tactics were justified by their pursuit of the larger public good.

Also noteworthy about the 1954 episode is how unusual it was for the middle decades of the twentieth century. Very few legislative battles generated serious obstructionism or cloture votes. While the atomic energy bill involved a classic filibuster with a senator holding the floor for hours, perhaps encouraged by a determined majority leader and taken up by an eager and media-savvy nonconformist, the floor extravaganza occurred *after* the minority leader and his followers had concluded that they were ready to move to other business. It was showmanship, pure and simple.

Southern Democrats, liberal Democrats, and the Republicans took distinctive positions on cloture. Taking account of their long-term interest in protecting the filibuster, southern Democrats refused to vote for cloture even if it threatened a bill they favored. Liberals, such as Minnesota's Hubert Humphrey, were quite willing to oppose cloture on the atomic energy bill and yet had advocated filibuster reform for years in order to get votes on civil rights and other measures. The frustrated Republican majority of 1954 simply favored cloture when confronted with minority obstruction.

## OBSTRUCTIONISM IN THE 1950s

While the decade of the 1950s was filled with important issues—the Cold War and Korean War, the reconstruction of Europe, the development of American science and technology, the creation of an interstate highway system—liberal Democrats were often disappointed by the lack of significant legislation on civil rights, education, labor, and other issues. On most issues, they simply lacked a majority. On civil rights, they often had a majority but faced conservative obstruction, which kept them agitating for filibuster reform throughout the decade.

By the 1950s, the floor management responsibilities of the majority leader were well established (Gamm and Smith 2002; Roberts and Smith 2007). Beginning with John Kern in 1913, the elected top leader of the majority party assumed responsibility for setting the agenda (with the assistance of a steering committee), propounding unanimous consent agreements to limit debate, expediting business, and, often, serving as the spokesman for the party. Thanks to a rule adopted in 1914, unanimous consent agreements were considered orders to the Senate to be enforced by the presiding officer, and therefore they became the most frequently used tool of the majority leader for orchestrating floor activity.

Equally important, a precedent recognized since the 1930s provided the majority leader the "right of first recognition." That is, if the majority leader and another senator are seeking recognition to address the Senate, the majority leader is given priority. With this privilege, the majority leader is in a position to offer motions, make unanimous consent requests, and ask for the cooperation of colleagues.

Johnson's Senate of the 1950s was one with only a few procedural innovations. Most major bills were considered on the floor by unanimous consent and debated under a "time agreement" that limited debate (Smith and Flathman 1989). Time agreements are unanimous consent agreements—"UCs" in Senate lingo—that can be used to supplant or substitute for standing rules and precedents governing floor procedure. The difficulty of limiting debate through Rule XXII leads the majority leader, bill managers, and others to seek unanimous consent to limit debate and amendments. Since 1914, unanimous consent agreements have been treated as orders of the Senate that are enforced by the presiding officer, but, because a single senator can object and prevent agreement, they require senators' tolerance of the limits proposed.

By the 1950s, the standard operating procedure on the Senate floor was for the majority leader to seek unanimous consent to limit debate on bills, amendments, nominations, and other business in order to gain action on his party's agenda as expeditiously as possible. Lyndon Johnson has been given credit for his innovations in parliamentary tactics, including his use of unanimous consent agreements (Caro 2002; Evans and Novak 1966). Most major bills during the late 1950s were subject to a unanimous consent agreement that limited debate on the bill, amendments, and motions and required amendments to be germane. Johnson was far more aggressive in seeking unanimous consent, and when he overcame objections he immediately went to the floor, gained consent for a time limitation, bullied colleagues into withholding amendments, and rushed the bill through the Senate.

Some evidence of Johnson's distinctiveness is evident in table 2.1. More frequently than his predecessors, Johnson successfully propounded time limitation agreements before the motion to proceed on a measure was offered. Then, also much more frequently than previously, Johnson's requests divided control of time for general debate on a bill between the floor leaders, giving Johnson more control over the flow of debate and an opportunity to offer amendments of his own in a timely way. Moreover, Johnson sought to keep the Senate focused on the bill at hand by barring nongermane amendments when he could. Finally, Johnson's requests were more likely than those of his predecessors to provide for special treatment of one or more amendments by allowing extra debate or allowing for action on a nongermane amendment that would otherwise be barred by the agreement (Smith and Flathman 1989).

The standard time agreement—the "usual form," as it was known in the Senate—included a requirement that amendments be germane. The statement was simply that "no amendment that is not germane to the provisions of said bill shall be received." The germaneness requirement, once senators agreed to it, prevented them from proposing unrelated legislation as amendments, a strategy that could help them circumvent committees that might be blocking action on their bills (Smith and Flathman 1989).

**Table 2.1.** Provisions of Senate Unanimous Consent Agreements (UCAs), 1935–2000

| | | | Percentage of complex UCs that | | | | | | | |
|---|---|---|---|---|---|---|---|---|---|---|
| Congress | Majority leader | Number of UCs | were offered before debate on measure began | assigned control of time for general debate to floor leaders | required amdmts to be germane | set one standard limit for debate on all amdmts | set a specific limit for debate on one or more amdmts | provided for certain amdmts without barring other amdmts | allowed only specified amdmts to be offered | barred second–degree amdmts |
| 74th (1935–1936) | Robinson (D-AR) | 20 | 5.0 | 0.0 | 0.0 | 55.0 | 0.0 | 0.0 | 0.0 | 0.0 |
| 77th (1941–1942) | Barkley (D-KY) | 12 | 0 | 0.0 | 0.0 | 50.0 | 0.0 | 0.0 | 0.0 | 0.0 |
| 82nd (1951–1952) | McFarland (D-AZ) | 45 | 11.1 | 4.4 | 57.8 | 68.9 | 11.1 | 4.4 | 2.2 | 0.0 |
| 83rd (1953–1954) | Taft (R-Ohio)/ Knowland (R-CA) | 30 | 6.7 | 13.3 | 63.3 | 73.3 | 0.0 | 0.0 | 0.0 | 0.0 |
| 84th (1955–1956) | Johnson (D-TX) | 92 | 27.2 | 81.5 | 79.4 | 78.3 | 4.4 | 1.1 | 6.5 | 0.0 |

| | | | | | | | | | | |
|---|---|---|---|---|---|---|---|---|---|---|
| 85th (1957–1958) | Johnson (D-TX) | 36 | 25.0 | 63.9 | 69.4 | 69.4 | 5.6 | 8.3 | 8.3 | 0.0 |
| 88th (1963–1964) | Mansfield (D-MT) | 96 | 17.1 | 36.5 | 31.3 | 38.5 | 35.4 | 13.5 | 2.1 | 0.0 |
| 92nd (1971–1972) | Mansfield (D-MT) | 378 | 37.0 | 10.1 | 11.9 | 32.8 | 47.9 | 1.6 | 0.3 | 1.3 |
| 96th (1979–1980) | Byrd (D-WV) | 407 | 47.2 | 1.2 | 3.0 | 10.8 | 46.9 | 0.0 | 7.1 | 5.9 |
| 98th (1983–1984) | Baker (R-TN) | 148 | 50.7 | 6.1 | 2.0 | 3.4 | 26.4 | 0.0 | 29.7 | 16.2 |
| 100th (1987–1988) | Byrd (D-WV) | 86 | 4.7 | 4.7 | 2.3 | 2.3 | 34.9 | 31.4 | 14.0 | 30.2 |
| 102nd (1991–1992) | Mitchell (D-ME) | 103 | 13.6 | 1.9 | 1.0 | 2.9 | 20.4 | 50.5 | 16.5 | 49.5 |
| 104th (1995–1996) | Dole (R-KS) | 98 | 7.1 | 26.5 | 5.1 | 4.1 | 10.2 | 28.6 | 18.4 | 27.6 |
| 106th (1999–2000) | Lott (R-MS) | 105 | 9.5 | 10.5 | 1.9 | 11.4 | 33.7 | 38.1 | 11.4 | 30.5 |

*Source:* Senate *Journal*, selected years.

Johnson's effectiveness in negotiating with his party's factions and keeping the Republicans at bay allowed him to keep some issues off the floor and push others to quick action. His success surely played an important role in limiting filibusters and the need for cloture. Indeed, few filibusters and cloture votes occurred in the 1950s, even after the 1949 cloture rule facilitated the application of cloture to procedural motions. Three mutually reinforcing factors seem to have been at work during the 1950s.

First, senators, journalists, and political scientists of the period gave considerable emphasis to informal norms of behavior that called for restraint in the use of procedural prerogatives. Political scientist Donald Matthews reported that the Senate of the 1950s was infused with a "spirit of reciprocity" (1960, 100–101). This resulted, he said, "in much, if not most, of the senators' actual power not being exercised. If a senator *does* push his formal powers to the limit, he has broken the implicit bargain and can expect, not cooperation from his colleagues, but only retaliation in kind." Senators who failed to exhibit the spirit of reciprocity "are the exceptions, the nonconformists to the Senate folkways" (101).

Second, the interests of the conservative majority that dominated the Senate on most issues were served by the norms restraining activism. This conservative majority seldom supported major new domestic policy initiatives, so there were not many occasions on which a minority of senators had occasion to block a majority's new initiative. Senior conservatives appeared to be the leading advocates of the restrictive informal norms that served their interests, while liberals were the most vocal critics of the norms (Huitt 1961).

The dominance of conservatives extended beyond the question of norms and cloture. Their acquisition of a large share of committee chairmanships meant that they were in a position to block or delay action on liberal legislation through control of their committee agendas (Finley 2008; Hinckley 1971). They acquired the chairmanships through the seniority norm, which had been in place since the late nineteenth century. Like the supermajority threshold for cloture, the seniority norm had developed a strong and credible rationale: the most experienced and expert legislators would lead standing committees, where most of the text of legislation was written. While liberals showed some sympathy for the seniority tradition, they were often critical of its consequences. Because civil rights bills were in the jurisdiction of the Senate's Committee on the Judiciary, its southern chairman, James Eastland of Mississippi, was the most frequent target of the critics of the seniority system.

Like the House of the era, this was a Senate that did much of its work behind closed doors. Typically, committees held markup sessions at which the details of legislation were written in private meetings at which the public and press were not allowed. There was a sense of mystery to the internal workings of committees and always considerable emphasis on the power of the committee chairmen to call meetings and set the agenda.

For strategic reasons, the southern Democrats kept filibusters and obstructionism to a minimum (Finley 2008). The "great cause," sustaining racial segregation and blocking civil rights bills, demanded that southerners preserve a high threshold for cloture in Rule XXII. In turn, preserving a high cloture threshold implied minimizing interest in filibuster reform, which meant limiting obstructionist tactics as much as possible on all other issues. Filibusters were reserved for civil rights, the one issue that mattered more than any other.

Third, Lyndon Johnson was at work. As majority leader during the 1953–60 period, Johnson worked to keep significant civil rights and other liberal measures off the floor. He accomplished much of this by simply endorsing the "regular order" of committee consideration. Many key Senate committees were run with a strong hand by conservative chairmen, so allowing them to handle legislation as they wished was sufficient for keeping divisive legislation off the floor. At times, however, Johnson used his powers of persuasion to find the votes to gain both liberal and conservative support for compromises that avoided open filibustering and left his party intact. And, as we have seen, Johnson often refused to bring a controversial bill to the floor until he had a time agreement—that is, until a filibuster was no longer possible.

This was an era in which informal norms, a conservative majority, and a majority leader's strategy were mutually supportive. They gave the Senate the appearance of a tranquil, tradition-bound men's club in which senators did not fully exploit their parliamentary weapons and consensus was required, at least within the majority party conference, to move legislation. To some observers, this was a well-adjusted, fully mature parliamentary body in a stable, modern democracy. It deserved to be the envy of the world. To others, the Senate remained a stuffy, antiquated, and oppressive institution.

## THE NIXON SURPRISE, 1957

Two weeks after the November 1956 elections, six Senate liberals announced their intention to seek filibuster reform and to renew their effort to gain consideration of the rules at the start of the 85th Congress in January. They observed, and newspaper editorialists reiterated, that Vice President Richard Nixon, a former California senator, would be called upon to rule on whether Rule XXII applied to a motion to adopt the rules. They were also more fully prepared than they had been in the past. They came to the floor with a long memorandum on the procedural arguments and precedents (*Congressional Record,* January 3, 1957, 24–30).

Within the first hour that the Senate convened on January 3, Clinton Anderson moved to have the Senate adopt its rules and Majority Leader Johnson responded with a motion to table Anderson's motion. Before moving his motion, Johnson observed that he, Anderson, and other liberals had agreed to a period of debate on the reform issue before the vote on the motion to table and offered a unanimous consent agreement to accomplish that.

During the debate, most of the arguments of the 1953 episode were rehearsed. Perhaps most notable about the liberals' arguments in 1957 was that they now asserted that the "continuous body" argument is irrelevant to the contention that a simple majority of the Senate has the right to consider the rules (*Congressional Record,* January 3, 1957, 14, 150). This set their argument apart from the well-established liberal line of reasoning that the Constitution implies that the right to consider the rules must apply to the start of a Congress. They certainly thought the start of a Congress was a good time to consider changes in the rules, but they now chose to counter the reform opponents' emphasis on the continuity of the Senate by insisting that the Senate, if a continuous body, still did not have continuous rules.

In response to a parliamentary inquiry from Hubert Humphrey (D-MN) about the rule under which the Senate was proceeding, Nixon offered an extended opinion on the status of Senate rules. He obviously had prepared for the occasion and surprised reform opponents. Reformers have cited Nixon's statement many times since then, and it warrants extended quotation:

> The question posed by the preliminary inquiry is, in effect: Do the rules of the Senate continue from one Congress to another?
>
> Although there is a great volume of written comment and opinion to the effect that the Senate is a continuing body with continuing rules, as well as some opinion to the contrary, the Presiding Officer of the Senate has never ruled directly on this question. Since there are no binding precedents, we must first turn to the Constitution for guidance.
>
> The constitutional provision under which only one-third of the Senate membership is changed by election in each Congress can only be construed to indicate the intent of the framers that the Senate should be a continuing parliamentary body for at least some purposes. By practice for 167 years the rules of the Senate have been continued from one Congress to another.
>
> The Constitution also provides that "each House may determine the rules of its proceedings." This constitutional right is lodged in the membership of the Senate and it may be exercised by a majority of the Senate at any time. When the membership of the Senate changes, as it does upon the election of each Congress, it is the Chair's opinion that there can be no question that the majority of the new existing membership of the Senate, under the Constitution, have the power to determine the rules under which the Senate will proceed.
>
> The question, therefore, is, "How can these two constitutional mandates be reconciled?"

It is the opinion of the Chair that while the rules of the Senate have been continued from one Congress to another, the right of a current majority of the Senate at the beginning of a new Congress to adopt its own rules, stemming as it does from the Constitution itself, cannot be restricted or limited by rules adopted by a majority of the Senate in a previous Congress.

Any provision of Senate rules adopted in a previous Congress which has the expressed or practical effect of denying the majority of the Senate in a new Congress the right to adopt the rules under which it desires to proceed is, in the opinion of the Chair, unconstitutional. It is also the opinion of the Chair that Section 3 of Rule 22 in practice has such an effect.

The Chair emphasizes that this is only his own opinion, because under Senate precedents, a question of constitutionality can only be decided by the Senate itself, and not by the Chair.

At the beginning of a session in a newly elected Congress, the Senate can indicate its will in regard to its rules in one of three ways:

First. It can proceed to conduct its business under the Senate rules which were in effect in the previous Congress and thereby indicate by acquiescence that those rules continue in effect. This has been the practice in the past.

Second. It can vote negatively when a motion is made to adopt new rules and by such action indicate approval of the previous rules.

Third. It can vote affirmatively to proceed with the adoption of new rules.

Turning to the parliamentary situation in which the Senate now finds itself, if the motion to table should prevail, a majority of the Senate by such action would have indicated its approval of the previous rules of the Senate, and those rules would be binding on the Senate for the remainder of this Congress unless subsequently changed under those rules.

If, on the other hand, the motion to lay on the table shall fail, the Senate can proceed with the adoption of rules under whatever procedures the majority of the Senate approves.

In summary, until the Senate at the initiation of a new Congress expresses its will otherwise, the rules in effect in the previous Congress in the opinion of the Chair remain in effect, with the exception that the Senate should not be bound by any provision in those previous rules which denies the membership of the Senate the power to exercise its constitutional right to make its own rules.

As Nixon emphasized, his opinion did not have the force of a ruling in response to a point of order and was merely advisory. Nevertheless, Nixon, a Republican whose party was the Senate minority, urged the Senate to rethink the inherited view of the Senate as a continuing body. Nixon's view was very plain: in choosing between the Senate's right to decide its rules, a constitutional prerogative, and operating under a rule inherited from a past Congress, the Senate had no choice but to allow the Senate to decide its rules.[2]

Nixon's opinion highlighted an issue on which reformers had spoken before but which remained unsettled in their arguments. Nixon emphasized the Senate's circumstances at the start of a new Congress. The implication of Nixon's statement is that the adoption or passive acceptance of a supermajority rule for changing rules at the start of a Congress binds the Senate to that rule. It is questionable whether Nixon's view that the Constitution empowers a Senate majority to revisit its rules would imply that this power is limited to the start of a Congress. After all, the composition and attitude of the majority can change during a Congress. Nixon's opinion reflected his immediate circumstances—the consideration of a motion to consider the rules at the start of a Congress—and represented a less radical change than the idea that the Constitution empowers the Senate majority to change the rules at any time.

Johnson surely knew that Nixon's ruling and the growing demand for both civil rights legislation and filibuster reform were important developments. He chose to address the Senate just before the vote with his longest and most carefully prepared comments on the subject yet. It was recognized as an important moment and the galleries were filled with staff and spectators (*Congressional Record,* January 4, 1957, 213–15).

Johnson began, as many reform opponents did, with the contention that the Senate risked becoming a House of Representatives if the reformers had their way. He observed that reform proponents were arguing that a continuing body need not have continuing rules, but he insisted that nothing in Article 1, Section 5, required that "a continuing body must change its rules every 2 years." He went on to argue that the rules could be changed under the continuing rules, as the adoption of the cloture rule illustrated. The cloture rule, he went on in his only reference to Nixon's opinion, "was adopted without going around Robin Hood's barn to obtain a ruling that the Senate is not a continuing body."[3] Surely reflecting his management role as majority leader and his concern about the fragile relations between the two wings of his party, Johnson said, "I cannot see the prudence of now opening the Senate to a prolonged and chaotic period by making a decision which would deprive us of all of our rules and all the things that go with those rules, including our committee structure."

The opening of the 1957 session produced no change. The motion to table Anderson's motion was adopted 55–38. Opposed by southerners and most minority party Republicans and therefore lacking a simple majority for reform, liberal Democrats had little choice but to let the issue be decided as Johnson intended. Nevertheless, 38 votes against the motion to table were 17 more than they had had in 1953, which was some consolation for liberals and a source of concern about the future for Johnson and the southerners. Moreover, Nixon's opinion was far more sweeping than Barkley's 1949 ruling on whether cloture applied to the motion to proceed, but the two rulings indicated the potential importance of the presiding officer in challenging supermajority cloture in the twentieth-century Senate. Nixon would be vice president in the next Congress, too.

With significant filibuster reform dead, Democratic liberals had little hope of passing a major civil rights bill. A modest bill proposed by the Eisenhower administration was passed by the House but faced procedural maneuvering in the Senate. The Republican minority leader, William Knowland, took the lead in promoting the House-passed bill, and Johnson, saddled with a divided party, was something of a procedural bystander while working to find some formula to pass a watered-down version. Knowland and civil rights advocates believed that referral of the bill to the Judiciary Committee would doom the legislation, so Knowland objected to referral under Rule XIV, which allows an objection to the referral of a House-passed bill to remain on the calendar for floor action. Russell raised a point of order that

Rule XIV conflicted with Rule XXV, which provides for referral to the committee of jurisdiction, but Nixon ruled against the point of order and the Senate sided with Nixon's ruling and against the point of order, 39–45.

Southerners' debate delayed a vote on the motion to proceed more than a week. Eventually a large majority favoring the administration bill passed the motion 71–18. Southerners focused on amending the bill and at first threatened a long filibuster if it was not amended. During Senate floor consideration, two key provisions, allowing federal troops to enforce existing civil rights laws and the attorney general to pursue civil actions for preventive relief in civil rights cases, were deleted by amendment. Added were amendments guaranteeing jury trials in criminal contempt cases and specifying juror qualifications, both of which were considered unfriendly to civil rights. In the meantime, southerners backed off filibustering with Senator Sam Ervin (D-NC), confessing that they were worried that to do so would kindle more support for filibuster reform.

Although southerners backed away from all-out obstruction, the 1957 debate produced the longest speech ever by a lone senator. South Carolina's Strom Thurmond, then still a Democrat but having been the presidential candidate of the segregationist Dixiecrat Party in 1948, held the floor for twenty-four hours and eighteen minutes. He was well aware that Morse had held the floor for twenty-two hours and twenty-six minutes in 1954. Thurmond's nonstop speech attracted throngs to the Senate gallery and forced the Senate to bring in cots from a neighboring hotel so that senators could rest. But his fellow southerners did not appreciate his filibuster, which brought even more unfavorable attention in the South to their willingness to allow the bill to come to a vote (Cohodas 1994; Finley 2008; Frederickson 2001).

## CLOTURE REFORM, 1959

The 1958 elections, occurring in an economic recession during the midterm of President Dwight Eisenhower's second term, yielded a net of 16 additional Democrats in the Senate and moved the Senate's party division from a 49–47 Democratic seat advantage to a 65–35 advantage (with the addition of seats for Alaska and Hawaii for the first time). With most of the new Democrats representing the liberal wing of the party, the result was a more liberal Democratic conference, one in which liberal Democrats outnumbered conservative Democrats, and a more liberal Senate. Liberals again focused on the procedural obstacles to moving civil rights legislation.

Anticipating a stronger and well-planned liberal effort, Johnson collaborated with several Democratic and Republican leaders to sponsor an alternative to the likely Anderson motion to consider the Senate rules. Joining with Johnson were his whip, Mike Mansfield (D-MT), president pro tempore Carl Hayden (D-AZ), the Republican leader Everett McKinley Dirksen (R-IL), and two other Republican leaders, Styles Bridges (R-NH) and Leverett Saltonstall (R-MA). Johnson's strategy was to have a modest reform proposal to promise his colleagues if they supported his effort to table the expected Anderson motion.

Johnson's resolution, S. Res. 5,

- changed the majority required for cloture from two-thirds of senators duly chosen and sworn to two-thirds of senators present and voting;
- extended cloture to a resolution to change the Senate rules; and
- provided that "the rules of the Senate shall continue from one Congress to the next Congress unless they are changed as provided in these rules."

The first provision reduced the threshold for cloture to the pre-1949 standard, while the second reestablished the pre-1949 expectation that cloture can be applied to rules reform. These were considered concessions to reformers. The third provision was an explicit response to the Nixon opinion, which, Johnson had reason to fear, would be the basis for the consideration of a more radical change to Rule XXII. It was interpreted as a guarantee to party conservatives that reform would go no further.

Events unfolded on the floor in a manner that probably neither Anderson nor Johnson predicted. Johnson sought unanimous consent to have his reform resolution considered, but

Anderson objected. Vice President Nixon then recognized Anderson, as may have been prearranged, but, with his right of first recognition, Johnson insisted that he retain the floor, which he used to move adjournment. The Senate supported the motion 73–23, with liberals opposed.

Having regrouped by the next day, Johnson indicated that he was willing to let Anderson make his motion, which Johnson expected to be able to table before moving to his own resolution. Anderson, however, offered a different motion than he had in the past: he now moved that the Senate adopt its rules, excluding Rule XXII, and consider Rule XXII following the adoption of his motion. In doing so, Anderson hoped to disarm critics who charged that his previous approach opened all Senate rules to revision. It turned out not to matter much because Johnson managed to attract the support of several freshmen for his limited reforms. The Anderson motion was tabled 60–36, and after several liberal amendments were rejected, the Johnson resolution was adopted 72–22. Two-thirds of the negative votes came from southerners who, while opting not to filibuster Johnson's resolution, chose to vote against any modification of the cloture threshold. Johnson had won the support of several freshmen and liberals. At least some southerners knew they had escaped another reform episode with minimal harm to their cause, and maybe some good had come from endorsement of abiding by Rule XXII for the purpose of reforming the rules in the future.

## 1960: CONSERVATIVE DEMOCRATS FILIBUSTER

After the Johnson resolution was adopted, it took a little more than a year for the first real filibuster to occur on a civil rights bill. The result was passage of a bill, but only after what is regarded as the most classic of all filibusters.

The Eisenhower administration advocated a civil rights bill that included a provision for federal referees to oversee elections in areas with a pattern of discrimination. Southerners made every effort to block the legislation, but circumstances had changed. Liberal forces were stronger and Johnson was preparing a campaign for the presidency. Johnson's stance on civil rights shifted—for a national audience, he wanted to be seen as an advocate of civil rights and took the lead in designing a procedural strategy. Johnson circumvented the need for cloture on a motion to proceed by inviting civil rights provisions as amendments to an unrelated bill—a measure to lease acreage in a Missouri military base to a local school district. Johnson then kept the Senate in the same legislative day for the duration of the debate so that dilatory motions that could be used at the start of a new legislative day could be avoided. He used motions to table to cut off debate and defeat unfriendly amendments. Moreover, once southerners made clear their intention to obstruct action, Johnson held around-the-clock sessions to wear them down; many were rather old. Some observers suggested that Johnson also was deliberately baiting the southerners into filibustering in order to draw attention to his support for civil rights.

Unlike the 1957 debate, when Thurmond struck out on his own, the 1960 filibuster was orchestrated by Russell as leader of the southerners. He organized three six-senator teams, with each team holding the floor for a day while the others rested and refused to be counted for quorum calls. Again, cots were brought into the rooms adjacent to the floor, and for a time senators answered quorum calls in pajamas and slippers. The quorum calls, demanded at all hours, forced civil rights supporters to muster a majority of senators to prevent the Senate from adjourning, which would have created a new legislative day and given the filibusterers time to rest.

The 1960 cloture vote was defeated 42–53, far short of the required two-thirds majority of senators voting. Morse and other liberals filed the cloture petition against the wishes of Majority Leader Johnson, who wanted more time to work on compromise legislation. Apparently, even a dozen northern Democrats and a majority of Republicans who were on record in favor of some legislation also wanted more time and sided with Johnson against cloture. Johnson worked on a Dirksen proposal to find compromise legislation that southerners might allow to come to a vote and, after the House passed its bill, moved to take up the House bill. Southerners allowed the bill to be considered and the Senate approved the Dirksen substitute 68–20, indicating more than two-thirds support for the compromise language. With votes to spare, Johnson moved to table a variety of amendments, which led to passage of the bill, 74–18, with southerners voting against.

In the end, the 1960 southern filibuster slowed the process, created opportunities for negotiations, and resulted in a compromise bill that suited Johnson's interests as a party leader and presidential candidate. Johnson appeared to be critical to the outcome. He wanted a new civil rights bill while minimizing the alienation of his southern colleagues. He successfully opposed cloture when a vote on cloture was forced on him by holding out the possibility of constructing a bill that would attract the support of a supermajority and make cloture moot. Southerners thought that the outcome was not nearly as bad as they had feared and was much preferred to the House bill; liberals were not excited by the result but were happy to claim victory. Demands for stronger legislation continued to build outside of the halls of Congress.

## THE JOHNSON YEARS IN RETROSPECT

Decades later, senators would cite the mid-twentieth century as a time when the Senate worked as it should. This was a Senate in which senators behaved. They minimized their partisanship, fully exploited the rules only in extraordinary circumstances, and resolved their differences over procedural matters informally through unanimous consent agreements. The filibuster was reserved for the most important issues of the day. The give-and-take of extended deliberations, when they occurred, yielded compromise outcomes. Civility reigned.

This characterization is a half-truth at best. Far more powerful forces than mere civility kept overt obstructionism to a minimum in the 1950s. Missing from the traditional account is that there was a conservative majority in most Congresses that did not have a large, positive legislative agenda, that the inherited system allowed many issues to be bottled up in committee, that a major faction of the majority party deliberately suppressed filibusters to reserve them for its own cause, and that a talented majority leader was proactively engaged in suppressing the issues that would divide his party and generate overt obstructionism on the Senate floor.

Throughout the 1950s, southerners weighed the costs and benefits of filibustering. Knowing that their success in opposing serious civil rights legislation depended on preserving a high threshold for cloture, they filibustered selectively so as not to stimulate more support for filibuster reform than was deemed to be a necessary risk. Only in 1960 did a unified southern bloc coordinate a filibuster for a lengthy period of time. Otherwise, usually with Lyndon Johnson's assistance, they sidestepped liberal efforts that might have produced protracted filibusters. Open filibusters were not common, but obstructionism on civil rights was real and effective.

Johnson was an important ally. He used his influence to slow and dilute civil rights measures and was a force for the procedural status quo. With the support of Republicans and southern Democrats, Johnson successfully avoided efforts by Democratic liberals in 1953 and 1957 to gain floor consideration of cloture reform resolutions. In 1959, he preempted the liberals with the modest proposal negotiated with Republican leaders and adopted after a simple-majority cloture proposal was defeated. The Senate entered the 1960s with liberals continuing to agitate for reform.

CHAPTER 3

# THE RISE OF INDIVIDUALISM, 1961–1976

AFTER THE JOHNSON YEARS, senators ascended as more prominent politicians. The Senate emerged as an institution that catered to individual senators' needs and aspirations. Individualism did not supplant parties and factions as forces in policy making, but respecting individual senators and adjusting the schedule and procedure to suit them became a self-conscious emphasis of the institution's leadership and reshaped everyday life in the Senate.

This was the era of Mike Mansfield, the Democratic leader from 1961 through 1976. Mansfield loved China and world affairs more than the day-to-day details of managing the Senate. His whip in the 1970s, Robert Byrd, was fully dedicated to the Senate, mastered its history, personified the transition of southern politics, and attempted to lend order to an increasingly disorderly institution. Both Mansfield and Byrd were openly and without reservation servants of their colleagues. Mansfield, at least, supported modest reform of the cloture rule but, critically, opposed the use of extraordinary means for getting to a vote on reform. His view appeared to reflect a pivotal position throughout this era—until 1975.

Party and faction did not disappear in this era. To the contrary, factional politics dominated policy making, and partisan interests remained central to most important issues. But there was an odd mix of individualistic, factional, and partisan politics. Senators were eager to exploit the opportunities the Senate created to express their views and pursue their policy and career interests. They less frequently resisted the temptation, often encouraged by organized interests outside of Congress, to push causes. The overlay of party and factions remained in the 1960s and 1970s and created tremendous challenges for party leaders in managing the floor.

The civil rights struggle continued and cloture reform remained central to it. The 1958 and 1964 elections greatly strengthened the liberal faction of the Senate majority party. In 1963, 1967, 1969, and 1971, efforts to invoke cloture on reform proposals received majority, but not two-thirds, support. Mansfield, who was not the taskmaster that Johnson attempted to be, sympathized with reformers but generally stood for Senate traditions and, in the absence of two-thirds support to invoke cloture on reform resolutions, opposed the use of extraordinary means to gain a vote on a reform resolution. The result was stalemate on cloture reform until 1975, when a nearly unique confluence of factors allowed liberals to successfully gain a vote on a reform resolution.

## FROM A FACTIONALIZED TO A POLARIZED SENATE, 1961–1988

During the 1960s and early 1970s, the divide between conservative and liberal Democrats deepened. This schism among majority party senators shaped Mansfield's strategies and continued to motivate senators' interests in procedural reform. Two aspects of the Senate's composition warrant careful attention.

First, the partisan balance waxed and waned. As figure 3.1 shows, after the very competitive 1950s, the Democrats retained majority control of the Senate through 1980. During the 1960s, Democrats enjoyed large majorities due to the success of northern Democrats and the retention of southern seats. Even with large majorities, Democrats achieved two-thirds of the seats only in the 88th and 89th Congresses (1963–66). Democrats maintained a majority until the Republicans won a Senate majority in the 1980 elections, which brought Republican Ronald Reagan to the White House. For three Congresses, the Republican majorities were small. In part, their success reflected gains in southern states, which proved to be lasting. Republicans lost their Senate majority in the 1986 elections, Reagan's second midterm election (figure 3.2).

**Figure 3.1.** Party Sizes as Percentage of Senate, 1951–2012

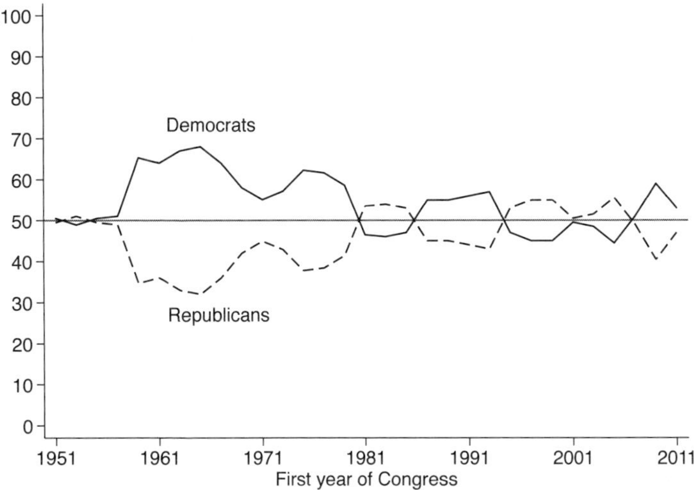


**Figure 3.2.** Number of Southern Senators, 1951–2012

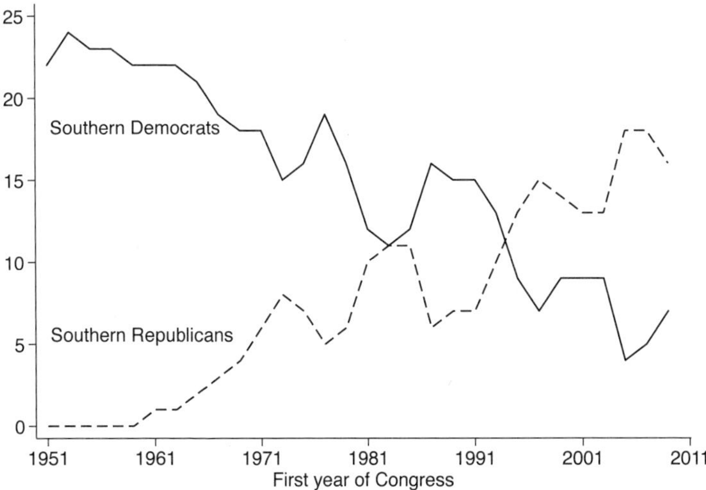

Second, the factionalism within the parties evolved in important ways. Factionalism is best understood in the context of the two major dimensions of congressional politics during the era—the liberal-conservative dimension and the civil rights dimension. Before the 1970s, southern Democrats separated themselves from other Democrats and most Republicans on civil rights issues, which yielded voting patterns quite different from those on other issues.

To see the significance of these dimensions, a little statistical background is helpful. Political scientists use statistical techniques to summarize the behavior of legislators on roll-call votes. The analysis defines mathematical scales on which legislators are ordered or ranked in a way that minimizes the errors in predicting their votes. A perfect scale is one that cleanly separates legislators who vote yea from those who vote nay. One scale, say a liberal-conservative dimension, might fit the observed behavior well, but often two or more dimensions are required to improve the accuracy of the predictions. The presence of two or more dimensions means that the alignment of legislators varies across the dimensions, with some groups voting alike on one dimension but differently on other dimensions.

Here and throughout this book, I report analyses based on the scaling technique used most frequently by political scientists. Figure 3.3 shows the percentage of senators' votes that are correctly predicted by just the liberal-conservative dimension and by adding a second dimension. That scaling uncovers a strong liberal-conservative dimension throughout the era and a significant second dimension in the 1950s and 1960s. During that period, the second dimension was defined by votes on civil rights issues. In the 1970s and later, this dimension was not associated with civil rights votes and was less important to the structure of the observed voting alignments. As this era ended in the late 1980s, the liberal-conservative dimension became more dominant and politics looked more unidimensional.

To illustrate the factionalism in the Senate of the 1960s, senators of the 89th Congress (1965–1966) have been scaled on the two dimensions. The scatterplots for each party, distinguishing

**Figure 3.3.** Percentage of Senators' Votes Correctly Predicted Using One or Two Dimensions, 1947–2010

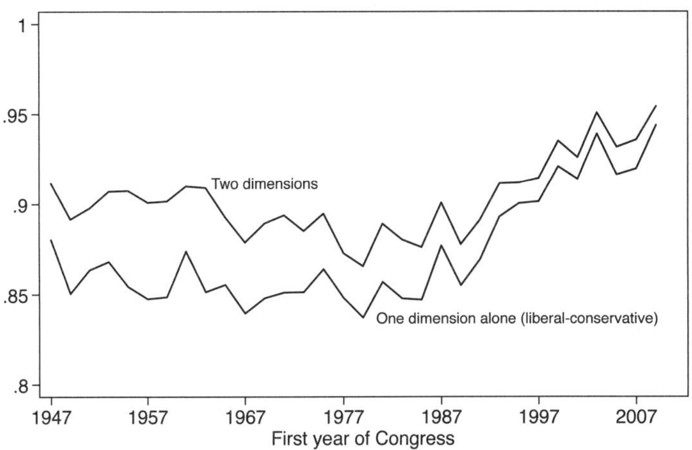


*Source:* Optimal classification. Keith Poole, www.voteview.com.

senators by region, are shown in figure 3.4.[1] The figure also shows several important features about voting alignments:

- On the liberal-conservative dimension, southern Democrats populated the moderate region between the parties' medians along with much of the Republican party, with northern Democrats more liberal and half of the Republicans more conservative.
- On the liberal-conservative dimension, with a large Democratic majority, the Senate's overall median and the Democrats' median were close. Simple-majority legislative outcomes would be expected to lie at the chamber median and near the center of the distribution of Democrats, with a few southern Democrats preferring outcomes at the Republican median over the chamber median.
- On the civil rights dimension, Republicans and southern Democrats were on opposite sides. This allowed a coalition of Republicans and northern Democrats to determine legislative outcomes, which would be expected to be located in the middle of the northern Democratic contingent.

**Figure 3.4.** Distribution of Senators on Liberal-Conservative and Civil Rights Dimensions, by Party and Region, 89th Congress (1965–1966)

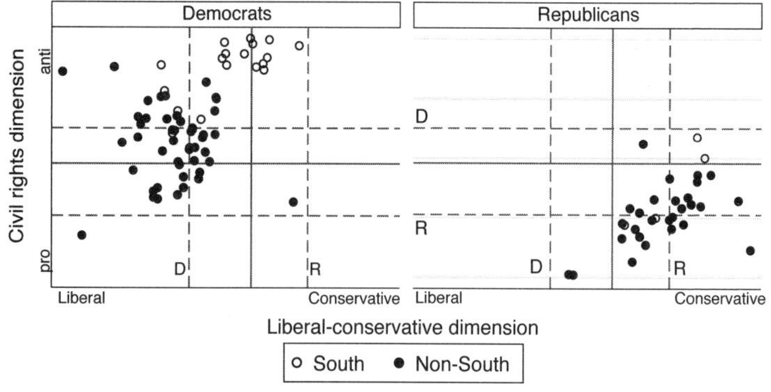


DW-NOMINATE scores. Dashed lines indicate the Democratic (D) and Republican (R) medians. Solid lines are Senate medians.

The distribution can be divided into quadrants using the Senate median on each dimension. For the majority party Democrats, it is notable that in no quadrant did the Democrats constitute a majority of the party. Although nearly all nonsouthern Democrats were on the liberal side of the liberal-conservative dimension, there were a few nonsouthern Democrats on the side of the southerners in resisting strong civil rights legislation. Southern Democrats were distinctive on both dimensions but more so on civil rights votes, where they were very cohesive at the anti–civil rights end of the scale.

The rise of the liberal Democrats, due primarily to the elections of 1958 and 1964, and the election of Democratic presidents Kennedy and Johnson promoted the liberal agenda. Beyond civil rights issues, liberals pushed a wide range of economic, environmental, and social programs that were associated with the Kennedy and Johnson administrations and continued into battles with the Nixon administration. The liberal agenda yielded more frequent opposition from the conservative coalition of Republicans and southern Democrats. The frequency of the appearance of that voting bloc, and the number of its victories, increased over the late 1960s and into the 1970s (see figure 2.1 in the previous chapter).

It was difficult for the Democratic leader, Mike Mansfield, to manage his party. Northern and southern Democrats found themselves on opposite sides of the Senate median on many issues. Unlike the Senate Democrats of the mid-1950s, northern liberals greatly outnumbered southern conservatives. Given the liberal leaning of his party's conference and Presidents Kennedy and Johnson, Mansfield did not have the option of ignoring or suppressing the liberal agenda. Nevertheless, on the central procedural question of filibuster reform, the party remained divided. I say more about this below.

The appearances of the conservative coalition—defined as votes on which a majority of southern Democrats and a majority of Republicans opposed a majority of northern Democrats—faded from their peak early in the Nixon administration. Over the 1970s and 1980s, as Republicans replaced many southern Democrats, the liberal Democrats continued to confront a conservative coalition, but the conservative Democrats became a smaller faction that could no longer win leadership contests and direct party strategy, at least not without the support of some northerners and liberals. Democratic conservatives were a source of considerable frustration for liberals, as they joined with Republicans on many issues to carry votes in the Senate throughout the 1970s and 1980s.

By the late 1980s, the divisions among senators on roll-call votes aligned more frequently with the liberal-conservative dimension. This process of polarization came with the realignment of the South and the sorting of the parties' electoral coalitions into liberal and conservative camps (Abramowitz 2010). By this time, as figure 3.5 shows, the remaining southern Democrats were to the left of nearly all Republicans, southern Republicans were the most conservative party-region group, and the parties were quite polarized. The senators at the Senate median were southern Democrats, but now their numbers were reduced and the remaining southerners were considerably more moderate than nearly all Republicans. Partisan

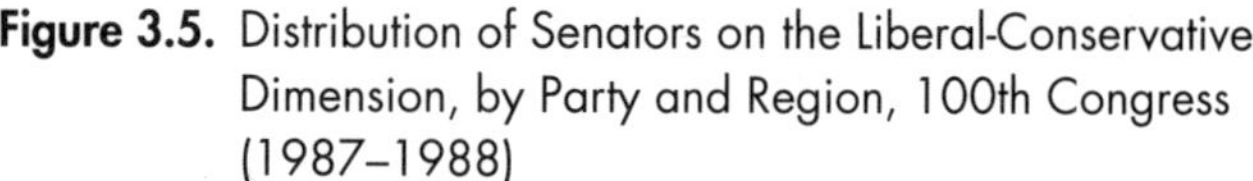

**Figure 3.5.** Distribution of Senators on the Liberal-Conservative Dimension, by Party and Region, 100th Congress (1987–1988)

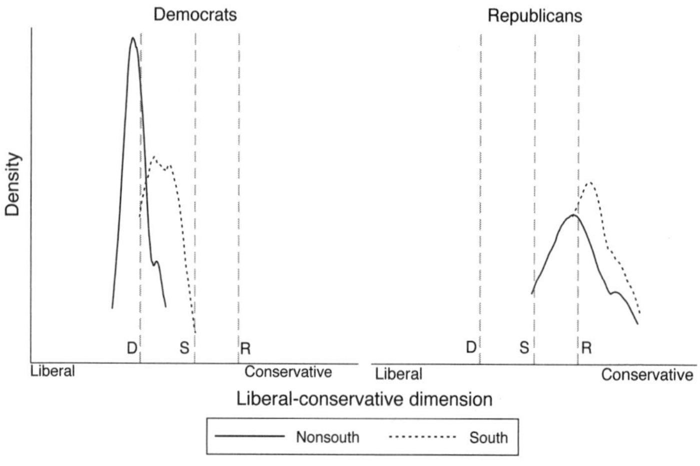


Kernel density distributions. DW-NOMINATE scores. Dashed lines: Party (D, R) and Senate (S) medians.

polarization did not eliminate internal factionalism, but dominant factions—liberals for Democrats and conservatives for Republicans—were well established as the 1980s came to an end.

## FROM THE CLUBBY TO THE INDIVIDUALISTIC SENATE

The clubby Senate of the 1950s, whatever its political foundations, could not survive the changes in its membership and the environment in which senators operated over the next decade. Evolving party alignments and factionalism were only a part of the story. The now-more-influential liberals were not interested in the slow, insular, norm-bound, midcentury Senate that was dominated by conservative southern Democrats, often in coalition with Republicans. And the political environment was changing, and changing quickly and dramatically:

- The emergence of television as the dominant medium of news created an opportunity for senators to become nationally recognized; they exploited it.
- Jet travel allowed most senators to be back in their states on a weekly basis. The speed of travel created opportunities for senators to attend events around the country and build a national following.
- The expansion of the Washington community—federal agencies, national associations, law firms, and lobbyists—created new pressures on and opportunities for senators.
- The rise of new electioneering techniques and technologies, the decline of party-run campaigns, and the rise of candidate-centered campaigns placed legislators in charge of developing their own organizations and raising their own campaign funds.
- The demise of party caucuses and conventions as the means for selecting delegates to the presidential nominating conventions, a process once dominated by governors, opened a path to nomination for more senators.

Many observers of American politics noted that the Senate of the 1970s and 1980s was very different from the Senate of the 1950s (Fenno 1989; Polsby 1989; Ornstein, Peabody, and Rohde 1977; Peabody, Ornstein, and Rohde 1976; Sinclair 1989; Smith 1989). Over the course of the 1960s, the Senate became a permeable institution filled with senators with a national and international outlook, broader policy interests, more committee and subcommittee assignments, larger staffs, and, commonly, an interest in the presidency and building a national audience. In the Senate of the 1970s and 1980s, senators showed little recognition of the previous informal norms that limited their participation, and no inner club was to be found. By the 1970s, even junior senators were eager to champion causes, attract nationwide audiences, and build coalitions, often across party lines, to pass legislation and advance their careers.

The Senate of the 1970s and 1980s was known for its individualism. Neither beholden to strong partisan bonds nor bound by norms that limited influence to senior committee leaders, senators adopted strategies that suited their personal political and policy interests. To expand and support their individual activism, senators created more committee and subcommittee chairmanships, created much larger personal and committee staffs, and expanded the congressional support agencies. They asked that committee and floor sessions be arranged to reflect their travel schedules. More important, senators came to be known for political entrepreneurship—for cultivating new policy ideas; attracting a national following, often testing the waters for presidential campaigns; and exploiting the opportunities under Senate rules and practices to push or oppose legislation.

As if to illustrate my point, Senator Fred Harris (D-OK) once said, "If I'm reincarnated I'd like to come back as Jim Abourezk. There I was, up there on that Hill, trying to be nice to everyone for five years, and the sixth year I realized it didn't make a damn bit of difference. All you do is become a member of the establishment and you still don't get all that much accomplished. Abourezk figured that out in the first two weeks he was up there" (Hightower 1989). Harris, first elected in 1964, made this observation about James Abourezk (D-SD), first elected in 1972. A new breed had arrived in the Senate and senators knew it.

The task of managing the floor—scheduling sessions, bringing bills to the floor, arranging time agreements—became much more difficult. Senators became more assertive on the floor (Smith 1989, 86–129). As the liberal agenda expanded, the volume of floor activity increased and created more openings for amendments and obstruction. By the late 1960s, senators were offering 50 percent more amendments than they were early in the decade and objecting more frequently to leaders' unanimous requests to limit their opportunities to debate and offer amendments. And they were more insistent that floor activity be scheduled to accommodate their numerous other activities.

Anyone attentive to the Senate of this era was quite aware of how reserved the new leaders were in comparison with the heavy-handed leadership of Lyndon Johnson in the 1950s. The majority and minority party leaders during this period—Mike Mansfield (MT) and Robert Byrd (WV) on the Democratic side and Everett Dirksen (IL), Hugh Scott (PA), and Howard Baker (TN) on the Republican side—assisted and facilitated the work of their colleagues more than they set directions and implemented central strategies. To be sure, these leaders were spokesmen for their parties, acting as the chief intermediaries with the president, and they supervised the small party organizations and staffs, managed floor activities, and coordinated party strategies, all tasks of considerable importance. Nevertheless, the leaders generally took a backseat to committee leaders and other senators in writing legislation and building coalitions on the important issues.

In the more individualistic Senate, parties were of considerable importance, but the parties of the 1960s and 1970s lacked the cohesiveness that allowed elected leaders to take much for granted. The divisions among Democrats were conspicuous. Through the 1980s, even Senate Republicans, long the more cohesive of the two parties, included a handful of northeastern and midwestern senators with more moderate or liberal policy preferences whose votes were often vital to Democratic liberals. In this context, a coherent, extended obstructionist strategy of filibustering and delay on the part of the minority was unthinkable. The minority party lacked a sufficient consensus to pursue any strategy for long, and without the backing of a cohesive party, the minority leader was not in a position to obstruct the majority without alienating a significant number of his fellow partisans. Neither party's leaders could punish defectors on any issue without alienating colleagues whose votes would be needed on other issues.

By the end of the 1980s, the Senate remained individualistic but showed signs of sharper partisan polarization. In the House at that time, Republican Newt Gingrich was advocating more disciplined and universal opposition to the majority party Democrats, who, he argued, had become more stridently partisan under Speaker Jim Wright (D-TX) (Sinclair 2006). Indeed, Gingrich's message seemed to play a critical role in his election as party whip in 1989. In the Senate, assertive senators, then divided sharply by party, were ready to fully exploit their procedural prerogatives.

## SENATE TIME AS A COMMON POOL RESOURCE

In his struggle with Senate individualism, Mansfield confronted what social scientists call the "common pool resource" problem. A common pool resource is a good that is difficult or costly to exclude individuals from exploiting. With unchecked access, individuals overuse the resource to the detriment of the group as a whole. In this chapter and the next, we will see that Senate floor time became scarcer as the congressional workload expanded in the late twentieth century. Contributing to the scarcity were senators' more aggressive use of amendments and obstructive tactics, more frequent debate, and, more often than seems possible, delays in getting senators to the floor to offer amendments and conduct the debate they demanded.

The primary solutions to common pool resource problems (Ostrom 2000) are voluntary coordination among individuals who recognize the costs of abusing access, "privatizing" the resource by dividing it and giving each part to an individual to manage, and formal regulation by some authority. Privatizing is not an option in the case of Senate floor time, so senators struggle with informal coordination approaches and more formal rules. In a relatively small, clearly defined group like the Senate, or at least the majority party, agreement about how to informally allocate floor opportunities seems to be a viable solution as long as there are meaningful sanctions for a senator who abuses his privileges.

Leaders realized that their tools for managing the floor and sanctioning colleagues were limited. The most effective means for structuring debate and amending activity was to gain unanimous consent for some limitations, but Senate individualism made this most important tool for managing the floor more difficult to employ. More and more of the majority leader's time became dedicated to gaining unanimous consent to improve the efficiency of floor proceedings. The succession of reform efforts in the 1970s and 1980s, implying the need for more formal regulation of floor activity, indicates how difficult it was for leaders to address the floor management issues on their own and how little freedom to maneuver individual senators were willing to give up to meet the demand for a more predictable schedule.

## ELABORATION OF UNANIMOUS CONSENT AGREEMENTS

In response to the expectations of their colleagues, majority leaders adjusted their strategies. This was obvious in the provisions of unanimous consent agreements, which were designed to structure floor action but also had to reflect senators' demands. Even before Johnson left the Senate to become vice president, the Senate began to change in ways that made the standard form unworkable in some situations. A major problem was that the standard form allowed intervening amendments and motions to lengthen floor consideration of a measure. A more assertive membership proved increasingly unwilling to accept unanimous consent requests to impose a general limit of debate on amendments and instead insisted on limits tailored to individual amendments. Most of this came to be done on an ad hoc, amendment-by-amendment basis, but sometimes it was accomplished in long agreements that listed many amendments. To further close loopholes that senators had learned to exploit, leaders began to offer agreements that barred intervening motions.

By the end of Johnson's service as majority leader, resistance to the routine inclusion of a germaneness requirement for amendments had begun to surface. During the 1960s and 1970s, leaders found that their "UC" requests were frequently questioned by colleagues and they could seldom gain approval of a blanket prohibition of nongermane amendments. Nonstop efforts to limit debate and amendments to lend some order to floor proceedings were frequently frustrated, as in this 1964 exchange on the floor between Mansfield, who had been trying for days to make progress in considering amendments to a bill, and Iowa Republican Bourke Hickenlooper (R-IA), with New York Democrat Kenneth Keating jumping in:

> MR. HICKENLOOPER: Following the pattern of the inquiry of the distinguished leader, would it be in order to ask that the amendment to which I have referred be put in the line of progression?
> MR. MANSFIELD: There is nothing to stop it.
> MR. HICKENLOOPER: May I ask that there be added to the Senator's list of developing programs the amendment relating to writing instruments to which I have referred so that it will follow the three or four amendments to which he has already referred?
> MR. MANSFIELD: Mr. President, I ask unanimous consent that the Dirksen-Hickenlooper amendment be considered sometime tomorrow.
> MR. HICKENLOOPER: Mr. President, reserving the right to object, that is not what I asked. I asked if the amendment could follow the succession of amendments which the majority leader has outlined.
> MR. MANSFIELD: If the Senator wishes to make such a unanimous consent request, it is satisfactory with me.
> MR. HICKENLOOPER: I hoped that, out of the charity of the Senator's heart, he would include the amendment in his request.
> MR. KEATING: Mr. President, reserving the right to object, I have an amendment—
> MR. MANSFIELD: I give up . . .
> (*Congressional Record,* February 4, 1964, 1890)

In fact, Mansfield was an exceptionally tolerant and service-oriented floor leader. He was quite willing to modify agreements once approved if a senator asked later to have his or her amendment included. Far more than his predecessors, often because there was no other way to proceed, Mansfield offered unanimous consent requests in a piecemeal fashion—relating to single amendments, an afternoon's session, or a set of speeches. He worked hard to arrange the schedule to the convenience of his colleagues and made unanimous consent agreements his primary tool for creating some predictability in the schedule. This task became increasingly difficult.

In the early 1970s, several senators objected to Majority Leader Mike Mansfield's standard request that agreements be in the "usual form," which included the germaneness requirement. This came to a head in 1971, when Senator Jacob Javits complained, "I have seen unanimous-consent agreements entered into in which the rule of germaneness was never mentioned here; but when we read it in the order the next day, the rule of germaneness was there"(*Congressional Record,* October 27, 1971, 37729). In fact, Mansfield, following Johnson, frequently asked for the agreement in "usual form" without mentioning the germaneness restriction. In response to objections, Mansfield promised to give the Senate notice of future requests for a germaneness restriction and indicated that he would consider eliminating the germaneness provision as a part of the usual form. I have been unable to find evidence of any follow-up action on Mansfield's part, but the Javits-Mansfield exchange exemplifies the resistance of activist rank-and-file senators to the standardized procedures that mid-twentieth-century majority leaders had relied on.

As senators insisted on protecting their procedural prerogatives, majority leaders' efforts to manage the floor required customized unanimous consent agreements that responded to a variety of senators' demands. Such agreements protected a senator's right to have an amendment considered, whether it was germane or not; guaranteed all senators an opportunity to debate an amendment; and, as the majority leader desired, still provided some order to floor consideration of amendments. Unanimous consent agreements became highly individualized and far more complex.

Senator Robert Byrd (D-WV), who became Mansfield's assistant leader in 1971 and was active on the floor before that, took the lead on a number of innovations. Byrd aggressively pursued a tactical use of time agreements, frequently offering multiple agreements for floor action of amendments for a single bill to speed floor action whenever possible. An agreement for a single amendment became common, as did agreements that barred second-degree amendments and subsidiary motions. The *New Republic* labeled him "The Efficiency Byrd," dedicated to "keeping Senate traffic moving," keeping unnecessary staff off of the floor, reducing the Morning Hour to prearranged speeches, and structuring floor action whenever possible (Wieck 1973).

## THE FAILURE OF REFORMERS, 1961–1973

In the 1960s, filibusters remained uncommon, but the few filibusters that occurred were usually quite notorious and shaped the Senate's public image. Southerners, guided by Georgia's Richard Russell until his death in 1971, continued to limit their use of the filibuster to legislation that imposed federal civil rights standards on their region. Successful cloture motions backed by liberal Democrats and Republicans paved the way for action on landmark bills related to race and civil rights—the Civil Rights Act of 1964, the Voting Rights Act of 1965, and open housing legislation in 1968. Liberals failed to gain cloture over southern and Republican opposition on a ban of literacy tests for voting (1962), state right-to-work laws (1965), a civil rights bill focusing on housing and jury selection (1966), and District of Columbia home rule (1966). In 1968, a Republican-led filibuster prevented cloture on President Johnson's nomination of Abe Fortas to the Supreme Court.

Although successful in gaining congressional action on major civil rights measures, liberals kept up their efforts, all unsuccessful, to reform Rule XXII. At the start of five Congresses—in 1961, 1963, 1967, 1969, and 1971—liberals sought cloture on proposals to reduce the threshold for cloture and were defeated each time by southern Democrats and, usually, half or more of the Republicans. Only after the 1964 elections, when liberal ranks swelled and Johnson won by a landslide over Barry Goldwater, did liberals proceed to their legislative agenda without first attempting cloture reform. In all four reform efforts, reformers coalesced behind a proposal to reduce the threshold for cloture from two-thirds to three-fifths of senators present and voting, although significant numbers of liberals favored a simple-majority threshold. In the 1963, 1967, 1969, and 1971 efforts, a majority of senators voted in favor of cloture on the reform resolutions.

As in the past, reformers sought favorable rulings from the vice president that would have allowed them to gain a vote on a reform proposal without the necessity of cloture being invoked to overcome obstruction. In each case, Anderson made a motion to yield a ruling that a simple majority had the power to bring a reform measure to a vote at the start of a Congress. The argument continued to be that, at least at the start of a Congress, the Constitution implies that a simple majority of the Senate has the power to determine the rules.

In 1963, Vice President Johnson submitted the parliamentary question to the Senate. Precedent, Johnson correctly observed, required that a question of the interpretation of the Constitution be decided by the Senate rather than the presiding officer. A submitted question was (and is) debatable under the rules, so the submission of the question placed liberals in the hopeless position of having to find a two-thirds majority to invoke cloture on the question. As a result, liberals agreed to a showdown vote on a motion to table the submitted question, which was passed 53–42 and doomed their effort. The 53-vote majority to table the question might be interpreted as a sign of majority opposition to reform. It should not be. The subsequent motion to invoke cloture on the reform proposal, now requiring a two-thirds majority, failed 54–42—that is, a majority favored getting a vote on reform. Six Republicans and five Democrats who supported cloture on reform, thereby appearing to endorse the reform proposal, had voted in favor of the motion to table the constitutional question, which left the two-thirds threshold in place. Democratic leader Mike Mansfield was among the eleven. It appeared that at least a few senators who favored reform of Rule XXII were not persuaded by the liberals' constitutional argument about simple-majority cloture at the start of a Congress (Binder and Smith 1997, 176–82).[2]

Throughout his service as the Democrats' leader (1961–76), Mansfield took the position that the Senate should change the rules under existing rules. He was quite willing to seek cloture on reform proposals, but he did not cooperate with liberals seeking favorable rulings from the vice president. His unfriendly stance on the constitutional question meant that liberals could not take advantage of the majority leader's right of first recognition in their parliamentary strategy. In 1963, Mansfield's attitude, backed by Johnson's predictable view of his obligation to submit the constitutional question to the Senate, blocked liberals' path to reform.

Conditions changed in 1967. Hubert Humphrey was vice president and, during his Senate service, had a long record of support for Anderson's view of the constitutional question as the leading advocate of civil rights legislation (*Congressional Record,* January 18, 1967, 910–33). Senator George McGovern (D-SD) offered a two-part motion to set up a Humphrey ruling on a point of order that certainly would be raised against it. McGovern's motion to proceed was accompanied by a provision that the Senate vote immediately to end debate on the motion and do so requiring only a simple majority of senators present and voting to pass. Dirksen, the Republican leader, raised the point of order that McGovern's motion violated Rule XXII, and Humphrey submitted the question to the Senate. Humphrey assisted the reformers by noting that the point of order could be set aside by a successful motion to table, decided by a simple majority. By wording his motion as he did and arranging for Humphrey's announcement that objections to it could be settled by the motion to table the submitted question, McGovern hoped that the point of order against his multipart motion would be set aside by a simple majority and a clear path for a simple-majority vote on the motion would be obtained.

Mansfield objected to the McGovern approach and the motion to table on the grounds that it would undermine the Senate as a continuing body. In making his short statement, Mansfield ignored the argument of reformers in the 1950s that the question of the continuation of the rules from Congress to Congress was distinct from the Senate as a continuing body. Mansfield's point of order against the motion to table prevailed, 37–61. Five Democrats and nine Republicans voted against the motion to table but for cloture on the reform resolution itself (which attracted 53 votes). Again, a number of reform supporters did not endorse the method of getting to a vote for reform that reformers pursued.

In 1969, with Humphrey's support in his last few days as vice president, the reformers' approach changed. Humphrey agreed to rule on a point of order, to be raised by liberal Frank Church (D-ID), that only a simple majority is required to invoke cloture on a motion to proceed to the consideration of a reform resolution at the start of a Congress. Furthermore, he agreed to rule that an appeal of his ruling was not debatable and thus set up a quick vote on his ruling. As planned by liberals, a cloture vote occurred on the motion to proceed with a 51–47 vote in favor, Humphrey ruled that the vote was sufficient to invoke cloture, and his ruling was appealed. The Senate reversed the ruling 45–53. Mansfield, Albert Gore (D-TN), and four Republicans voted in favor of cloture and against the ruling.

In 1971, 51 senators cosponsored the reform resolution, but reformers no longer had a cooperative presiding officer. Republican vice president Spiro Agnew ruled that Rule XXII applied to the motion to proceed to the consideration of the resolution. With liberals refusing to give up, at least at first, southerners held the floor for most of three weeks, during which four cloture motions, all supported by a majority, failed. After the fourth vote, when President Pro Tempore Allen Ellender (D-LA) was presiding, liberal Republican Jacob Javits (R-NY) appealed the ruling that the vote failed on the grounds that a simple majority should decide the question. A Mansfield motion to table the appeal was adopted, 55–37, with the support of thirteen Republicans and three other Democrats who had supported cloture on the reform resolution.

With this somewhat tortured effort by reformers, the Senate entered the 1970s with the 1959 version of Rule XXII intact. Divisions on reform were largely the same as in the 1950s—liberal Democrats in favor, southern Democrats and most Republicans opposed. Nevertheless, at least a few liberal Democrats were beginning to have second thoughts about reform. President Richard Nixon, sworn into office in 1969, was making moves to enhance the power of the president at the expense of Congress. He had a legislative agenda that included many measures liberals opposed, and he appealed to fellow Republicans and southern Democrats for support. By the end of 1971, liberals had used the cloture rule to delay or block action on several bills and a Supreme Court nominee and were openly considering the importance of retaining the filibuster as a procedural option for their own use (Orfield 1975).

## THE END OF SOUTHERN RESTRAINT

In fact, 1971 marked an important development for southern Democrats. For many of them, the vote to invoke cloture on a bill to extend the military draft, which they favored, was the first time they had ever voted for cloture. Some of the old-timers had never voted for cloture in three decades of Senate service. The cloture motion, adopted 61–30, required the support of conservative Democrats because liberal Democrats who opposed the Vietnam War refused to allow a vote on the conference report. The world of obstructionism was becoming more complicated.

Nevertheless, by the end of Nixon's time in the White House (he resigned in August 1974 under the cloud of the Watergate affair), liberals had refocused their attention on filibuster reform. In 1973 and 1974, in what seemed at the time to be an eruption of obstructionism, liberals' legislation on voter registration, legal services, campaign finance reform, and the boycott of Rhodesian chrome were narrowly defeated when the two-thirds majority required for cloture could not be mustered. Seventeen measures were subject to cloture votes, far more than in any Congress until then. One issue—voter registration—had the flavor of the civil rights fights, but other legislative battles on legal services, the boycott of Rhodesian chrome, campaign finance reform, the Genocide Treaty, and debt limit generated other divisions—usually simple liberal-conservative divisions.

Plainly, southern Democrats had given up their long-standing policy of limiting filibusters to civil rights issues, opposing cloture on principle, and being attentive to the need to protect a high threshold for cloture in Rule XXII. The list of possible explanations for southerners' change of heart is quite long. Russell's death in 1971 may have removed a cautious southern leader and emboldened southerners, like James Allen (D-AL), to take the lead on the floor. The passing of the major civil rights bills in the 1960s meant that the "great cause" was lost, and there was therefore little reason to hold the filibuster in reserve for major civil rights bills.

Southerners were not operating in a political vacuum. A Republican president and the Republican senators were often teammates in obstruction. Dirksen, an assertive Republican leader who sought to maintain good working relations with Democratic leaders and supported key civil rights measures, died in 1969 and was replaced by Hugh Scott, a leader who was less influential with party conservatives. Perhaps most important, the frequency with which a liberal majority could be mustered for legislation increased the incentive to obstruct.

Political scientist Bruce Oppenheimer (1985) emphasized a feature of Senate decision making that may have contributed to the surge in filibustering and was only indirectly associated with factional politics. Oppenheimer observed that the congressional workload expanded in the aftermath of enacting the Great Society programs of the 1960s, which created a serious time management problem for the majority leadership. We have also observed that senators became more active on the floor. Time became scarce and more valuable, particularly for the majority party leader charged with passing his party's program and getting the work of the Senate done. Squeezing more legislative activity into a fixed two-year schedule gave filibustering senators more leverage with the majority leader and their colleagues. This additional leverage, the argument goes, increased the incentive to filibuster.

Another factor, not mentioned by Oppenheimer, is the emergence of Senator Robert Byrd as the de facto floor manager for the Democrats. Elected assistant leader (whip) in 1971, Byrd began to assist Mansfield in the day-to-day management of floor activity. From the start, Byrd looked to improve efficiency and was impatient with extended debate (*Congressional Record,* February 12, 1971, 366). Byrd's colleagues were both eager to offer more debate and amendments and insistent on attending to more activities away from the floor and even away from D.C., so Byrd's emphasis on efficiency was much appreciated. Byrd urged quicker and multiple cloture votes to move legislation as rapidly as possible and to increase public exposure to obstructionist opponents.

Of course, obstruction, cloture votes, factional strength, and majority party leadership strategies interact in ways that make sorting out cause and effect difficult. A large majority agenda may abbreviate the time available for each measure, create more opportunities for obstruction, and give obstructionists more leverage. Leadership impatience may yield quicker and more frequent cloture votes on more issues. The majority party

**Figure 3.6.** Number of Cloture Petitions, 1961–2010

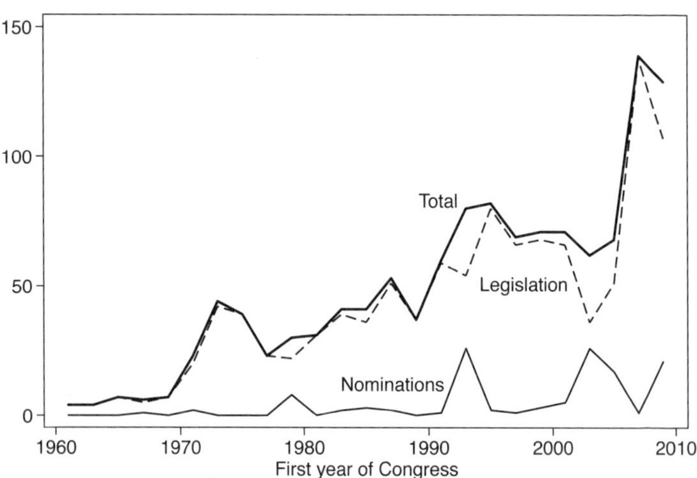


*Source:* www.senate.gov.

may deliberately stage cloture votes to highlight the policy stance of the opposition.

One thing was clear: southern Democrats were joining Republicans to block votes on liberals' agenda with a frequency that living senators had not seen before. The result was a step increase in the number of episodes in which the majority party leadership resorted to cloture. The new plateau of obstructionism and cloture would last through the 1980s and into the 1990s. This is reflected in the number of cloture petitions filed (see figure 3.6). Cloture petitions do not directly represent the number of filibusters, of course, but their frequency reflects the efforts of the majority to overcome minority obstruction.

## TRACKING AND HOLDS

The modern practices of tracking, holds, and clearance emerged under Mansfield with Byrd's guidance. Tracking—sometimes called the "two-track system"—emerged in 1972. Arranged by unanimous consent, debate on the filibustered bill is limited to certain hours of the day, while at other times, the Senate may debate and act on other legislation. The filibustering senators often find this acceptable because it saves them from organizing long floor speeches. The majority leader gets to move on with other parts of his floor agenda.

Observers have noted that tracking reduces the price that filibustering senators might pay for obstructing action. They are spared the burden of mounting hours of floor debate and they avoid blame for creating a backlog of other legislation. If so, tracking may encourage filibustering, an inference that has led senators and outsiders to demand that the majority leader force filibustering senators to conduct real, extended debate. In fact, Byrd did this for a labor bill in 1977 and again on a campaign finance reform bill in 1988, to no good effect.

In practice, only one filibustering senator needs to be on the floor, and senators on neither side of an issue want to sit through extended debate. The filibustering senator can buy a break by noting the absence of a quorum, which produces a quorum call and forces the bill's supporters to muster a quorum. If they fail to produce a quorum, the Senate must adjourn and the obstructionists may get the night off. If a quorum is achieved by getting senators to the floor, then another filibusterer can take over the debate and later note the absence of a quorum. This can continue indefinitely unless cloture is invoked or another arrangement is made by unanimous consent. In the meantime, C-SPAN viewers see little debate and a frequently empty Senate with "quorum call" splashed on the screen. Tracking often seems to be a less costly alternative.

Holds and more formal clearance practices emerged in tandem in the early 1970s as Byrd assumed a central role in floor proceedings (Smith 1989). Holds are requests to the floor leader that a measure not be considered on the floor, perhaps until some condition is met. For a minority senator, a hold represents an expectation that the floor leader will object to a majority-side request to proceed to the consideration of a measure. The practice became regularized in the 1970s as leadership staff recorded holds on their copies of the Senate *Calendar of Business.* Lobbyists began to request that senators place holds on bills to delay action. And senators found that they could use a hold to hold hostage a bill for some unrelated purpose, such as to get a committee chair to commit to considering another bill.

At about the same time, the majority leadership began to clear their plans for taking up measures on the floor in advance with their own membership and with the minority leader. Clearance helped the majority leader avoid surprise objections to his request to consider a measure. The regularization of the clearance practice also contributed to making holds appear to be a right and prompted more holds to be registered.

From the start, floor leaders kept confidential the identity of a senator placing a hold. At times, floor leaders may have used the secrecy to their advantage by privately addressing the concern of the senator or even using a hold as an excuse to delay floor action on a matter. But on the whole, holds became a serious problem for majority leaders. During the 1970s and 1980s, repeated announcements by majority leaders that holds were not a right and could be ignored did not make much difference. Leaders still wanted advance notice of problems, and senators appreciated the opportunity to exercise something approaching a personal veto, at least for legislation of only modest importance (Smith 1989). Whenever they could, Mansfield (with Byrd's assistance), Byrd, and Howard Baker, the Republican majority leader for the 1981–86 period, sought a time agreement before debate on a bill started and gained agreement to a debate limit for all amendments.[3]

Holds gained their effectiveness as implicit threats to object to a unanimous consent request to proceed to the consideration of a bill and then to filibuster. The threats became more credible and the floor leader's need for predictability increased as the number of actual filibusters increased.[4] It seems likely that more severe time constraints, a greater willingness to obstruct, and leadership practices were mutually reinforcing.

## AMENDMENTS AND THE EXPANDED USE OF MOTIONS TO TABLE

The increase in obstructionism in the early 1970s was accompanied by an increase in the number of amendments offered to measures on the Senate floor. In the 84th (1955–56) and 88th (1963–64) Congresses, for example, 600 to 700 amendments were offered on the floor, but only 10–15 percent yielded a contested vote (60–40 split or closer) and a large majority were accepted by voice vote. In contrast, in the 92nd (1971–72) and 96th (1979–80) Congresses, nearly 1,300 and 1,800 amendments were offered, respectively, with some increase in the fraction that were handled by voice vote but little change in the fraction that were contested (Smith 1989, 91). We will consider this development further in the next chapter.

The burden of obstructionism and the tidal wave of floor amendments on senators, bill managers, and especially floor leaders was enormous. Floor time became scarcer and needed more careful management. Aggressive use of time agreements to order consideration of amendments and bills was an essential tool, but in a chamber filled with assertive senators, the necessity of obtaining unanimous consent limited its utility. Floor leaders had good reason to look to other devices.

One place they looked was to the motion to table. A motion to table is not debatable. When offered, such as a motion to table an amendment, the vote occurs immediately, thereby preventing or ending any debate on the amendment. If adopted, the motion to table kills the amendment. If defeated, debate continues on the amendment, which usually ends with either a roll-call vote or voice vote to approve the amendment. With the Senate's sentiment registered on the motion to table, a voice vote on the amendment is often all that is requested.

Some scholars have emphasized that the motion to table is a procedural motion that, when adopted, avoids a direct vote on an amendment. This, they correctly observe, might insulate some senators from criticism for opposing an amendment and make it easier for the majority leader to find the votes necessary for killing an unfriendly amendment. As a result, the argument goes, the motion to table is central to the ability of the majority party to exercise an extra pound of influence over legislative outcomes (Den Hartog and Monroe 2011; Carson, Madonna, and Owens, 2011; King, Orlando, and Rohde 2010). In doing so, the Senate majority party has more control over what comes to a vote than is sometimes credited to it.

The historical pattern in the use of the motion to table to dispose of amendments suggests a different story (Smith, Ostrander, and Pope 2011). The frequency of motions to table amendments is mapped over recent decades in figure 3.7. Motions to table did not become an everyday feature of Senate floor action until the 1970s. The drop in their use in the most recent Congresses will be addressed in chapter 6. Plainly, there is more to the story of the use of motions to table than their occasional utility for attracting more votes against an amendment than the majority party leadership might otherwise acquire.

In the mid-twentieth century, senators seldom used the motion to table to dispose of amendments and seemed to prefer to avoid its use. In 1952, for example, a bill manager observed: "Mr. President, as a rule I do not favor the use of a motion to

**Figure 3.7.** Number of Motions to Table Amendments That Received Roll-Call Votes, 1949–2010

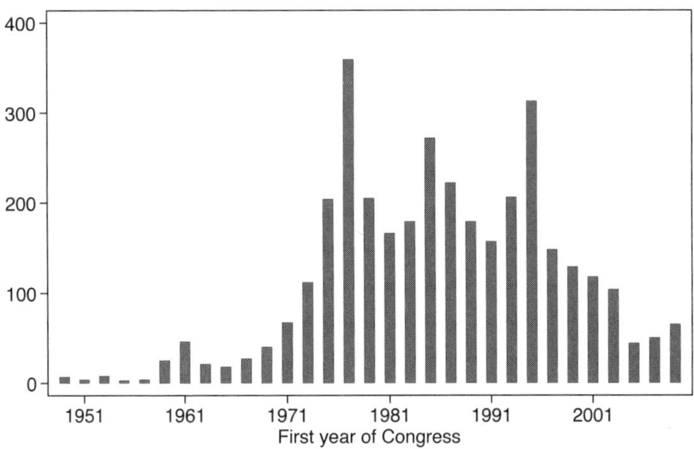


*Source:* Senate roll-call votes.

lay on the table. However, in this case two distinguished Senators have amendments which they wish to propose to the Hill amendment in the event the Hill amendment is not laid on the table. Therefore, since the easiest way to meet the issue at this time is by making such a motion, I move to lay on the table the amendment" (*Congressional Record,* April 2, 1952, 3346).

A motion to table an amendment was uncommon in the 1950s. Even Johnson, known for his parliamentary prowess, seldom used it. Through the 1960s, obstructionist episodes, such as debates on civil rights measures and cloture reform, were the few times that leaders, often including the minority leader, resorted to motions to table. The first episode of repeated use of the motion to table in the modern Senate occurred in 1960 during consideration of the civil rights bill. Johnson and Dirksen used several motions to table procedural motions and a few amendments of southerners who were throwing up obstacles to completing work on the bill.

The 1970s surge in amending activity was accompanied by more frequent use of the motion to table as the method to dispose of amendments. The efficiency of limiting debate on amendments, many of which would have been considered unfriendly to the interests of the majority leadership, surely was the major factor in this tactical adjustment. The Mansfield-Byrd team, operating under severe time constraints, wanted to clear the path to final action on bills and often found the motion to table indispensable for doing so, at least in the absence of unanimous consent to limit debate.

To say that efficiency was at stake is not to attribute the trend in motions to table amendments to an apolitical or nonpartisan cause. To the contrary, in a legislative institution, efficiency is charged with partisan implications. A majority leader confronting a minority that delays action by offering a succession of amendments may, in the end, find that the session expires before the Senate can act on much of his party's agenda. Sympathy for the leader's efforts may predispose his colleagues to support his motions to table. The important point is that the use of the motion to table, particularly for amendments, should be viewed in the context of the majority party's struggle to move Senate business. Its leaders sought to structure debate and amending activity by unanimous consent whenever possible, but when unanimous consent was not acquired, they turned to tabling motions to expedite business.[5]

These various considerations came into view during a 1978 debate over a treaty to give ownership of the Panama Canal to Panama. The debate extended for several weeks while senators proposed many reservations, which took the form of amendments to the resolution of ratification.[6] After agreeing by unanimous consent to a time for a vote on the treaty, senators were eager to have their amendments considered before time expired. With only a day before the final vote, Majority Leader Byrd sought unanimous consent to structure debate on the eleven amendments that his colleagues (of both parties) demanded receive consideration and a vote. His request provided for votes "with respect to" each of the amendments, which allowed a motion to table. Carl Curtis (R-NE), whose amendment was included in Byrd's request, threatened to object, indicating that he wanted a direct vote on his amendment. He observed that "when we are short of time" the Senate "should forego the idea of tabling amendments because some of them might require two rollcalls," which would happen if a motion to table was defeated by a roll-call vote and then the amendment was subject to a roll-call vote (*Congressional Record,* April 17, 1978, 10290).

Byrd responded:

> If we agree that we will waive the rights of senators to move to table the amendment by Mr. Curtis, there are other senators who, I think, would have justification for criticizing the leadership and for complaining that they were not given the same right of an up-and-down vote. That is the problem.
>
> We do have only a limited time tomorrow. Mr. Laxalt, Mr. Sarbanes, the minority leader, Mr. Helms, and others have tried to work out a schedule which is very tight and very close, indeed, in order to give every senator who has an amendment a chance to call it up and have a certain amount of time to debate it, so that no senator, when 6 o'clock arrives, will have been deprived of the opportunity to call up an amendment and to have some time for debate on it. . . . I hope the senator will not press his point, because if he does object, some senator will conceivably be shut out of time for debate on their [*sic*] amendments tomorrow. (*Congressional Record,* April 17, 1978, 10291)

Byrd withdrew his request and then plainly had an off-the-record conversation with Curtis and probably Paul Sarbanes (D-MD), the treaty manager for the majority. A few moments later, Byrd renewed his request and Curtis did not object. But later, after conferring with affected senators, Byrd asked for unanimous consent to modify the agreement to allow a direct vote on the Curtis amendment, which was done. The Curtis amendment was defeated, 33–65.

This minor episode illustrates several features of floor action typical of the 1970s Senate. The majority leader gave heavy emphasis to efficiency, fairness, and accommodation in a context of high demand for floor time. A senator preferred a direct vote on his amendment but seemed willing to accept a motion to table. And, as senators knew, the motion to table would have made no difference in the outcome on the amendment.

A systematic test of the view that motions to table amendments give the majority party extra influence is difficult to construct. The reason is that amendments that are killed by motions to table are not subject to a direct vote, which prevents an examination of vote outcomes on paired amendments and motions to table. Nevertheless, we can contrast votes on motions to table and votes on (unpaired) amendments to determine whether there are systematic differences in the distributions that seem to favor the side wanting to kill an amendment. If the argument is correct, we would expect to see more close votes and more partisan alignments on motions to table, which would be used to win a few extra votes to table amendments that might otherwise be adopted (Smith, Ostrander, and Pope 2013).

Figure 3.8 shows amendment and motion to table vote outcomes for the four Congresses of the 1969–76 period, during which motions to table amendments became so common—the

**Figure 3.8.** Distribution of Vote Margins for Amendment Votes and Motions to Table Amendment Votes, 1969–1976

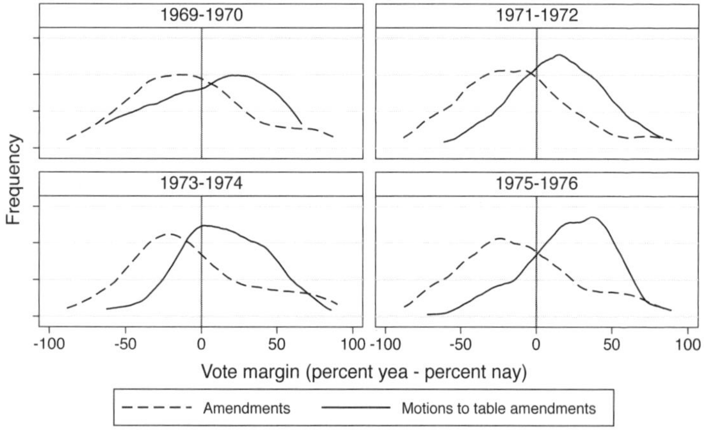

Kernel density distributions.

Mansfield period in which Byrd took a leading role in managing the floor.[7] The height of each line indicates the relative frequency of votes with that margin—the percentage voting yea minus the percentage voting nay. A value greater than zero indicates that the motion passed, so the modal case is for an amendment to fail and for a motion to table an amendment to pass. Amendment votes are shown to have a distribution very similar to motions to table. The proportion of votes that are closely divided—those in which some extra party influence might make a difference—is not significantly different for the two kinds of votes. Thus, it is reasonable to infer that few outcomes pivot on the difference between a motion to table and a direct vote on an amendment. Efficiency, rather than vote-by-vote partisan advantage, seems to be the primary motivation for more frequent use of the motion to table.

## LIMITS ON DEBATE IN BUDGET MEASURES

In the early 1970s, liberal-conservative conflict did more than pit Senate factions against each other and generate more filibusters than had ever been experienced before. It also pitted the Republican President Nixon against the Democratic majorities in the House and Senate. The Vietnam War stimulated end-the-war efforts on Capitol Hill, legislative battles over the military draft, and other subsidiary conflicts. Also central to interbranch conflict was President Nixon's use of impoundment and vetoes to counter spending on domestic programs, many of which had been created as a part of Johnson's Great Society programs in the mid-1960s when Democrats had a sizable majority. The impoundment battle involved the president's ability to withhold funds from programs that had received appropriations—spending bills signed into law or forced into law over the president's veto. The president was on weak constitutional grounds in doing so, at least most courts found, but he was winning the battle of public opinion on the question of whether the Democratic Congress was fiscally responsible.

It was in this context that the Senate adopted debate limits for budget measures as a part of the Budget Act of 1974 (Schick

2000).[8] The Budget Act created a schedule under which budget resolutions and reconciliation measures were considered. The Act included a fifty-hour debate limit for budget resolutions, a twenty-hour debate limit for reconciliation measures, debate limits for conference reports, and a prohibition on nongermane amendments.[9] It also created points of order to protect restrictions on the content of budget measures and floor action, restrictions that were expanded by the Budget Enforcement Act of 1985 and subsequent amendments thereto. Most notable about the enforcement mechanisms was that a point of order could be waived, or a ruling of the presiding officer overturned, only with a three-fifths majority. These mechanisms included the "Byrd rule," which provided for a point of order for violation of limits on the content of reconciliation bills.[10]

The new budget process turned Senate tradition on its head. In the Budget Act, senators accepted debate and amendment restrictions for one of the most important classes of legislation. They did so at a time when Senate minorities were exhibiting a penchant for filibustering important legislation, and budgets surely were among the most controversial legislative measures the Senate considered each year. Since then, senators have continued to accept new special procedures that limit their procedural options in order to address budget challenges.

While the Senate traditionally allowed extended debate, it also traditionally allowed a simple majority to overturn or uphold rulings of the presiding officer on procedural matters. To add teeth to the Budget Act's provisions, the Senate accepted a three-fifths majority requirement for sustaining an appeal of the ruling of the presiding officer or waiving points of order related to the most important features of the Act. For this class of legislation, senators had bound themselves more tightly to formal rules and procedural rulings than they had in the past.

## THE 1975 REFORM

In late 1974, liberals got lucky. In the aftermath of the Watergate scandal, the November elections boosted the number of Democrats to 61 and brought in several new liberals. Moreover,

Nelson Rockefeller, a liberal New York Republican, became vice president in December 1974 after Spiro Agnew resigned in response to a corruption investigation. Rockefeller would preside over the start of the new Congress in January 1975. For the first time since 1967, a proreform majority would have a friendly vice president at the start of a Congress and have a chance to revise Rule XXII.[11]

Reformers again offered a two-part motion to proceed to the consideration of their reform resolution and to require an immediate simple-majority vote on the motion to proceed.[12] Predictably, Mansfield raised a point of order against the motion on the grounds that it violated Rule XXII. Because the reformers defended the motion on constitutional grounds, Rockefeller submitted the question to the Senate, but he observed that he would interpret the Senate's decision on the Mansfield point of order "as an expression by the Senate of its judgment that the motion to end debate is in all respects a proper motion." Under this interpretation, tabling the Mansfield point of order would endorse the motion that provided for a simple majority to get a vote on the reform resolution, contrary to the letter of Rule XXII. Reformers then moved to table the Mansfield point of order.

In his argument against the reformers' motion to table the Mansfield point of order, Byrd outlined the implications of the Rockefeller interpretation for his colleagues (*Congressional Record,* February 20, 1975, 3841–45). He observed that if the reformers' strategy worked, senators could expect more multipart motions in which one part of the motion provides for an immediate vote without debate on the other parts. By tabling a point of order against such a motion—and a motion to table cannot be debated and is decided by a simple majority—the Senate would be prevented from debating the substance of the motion, which might be to pass a bill or amend the rules. Byrd warned reform Democrats, "May I say to those of us on our side that the day may come—although I hope it will not be in my time—when we will be in the minority, and it will take only 51 Senators from the other side of the aisle to stop debate immediately, without one word, on some matter which we may consider vital to our States or to the Nation." Going on, he said, "If this is done today, it can be done any day. If it can be done on this constitutional question, it can be done on another constitutional question. It can be done on any other point of order the Chair wishes to refer to the Senate for decision."

Byrd raised a question that would continue to hover over Senate reform debates. A presiding officer and a simple majority of senators might use ruling of the presiding officer to reform the rules without having to muster a supermajority for cloture as provided in Rule XXII. At the extreme, Byrd was cautioning, Senate majorities could be expected to modify the rules to suit their immediate convenience. For Byrd and others, this would turn the Senate into a "small House of Representatives."

Mansfield and Byrd lost the argument. A motion to table Mansfield's point of order was adopted 51–42, thereby clearing a path to invoke cloture on the motion to proceed by a simple majority. This was the first time that a Senate majority accepted the principle that a simple majority could invoke cloture on the motion to proceed to the consideration of a reform resolution.

Southerners, led by Allen, maneuvered to delay action by quorum calls, motions to recess, and motions to reconsider while they sought the votes to reverse the decision on tabling Mansfield's point of order. A few days later, reformers offered another motion and again set aside a Mansfield point of order, this time by a 46–42 vote. With the outcome on Mansfield's point of order reconfirmed, some southerners, led by Russell Long (D-LA), discussed a compromise on a temporary cloture threshold—a three-fifths majority of all elected senators (duly chosen and sworn) for only the 94th Congress. The reformers, of course, did not want to limit the reform to one Congress and preferred a threshold of three-fifths of senators present and voting. Mansfield, anxious to resolve the matter, quickly endorsed Long's approach, but he later accepted the reformers' demand that the rules change not be limited to one Congress and the opponents' demand that the old two-thirds of senators present and voting be retained for proposals to change the rules.

The compromise attracted a few southern votes and placated other southerners enough to suppress significant additional obstruction.

Mansfield did something else as he extricated himself from a difficult situation. As southerners requested, and he certainly approved, Mansfield moved and the Senate agreed, 53–38, that the Senate reconsider the motion to table the Mansfield point of order concerning ending debate on a reform resolution at the start of a Congress by a simple majority. The Senate then defeated the motion to table, 40–51, and sustained the point of order, 53–43. In this process, Senator Long and others elaborated on the implications of Rockefeller's ruling, observing, among other things, that the reformers' motion for an immediate vote set aside rules beyond Rule XXII, including the rules that require the presiding officer to recognize a senator who seeks to be recognized to speak, give precedence to motions to adjourn or recess, or allow a senator to observe the absence of a quorum.

Nine senators—eight Democrats—had switched their votes on the Mansfield point of order. Several of the switchers were reform Democrats who reported that they did so to facilitate the compromise and remained committed to the constitutional principle that a simple majority can get a vote on a reform resolution. Senator Alan Cranston (D-CA) was among them: "We have the opportunity to amend Rule 22 if we can get the reasonable leadership compromise up for a vote. Upholding the Mansfield point of order only adds one tree to the jungle of precedents we reside in. But above and beyond that jungle stands the Constitution. And no precedent can reverse the fact that the Constitution supersedes the rules of the Senate—and that the constitutional right to make its rules cannot be challenged" (*Congressional* Record, March 5, 1975, 5251). None of the switchers seconded the warnings of Byrd and Long about possible abuse of the process they initially supported.

With the compromise endorsed by the leadership of both parties and a handful of southerners, 73–21 votes to invoke cloture on the motion to proceed and later on the resolution cleared the way for a final vote, 56–27, in favor of the reform. Most southern Democrats voted against the measure or abstained; 16 Republicans voted against the resolution.

The developments of 1975 bear careful consideration. With a large proreform bloc and a presiding officer willing to endorse the reformers' interpretation of tabling the Mansfield point of order, the conditions that seemed necessary for filibuster reform were in place. At least a simple majority for a three-fifths threshold for cloture had been in place for several Congresses. Still missing was a majority—and a majority leader—that favored the use of a constitutional ruling to allow a simple majority to get to a vote, but the proliferation of obstructionism and the 1974 elections created a majority for the constitutional ruling that liberals had advocated since the 1940s. Also present was a presiding officer who allowed a simple majority to circumvent the two-thirds majority threshold for cloture on a motion to proceed to the consideration of a reform resolution, as provided in Rule XXII. Mansfield, bending to this reality, negotiated a way out and, consistent with his own views, attempted to reverse the presiding officer's ruling. He seemed to do so successfully as a part of the final compromise arrangement, although, at the critical moment, a Senate majority appeared to endorse the constitutional argument in favor of simple-majority cloture in tabling the Mansfield point of order.

## A NEW POST-REFORM SENATE?

Senators were quickly disabused of the hope that the trends in filibustering in the early 1970s would be reversed by the 1975 reform of Rule XXII. While the number of filibusters and cloture petitions dropped a little (see below), new tactics forced consideration of additional reforms before the 94th Congress (1975–1976) was over. The primary issues were amending activity and dilatory motions in post-cloture debate. Even under the 1975 rule, time taken for quorum calls, procedural motions, and roll-call voting was not counted against the 100-hour limit for post-cloture debate. With a lower threshold for cloture, post-cloture obstructionism now seemed more likely to be exploited—and it was, almost immediately.

After the death of Richard Russell in 1971, Alabama's Allen soon became the leading southerner in opposing a wide range of liberal legislation. First elected in 1968, Allen quickly mastered Senate procedure and became the chief strategist for southerners in efforts to block postcard voter registration legislation and other measures before the end of his first term. He was reelected in 1974 with nearly 96 percent of the vote. In Mansfield's last Congress as majority leader, Allen threatened filibusters on several bills, carried out his threat a few times, prompted preemptory cloture petitions from Mansfield, and employed parliamentary tactics that provided a motivation for new cloture reform proposals.

Allen played a leading role in a mid-1976 episode that is particularly noteworthy. The episode followed a little-noticed change in Rule XXII in April of that year. Under the previous rule, a germane amendment had to have been read before cloture was invoked in order to be eligible for consideration after cloture was invoked, but it was common for all germane amendments submitted to the desk before cloture to be allowed by unanimous consent. After an unread amendment was ruled out of order in the post-cloture period in the fall of 1975, Edward Kennedy (D-MA) proposed to change the rule so that all amendments submitted in writing prior to cloture would be allowed. Endorsed by Byrd, the Kennedy proposal was adopted. As senators observed, the new rule made it easier for amendments to be eligible for post-cloture consideration, but, by not requiring that amendments be read before cloture, the rule also made it less likely that senators would know much about the amendments that might be considered after cloture was invoked.

It took only a few weeks for the importance of the rule to be recognized. At issue was an important and fairly popular anti-trust bill that, among other things, authorized state attorneys general to file anti-trust suits on behalf of citizens. Proof of the popularity of the bill came early when a cloture petition, endorsed by both parties' leaders, was filed almost immediately and cloture was easily invoked, 67–22, with the most conservative Democrats and Republicans voting against. Before and after cloture was invoked on the bill, Allen pursued a variety of delaying tactics. He frequently noted the absence of a quorum; moved to reconsider votes (with no expectation of the outcome changing); forced roll-call votes on many routine amendments and motions to reconsider or table; and objected to routine unanimous consent requests for the reservation of leaders' time, for recessing until a certain time, and for other purposes. And, of course, he took advantage of most opportunities to speak at length. At one point, with Allen's help, the Senate cast a roll-call vote on a motion to table the motion to reconsider the vote by which a motion to table an amendment was rejected. I am not kidding.

Before cloture was invoked, Allen and other opponents of the legislation submitted nearly seventy amendments, none of which had to be read, that would be in order during the post-cloture period. This allowed the opponents to claim an hour to debate each of their amendments after cloture was invoked, as Rule XXII provided. When combined with various motions and demands for roll-call votes, none of which counted against post-cloture debate limits, the dilatory tactics created the possibility that the bill could not be brought to a vote even after cloture was invoked.

The bipartisan support for the measure made Allen's dilatory tactics particularly frustrating for Mansfield and Byrd, who were eager to complete work on a large legislative agenda in an election year (*Congressional Record,* June 4, 1976, 16724–27). Warning that "delay and stalling" would cause great inconvenience for all senators, Mansfield and Byrd held the Senate in session for long daily sessions and extra days and even denied committees the authority to meet while the Senate was in session (*Congressional Record,* June 7, 1976, 16821). Their arguments did not persuade Allen to give up his dilatory moves and produced loud complaints about both the Allen tactics and leaders' scheduling decisions. Senators spoke of "tremendous harm to personal relationships" and complained that dilatory tactics were prohibited under Rule XXII (*Congressional Record,* June 8, 1976, 16941; June 9, 1976, 17241). Senator John Pastore (D-RI) griped, "You can talk about the tyranny of the majority against the minority, but why do we not talk about the crucifixion by the minority against the majority? That is what we are getting into here" (*Congressional Record,* June 9, 1976, 17241).

Pastore raised a point of order that Rule XXII prohibits dilatory motions after cloture is invoked. Pastore was right about the provisions of the rule, but the Senate had had very few occasions in which post-cloture dilatory moves were a problem. His move prompted discussion about the need for the minority to recognize the will of the majority and to resist the temptation to exploit opportunities to deny a final vote. After several senators of both parties endorsed the tenor of Pastore's remarks, Pastore acceded to the desire of some colleagues to avoid forcing the issue and withdrew his point of order. Allen persisted. Byrd then raised a point of order about a dilatory motion and the presiding officer noted that he intended to submit the question to the Senate, but confusion about which motion was pending when the point of order was made led the presiding officer to move on to a vote on a motion to table and the matter was dropped. The crisis atmosphere that Allen's move spawned seemed to have deterred further dilatory motions (although not dilatory demands for roll-call votes) and encouraged the development of a compromise amendment that was adopted and cleared the way for a final vote.

After the House passed parallel legislation in July, time became a more critical factor. Allen threatened to filibuster motions to appoint conferees and the subsequent conference report. To avoid the delays that Allen and other opponents could impose, bill sponsors, with leadership backing, conducted informal negotiations with House bill sponsors and prepared a compromise substitute that would be introduced in each house as a new bill. Byrd simultaneously introduced the new bill and filed a cloture motion, which was adopted as expected. Opponents complained bitterly about the unusual procedure and returned to post-cloture stalling tactics. Byrd again threatened a point of order.

Until then, Mansfield had left floor management of the bill to Byrd and committee leaders. Now, just a few months from retirement after years of defending minority rights under the terms of Rule XXII, he took the floor to again express his sorrow about developments in the Senate.[13] He is worth quoting at length.

> Mr. President, I think that the Senate has seen an indication and an illustration of how the cloture rule can be abused, how dilatory tactics can be put into effect, and how the will of the overwhelming majority of this body can be negated. We have had 13 votes so far since cloture was invoked.
>
> My mind goes back to the days of Dick Russell and others who undertook to make their position substantially known on matters of great import affecting not only their part of the country, the South, but the Nation as a whole, and I refer specifically to the great civil rights debates in this body.
>
> We do not have those kinds of debates anymore. But what has developed in the last 2 years has been a policy by means of which cloture is almost forced on the Senate on practically every piece of legislation of major significance which comes before this body. Not only that, but the substantial way Dick Russell and his colleagues used to handle the imposition of cloture, once it was invoked, has gone by the board.
>
> Substance has disappeared and form has taken its place. Dilatory tactics are the norm. They are not unusual anymore.
>
> I agree with the distinguished Senator from North Carolina (Mr. Morgan) that if the Senate keeps on in this way, what it is going to end up with is majority cloture, and those who are so much against cloture will be the ones who will be responsible for bringing it on this body.
>
> I do not believe in majority cloture. I had my doubts about three-fifths; but when the Senate makes a rule, I believe in that rule, and I tell you, my colleagues, this: If this kind of dilatory tactics continues, you are going to have "reforms" in this body the like of which you have never seen before.
>
> The idea of calling up a 47-page substitute and having it read and not charged against the [the time of the] Senator who asked that it be read is ridiculous and is demeaning. The same

> effort was made on another 47-page amendment—a few words changed here and a few words changed there. And when the question was raised about whether or not that was dilatory and it looked as if the Senate were going to decide that it was, what did the author of that amendment do? He withdrew it. . . .
>
> I hope that the minority, which for 8 days kept the Senate in thrall, once cloture was invoked some months ago on the antitrust bill—8 days under cloture—violating the intent, the letter, and the spirit of the rule—I hope this minority will be aware of its responsibility to the majority and recognize that on every vote passed today, an overwhelming majority voted against what the minority was attempting to do.
>
> The minority has its rights. They will be protected; they should be protected.
>
> But there is a breaking point. I hope that the Senate, both the majority and the minority, and members singly and in groups, will recognize that the institution means a great deal more than any of us. Because if you do not face up to your responsibility, then you are going to have to pay the penalty in the months and in the years ahead.
>
> It is my belief that, if this procedure, which has become normal, is allowed to continue next year, you will have a cloture rule which will be ironbound, under which no Member will be able to call up an amendment or a substitute or put in a quorum call and not have it charged to him. And I, for one, hope that, next year, the Senate does tighten up the cloture rule so that no Senator can put in a quorum call and not have it charged to him; that no Senator can have an amendment read and not have it charged to him. Because we have gone far beyond the bounds of parliamentary decency and what a minority is doing to the majority is, I must say once again, most demeaning to the Senate. (*Congressional Record,* August 31, 1976, 28600)

Allen again backed off and the Senate (and House) eventually passed the bill. But Allen had stirred his colleagues' passions about the use of the rules.[14] It became obvious to Byrd and others that Rule XXII had loopholes that needed filling and a new rule would be proposed in the next Congress. The need to manage the floor with care and expertise brought Byrd, as a party leader, to nearly full-time floor surveillance. And the desire to avoid the multiple votes required to go to conference motivated a strategy—negotiating a new bill with the House and avoiding conference—that came to be more common a quarter of a century later.

## THE MANSFIELD ERA IN RETROSPECT

During the 1961–76 period, the majority party Democrats became more liberal and often had the majority for passing their legislation. What they often lacked was the two-thirds majority to gain cloture and move to a final passage vote. They found that the combination of Rule XXII and the assertiveness of the minority was a severe constraint on the majority party influence. During Mansfield's service as majority leader through the 1975 reform, the 81 cloture votes received, on average, a vote of 55–36. Nearly three-fifths of cloture votes produced majority support, but these had less than the required two-thirds majority. Support of a majority of the majority party *and* a majority of the full Senate was no guarantee that a measure could receive a vote. For the typical majority party, procedural limbo remained a common condition.

Plainly, as the Mansfield era came to an end, Senate individualism was reaching a fever pitch. Senators were exploiting the common pool resource of the Senate—time for its floor proceedings—in ways that were widely recognized as abusing the rules and personal privilege at the expense of all senators and the institution. Majority leaders' efforts to adapt had only a marginal and temporary effect.

Not surprisingly, frustrated liberal Democrats, constituting a majority of the majority party, pushed reform. During this period, a majority of senators voted for cloture on reform resolutions on many occasions. They were stymied not only by opponents to reform but also by a few senators who endorsed reform but opposed changing the rule by means other than under the terms of the existing rule. The primary argument of Mansfield, Gore, Long, and a few others was that the Senate, as a continuing body with continuity in its rules, should abide by Rule XXII even if the rule was an obstacle to gaining a vote on a resolution to change the rule. They feared that temporary majorities and a cooperative presiding officer could interpret the Constitution to get any rule they pleased, whatever the Senate's adopted standing rules. Plainly, majority party Democrats did not share a single vision of the procedural Senate.

A reasonable hypothesis is that the institutional context—in this case, the inherited cloture rule—limited the degree to which majority party senators could settle procedural questions within their party conference. In most Congresses, under the terms of the rule, a cohesive minority party alone could block a change in the rules. In most Congresses, the majority party cannot guarantee Senate approval even when the majority party favors an action unanimously.[15]

Nevertheless, and hardly noticed at the time, the Senate accepted debate limits for budget resolutions and reconciliation bills in 1974. Senators, in their effort to regain control over a budgeting process that was central to their institution's power, accepted debate limits—for limited purposes—without serious debate or objection. In time, the budget rules would come to be recognized as among the most important considered by Congress. Majority party strategists would exploit the debate limits to avoid cloture votes on legislation that otherwise would be subject to obstructionism.

The Mansfield era ended with reform but also with a sense of foreboding. Mansfield recognized the procedural fragility of the Senate when he took the floor to warn his colleagues about the dangers of fully exploiting the rules. While Allen backed off and the anti-trust bill was passed, the procedural tension in the Senate was palpable as the 1976 session came to a close.

CHAPTER 4

# THE INTENSIFICATION OF INDIVIDUALISM AND OBSTRUCTIONISM, 1977–1988

THE SENATE INSTALLED A royal blue carpet in its chamber before the 94th Congress convened in January 1975. The new carpet was sprinkled with small, abstract swirls of yellow and black. Very '70s. Some observers took the new look to be symbolic of the passing of the venerable but clubby mid-twentieth-century Senate and the arrival of a different kind of institution.[1] The old red carpet was cut up for use in various Senate offices.

In February 1975, as the Senate started considering cloture reform, Senator Jim Allen of Alabama warned that once Rule XXII was amended, the damage could not be undone. "You cannot capture the things that go away," he said, "any more than you can pick up the color from a bottle of red ink spilled on this blue carpet" (*Congressional Record,* February 20, 1975, 3863). The Senate did not heed his warning that month and moved ahead with a new, three-fifths majority threshold for cloture, which remains in place today.

In many respects, the 1970s were the Byrd era. While Mike Mansfield (D-MT) continued as majority leader through 1976, when Robert Byrd (D-WV) replaced him, Byrd had already become the floor tactician for his party. In fact, from at least as far back as 1969, when he was still conference secretary, Byrd took an active role in floor management when Mansfield and his whips showed impatience with that everyday burden. He continued to serve as minority leader for his party after the Republicans won a Senate majority in the 1980 elections, the first

Republican majority since 1955. Byrd returned to his position as majority leader after the 1986 elections and served just two more years in the post because it became clear that his party was looking for a more effective spokesman.

In 1975, Byrd surmised, and surely hoped, that the adoption of the compromise cloture rule and reversal of the vote on the Mansfield point of order would put to rest debate about simple-majority cloture (*Congressional Record,* March 5, 1975, 5248). He was half right. The 1975 reform did end the biennial effort to reduce the threshold for cloture, but delay and obstructionism did not end, and new dilatory tactics, evident in the 1976 antitrust bill episode, spawned demands for additional reform. In fact, the willingness of individual senators to exploit their parliamentary rights had not yet peaked. Majority party leaders' challenges of managing the floor continued to intensify.

## INDIVIDUALISM, OBSTRUCTIONISM, AND FLOOR MANAGEMENT

Individualism blossomed in the Senate of the 1970s. Considerable party differences existed, but the sharp polarization of the parties would not arrive until the end of Byrd's leadership tenure. The conservative coalition was vibrant through the 1970s and an important source of obstruction to Byrd's legislative agenda. But the Senate was known for its individualism. Senators exploited holds with increasing frequency, with some senators like Howard Metzenbaum (D-OH) taking great pride in delaying action on legislation that they deemed foolish. They offered record numbers of floor amendments—there were nearly three times more amendments offered in the Congresses of the late 1970s and 1980s as in the 1950s and early 1960s (Smith 1989, 91).

The 1975 cloture reform brought a new pattern of obstructionism and cloture. Although it varied widely from year to year, the failure rate for cloture motions dropped measurably after the adoption of the lower threshold for cloture at the start of the 94th Congress (1975). During the 1961–74 period, a large majority—71 percent—of cloture petitions yielded a defeated cloture motion. For the fourteen years after 1975, 38 percent of cloture petitions resulted in a defeated cloture motion.

The success of cloture motions appears to be due primarily to the lower cloture threshold, although a slight increase in the support for cloture contributed, too. In the 1961–74 period, the average percentage of senators favoring cloture was 59.7, about seven votes short of the two-thirds of voting senators usually required for cloture. In the 1975–88 period, the mean was 62.9 percent in favor of cloture, or nearly three votes above the threshold of three-fifths of all senators when 99 or 100 senators were in office. The threshold was lowered more than the average support for cloture increased. Rules matter.

The lower cloture threshold, it is reasonable to hypothesize, would produce fewer successful filibusters, reduce the incentive to filibuster, and produce fewer cloture motions. Certainly that is what reformers argued in 1975. It did not turn out that way. As we saw in previous chapters, the frequency of cloture petitions dipped in the late 1970s but returned to an upward climb during the 1980s. Over the period that Byrd served as Democratic leader, 1977 through 1988, the number of petitions filed reached a new high. About 40 percent of the most important measures involved cloture petitions in 1987–88, up from 10 percent in the early 1960s. I return to variation in cloture success rates in chapter 8.

Why would senators obstruct when cloture was likely to be invoked? The simple and probably correct answer is that senators continued to benefit from fighting for the good cause, even if it was a losing one. The trends in place at the end of the 1960s—an expanding lobbying community, increasing demand for campaign contributions, intensifying individualism—did not change with the adoption of cloture reform. The political incentives for manipulating parliamentary procedure for tactical advantage remained strong or even strengthened as the probability of successful obstruction dropped. Exploitation of parliamentary prerogatives—holds, amendments, extended debate—continued apace.

It is hard to exaggerate the difficulty that majority leaders experienced in managing the Senate floor in the 1970s and 1980s. Not only did managing the expanding workload and dealing with obstructive tactics create uncertainty for the daily schedule, but senators made many mundane aspects of floor activity a challenge. While senators sponsored more floor amendments than ever, the leader frequently found it nearly impossible to persuade colleagues to come to the floor to formally offer, debate, and dispose of their amendments. Gaining unanimous consent to structure debate and amending activity took more effort and time as senators insisted on arrangements that accommodated their amendments and personal schedules. In the previous chapter, the expanded use of motions to table to dispose of amendments is described. Byrd responded in several other ways, too.

## ELABORATION OF UNANIMOUS CONSENT AGREEMENTS

As whip and then majority leader, Byrd worked tirelessly to get agreement on how floor action would be structured before placing a bill before the Senate. More often than Johnson and Mansfield before him, Byrd sought unanimous consent to limit debate and amendments before making a motion to proceed. This required that he consult with colleagues who might object and led him to develop a more standardized method for clearing bills for floor action and avoiding objections to unanimous consent requests.

As much as Byrd would have liked to gain unanimous consent to structure the entire debate and amendment process for a bill, he often found that impossible. Consequently, Byrd frequently made multiple unanimous consent requests to structure debate during the course of debate on a single measure. Comfortable with his mastery of the procedural details, Byrd would formulate and make unanimous consent requests on the fly as he attempted to move the Senate to act on bills. Overall, time agreements became far less comprehensive and often dealt with a single amendment or short period of time. And when a time agreement was not possible, he sometimes turned to the nondebatable motion to table to efficiently dispose of amendments (see chapter 2, table 2.1).[2]

Unlike the standardized unanimous consent agreements of the Johnson era, modern agreements come in all sizes, big and small. While agreements are often tailored to individual measures and often to brief periods of debate and a single amendment, they have also been used to establish a comprehensive floor agenda for a measure, or even a set of measures, in delicate legislative situations. Unanimous consent agreements have the virtue of being difficult to modify (only by unanimous consent, of course), so they provide a particularly useful means for cementing arrangements intended to guarantee votes on certain measures or amendments or to preclude votes on others.

The move to more omnibus measures—particularly budget measures, which were debated under time limitations established by statute—reduced the number of unanimous consent agreements propounded by leaders. Beginning in the mid-1980s, agreements providing for the consideration of a single amendment were more common. The greater frequency of provisions barring second-degree amendments reflected the leaders' efforts to more fully structure the floor agenda when possible and senators' insistence that their first-degree amendments receive a direct vote. In more comprehensive agreements, such provisions were almost always accompanied by provisions barring other motions, appeals, and points of order. At times, although for only a small fraction of bills, amendments to certain sections of bills were barred by unanimous consent.

A typical episode in the Byrd years, although one that generated unusually emotional exchanges, was the 1978 debate over tuition tax credits, including controversial provisions to extend tax credits to tuition for private elementary and secondary education (*Congressional Record,* August 14, 1978, 25862–65). An excerpt from the floor discussion is provided in the adjacent box. This is worth reading to get the feel for Senate floor action in this period. Two senators sought consideration of their amendments. Ernest Hollings (D-SC) led the fight against the extension and offered an amendment to strip the extension provision. Bob Packwood (R-OR), a coauthor of the bill, wanted consideration of an amendment to the preamble of the bill to declare the sense of the Senate that, effectively, tax credits for private school tuition are constitutional. One senator, Ohio's Metzenbaum, wanted the vote scheduled so he could be present. Majority Leader Byrd merely wanted to expedite matters by gaining unanimous consent for a vote at a certain time on the first amendment.

**The Chores of the Modern Floor Leader**

Mr. PACKWOOD. Mr. President, I send to the desk an amendment and ask for its immediate consideration.

The PRESIDING OFFICER. The amendment will be stated.

*The assistant legislative clerk read as follows: . . .*

Mr. PACKWOOD. Mr. President, I shall not take long. I would enter into a time agreement on this.

Mr. EAGLETON addressed the Chair.

The PRESIDING OFFICER. The Senator from Missouri.

Mr. EAGLETON. Will the Senator yield?

Mr. PACKWOOD. Yes.

Mr. EAGLETON. Mr. President, is there a unanimous-consent agreement on this amendment?

The PRESIDING OFFICER. There is none.

Mr. EAGLETON. I will object to any unanimous-consent agreement on this matter. This goes to the very vitals of the constitutional debate. I intend to address myself on that issue tomorrow. We can debate it for 6, 7, 8 hours tonight, but I will enter into no unanimous-consent agreement.

I thought, at first blush, that this amendment was as innocuous and meaningless as the previous Moynihan Amendment which has commanded our presence here tonight. I thought that this was yet another exercise in egocentricity by Senator Moynihan whereby he could chalk up another unanimous vote.

Mr. SCOTT. Will the Senator yield?

Mr. PACKWOOD. I believe that I have the floor.

The PRESIDING OFFICER. The Senator from Oregon has the floor.

Mr. PACKWOOD. Mr. President, I have no desire to delay the Senate. I was willing to enter into a time limitation of 15 minutes on a side. That is obviously going to be objected to.

We have been in session 10 hours today. I am perfectly willing to debate with the Senator from Missouri at whatever length he wants tomorrow on this amendment, or I will stay with him tonight, if he wants to debate. But if there is going to be no vote on this particular amendment, and if it is now the pending business, I am not sure there is much point in any of the other Senators staying . . .

Mr. ROBERT C. BYRD. It is my understanding that there are Senators who wish to talk on this amendment before a vote is reached. Let me see if I understand the temper of the Senate correctly at this point.

Could we agree on a time to vote on this amendment this evening or in the morning, sometime tomorrow?

Mr. HOLLINGS. If there is a time agreement to vote on my amendment up or down. That is what I have been trying to do.

Mr. ROBERT C. BYRD. Is there a possibility that we could get an agreement to vote on the pending amendment and then on the amendment by Mr. Hollings, both tomorrow?

Mr. PACKWOOD. I would agree to a 40-minute limitation on the pending amendment.

Mr. EAGLETON. I would object.

Mr. ROBERT C. BYRD. Can we agree to vote on the pending amendment tomorrow morning or tomorrow at some point, and then an agreement to vote on the amendment by Mr. Hollings following that? . . .

Mr. PACKWOOD. I know that the Senator from Ohio (Mr. Metzenbaum) has an amendment to the Hollings amendment. He spoke to me about it. So I could not enter into that agreement.

Second, if the amendment is not tabled, Senator Moynihan and I have one or two amendments to offer to the Senator's amendment. So we would not want to vote up and down.

Mr. ROBERT C. BYRD. Could we agree for a time to vote on the amendment by Mr. Packwood, to be followed after a period of time tomorrow with a vote on the amendment by Mr. Hollings?

Mr. PACKWOOD. Yes.

Mr. ROBERT C. BYRD. Could we agree for a time to vote on the amendment by Mr. Packwood, to be followed after a period of time tomorrow with a vote on the amendment by Mr. Hollings?

Mr. HOLLINGS. They will not give me an up-and-down vote. If he objects to mine, I object to his.

Mr. ROBERT C. BYRD. Could we agree to an up-and-down vote on the amendment by Mr. Hollings?

Mr. MOYNIHAN. The fact is that we propose to move to table the amendment by Mr. Hollings; and in the event the motion to table does not succeed, we propose to submit one or more amendments to his amendment.

Mr. ROBERT C. BYRD. Could we agree to a time to vote on the Packwood amendment at a reasonable time tomorrow, so that Mr. Hollings could call up his amendment, and we could let developments take their course?

Mr. PACKWOOD. I am amendable to a time limit to vote on—

Mr. MOYNIHAN. There seems to be no reason why we cannot conclude this matter tomorrow. We have some votes we want to take, but they could go in sequence.

Mr. SCOTT. If the Senate will yield, the distinguished Senator from New York sees no reason why we cannot have a vote, if we do things his way.

Mr. President, I have spent the whole weekend working on this matter and preparing some comments directed at an amendment I have prepared. Now that has been changed by the amendment before us and the amendment that has just been agreed to by unanimous vote, the so-called harmless amendment . . . Now I have to reword my amendment, because of these harmless amendments. This will take some time. I also will have to revise my remarks because of these harmless amendments.

So there has to be a little quid pro quo here. If the distinguished floor managers want cooperation, they should not spring the so-called innocuous amendments before us, when we have amendments, too. I have often heard that we are a body of 200 coequal Senators, and I submit that the two distinguished floor managers are not more equal than the other 98 . . .

Mr. PACKWOOD. I am perfectly willing to get an agreement on this amendment or to start early in the morning and talk, as long as somebody wants to talk on this amendment until we are talked out, and then we will vote on it.

Mr. ROBERT C. BYRD. Let me at least make the effort.

Mr. President, I ask unanimous consent that a vote occur on the amendment by Mr. Packwood tomorrow at 11 A.M.

Mr. METZENBAUM. I object. I do not object to the vote being taken. I just would like to be able to be present to vote on it. Could we make the hour 2:30?

Mr. ROBERT C. BYRD. I will not be present either, but the Senate can work its will without me.

Mr. METZENBAUM. It seems to me that it does matter whether the amendment is acted upon at 11 or 2:30.

Mr. ROBERT C. BYRD. Provided it is not too late. I hope the Senate will complete action on this bill tomorrow. We have been on it Friday and today.

Mr. METZENBAUM. I am not trying to delay the matter.

Mr. ROBERT C. BYRD. I will give the Senator a pair.[1] Whatever way he wants to vote, I will vote the opposite.

[LAUGHTER.]

Mr. HOLLINGS. You cannot beat that.

Mr. ROBERT C. BYRD. I will be here. I will give the Senator a pair, if we can reach an agreement to vote at 11 o'clock, so that we can get to the amendment by Mr. Hollings.

Mr. EAGLETON. I have have no objection if we could get some tentative agreement as to when Senator Hollings will be able to get a vote on his amendment, so that we can bring this matter to a conclusion . . .

Mr. HOLLINGS. The Senate says, "I do not mind—just give me an up-and-down vote on mine and I would like to table yours; and if I cannot table it, I would like to amend it and substitute it and harass you for another 2 days around here." That is what he is saying.

Mr. ROBERT C. BYRD. I do not believe the Senator is willing to go another 2 days.

The PRESIDING OFFICER. Is there objection?

Mr. METZENBAUM. Reserving the right to object . . .

Mr. DURKIN. Mr. President, reserving the right to object, will the Senator from West Virginia be willing to propose the vote on the Packwood amendment, say, at 11 o'clock rather than 1 o'clock?

Mr. METZENBAUM. I object.

Mr. ROBERT C. BYRD. Mr. President, would the Senator from Ohio be willing to have the vote, say, at 12 o'clock? That would give us more time during the afternoon to settle the issue . . .

Mr. EAGLETON. Is it the customary practice that a Senator object to any amendment because of the personal social agenda appointments for him not to be here at the appointed hour and thereby require the Senate to stay in session for 3 extra hours to accommodate the social engagement? I have never delayed the Senate for such an occasion.

Mr. METZENBAUM. I say to the Senator if I were going to Cleveland for a social matter I would accept it. But the fact is I am going to testify in an environmental protection miner hearing involving 15,000 Ohio miners and people of southeastern Ohio, and I believe it is part of the senatorial responsibilities to be there.

Mr. EAGLETON. The point is the Senator is willing to delay 99 other Senators. We could vote at 11 o'clock. The Senator is going to delay 99 other Senators for his own personal convenience.

Mr. METZENBAUM. Ninety-nine other Senators will not be delayed.

Mr. EAGLETON. This amendment of Senator Packwood is just as useless as any amendment I know of . . .

Mr. ROBERT C. BYRD. Mr. President, let me put the request once more to vote on the amendment by Mr. Packwood at 1 o'clock tomorrow.

> This will allow the amendment to be set aside by unanimous consent. In the meantime other amendments will be called up and allowed to make some progress. And I would hope then following that vote we could get on with the amendment by Mr. Hollings, with all reasonable men working together, and complete action on that bill tomorrow night.
>
> I make that unanimous-consent request.
>
> The PRESIDING OFFICER. Is there objection?
>
> The Chair hears none. Without objection, it is so ordered.
>
> (*Congressional Record,* August 14, 1978, 25862–5)
>
> A pair is an announcement by a senator of how he or she would have voted if present. Pairs of senators who vote yea and nay would have no effect on the vote outcome.

## TAMING THE POST-CLOTURE FILIBUSTER

Byrd, upon assuming the post of majority leader in January 1977, was eager to prevent a recurrence of the post-cloture gamesmanship in which Allen had engaged on the 1976 antitrust bill. While he opposed a reduction of the threshold for cloture from the three-fifths constitutional majority required in the 1975 rule, Byrd urged a revision of the rules to deal with post-cloture dilatory tactics. Allen, fearing even stronger reform, endorsed Byrd's effort (*New York Times,* May 10, 1977, 13). The Committee on Rules and Administration reported, on a party-line vote, a resolution (S. Res. 5, 95th Congress) that

(a) limited post-cloture debate to fifty hours (thirty minutes per senator),
(b) included quorum calls and votes in the fifty hours,
(c) provided that a two-thirds majority could extend the fifty hours,
(d) provided for a nondebatable motion to suspend the reading of the *Journal,*
(e) eliminated the reading of printed amendments, and
(f) provided that a cloture petition could not be presented until twenty-four hours after the beginning of consideration of the measure or motion.

The last provision was a concession to the minority Republicans who were concerned that cloture could be invoked before senators had an opportunity to debate a measure or motion.

With 38 Republicans backing Minority Leader Howard Baker (R-TN), Republicans were in a position to prevent a two-thirds majority from invoking cloture on the motion to proceed on the resolution. (Keep in mind that the 1975 rule continued the threshold of two-thirds majority of senators present and voting for cloture on a resolution to change Senate rules.) Baker's primary objection was that the majority could fill the fifty hours of post-cloture debate with quorum calls and voting on various motions without giving the minority a real opportunity to offer amendments. Byrd worked with Baker to formulate compromise language that provided guarantees on debate and the treatment of amendments. The new text provided that

(a) after the fifty hours expired, every senator would have time to use his or her remaining allocation of thirty minutes,
(b) a vote on any qualified amendment that had not yet been considered would be allowed,
(c) after twenty-four hours of post-cloture debate, a two-thirds majority could reduce additional debate to a minimum of ten hours,
(d) a nondebatable motion could suspend the reading of the *Journal,*
(e) requests for the reading of amendments and conference reports could be waived on a nondebatable motion when printed documents were available, and
(f) a cloture petition could not be presented until twenty-four hours after the beginning of consideration of the measure or motion.

Although Baker supported the modified resolution, liberal Democrats objected to the concessions to the Republicans and Byrd let the issue drop.

Press accounts give no clues about which Democrats opposed the Byrd-Baker compromise, but we know that liberals James Abourezk (D-SD) and Howard Metzenbuam (D-OH) soon exploited the post-cloture opportunities for obstructionism. Abourezk, in fact, wrote later that his experience fighting Allen's filibusters helped him develop the parliamentary expertise that Metzenbaum needed in opposing legislation to deregulate natural gas prices in September 1977.[3] Abourezk and Metzenbaum, knowing that they lacked the votes to prevent cloture, submitted 508 amendments before cloture was invoked. The bill and cloture were supported by a large bipartisan majority—cloture by 77–17. After cloture was invoked, Abourezk and Metzenbaum called up the amendments one after another, forced roll-call votes on motions to reconsider and table, and demanded a live quorum each time their colleagues drifted away from the floor.

Abourezk described his strategy to delay by forcing quorum calls:

> I assigned Maine Senator Bill Hathaway the job of "chaser," making certain that there was never a quorum of senators on the floor. If I could keep enough senators off the floor, I would be able to demand a quorum call, then a vote on requiring the sergeant-at-arms to round up senators, then a vote to table this motion, then a vote to reconsider the motion to table. Because I was not debating, and because the votes were not charged against the one hour of time allotted to me, under the postcloture rules, chasing a quorum off the floor was a valuable tool. To this end, Bill Hathaway read from a tome in the most boring voice he could muster each time there were too many senators on the floor. It would not take him more than thirty seconds of reading to literally empty the Senate. And each time he did, I would call for another quorum count. (Abourezk 1989)

In response, Byrd kept the Senate in continuous session for thirty-seven hours, but Abourezk and Metzenbaum, with a little help from their friends, did not give up. Byrd and the committee chairman, Henry (Scoop) Jackson (D-WA), made a successful effort to find compromise provisions that would be acceptable to Abourezk and Metzenbaum but were unable to keep the support of deregulation advocates. The advocates then showed that they were willing to call up the Abourezk-Metzenbaum amendments and demand votes in order to keep the bill from coming to a vote. In the absence of agreement, Abourezk and Metzenbaum returned to their filibuster.

The impasse motivated Byrd to resort to an argument made in 1976. Vice President Walter Mondale was presiding, as was prearranged with Byrd and the White House. Byrd made a point of order that an Abourezk amendment violated the provision of Rule XXII that barred dilatory amendments and motions in post-cloture debate.[4] Historically, points of order against amendments on the grounds that they are dilatory were not raised. Until Allen in 1976, no systematic obstructionist efforts had been attempted in post-cloture debate. Byrd argued further that "when the Senate is operating under cloture the chair is required to take the initiative under Rule XXII to rule out of order all amendments which are dilatory or which on their face are out of order" (*Congressional Record*, October 3, 1977, 31916–18).

Byrd's point of order is noteworthy for two reasons. First, it raised the question of how a presiding officer was to determine that an amendment (or, for that matter, a motion) was dilatory, a point quickly raised by other senators. Byrd responded by noting that Abourezk had waited "13 days and one night" to call up an amendment to perfect the bill and was doing so at this late stage only for dilatory purposes. He also observed that cloture had been applied to a substitute for the bill, which, if adopted, would supplant the bill and any amendments, like Abourezk's, that were directed to the bill. If the substitute was not adopted at the end of the post-cloture period, Abourezk would still be able to offer his amendment to the bill.[5] Therefore, in Byrd's view, an amendment to the bill at that stage in the consideration of the substitute was clearly dilatory.

The response of Senator Paul Sarbanes, the Maryland Democrat, and others was that amendments to the bill could alter their view of the choice between the substitute and the bill. Therefore, such amendments could not be considered dilatory merely because the substitute, if adopted, would make them moot. Senator Stevens, the Alaskan Republican, reinforced

Byrd by observing that, while subjective, the aggregate record of forced roll-call votes, live quorums, and forty hours of debate led to the reasonable judgment that the amendment was dilatory, which created an obligation under Rule XXII for the presiding officer to rule (*Congressional Record*, October 3, 1977, 31918).

Second, Byrd's point of order raised the question of whether the Senate had the right to settle procedural questions for itself. Senators Edmund Muskie (D-ME), Russell Long (D-LA), and others observed that the Byrd argument might imply that (a) the presiding officer could rule an amendment dilatory without a point of order being raised and (b) an appeal of a ruling about a dilatory amendment or motion might be ruled dilatory. In which case, they complained, the Senate would lose control of its own proceedings to the presiding officer (*Congressional Record*, October 3, 1977, 31916, 31918).

Mondale ruled in favor of Byrd's interpretation on both counts—the amendment was dilatory, and under cloture, the presiding officer is obligated to take the initiative to rule out of order dilatory amendments (that is, without waiting for a point of order to be raised from the floor). In further elaboration, Mondale indicated that the presiding officer would take the initiative when an amendment was called up for consideration. A motion to table an Abourezk appeal was adopted 79–14, which reflected the deep bipartisan frustration with the post-cloture obstructionism.

Byrd, using his right of first recognition, then called up amendment after amendment, with each being ruled dilatory by Mondale. Abourezk, Muskie, Sarbanes, and others tried to interrupt to raise a point of order, appeal Mondale's rulings, or note the absence of a quorum, but they were ignored as Byrd gained recognition each time to bring up another amendment. Emotions ran as high as ever, with many of Byrd's party colleagues outraged by his "steamroller." After Byrd paused, Muskie complained about the lack of precedent for the rulings. Frank Church (D-ID) and Sarbanes objected to the use of the right of first recognition to prevent an appeal of the presiding officer's rulings, noting that Byrd had said that the right to appeal was not touched by the Byrd point of order. Gary Hart (D-CO) called the Byrd-Mondale procedure an "outrageous act" (*Congressional Record,* October 3, 1977, 31929).

Byrd eventually responded to open complaints about the abuse of leadership. Exhibiting both anger and sorrow, Byrd emphasized "the abuse of the Senate itself" and called attention to his years of efforts to prevent such abuse. He concluded with the observation that "it is self-evident that the ending of such abuse is long overdue." He also justified his action by noting that the amendments he called up and ruled as dilatory were all either nongermane or addressed more than one section of the bill and so were plainly out of order for reasons other than being dilatory (*Congressional Record,* October 3, 1977, 31930–31).

Byrd did not persuade many of his colleagues about the propriety of avoiding appeals, but his move seemed to end the filibuster. Jacob Javits (R-NY) made a point of order challenging the right of the presiding officer to repeatedly recognize the majority leader so as to deny other senators the right to appeal a ruling of the presiding officer. In an effort to defuse the issue, Allen appealed to Javits to withdraw the point of order, which Javits did after Byrd indicated that he intended to call up no more amendments. In a couple of hours, Abourezk and Metzenbaum, responding to requests from colleagues and perhaps because Byrd remained serious about ending the dilatory moves, announced they were discontinuing their filibuster. A day later the substitute was approved and the bill passed by voice vote.

The 1977 episode demonstrated the fragility of the procedural Senate. Senators were plainly uncomfortable with Byrd's use of a clear precedent on the right of recognition in a manner contrary to senators' expectations that rulings of the presiding officer can be appealed. Yet the bipartisan support for a new rule, exhibited by the Byrd-Baker agreement in May 1977, and the large majority favoring Byrd's point of order in the deregulation battle indicated that a large majority of senators accepted the principle that successful cloture should mean a clear and enforceable limit to debate on the legislation at hand.

## THE 1979 REFORM

Byrd sought to tighten the cloture rule in several ways when a new Congress convened in 1979. The 1976 and 1977 post-cloture filibusters, led by majority party senators, were still on his mind, but by the end of 1978 Byrd had experienced numerous minority party threats to exploit post-cloture opportunities that he said represented a new and dangerous "mindset" among senators. Republicans' obstructive tactics in 1978—killing labor law and campaign finance legislation with filibusters and stalling action on other measures with filibuster threats—motivated renewed interest in filibuster reform among majority party Democrats (Ayres 1979).

Byrd was serious. His view on the right of a majority to get a vote on the rules at the start of a Congress had changed. In a letter addressed to Democrats and shared with Minority Leader Baker in which he outlined his proposals, Byrd observed that he was now accepting the view that a simple majority of senators can acquire a vote on reform of the rules at the start of a Congress. In introducing his legislation on the floor, Byrd reiterated this view and observed that "the experience of the last few years has made me come to a conclusion contrary to the one I reached some years ago" (*Congressional Record*, January 15, 1979, 144). His party, which had a 59-seat majority, still lacked the two-thirds majority required by Rule XXII for cloture on a rules package.

Republicans were on alert when Byrd was recognized to introduce his resolution, which led him to observe, "I would hope to have the attention of the members at this point. They may relax. I do not intend to pull any fast ones at this point" (*Congressional Record*, January 15, 1979, 143). Byrd recessed (as opposed to adjourned) the Senate from day to day in order to keep the Senate in the first legislative day and thereby keep this implicit threat viable. He did this for most of three weeks while keeping the Senate on his resolution most of the time, but he also appointed three Democratic colleagues to work with three Republicans named by Baker to see if agreement on reform could be reached ("Byrd Seeking Changes" 1979).

The one proposal that attracted minority party interest was a 100-hour limit on post-cloture debate that included time spent on votes and quorum calls. With a firm 100-hour limit, post-cloture dilatory moves would not prevent final action on a bill in a few days. The proposal also

- allowed a three-fifths majority to extend the 100-hour period for a specified time, to be equally divided between the majority and minority;
- prohibited a senator from calling up two amendments until every senator had an opportunity to call up an amendment;
- waived the reading of any amendment that was available in printed form twenty-four hours in advance; and
- guaranteed ten minutes of debate for each senator who had not spoken before the 100-hour limit was reached.

In addition, to clarify the eligibility of amendments in the post-cloture period, Byrd proposed that all first-degree amendments be submitted by 1:00 P.M. of the day after the filing of a cloture motion and that all second-degree amendments be submitted at least one hour before the cloture vote. These features of the Byrd proposal were adopted.

Republicans opposed other cloture-tightening elements of the Byrd proposal:

- allowing a three-fifths majority to reduce the 100-hour cap to 30 hours, which would speed action on filibustered measures;
- limiting debate on motions to proceed to thirty minutes, which would eliminate one step in the normal process for considering legislation at which a filibuster could be conducted;
- permitting a cloture motion filed after September 1 each year to receive an immediate vote, rather than ripening only after two days, which would allow the majority to deal with obstructionism more rapidly at the end of sessions; and

- allowing a three-fifths majority to require amendments to be germane, even without cloture, which would limit dilatory amendments and the circumvention of majority-controlled committees.

Facing enough Republican votes to block a vote on his proposal, Byrd and the Democrats agreed to drop these provisions from the resolution.

Republicans asserted that an abbreviated post-cloture debate period would make it easy for a senator—someone like Senator Allen or even the majority leader—to control the floor and prevent minority party senators from conducting debate and calling up amendments after cloture was invoked. In place of the 100-hour cap, Republicans proposed that time for votes and quorum calls be charged against a senator's one-hour debate limit. They also supported proposals to allow a senator to transfer his or her time to another senator and to limit post-cloture sessions to eight hours in a calendar day. The Republican proposals were tabled on nearly party-line votes.

The stripped-down resolution was approved 78–16, and the short life of post-cloture filibustering ended. All but one vote against came from conservative Republicans. Plainly, the vast majority of senators, both majority and minority party, wanted to revise Rule XXII to prevent post-cloture obstructionism. Even most minority Republicans, who had reason to be concerned about the way a firm post-cloture time limit might be used to narrow their opportunities to bring up amendments, supported the more rigid limit. Nevertheless, with the votes to prevent cloture, Republicans readily prevented the Senate from adopting Byrd's more expansive set of reforms.

Byrd accepted the pared-down reform package. He set aside his threat of making a constitutional point of order that a simple majority could invoke cloture on his more extensive reform proposal. It appears that Byrd simply decided not to force the issue once he achieved his primary objective to end post-cloture obstruction. His threat may have encouraged the minority Republicans to agree to amend Rule XXII as much as they did.

## NEW PRECEDENTS LIMITING DEBATE

The post-cloture obstructionism in 1977 was the first of several episodes in which the presiding officer was instrumental to Byrd's response to obstructionist tactics that he found troublesome. In most cases, the presiding officer sustained a point of order that provided a new interpretation of a standing rule and was backed by a simple majority of the Senate that agreed to table an appeal. It also happened when a point of order was overruled by the presiding officer, who was then overturned on appeal by a simple majority. In each case, Byrd successfully altered Senate practice with a point of order backed by a simple majority without amending the standing rules.[6]

In the fall of 1979, Senator William Armstrong (R-CO) offered an amendment to a defense appropriations bill, first passed by the House, that would increase the cap on military pay already in law, a matter not addressed in the House-passed bill. The amendment would force spending above levels specified in that year's budget resolution and was opposed by the chairmen of the defense appropriations subcommittee, Armed Services Committee, and Budget Committee. The appropriations subcommittee chairman raised a point of order that the amendment violated Rule XVI(4), which bars legislative amendments on appropriations bills and is intended to preserve the difference between appropriations and authorizations bills. In response, Armstrong raised the defense of germaneness—implicitly arguing that his amendment was germane to the language of the underlying House bill. Armstrong expected the matter to be referred to the Senate under the terms of the rule, which provided that "all questions of relevancy of amendments under this rule, when raised, shall be submitted to the Senate and be decided without debate." Armstrong knew that the Senate frequently deemed popular legislative amendments to appropriations bills as relevant even if it was obvious that they were not.

Byrd had long been frustrated by his colleagues' approval of irrelevant and legislative amendments to appropriations bills.

They lengthened Senate debate of appropriations bills, angered the authorizing committees, and often complicated the task of passing the bills. Even so, Armstrong surely was surprised when Byrd responded to the germaneness defense by raising another point of order: "I make the point of order that this is a misuse of the precedents of the Senate, since there is no House language to which this amendment could be germane and that, therefore, the Chair is required to rule on the point of order as to its being legislation on an appropriation bill and cannot submit the question of germaneness to the Senate" (*Congressional Record,* November 9, 1979, 31893). Byrd argued that, in a case in which there is no House language to which the amendment could be germane, the presiding officer was obligated to rule directly on germaneness rather than submitting the question to the Senate. While Rule XVI does not provide that only some questions of relevancy be submitted to the Senate, the presiding officer ruled in Byrd's favor and Armstrong's appeal was tabled, 44–40 (*Congressional Record,* November 9, 1979, 31893). The presiding officer then ruled the Armstrong amendment out of order.

The Armstrong amendment received little attention. Other than Armstrong and the bill manager, senators refrained from commenting on Byrd's point of order. Byrd concluded that "this is one way to stop this business of legislating on appropriations bills when there is no House language to which a Senate amendment can be germane" (*Congressional Record,* November 9, 1979, 31894). Remarkably, after he voted against Byrd because he did not want his amendment killed, Armstrong observed that he supported the precedent that a ruling on germaneness would short-circuit submitting a question of relevancy to the Senate. A reasonable inference is that Byrd and Armstrong endorsed a pragmatic solution to an irksome procedural problem.

Byrd took a similar approach to another nagging problem a few months later. The standard approach for taking up a presidential nomination was a two-step process: The Senate first adopted a nondebatable motion to go into executive session and then adopted a debatable motion to consider a particular nomination (or treaty) on the Executive Calendar. Treaties are listed first on the Executive Calendar, so the second motion—to move to an item beyond the first treaty listed—was required, unless the Senate adopted some other order by unanimous consent.[7] Because a nomination is debatable, senators could filibuster both the motion to consider the nomination and the nomination itself.

In March 1980, Byrd combined the two standard motions in moving that "the Senate go into executive session to consider the first nomination on the Executive Calendar," which was a nomination for ambassador to El Salvador. In Byrd's view this was a logical extension of the nondebatable motion to proceed to executive business and made the combined motion nondebatable. Jesse Helms (R-NC) raised a point of order that the combined motion violated precedent. In this case, the presiding officer (a Democrat) sustained the point of order and Byrd appealed. The Senate failed to support the presiding officer's ruling, 38–54.

The effect of the Senate's verdict on Byrd's point of order was, and still is, to treat legislation differently from matters on the Executive Calendar. Whereas a motion to proceed to the consideration of a bill is debatable and thus open to filibuster, a motion to go into executive session to consider a particular nomination or treaty is not debatable and not subject to a filibuster. The nomination or treaty is itself debatable and so open to extended debate, but Byrd had successfully reduced the number of filibusters on a nomination or treaty from two to one.

Plainly, while he expressed doubts about the wisdom of reducing the threshold for cloture to a three-fifths majority, Byrd was moving to eliminate opportunities for delay. Byrd's "reform by ruling" efforts were not the first or last, but they were motivated by the more complete exploitation of procedural options by senators of both parties during the 1970s. While none of the resulting precedents concerned the essential features of Rule XXII, they reinforced a precedent that certain limitations on senators' rights, which could reasonably be viewed as important interpretations or elaborations of the standing rules, could be accomplished through a point of order and the support of just a simple majority.

At the time, a few senators recognized that the new precedents had potentially important implications for the credibility of the standing rules. In 2005, when a Republican majority was looking for a way to circumvent Democratic obstructionism on judicial nominations, Republicans looked to Byrd's points of order as a model for circumventing the letter of Rule XXII and using points of order and a cooperative presiding officer to get simple-majority cloture on judicial nominations. The prominence of the issue—and the more direct limitation on the reach of Rule XXII that Republicans proposed—motivated threats of retaliatory obstructionism from the minority. We will return to the events of 2005 in chapter 6.

## NEW STATUTORY LIMITS ON DEBATE

Other new limits on debate adopted in the 1970s were, on the whole, even less visible and controversial. On many occasions, the Senate has accepted debate limits for specific purposes by placing the rule in a statute. Typically, these statutory rules give the specified legislation privileged status so that it is easily made the pending business; limit debate so that a filibuster is not possible; and ban amendments and extraneous motions so that the proposed measure receives an up-or-down vote. The Reorganization Act of 1939 was the first use of this approach to limit Senate debate. Congress wanted to restructure executive departments and give the president discretion to redesign agencies, and yet retain congressional power to block his plans. The act provided for a joint resolution of approval of a presidential plan on which the Senate agreed to a ten-day limit on debate. Southerners objected but their amendment to remove the debate limit was defeated.

Such provisions became the staple of trade measures after the 1930s. Between the 1930s and 1970s, presidents requested and received authority to implement international trade agreements by making tariff and other changes in law. When the

Nixon administration sought renewal of such authority, the Senate balked and insisted that the president submit the agreement to Congress. The agreement would be embodied in a resolution of approval that would be considered under "fast track" procedures—a privileged resolution, debate limits, and no amendments. This represented a new balance—the president had to submit the plan to Congress, but both houses agreed to consider an implementing resolution in a limited period of time and without amendments. Congress reenacted fast-track procedures several times for trade measures through 1994, but Republican Congresses refused to renew them for President Bill Clinton. The process was restarted in 2002 for President George W. Bush and allowed to expire in 2007. It has not been renewed.

Provisions to limit Senate debate were particularly common in the 1970s, when Congress sought to achieve a new balance in the exercise of power by the executive and legislative branches. Binder and Smith (1997, 189) listed nearly three dozen statutes with debate limits, primarily in policy areas in which Congress sought to balance a delegation of power to the president with a resolution of approval or disapproval. Arms sales, foreign assistance, energy regulations, and, perhaps most notable, war powers, among other things, are governed by limits on debates and amendments. The practice continues: the 2010 health care reform bill included fast-track provisions for a commission's recommendations for programmatic changes in Medicare.

Statutes addressing Senate procedures nearly always incorporate a statement that the provisions are enacted

> as an exercise of the rulemaking power of the House of Representatives and the Senate, respectively, and as such are deemed a part of the rules of each House, respectively, and such procedures supersede other rules only to the extent that they are inconsistent with such other rules; and with the full recognition of the constitutional right of either House to change the rules (so far as relating to the procedures of that House) at any time, in the same manner, and to the same extent as any other rule of that House.

Senate precedent, what little there is, treats statutory provisions for Senate procedure as regular legislation that is not subject to Rule XXII's two-thirds threshold for cloture on a measure to amend the Senate rules (*Congressional Record,* December 21, 2009, S13708–9). It appears that the Senate can amend such statutory procedural provisions with a resolution that establishes a standing order and, if necessary, will be subject to a three-fifths cloture vote, just as the original bill. Thus, for important classes of legislation subject to fast-track procedures for resolutions of approval or disapproval, the Senate applies the standard cloture threshold for changing the rules.

Perhaps the most important class of legislation for which Senate debate is limited is budget measures, which are governed by the Budget Act of 1974 and amendments to it (see chapter 3). During the early 1980s, committees began to use reconciliation bills, originally designed to reconcile appropriations, revenue, and budget targets, as vehicles for enacting a wide range of nonbudget legislation, some of which intruded on the jurisdictions of other committees and some of which may have faced filibusters if not protected by debate limits. In 1981, the Senate agreed with Majority Leader Howard Baker and Minority Leader Byrd to strike extraneous matter—matter not related to spending, revenues, and deficit reduction—from a large reconciliation bill. Baker feared that allowing such extraneous provisions to be included in a reconciliation bill "would evade the letter and spirit of Rule XXII" and "create an unacceptable degree of tension between the Budget Act and the remainder of Senate procedures and practice" (Dauster 1993). Nevertheless, the practice continued and Byrd eventually responded in 1985 with an amendment to a reconciliation bill that barred extraneous matter. The amendment was adopted 96–0. Similar provisions were incorporated into reconciliation bills in subsequent years, and in 1990, the "Byrd rule" provisions were formally incorporated into the Budget Act. The Byrd rule, which was designed to limit the range of legislation protected from unlimited debate, would prove central to senators' procedural strategies in the future (see chapter 5).

## THE BAKER YEARS: TELEVISION AND THE SENATE'S QUALITY OF LIFE

Howard Baker (R-TN) became majority leader after the Republicans gained a Senate majority in the 1980 elections, the first time since their 1953–54 stint as the majority party. Baker hoped to refurbish the Senate. After years in the minority and with a new Republican president, Senate Republicans had a sizable agenda and yet they faced the same individualism and minority tactics that had plagued Byrd and the Democrats. In his two Congresses as majority leader—he retired from the Senate at the end of 1984 and Robert Dole became majority leader—Baker struggled with dilatory motions, holds, proposals to televise sessions, and scheduling challenges. He ultimately left office with his institutional renovation far from complete. Senate individualism, far more than partisanship, seemed to be the primary challenge.

Baker promised to bring television to the Senate chamber but found his efforts blocked by filibusters conducted by traditionalists.[8] Richard Russell (D-LA), who led the opposition to television, argued that "the whole method of operation, the structure of debate, what we do as United States Senators will change" (*Congressional Record,* April 15, 1982, 3584). Traditionalists expressed concern that their colleagues, already too individualistic and quick to exploit media attention, would play to the cameras and the national audience, which would spur speechmaking, lengthen debate, and reduce the quality of interaction on the floor. The role of committees would be further undermined. And, perhaps most important, the pressure to limit debate and change the character of the Senate would become irresistible. The special role of the Senate in the constitutional system—the Senate as a deliberative institution—would be undermined.

Baker and others argued that the Senate was obligated to open floor sessions to television coverage and risked being superseded by the House and other forums for public discourse if it did not join the electronic world. Some proponents did not deny that additional changes in Senate rules were desirable, which may have added weight to the argument that Rule XXII was in the sights of reformers. But they insisted that public interest was served by putting the great debates of the Senate in public view. The effort failed. Cloture on the 1982 television resolution failed 47–51, short of even a simple majority.

Baker's first Congress as majority leader ended with widespread frustration about how the Senate was run. The minority blocked several bills, but perhaps most frustrating for Baker was the delay in acting on a gasoline tax bill that was generated by the tactics of Baker's fellow Republican Jesse Helms (R-NC). Long sessions, produced by a combination of obstruction and Baker's insistence on completing action on some measures, caused personal inconvenience and discomfort and generated demands for reform from senators of both parties. Baker appointed a task force, headed by former senators James Pearson (R-KS) and Abraham Ribicoff (D-CT), to address the "quality of life" issues that were being expressed by many senators.

The Pearson-Ribicoff report received a committee hearing in the spring of 1983 amid considerable agitation about "chaos" on the floor. Runaway individualism, more than partisan obstructionism, was the perceived problem of the time. Wendell Ford, then the ranking minority party senator on the Committee on Rules and Administration, complained that Senate rules "have been distorted and exploited, putting serious strains on floor procedures" (*CQ Almanac* 1983). While the report motivated the committee to endorse a reform resolution, Baker did not have the votes or the time to give the resolution consideration on the floor.

Nevertheless, the Pearson-Ribicoff report and the committee response reflected the depth of many senators' unhappiness about how the Senate was operating. In response to concerns about the lack of order on the Senate floor, the report recommended the election of a permanent presiding officer whose efforts to maintain order would be more fully respected than the efforts of the junior senators who took turns presiding during most sessions. The new presiding officer would be empowered to count the presence of a quorum, thereby undercutting the dilatory tactic of observing the absence of a quorum and forcing a call of the roll. The Pearson-Ribicoff report also recommended an hour limit for debate on a motion to proceed, a limit of two amendments for each senator after cloture was invoked, and a change from the annual budget process to a two-year cycle for appropriations bills. These reform proposals were intended to improve efficiency and reduce sources of delay, but Baker judged them to be too controversial to risk bringing them to the floor.

Baker did not give up on television, but he did not see it authorized before leaving the Senate at the end of 1984. That year, cloture on the television resolution failed 37–44. Only in the next Congress, with the new majority leader, Bob Dole, allowing Minority Leader Byrd to take the lead, did a sizable majority materialize. Newly elected senators were instrumental to Byrd's success. The television resolution eventually passed 67–21 in 1986. After a six-week trial period, television was permanently authorized on a 78–21 vote.

Once it was clear in 1986 that a Senate majority favored some kind of television resolution, the debate focused on the package of amendments to the standing rules that Byrd and Dole sought to incorporate in the resolution. Most of their proposals had a long history. One proposal, strongly endorsed by Majority Leader Dole, was to limit debate on the motion to proceed to two hours. Another would allow a three-fifths majority to require that amendments be germane and set a two-thirds majority threshold for overruling the presiding officer on a point of order that an amendment was not germane.[9] Another provision would make the motion to approve the Senate *Journal* nondebatable. Byrd also proposed, to the chagrin of many Democrats, that the cloture threshold be raised to two-thirds of senators voting, which he saw as a trade-off with a proposal to reduce post-cloture debate from one hundred to twenty hours. With the exception of a modified proposal to reduce post-cloture debate to thirty hours and make the motion to approve the *Journal* nondebatable, the other proposals were either defeated by a bipartisan majority or dropped by Byrd and Dole.

Russell Long (D-LA), like Byrd, was a minority party senator and yet was the chief advocate of the proposal to allow a three-fifths majority to require that amendments be germane.[10] He argued that it was desirable to lend more order to floor debate, particularly with a public audience through television. Separating the imposition of a germaneness requirement from cloture, Long insisted, was desirable because cloture brought unnecessary debate limits, implying that some senators might favor the additional predictability of a germaneness requirement even if they opposed cloture.

Long's opponents argued that more frequent imposition of a germaneness requirement would rule out common-sense policy alternatives that the Senate ought to consider. Then as now, Senate precedents provided for a very narrow definition of germaneness that severely restricted the range of amendments that were allowed when germaneness was required. In any event, Long's opponents insisted, even a small minority should be allowed to freely offer amendments in the absence of cloture. This view prevailed when an amendment excising the germaneness provisions was adopted on a 60–37 vote.

The division among senators on the germaneness issue was extraordinarily idiosyncratic. The balance of opinion in the parties seemed contrary to expectation based on majority and minority status. The majority party might be expected to be more eager to prevent nongermane amendments, yet the opposite proved true. Minority party Democrats were divided 16–29 against the amendment (and for the germaneness provision), while Republicans were divided 44–8 in favor of the amendment (and against the germaneness provision). Perhaps their long-term minority status shaped Republicans' views. Among Republicans, moderate Bill Cohen (R-ME) and conservative Barry Goldwater (R-AZ) voted against the amendment, but moderate Lowell Weicker (R-CT) supported it. Among Democrats, liberals Howard Metzenbaum (D-OH) and Carl Levin (D-MI) voted with Long against the amendment, while liberals

Ted Kennedy (D-MA) and Patrick Leahy (D-VT) voted for it. It appears that balancing partisan, personal, and institutional interests led senators who were similarly situated to take different positions on the issue.

The outcome on the germaneness proposal discouraged Byrd and Dole, who scaled back their proposal. They dropped the proposal to limit debate on motions to proceed. Byrd also dropped the proposal to increase the threshold for cloture after receiving considerable criticism from fellow Democrats.

The length of post-cloture debate has an interesting history. After the late 1970s brought post-cloture filibustering to an end, it seemed inconceivable that the Senate would soon perform radical surgery on post-cloture debate again. Byrd and others argued that retaining the 100-hour limit would either produce tedious television or generate too much grandstanding on tendentious matters when the outcome was settled, and in either case would harm the reputation of the Senate. This view was not given serious challenge. Byrd's initial proposal for a twenty-hour limit was changed to a thirty-hour limit during floor consideration of the resolution in response to senators concerned about having enough time to debate and offer amendments after cloture was invoked (*Congressional Record,* February 27, 1986, 3146).

## THE PROBLEM OF HOLDS

Holds, perhaps even more than filibusters, symbolized Senate individualism and created daily problems for party leaders seeking to move legislative business to the floor. The term "hold" is used to describe a senator's notice of objection to floor consideration of a legislative measure, nomination, or treaty. This is an informal process between senators and their floor leaders that, until recently, was not recognized in Senate rules. A hold is often treated as notice of intention to object to a unanimous consent request to proceed to the consideration of a measure. A leader who wants nothing to upset his floor schedule wants to know about possible objections in advance and so naturally pays attention to holds. He can ignore a hold, but he risks facing an objection to taking up a bill or alienating a colleague. Holds were kept confidential by floor leaders, who, even in the 1960s, maintained a record of holds on a "marked calendar"—a copy of the daily *Calendar of Business* on which senators' holds were noted in the margins, usually by the leaders' floor staff.[11]

In the 1970s, holds became a more central feature of floor scheduling and were closely connected to obstructionism, innovations in unanimous consent agreements, and scheduling practices. In his attempt to lend order to a quite complicated, unpredictable process, Byrd worked hard to anticipate objections. It has been observed that holds were encouraged by procedures established under Byrd's guidance to formally clear items with his party colleagues. The formal notice from the leadership brought items to the attention of senators and staff members, who then took advantage of the routinized process to indicate that they had an objection to the consideration of a bill or nomination. Lobbyists noticed the practice, too, and then pressed senators to use holds to slow action on some matters. As early as 1973, Byrd complained about senators exploiting holds, objected to staff members placing holds without the knowledge of their principals, and observed the serious problems that holds were creating for the majority party leadership (*Congressional Record*, December 20, 1973, S23611).

Holds came to be used for a wide variety of purposes: to receive personal advance notice of floor action, to make sure that any unanimous consent agreement related to a bill accommodated a senator's amendment, and to simply block action. "Rolling" holds were sometimes orchestrated by a set of senators intent on delaying action by taking turns placing holds on a measure. Holds also became all-purpose hostage-taking devices that senators used to gain leverage with a party leader, a committee chair, or others to accomplish a legislative objective on unrelated matters. Further complicating things, minority party senators registered their holds with their party's leader, who, in turn, would note their objections to the majority leader and usually keep secret the identities of senators placing holds. It was left to the majority leader to work with senators to get holds removed.

Democrat Howard Metzenbaum, who had been elected in 1974, built a reputation around his use of holds. He became known as "Senator No" for his holds on legislation, often the pet bills of his colleagues. In his piece "Every Man Is an Island," reporter Alan Ehrenhalt observed that Metzenbaum's tactics embodied the individualism of the era.[12]

Individualism was not the only force at work in the expanded use of holds. Minority obstructionism contributed, too. In the late 1970s, with the Democrats in the majority, the "Steering Committee," a caucus of the most conservative Republicans, served as an informal clearinghouse for holds on Democrats' bills and nominations. Its leader, James McClure (R-ID), was happy to place holds for his colleagues, adding a layer of anonymity to the senator initiating the hold. In 1977–78, by one count based on examination of marked calendars, nearly all minority Republicans placed holds intended to delay action. They averaged more than seven holds per senator, excluding McClure, who managed to register nearly ninety holds for himself and colleagues (Evans and Lipinski 2005).

In the early 1980s, Republican leader Howard Baker discovered how troublesome holds could be. Metzenbaum intensified his scrutiny of legislation ready for floor consideration, and the Steering Committee, although exclusively Republican in membership, kept up its objections to the consideration of measures that did not meet conservative standards. By late 1982, Baker was fed up and announced on the floor that he would no longer treat holds as binding (*Congressional Record,* December 6, 1982, S28790). In 1983, the Pearson-Ribicoff report fruitlessly recommended steps to eliminate holds.

Little had changed by the time the Democrats regained a majority in the 1986 elections. In fact, while Dole, Byrd, and Mitchell reinforced Baker's pronouncement on holds, the fact that the issue had to be addressed repetitively reflected the basic logic of the situation: floor leaders needed to plan floor sessions and clear legislation with their colleagues, which created an opportunity for individual and factional obstructionism. The Senate did not address the issue of holds by rule until 2007 (see chapter 6).

## FAILED MAJORITY TACTICS, 1987

The 1986 elections returned the Democrats to majority status, but with only a 54–46 advantage. It would be the last Congress (the 100th) in which Robert Byrd served as floor leader for his party. Sensitive to the quality of life concerns of his colleagues, Byrd attempted to create more order in Senate proceedings, promising a week off each month in exchange for longer sessions. He attempted to limit roll-call votes to the official fifteen-minute limit to speed proceedings, and, to encourage senators to be present for full-day sessions, he held roll-call votes in the early morning—called "bed checks" by some of his colleagues. Byrd's success was limited and Republicans became weary of his surprise parliamentary moves. As Byrd's service ended, the Senate parties were more sharply polarized than they had been for many decades, and senators continued to be frustrated with long sessions, an often unpredictable schedule, and frequent periods of inaction when senators did not come to the floor to call up amendments they had submitted.

Republicans, discouraged with renewed minority status and committed to stopping the wave of Democratic legislation, objected with greater frequency than ever before proceeding to the consideration of bills. In fact, the 100th Congress (1987–1988) witnessed the most cloture votes of any Congress to that time—43 cloture votes, one every two weeks. Only 12 were successful. Commentary on the Senate returned to the "trivialization" of the filibuster for the first time since 1975. Even moderate Democrats with a track record of tolerance for the minority expressed regret about what was happening to their institution. David Pryor (D-AR) complained, "The problem with the Senate today is that the filibuster is very, very debilitating. And the threat of a filibuster is almost as deadly" (*CQ*

*Almanac* 1987). Pryor proposed a one-hour limit on debate for the motion to proceed and hoped that the wave of Democrats moving from the House to the Senate after the 1986 elections would help the cause, but Byrd showed little interest in pursuing the matter after the Democrats regained majority control.

### *The Morning Hour Strategy*

Byrd tried another tactic to respond to obstruction. Again, he failed. Republicans were resisting floor action on a defense authorization bill that included a ban on testing a space-based missile defense system (Towell 1987; Hook 1987). Rule VIII provided that "all motions made during the first two hours of a new legislative day to proceed to the consideration of any matter shall be determined without debate, except motions to proceed to the consideration of any motion, resolution, or proposal to change any of the Standing Rules of the Senate shall be debatable." The "without debate" clause prevented a filibuster, and if a motion to proceed was adopted, the matter became the pending business of the Senate if no other matter was being considered. The general practice of majority leaders was to preclude motions to proceed during Morning Hour by gaining unanimous consent the previous day to use the time for senators' speeches. On May 12, Byrd deliberately did not make the usual unanimous consent request, presumably with the intent to offer a motion to proceed to the consideration of the defense bill.

Aware of Democrats' eagerness to gain action on the defense bill, Minority Leader Bob Dole's staff noticed the absence of the usual unanimous consent request for the use of Morning Hour and the next day came prepared. Their strategy was to fill the time allocated to Morning Hour with the consideration of procedural motions so that the period would expire without giving Byrd an opportunity to offer the motion to proceed. They succeeded. Republicans exploited time and a little-known rule, Rule XII(2), which provided that "when a Senator declines to vote on call of his name, he shall be required to assign his reasons therefor, and having assigned them, the Presiding Officer shall submit the question to the Senate: 'Shall the Senator for the reasons assigned by him, be excused from voting?' which shall be decided without debate." On the usually routine motion to approve the *Journal*, three senators announced that they declined to vote, which then required a fifteen-minute vote on each case. Byrd objected to these dilatory moves, but that was followed by a series of appeals, votes, and quorum calls that used up Morning Hour and prevented Byrd from making a nondebatable motion to proceed. Byrd was able to establish a precedent that a refusal-to-vote explanation cannot prevent the announcement of the vote on the *Journal*, but he was unable to overcome Republican obstruction on the bill for the time being.

Byrd's 1987 effort to use Morning Hour to force a vote on a motion to proceed was the last time the tactic was attempted. With some regularity, senators and others have suggested the Morning Hour strategy for getting a vote on a motion to proceed. However, as Martin Paone, the Democrats' chief floor aide in the 1980s and 1990s explained, minority staff prepared other procedural strategies to run out the clock if a majority leader again tried to circumvent minority obstruction in that way.[13] Of course, it should not be forgotten that a bill can be filibustered even if the motion to proceed should be adopted during Morning Hour or at any other time.

### *The Real Filibuster Strategy*

By the mid-1980s, a complaint heard from some senators and many outside observers was that the old-fashioned filibuster had disappeared from the Senate. That complaint had been registered since the early 1970s, when obstructionism seemed to become more routine, and it continues to be heard. The argument is that filibustering could be minimized, and even beaten back, by forcing obstructionists to take the floor, conduct extended debate, and expose their behavior to public view. By making obstructionists pay a higher price in personal time and public opprobrium, the argument continues, the majority would discover that some obstructionists would give up quickly or even avoid filibustering in the first place.

Leaders and others observe that the strategy is unlikely to succeed. In the first place, the burden of extended debate falls most heavily on the majority. The obstructionists have to create a tag team of senators to control the floor, but the majority has to marshal its troops to maintain a quorum or the Senate must adjourn. As the extended debate continues, a backlog of other legislation is created and pressure builds on the majority to set aside the obstructed measure and move to other public business. As the days pass, questions arise about the judgment of the majority leader and the priorities of the majority party. Only public pressure is likely to break the obstructionism, but the minority is likely to have judged that an open filibuster is not likely to cost them much at home.

In 1987, just weeks after the Morning Hour episode, a frustrated Byrd was willing to try the "real filibuster" approach—and probably regretted it. Byrd had already shown much less patience with filibusters than Mansfield and had a quick trigger when filing cloture petitions. The subject of the real-filibuster trial was a campaign finance reform bill, authored by Senator David Boren (D-OK), that would have capped the total donations a Senate candidate could receive from political action committees and provided public financing to a Senate candidate who accepted spending limits. The bill faced obstruction after it was taken up on the Senate floor. Over ten days, Byrd forced five cloture votes, gaining a majority of senators voting each time but never receiving more than 52 votes. Byrd moved to other business and returned to the issue in September when he got two more cloture votes, one of which attracted 53 votes, still far short of the 60 required. The seven cloture votes stand as a record number on a single bill.

It was in this context of deep Democratic frustration with Republican obstructionism that the Senate considered President Reagan's 1987 nominee to the Supreme Court, Court of Appeals judge Robert Bork. Bork, who authored a sizable body of legal scholarship before being named a judge, was criticized for his views on civil rights, abortion and the right to privacy, free speech, and other issues. Now somewhat famously, outside groups mounted large lobbying and public relations campaigns against the nomination, which has since been labeled being "borked." The Judiciary Committee opposed Bork's confirmation to the Supreme Court, 5–9, and liberals made clear that they would filibuster the nomination on the floor. To be sure, judicial nominations had become a sharply partisan issue on their own accord, but the Bork nomination came at a time when Republicans were blocking high-priority Democratic legislation. As it turned out, opponents to Bork attracted enough votes to defeat the nomination on a direct vote without a filibuster.

## UNORTHODOX APPROPRIATING, PART 1

The 1980s brought large continuing resolutions (technically, joint resolutions) for appropriations that were entwined with procedural developments in the Senate. Looming deficits, long-delayed budget resolutions that guided appropriations bills, unpopular spending cuts, divided party control of the House and Senate, and threatened presidential vetoes were blamed for untimely or no action on appropriations bills in the Senate. Election year concerns about casting unpopular votes also motivated the majority party leadership to avoid consideration of separate bills at times. In 1982, the Senate had passed just six of the bills, which meant that seven bills were covered by a continuing resolution for the full Fiscal Year 1983. That was topped in 1984, when nine bills, five of which were not considered on the Senate floor, were included in a year-long continuing resolution. And then in 1986 all thirteen bills were placed in one measure, four of which had been agreed to in conference; the other nine were negotiated as a part of the continuing resolution, seven of which were not considered on the Senate floor (*CQ Almanac*, 1982, 1984, 1986; Sinclair 2000; Krutz 2001; LeLoup 2005; Hanson 2009).

The importance for Senate procedure was that many of the regular appropriations bills were not considered on the Senate floor and escaped the normal debate and amending process. The large continuing resolutions were negotiated in conferences dominated by appropriations committee members with some oversight by party leaders but little input from other legislators. The legislation was then considered on the Senate floor under severe time constraints, sometimes in a lame duck session, as a conference report. A conference report is privileged so that the motion to consider it is not debatable or subject to a filibuster. The report cannot be filibustered, but the necessity to keep agencies funded kept senators operating under severe time constraints. And a report cannot be amended, which handed substantial discretion over the details of the legislation to conferees.

Plainly, with divided party control of the House and Senate and both houses agreeing to the approach in the early 1980s, the primary purpose of omnibus continuing resolutions was not to close amending and debate opportunities for the Senate minority. A lack of time for considering these must-pass bills, interparty and intraparty differences, and a desire by both parties to avoid difficult votes seem to have generated the conditions that produced a reliance on omnibus bills and the conference process. Indeed, because of dissension within the Senate majority party, some of the bills may not have passed as separate measures without being packaged in larger measures.

## PRESIDING OFFICERS AND TROUBLED PARLIAMENTARIANS

The parliamentary warfare of the 1980s placed the Senate parliamentarian in a difficult position. The Senate parliamentarian's post is a relatively new formal office. In the 1920s, Charles Watkins, then serving as the journal clerk, became the informal adviser to the presiding officer on procedural matters by virtue of his mastery of Senate history and rules. He became so accustomed to swiveling his chair below the presiding officer to whisper his advice, which was usually repeated verbatim to the Senate, that he became known as the "Senate ventriloquist." In 1935, the Senate transformed Watkins's informal role into a formal position when it made him Journal Clerk and Parliamentarian, a post that was split into two positions in 1937 (Ritchie 2000). Although Watkins came to the Senate under the patronage of Arkansas Democrats, the position was considered nonpartisan, and Watkins served under Democratic and Republican majorities until 1964, when, at age eighty-five, he was asked to step down as parliamentarian. He was replaced by his assistant, Floyd Riddick, who served until he retired in 1974.

Parliamentarians' recommendations to the presiding officer are often mistakenly called "rulings." They are not. The presiding officer and the Senate decide procedural questions. The parliamentarian merely advises the presiding officer—and, in private, any senator who seeks advice. Nevertheless, the presiding officer is normally far less well prepared to rule on questions of order and so is quite dependent on the parliamentarian. The perceived legitimacy of the presiding officer's rulings among senators, as well as among opinion leaders outside the Senate, in the media, and in the public, is maintained when they square with the recommendations of the parliamentarian, which can hardly be kept secret.

Watkins's successors served as nonpartisan advisers to the Senate, but the task of advising the presiding officer became more challenging. Senators' exploitation of the rules and precedents raised more parliamentary questions on the floor. New features of the rules, including statutory rules within the Budget Act, increased the complexity of the parliamentary situations about which parliamentarians were asked to give advice.

In the late 1970s, sensitivity to parliamentary rulings and the behavior of the presiding officer intensified. Historically, junior senators of both parties took turns presiding over the Senate in the absence of the vice president, who serves as the president of the Senate, and the president pro tempore, the Senate's elected replacement for the vice president. In 1975, when the extension of the Voting Rights Act was about to be brought up for consideration, Republican Jesse Helms was presiding when he recognized his ally Jim Allen, who was intent on delaying action by asking for the consideration of another bill, instead of Majority Leader Mansfield, who was seeking recognition simultaneously. Byrd vowed that that would not happen again and changed the practice of allowing minority senators to preside after he became majority leader in 1977. The practice of appointing only majority party senators to preside has been followed since then ("Congress Clears" 1976; "Presiding" 1988).

When the Republicans assumed majority status in 1981, Majority Leader Baker replaced the parliamentarian, Murray Zweben, who had replaced Riddick in 1974. Baker's motivation for the replacement was never justified in a public forum, but the speculation was that Baker did not trust a parliamentarian who had served at the pleasure of Byrd. Robert Dove, Zweben's assistant, was promoted to parliamentarian, but in 1987, when the Democrats regained a Senate majority, Byrd replaced Dove with his assistant, Alan Frumin. Minority Leader Bob Dole placed Dove on his leadership staff until the Republicans regained a majority after the 1994 elections, when Dove was made parliamentarian again. As a staff member, Dove was at Dole's side during the 1987 Morning Hour episode. Each of these parliamentarians was endorsed by senators for his nonpartisan service, and each professed a commitment to independent judgment, but leaders were plainly uncomfortable with parliamentarians who had a significant history with the leader of the opposite party.

## BYRD'S VIEWS OF THE SENATE AND CLOTURE

Just weeks before he died in 2010, Robert Byrd appeared at a hearing of the Committee on Rules and Administration to read a statement that summarized his views of the Senate and cloture. I was there, waiting for a turn to testify with Norman Ornstein after former vice president and senator Walter Mondale and former senator Don Nickles took their turns. Byrd, who was the recognized parliamentary expert of his Senate generation but whose body was failing his sharp mind, grabbed the attention of all who were in attendance for what they realized might be one of his last public appearances. He opposed lowering the threshold for cloture, urged his colleagues to exercise self-restraint in using the rules, and counseled the majority to be patient and, when necessary, to use the existing rules to gain control of the process. His views were not surprising to the more senior senators present because they had heard Byrd lecture them on the Senate at least a few times, but his tone was considerably different from what it had been in the late 1970s when he was struggling with post-cloture filibusters and other forms of obstruction.

Byrd's perspective on the Senate and cloture came to be associated with his understanding of the Senate's role in the American system of government. Borrowing from George Washington's comment to Thomas Jefferson, Byrd often reiterated the view that the Senate is "intended to cool the cup of coffee from the House," claiming that only "as long as the Senate retains the power to amend and the power of unlimited debate, the liberties of the people will remain secure."[14] He sometimes added the line from Vice President Adlai Stevenson I's 1897 farewell address: "Great evils often result from hasty legislation; rarely from the delay which follows full discussion and deliberation" (*Congressional Record,* October 2, 1992, 30315).

In spite of his long struggles with filibusters as majority leader, Byrd considered extended debate and cloture to be defining, essential, and treasured features of the Senate. They were to be prized, not despised, and he cautioned against reforms intended to improve efficiency. He argued that "we ought to forget about streamlining . . . the Senate was not meant to be streamlined" (*Congressional Record,* January 4, 1995, 44). He complained of new senators lacking institutional patriotism, "coming over here from the House of Representatives and immediately trying to make this a second House of Representatives" (*Congressional Record,* January 4, 1995, 41).

Byrd was very much aware that there were limits to the majority's tolerance of obstructionism. He favored a high threshold for cloture, but he also favored a clear means for getting to a vote once a supermajority was mustered to impose cloture. In his career, particularly as majority leader, he was a leading advocate of reform when the filibuster threatened to mutate from a guarantor of the rights of sizable minorities to an instrument for obstruction and extortion by a few senators. In this, he was an heir to the tradition of southern senators who believed that in order for the filibuster to be respected on matters of great significance, it must be exercised with restraint at other times.

Byrd saw his tightening of the rules and precedents governing floor debate as defending the integrity of Rule XXII. He saw too many filibusters on matters of relatively modest importance and resented obstructionist tactics that created "ill feelings and deep divisions in the Senate" while making "the Senate a spectacle before the nation." In the post-cloture episode of 1977, he observed that "three-fifths of the senators who vote in a given instance to invoke cloture are entitled to fair play" (*Congressional Record,* January 15, 1979, 143). He expressed similar views in other contexts, such as the reform-by-ruling episodes noted above. Again in 1987, when he raised a point of order against dilatory tactics being employed in approval of the Senate *Journal,* he sought to prevent abuses in the interest of preserving the principle of supermajority cloture (*Congressional Record,* May 13, 1987, 12259).

Republicans and others sometimes viewed Byrd as duplicitous on parliamentary procedure. Byrd, of course, was willing to use the existing rules, whatever they were, to move or oppose legislation. As majority leader, he was a strong advocate of certain scheduling tactics to evade filibusters on the motion to proceed, such as using Rule VII ("that a motion to proceed to take up a matter other than a rules change during the first 2 hours of a new legislative day shall be determined without debate"; *Congressional Record,* January 4, 1995, 39). And his use of points of order to alter the rules of the game was particularly nettlesome to his opponents.

A fair reading of Byrd's record is that he generally was not duplicitous. He was ready and willing to work against trivial uses of the filibuster, but he also maintained a passionate belief that supermajority cloture served the interests of the Senate and the nation. He often noted that extended and high-profile legislative debate allows a minority of legislators the chance to rouse a latent majority in the nation and change the winning view in the Senate. In early 2009, Byrd made his case:

> The filibuster is a device by which a single Senator can bring the Senate to a halt if that Senator believes his cause is just. But our partisan warfare has often transformed this unique,

> fundamental Senate tool into a political weapon which has been abused. As a result, there have lately been efforts to abolish it. If this should ever happen, a vital and historic protection of the liberties of the American people will be lost, and the Senate will cease to function as the one institution that has provided protection for the views and the prerogatives of a minority. (*Congressional Record,* January 6, 2009)

As he had done many times before, Byrd beseeched his colleagues to restrain themselves so that Rule XXII could serve the Senate and the nation.

## THE BYRD ERA IN RETROSPECT

The era of Byrd's floor leadership for the Democrats, 1977–88, ended with deeper frustration among senators about their institution than when it started. In the eyes of many senators, the Senate was failing to manage a precious resource: time. In the previous chapter, the individualistic Senate was observed to have a common pool resource problem—senators tended to exploit the rules and practices at the expense of the Senate and their colleagues. Individual senators and factions frequently took advantage of opportunities to offer amendments, object to unanimous consent agreements, place holds, conduct filibusters, and insist that floor schedules be adjusted for their personal convenience. Senators were unhappy with unpredictable schedules, long sessions, obstructionism, and selfish colleagues. Individualism was more acute when Byrd stepped aside as majority leader at the end of 1988 than it was when he became leader in 1977.

Informal adjustments helped. Leaders' efforts to improve bill clearance, to track legislation to allow consideration of other business during a filibuster, to expand use of motions to table, and to elaborate unanimous consent agreements gave some order to a potentially chaotic process. These steps also may have made it easier to register objections and less painful to conduct filibusters. At least as important were direct responses to the exploitation of Rule XXII: the reduction in the threshold for cloture, abbreviation of post-cloture debate, and acquisition of a few new precedents on debatable motions. A few opportunities for obstruction were eliminated by rule or precedent. Cloture was invoked more frequently.

The period ended, awaiting a new majority leader, with tension among senators about everyday life in their institution. Some senators looked to Rule XXII as a major source of their problems, but many also believed that a combination of selfish and partisan behavior made life under Rule XXII increasingly unbearable. For personal and sometimes political reasons, individual senators were exploiting courtesies of advance notice, placing holds, and waiting for other senators to offer promised amendments. The minority party was more actively asserting its rights, complaining of the majority leader's impatience, and orchestrating obstructionism. The unease about the institution was palpable.

The frustrations yielded another set of studies and reports in 1987 and 1988. The Committee on Rules and Administration held hearings, a "Quality of Life" task force was appointed by the party leaders, and some of the senators' wives formed a group to recommend improvements—all producing only modest changes in how business was conducted. Senators attributed their problems to a variety of causes: runaway individualism and minority obstructionism were the top candidates. An epidemic of holds, waves of floor amendments, large staffs with time to manufacture bills and amendments, schedules set to the convenience of individual senators, and simple selfishness in everyday behavior characterized this era. These features, viewed by many as serious problems, figured prominently in the contest to replace Byrd, which involved Senators Daniel Inouye (D-HI), George Mitchell (D-ME), and J. Bennett Johnston (D-LA) promising shorter and more regular hours, a more predictable annual and daily schedule, and greater effort to keep senators informed and cooperative. Mitchell won that contest.

CHAPTER 5

# RISING PARTISANSHIP, 1989–2004

SENATORS YEARNED FOR A MORE civil workplace as Byrd stepped down from his leadership post and George Mitchell (D-ME) became the majority leader after the 1988 elections. They did not get it. Fifteen years later, senators were even more fully entangled in partisan polarization and procedural gamesmanship, and many of them seemed to be resigned to service in an institution incapable of changing.

Under Byrd, senators were frustrated with the unpredictable schedule and the frequent night sessions that Byrd held to complete the Senate's business. Democrats hoped that Mitchell's greater willingness to share power with colleagues and to consult with the minority Republicans would pave the way for a smoother flow of legislative business, yield a more regular floor schedule, and improve interpersonal relations among senators. Mitchell observed, "We're going to try to run it that way and see how it works. But there has got to be an exercise of common sense and self-restraint and comity on the part of senators."[1] The election of President George H. W. Bush, who had served in the House and developed a somewhat nontraditional voting record before serving in foreign policy positions and as director of Central Intelligence, contributed to the hope that a good working relationship would emerge between the Republican president and the Democratic majorities in Congress.

By the time Mitchell retired from the Senate at the end of 1994, "common sense and self-restraint and comity" had given way to sharper partisanship and elevated obstructionism. Neither Mitchell nor President Bush was particularly partisan, but their ability to hold back partisan forces in Congress was limited. After Democrat Bill Clinton was elected in 1992,

Republicans became a more aggressive minority in seeking to block Democratic legislation and nominations. From that point on, the intensity of procedural battles between majority and minority parties ratcheted upward.

Over the 1989–2004 period, majority leaders responded to minority obstruction with greater determination, innovations in parliamentary tactics, and new precedents. Still, by 2005, when President George W. Bush's judicial nominees were contested, nothing was settled and frustration with minority tactics was more intense than at any time since the struggle over civil rights legislation nearly a half century ago. Even the language of threatened procedural moves—such as the "nuclear option"—reflected the depth of partisan divisions and the procedural threats that they produced. The developments that accumulated to increase partisan tensions during this period are detailed in this chapter.

## ELECTIONS AND PARTY POLARIZATION: 1989–2005

Party control of the Senate (and the House and presidency) was contested throughout this period. After the Democrats regained a majority in the 1986 elections, they held it until the 1994 elections, Clinton's first midterm election, and retained their majority until early 2001. The 2000 elections produced a 50–50 tie that allowed the Republicans to retain control with a Republican vice president, but in May 2001 Senator James Jeffords (VT) left the Republican party to caucus with the Democrats and gave the Democrats a majority for the remainder of the Congress. Republicans regained control in the 2002 elections and held a majority until the 2006 elections.

The partisan divide was showing signs of deepening before Mitchell was elected majority leader, but he struggled with a greater divide than the Senate had experienced for many decades. Figure 5.1 shows the distribution of senators on a liberal-conservative scale based on their aggregate voting records in selected Congresses since the early 1960s. During the 1960s and 1970s, a considerable number of senators were in the middle of the distribution, where there was overlap in the distributions

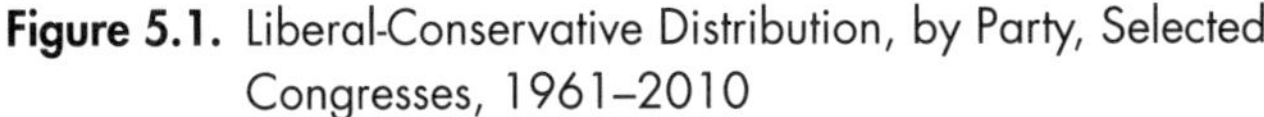
**Figure 5.1.** Liberal-Conservative Distribution, by Party, Selected Congresses, 1961–2010

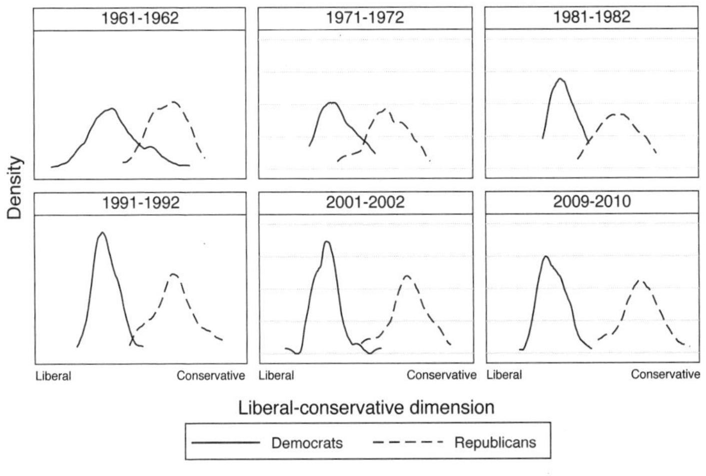


Kernel density distributions, DW-NOMINATE scores.

for the two parties. By the time Mitchell became leader, conservative Democrats and liberal Republicans were shrinking in number, the variation in each party was shrinking, and the number of senators in the middle range was declining. The polarization of the parties continued throughout the period.

A strong case can be made that the process of partisan polarization started in the House, specifically among House Republicans, and migrated to the Senate. In the House, it appears that Republicans moved much more to the right than Democrats moved to the left, in part because of the replacement of southern Democrats with Republicans in the late 1970s and 1980s, a process that shaped membership in the House more rapidly than in the Senate (Sinclair 2006). Among the new House Republicans was Newt Gingrich (R-GA), who in 1983 organized young, conservative Republicans into the Conservative Opportunity Society and then was elected Republican whip in 1989.

Gingrich advocated more than adherence to conservative policy principles. He also successfully promoted the sharpening rhetorical differences between the parties, party discipline in floor voting, hunting for and exploiting ethics violations by Democrats, and stronger public relations efforts as a part of a strategy to win a House majority for the Republicans. To be sure, Democrats' tactics, especially those of Speaker Jim Wright in 1987–88, displayed plenty of partisanship, but the conservative movement headed by Gingrich proved the most important. Many Republicans credited Gingrich's force-the-issue, offer-no-compromise, take-no-prisoners mentality for the election of new Republican majorities in the House and Senate in 1994. The apparent success of the Gingrich strategy encouraged Democrats to advocate a similar strategy with their own leaders.

In time, many of the conservative Gingrich-era Republicans were elected to the Senate (Theriault and Rohde 2011). Not quite half of them represented, like Gingrich himself, the success of Republicans in southern states in which Democrats had held nearly all congressional seats since Reconstruction, which contributed in a major way to the Republicans' chances of winning Senate majorities. Once in the Senate, these "Gingrich senators" urged more aggressive Republican tactics. Using the procedural tools available to individual senators, these junior Republicans could pursue tactics without the cooperation of elected party leaders. And Republican leaders—Bob Dole, Trent Lott, and Bill Frist—found themselves pressured to be more aggressive in pursuing party interests.

The result was that roll-call voting patterns showed signs of polarization along party lines earlier in the House than in the Senate, and eventually, a significant part of the Senate polarization was associated with House Republicans of the Gingrich era who won Senate seats in the 1990s and into the twenty-first century (Theriault and Rohde 2011).

The process of polarization in Senate parties involved a larger set of forces in American politics. In fact, a majority of the Gingrich senators contributing to intensified partisan polarization were elected from states outside the South. Congressional polarization was promoted by the expansion of networks of ideological groups on the right and left who heavily influenced nomination processes, the political mobilization of religious groups, an emerging partisan voice in talk radio and cable television, and, eventually, the sorting of the public into partisan groups with more polarized views on the issues. Intraparty nomination politics made it increasingly difficult for moderate candidates to gain a place on the ballot. Not all of this was clearly visible in the early 1990s, but a decade later it was plain that the pluralistic politics of the mid-twentieth century had given way to a far more polarized polity and Congress.

## POLARIZATION, INDIVIDUALISM, AND LEGISLATIVE STRATEGY

Let us pause to think about how a hypothetical legislative body is expected to operate when its members are deeply polarized over the issues before it. In the abstract, fully polarized parties can be said to be at opposite ends of a policy spectrum—say, one party at the conservative end and the other at the liberal end. There are no legislators in the middle. There are no legislators whose own policy interests motivate cross-party compromise and coalition building. On matters of even modest controversy, members of the minority party expect that they will not be a part of a majority coalition to pass legislation. There is no expectation of cooperation from members of the other party except on either routine or extraordinary matters on which there is unanimous agreement.

In a fully polarized legislative body, seemingly extreme legislative strategies will appear justified to both sides. For the minority, this will include a general strategy of delay and obstruction. The minority legislators will operate on the assumption—we could call it a strategic premise—that they will have no influence over policy unless they take steps to (a) obstruct the majority party or (b) make the majority party suffer in public opinion. By obstructing, the minority party may be able to block the majority, force concessions from the majority, and make it appear that the majority party is incompetent at governing. By offering popular alternatives to majority party proposals, the minority party may be able to force the majority party, or at least some of its members, to suffer reputational harm that will enhance the probability of a change in party control of the chamber.

Minority party legislators must account for the possibility that they will suffer in public opinion by offering unpopular policy proposals or obstructing popular majority party proposals. The minority party leadership, in particular, will be cognizant of the reputational costs that the party will suffer if it appears to operate in a manner contrary to public interest. There may be times when the leadership will seek to avoid the appearance of being obstructionist to protect the party's image.

Nevertheless, in a legislative body that empowers legislators with resources and a political environment that rewards individual legislators who strike out on their own with media attention and campaign support, the minority party leadership has few means to restrain fellow partisans. Even within a quite homogeneous minority party, there will be legislators whose personal views, home constituencies, and political ambitions will motivate them to pursue more uncommon, precedent-setting strategies that party leaders would not otherwise pursue. The minority party leadership will find that floor strategies are driven by the day-to-day tactics of more extreme legislators.

The majority party will respond. Lacking the alternative of building a coalition from the middle with the help of opposition-party legislators, the majority will pursue strategies of its own, some of which parallel minority strategies. Majority party strategies include:

- reducing or compromising on its policy agenda;
- using legislative proposals desired by the minority party as a source of bargaining leverage;
- drawing public attention to the minority party's strategies;
- offering proposals that force the minority party to suffer in public opinion if minority legislators oppose them;

- minimizing the opportunities for the minority party to propose policy alternatives that are costly for the majority legislators to oppose; and
- changing the rules or precedents that empower the minority.

The higher the price imposed on the majority party by the minority party's tactics, the farther the majority party will go in pursuing these responses.

A procedural arms race takes place as partisan moves and countermoves play out over time. Rhetoric about procedural matters becomes more charged. Adherence to tradition, constitutional design, and fairness are questioned. Advocates for bipartisanship, for more sensible legislators, for the defeat of all incumbents, and for procedural reform compete for attention.

In the Senate, polarized parties, individualism, supermajority cloture, and a less-than-supermajority majority party are the ingredients of legislative gridlock, strategic innovation, and deepening frustration. More than at any time since the first decades of the twentieth century, this describes the Senate in the period between the early 1990s and the present.

## MITCHELL AND INTENSIFYING OBSTRUCTIONISM

In hindsight, it is almost obvious that the partisan polarization in policy preferences generated new procedural strategies by senators and their parties. With so few minority party senators disadvantaged by organized efforts to delay or block majority party legislation, the resistance to obstructionist tactics weakened within that party. Moreover, majority party leaders faced less resistance from within their party to their efforts to limit obstruction and speed action on the party's legislative priorities.

In context, the late 1980s seemed to be a mix of hyperindividualism and partisanship that leaders struggled to manage. At times, Robert Byrd seemed to think that the Senate had to live with this. "We could make (serving in the Senate) a 9-to-5 job," he observed, "but it would no longer be the United

States Senate." Mitchell, in contrast, pledged and proceeded to institute more regular and predictable working hours for the Senate. At the start, no roll-call votes were to be held after 7:00 P.M., except on Thursdays, and few sessions went past 9:00 P.M. (Hook 1989). Most votes were taken in the middle of the week, allowing members to visit their states and take care of other responsibilities over long weekends ("Shifting Power" 2008). Mitchell also continued a popular innovation begun by Byrd: holding the Senate in session for three weeks at a time, then having a full week off for senators to tend to home-state business. As a result, Senators' voting participation, in his first year as majority leader, hit an all-time high of almost 98 percent (Hook 1989).

Mitchell promised a more consultative leadership style and pledged to avoid surprise parliamentary moves. Initial reports compared his approach to that of Howard Baker—unwilling to commit himself to any activity without widespread prior consultation (Hook 1989). For a while, this tempered approach seemed to pay dividends, although cooperation with the White House played a role. Mitchell worked particularly closely with Minority Leader Bob Dole to pass an anticrime bill, clean air legislation, and the Americans with Disabilities Act. Of the first 17 attempts to end filibusters when Mitchell gained his post as majority leader, Dole favored 13. By comparison, in 1987–88, when Byrd was majority leader, Dole voted for only 7 of 36 cloture attempts (Cohen 1990).

Mitchell's moves were soon overcome by events. The minority Republicans began to deliberately and collectively use the filibuster to obstruct the Democrats. In 1991–92, Mitchell's second Congress as leader, 60 cloture motions received votes, up from 37 in the previous Congress. This would prove to be a modest level of minority obstruction, but it was a record for the time and seemed to reflect more frequent efforts orchestrated by the minority party leadership. Mitchell was particularly frustrated with the Republican objections to his efforts to bring bills to the floor. From 1961 through 1990, 18 percent of all cloture petitions concerned motions to proceed, but in the 102nd Congress (1991–1992), the figure jumped to 55 percent.

Even Byrd, who was no fan of cloture reform at the time, observed that the minority party's procedural moves represented a "basic change" in how senators were behaving (Hook 1992).

In October 1992, the Senate experienced the second-longest one-person filibuster in its history. Senator Alfonse D'Amato (R-NY) stood for fifteen hours and fourteen minutes during an all-night filibuster, sipping tea to the dropping of a provision in a tax bill that would have tightened rules to prevent circumvention of antidumping rules for foreign producers of typewriter parts. With the provision, D'Amato had hoped to persuade Smith-Corona, a typewriter company, to keep a manufacturing plant open in upstate New York. He gained a concession for a stand-alone bill, which the Senate adopted, but the House adjourned for the year in a few hours without acting on it (Cloud 1992). Making the effort all the more futile, President George H. W. Bush pocket vetoed the tax bill as the November elections approached, as everyone expected.

It is hard to exaggerate how common holds had become by the late 1980s, when Byrd and Mitchell served as majority leaders. The archived papers of Republican minority leader Bob Dole, who served as leader from 1985 until mid-1996, give us some idea of the volume of objections during this period. Political scientists Jason Roberts and Nicholas Howard have examined the letters submitted to Dole to place holds (Howard and Roberts 2012). Figure 5.2 summarizes their data. The figure indicates the number of hold letters that placed a hold without qualification or sought to delay action for some reason (simple hold), those that conditioned removing the hold on getting an opportunity to offer an amendment or having some provision removed from the bill (amendment/remove), and those that requested advance notification before a time agreement was made (notification request).

As the figure shows, 400 or more holds—just from the Republican side—were registered with Dole in nearly all of the Congresses in which he served as floor leader. Many of the holds were placed by members of the "Steering Committee," formed by conservative Republicans in the 1970s, who coordinated their efforts to block or delay action on bills. The

**Figure 5.2.** Number of Hold Requests Received by Republican Leader Bob Dole, by Type, 1985–1996

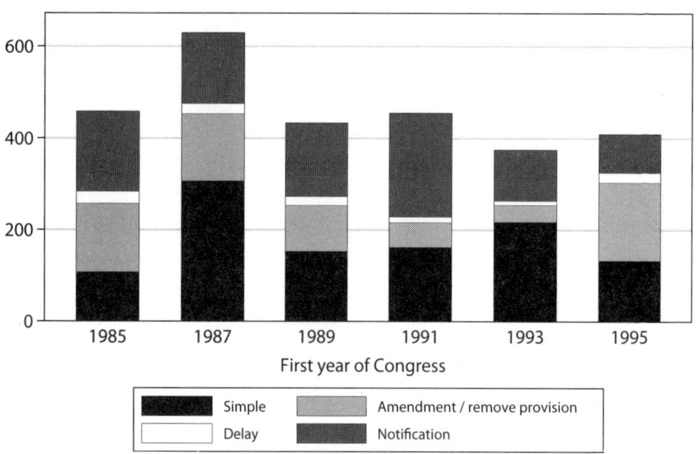


*Source:* Howard and Roberts (2012).

champion of holds was Jesse Helms (R-NC), who placed more than 400 holds during Dole's tenure and managed to submit more than 100 hold letters in the 101st Congress (1989–1990), Mitchell's first as majority leader.

By mid-1992, many Senate Democrats, backed by outside groups led by union labor, were eager to reform the rules to address minority obstructionism. A Joint Committee on the Organization of Congress was created late that year and met through 1993. Early in the process, Mitchell proposed several reforms:

- limiting debate to two hours on the motion to proceed;
- requiring three-fifths of the Senate to overturn a ruling of the chair under cloture;
- allowing committee-reported amendments to be considered germane in order to avoid the need for separate cloture votes on them;

- counting post-cloture time consumed by quorum calls against the senator who suggested the absence of a quorum;
- allowing the Senate to go to conference with a single motion to proceed;
- dispensing with the ability of any senator to demand a full reading of a conference report; and
- allowing a three-fifths majority to rule amendments nongermane pre-cloture.

The Senate members of the Joint Committee approved a number of recommendations that would affect Senate floor procedure, the committee system, and the budget process. Agreeing with Mitchell, they produced a proposal including limited debate on the motion to proceed, a three-fifths majority for overturning a ruling of the chair under cloture, and counting quorum call time against the senator who called for a quorum. In addition, they proposed a two-year budget and appropriations process. Senator David Boren (D-OK) chaired the committee for the Senate, but he and Mitchell had announced their plans to retire from the Senate by the time the Committee on Rules and Administration scheduled hearings on the Joint Committee's recommendations, which may have reduced the effectiveness of their efforts to generate support for their proposals.[2]

In 1993, Mitchell confronted more obstructionism—more holds and filibusters that now involved many nominations to executive branch posts. In the 102nd Congress (1991–1992), with Republican president Bush in the White House, only one cloture petition was filed on a nomination, but, with Democratic president Clinton in the White House during the 103rd Congress, Republicans placed holds on or objected to many nominations, with sixteen cloture petitions filed on nominations.

In response, Mitchell announced a change in his practices. He challenged numerous holds by asking for consideration of several nominations without gaining clearance from the senators placing the holds. Most notable was a bitter and protracted debate on the confirmation of Roberta Achtenberg as assistant secretary of Housing and Urban Development. Achtenberg was the first openly homosexual official to be confirmed by the Senate. Moreover, Mitchell put senators on notice that he could reverse his practice of avoiding procedural votes and unannounced votes. This would force senators to be available for votes and make the minority pay a price for delaying action on the majority's agenda. It was observed that this was a return to some of Byrd's tactics for trying to motivate senators to agree to schedule votes on legislation and nominations by unanimous consent (Donovan 1993).

In mid-1994, when it appeared that Republicans intended to block all important legislation before the upcoming elections, the Committee on Rules and Administration followed up on the Joint Committee recommendations by approving a reform resolution. The resolution included provisions for limited debate on the motion to proceed and a three-fifths majority to overrule the chair under cloture. At Byrd's urging, the committee turned down the proposal on quorum call time under cloture. It added a Byrd proposal to bar nongermane amendments to appropriations bills unless three-fifths of all senators agreed to overturn a ruling of the chair. The committee also endorsed a separate bill providing for a two-year budget cycle but, at the insistence of Byrd, who then chaired the Appropriations Committee, retained annual appropriations bills.

Many Republicans and some Democrats objected to provisions on motions to proceed and other provisions in the reform resolution and prevented its timely consideration in the last months of the 103rd Congress. Frustrated with the lack of action on their reform proposals as the Congress was nearing an end, cochairs Boren and Pete Domenici (R-NM) attempted to have the Joint Committee's proposals added as an amendment to the District of Columbia appropriations bill late in the Congress. Byrd, who still opposed several of the reform proposals, raised a point of order that the amendment violated budget rules, and the Senate came two votes short of the three-fifths majority required to waive the rules and consider the amendment. Republicans supported the waiver, 36–8, but Democrats voted against it, 22–33. Even Mitchell voted against Boren on the motion to waive. At least several Democrats favored the Rules and Administration version but feared that a long debate on the controversial amendment would delay the end of the session at a time when many Democrats were eager to go home to campaign, and so they voted against Boren on the motion to waive (*Congressional Record,* September 29, 1994, S13695–701). The proposals died and the Democrats lost their Senate majority in the November 1994 elections.

## SIDE-BY-SIDE AMENDMENTS

The new practice of side-by-side amendments emerged in this era and reflected common characteristics of the period: the majority leader's need to acquire unanimous consent for time agreements, senators' willingness to exploit the leverage they gained from the majority leader's need for unanimous consent to structure amending activity, the frequent partisan use of the practice, and the majority leader's search for procedural fixes. In this case, a senator insists that the Senate act on his first-degree amendment without considering a second-degree amendment, while an opponent of the amendment refuses to allow the first-degree amendment to be the only alternative considered. A solution is to provide, by unanimous consent, for votes on two first-degree amendments that represent different approaches to the issue. This creates the possibility that the Senate can approve both amendments and place incompatible provisions in the bill. It is usually hoped that only one is passed, but if both versions are passed, the problem would have to be addressed later in the process, perhaps in conference.[3]

The practice is reported to have emerged during Mitchell's watch as floor leader in the battles between Senator Ted Kennedy (D-MA), then chairman of the Committee on Labor and Human Resources, and Jesse Helms (R-NC) over social policy.[4] The first instance that I have found occurred in 1990 when Kennedy sponsored legislation to authorize funding for programs to fight the AIDS epidemic. Helms offered amendments to make the knowing donation of infected blood a federal crime and to prohibit funding for cleaning the needles used by drug users. Helms insisted on direct votes on his amendments as a condition for limiting debate, and Kennedy responded with a unanimous consent request to arrange side-by-side amendments. The agreement on the criminalization amendment provided that

> Senator Helms be recognized to offer an amendment with respect to criminalization of blood donations; that there be 30 minutes of debate, equally divided, on the amendment; that no second-degree amendment be in order; that following the conclusion of time for debate on the Helms amendment, the Helms amendment be laid aside and that Senator Kennedy be recognized to offer a Kennedy-Hatch amendment relating to the same subject matter of the Helms amendment on which there be 30 minutes of debate equally divided; that no second-degree amendment be in order; that, following the conclusion of the debate on the Kennedy-Hatch amendment, there be a vote, on or in relation to, the Helms amendment, to be followed, without any intervening action or debate, by a vote on, or in relation to the Kennedy-Hatch amendment. (*Congressional Record*, May 16, 1990, 6293)

In this case, the Kennedy-Hatch amendment was adopted, 99–0, and the Helms amendment was rejected, 47–52.[5]

The practice appears to have acquired its name, side-by-side amendments, in the late 1990s. It was first mentioned on the Senate floor in 2000, but use of the term, sometimes shortened to "side-by-sides," became very common in the following decade.[6] The minority came to demand the practice with great frequency in order to preserve a minority senator's opportunity to get votes on an amendment worded just as he or she crafted it—that is, free of a motion to table and an unfriendly second-degree amendment that could alter the amendment before it got a vote.

The term came to be so well understood that it was eventually incorporated into formal unanimous consent agreements.

For example, in 2008 the majority leader received unanimous consent for a time agreement that provided, in part, "that if the Managers and Leaders, acting jointly, have determined that a side-by-side amendment strategy is the appropriate approach for the listed amendments, it then be in order for side-by-side amendments to be offered, with the Majority amendment getting the first vote in any side-by-side arrangement" (*Senate Calendar,* July 16, 2008). In this case, the agreement specified numerous amendments and left it to the joint leadership to determine whether side-by-side amendments would be used. By this time, the side-by-side process was so well understood that much of the detail in the 1990 agreements was not necessary.

Very quickly, the side-by-side practice, which originated as an adjustment to the demands of individual senators, became a regular demand of minority party senators. In 2002, to cite just one of many episodes, Democratic majority leader Tom Daschle struggled to get action on an Interior appropriations bill. A pivotal issue was an amendment on burning policy for national forests sponsored by Republican Larry Craig (R-ID). Craig indicated that he would agree to time limits on his amendment and cloture on the bill only if he was free to have his amendment considered without second-degree amendments or a motion to table, and, at most, be subject to a side-by-side process. He explained, "I ask for a vote on it, an up-or-down vote, as it is entitled to. I would accept a side-by-side debate with Senator Bingaman's alternative" (*Congressional Record,* September 17, 2002, S8661).[7] The entitlement was a by-product of the leverage the minority had with the majority under the Senate's rules.

## LOTT AND FILLING THE AMENDMENT TREE

Republicans won majorities in both houses of Congress in the 1994 elections. The outcome returned Bob Dole to the post of Senate majority leader, with Trent Lott (R-MS) as the whip. The elections also put House Republicans in the majority for the first time since 1954. House Republicans took control of the House armed with the "Contract with America," a list of legislation that they promised to pass in the first one hundred days of the new Congress. The House passed the last of the Contract items on the ninety-second day of the session.

The open question was the fate of Contract items in the Senate, where Republicans held only 52 seats, some moderate Republicans held key committee chairmanships, and, of course, a sizable Democratic minority could obstruct or delay action. By the end of 1995, only three relatively minor items had been enacted into law, the constitutional amendment to require a balanced budget had been defeated in the Senate, and significant pending items were deemed unlikely to pass the Senate ("Contract Score Card" 1995). By the fall of 1995, House Republicans had lost their political momentum. Republicans held appropriations hostage to accepting their long-term budget plan, forcing the closing of federal agencies, which proved unpopular with the public and undermined their ability to push their agenda in 1996, a presidential election year.

Lott replaced Dole as majority leader in June 1996 when Dole resigned from the Senate to become a full-time candidate for president. Lott soon found his agenda frustrated by Democratic parliamentary moves. A month after becoming leader, sounding much like Mitchell in 1993, Lott took the floor to complain about slow action on a defense appropriations bill:

> We are now in a rolling filibuster on every issue, which is totally gridlocking the U.S. Senate. That is wrong. It is wrong for America. We cannot get the appropriations bills done. We cannot get the taxpayers' bill of rights done. We cannot get the White House Travel Office bill for Billy Dale done. We cannot get the gaming commission issue up. I do not support all of these bills, but we have an obligation to allow the Senate to do its work. That is not happening.[8] (*Congressional Record,* July 11, 1996, 16732)

Later in the day, even more exercised, Lott continued his diatribe on minority tactics. "Apparently, Mr. President," Lott surmised, "there is a planned concerted effort to have gridlock in the U.S. Senate." He complained about the objections to appointing conferees and taking up nominations and various bills, saying in the end that "we are completely balled up, and it is not my fault" (*Congressional Record,* July 11, 1996, 16735).

The immediate problem for Lott, who was anxious to get work done as an election approached, was the obstruction orchestrated by Nevada's senators, Richard Bryan and Harry Reid, both Democrats. The Nevadans were attempting to block action on a measure to place nuclear waste in their state. Lott claimed to have the votes for cloture on the nuclear waste measure, but Bryan and Reid were holding up other high-priority legislation to delay the time at which the Senate could move to the nuclear waste bill. The result was that action on a defense appropriations bill, a tax measure, and other matters was being delayed, as senators were eager to finish their business and go home to campaign. The calendar worked to the advantage of the Nevada senators.

Tom Daschle (D-SD), the minority leader, observed the irony of Lott's complaints. "I am delighted," he said, "that [the majority leader] has taken the speech that I put in his desk from George Mitchell from about 2 years ago and used it almost verbatim" (*Congressional Record,* July 11, 1996, 16735). He continued by objecting to the quickness with which Lott was filing cloture motions, thereby reducing the time for debate and amendments; to the conduct of conferences by majority party members without the participation of the minority; and to the need to object to the consideration of bills until opportunities to offer amendments were guaranteed. Bipartisanship in floor proceedings, Daschle insisted, was not possible without meaningful opportunities for the minority to offer amendments.

Lott responded by observing that the Republicans were doing nothing that the Democrats had not done. In the previous Congress, Lott noted that, even more frequently than the Republicans, Mitchell had filed cloture motions on the first day a motion to proceed was made. Excluding minority senators from conference negotiations was nothing new. He then tried unsuccessfully to gain unanimous consent to bring up the bills that were being blocked, and Democrats objected to each request. The next week, cloture was invoked, 65–34, on the nuclear waste bill and it passed the Senate with 63 votes two weeks later. However, the House leadership eventually dropped the bill when it became clear that there was not enough time remaining in the Congress to find the votes in both houses to override a promised presidential veto.

Lott muddled through the remainder of the Congress, but he became more aggressive than his predecessors in responding to the minority obstruction. Frequently drawing complaints from the Democrats, Lott filled the schedule with conference reports and unamendable vehicles, filled the amendment tree to block amendments, constructed omnibus bills to limit the opportunities for obstruction and raise its costs, and, with some frequency, pulled bills from the floor when they attracted too many amendments that would create political problems for his party colleagues.

Of Lott's various tactics, "filling the amendment tree" received the most attention and the most severe criticism from the minority. Senate precedents identify the types of amendments that may be pending simultaneously.[9] Figure 5.3 shows the simplest situation in a graphic representation, an "amendment tree," of the permissible amendments. In this case, an amendment to a bill is offered, followed by a substitute amendment and a perfecting amendment to the first amendment. The original amendment is called an amendment in the first degree and the other two are amendments in the second degree. No amendment in the third degree is allowed. In this simple case, no other amendment can be offered until the Senate disposes of one of the pending amendments by voting on it or having it withdrawn.[10]

The majority leader can fill the amendment tree by virtue of his right of first recognition. By seeking recognition to offer a series of amendments, the majority leader can fill the tree and prevent other amendments from being offered, at least temporarily. If he can gain cloture on a bill, he can prevent consideration of other amendments by filling the tree both before and after cloture is invoked.

The majority leader's ability to block amendments altogether depends on his ability to gain cloture on a measure. If he

**Figure 5.3.** Example of a Senate Amendment Tree

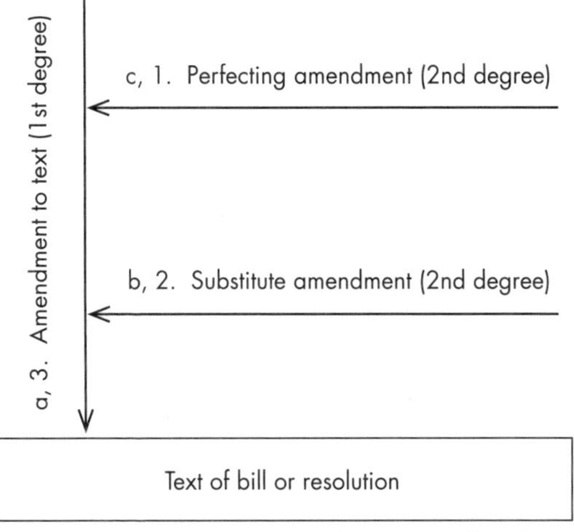


cannot gain cloture and chooses to keep the bill on the floor, he must eventually withdraw his amendments to gain additional action on the measure, at which time other amendments would be in order. Moreover, the majority leader may have to promise opportunities to offer amendments to senators whose votes he needs for cloture.

At a minimum, filling the tree stalls the amendment process, which may be all that the majority leader expects and wants. He may want to buy time to negotiate an agreement to limit or order amendments, or he may need time to find additional votes for cloture and the bill. In the meantime, filling the tree allows the leader to delay consideration of unfriendly, irrelevant, or embarrassing amendments and to avoid the exposure of divisions within his party to public view.

While the amendment tree is filled, amendments may be offered only by acquiring unanimous consent to temporarily set aside the pending amendments. This creates a situation in which the permission of the majority leader is required to have an amendment considered. In some circumstances, senators of both parties resent this. Minority party senators, who may be eager to publicize their differences with the majority, may be frustrated by the ability of the majority leader to delay consideration of their amendments.

The tree was filled once in 1993 while Mitchell was majority leader, and then at the initiative of Byrd, who was the Appropriations Committee chair and bill manager at the time. Lott filled the tree twice in the 105th Congress (1997–1998) but became more aggressive in the next Congress (106th, 1999–2000), when he filled the tree fully or partially eight times, more than in any previous Congress.[11] Plainly, the tactic was not employed for the vast majority of measures, but it was used on many important measures. Democrats interpreted the use of the tactic as inconsistent with the "regular order" and an unnecessarily partisan use of the right of first recognition.

In 1999, when Lott filled the tree six times, each side justified its procedural moves by citing the abuses by the other side. On one occasion in which he filled the amendment tree, Lott declared, "I have learned a lesson. If we are going to pass legislation, whether it is on bankruptcy or financial modernization, FAA reauthorization, or this legislation, Y2K legislation, which is important, I am going to have to take actions to block irrelevant, non-germane amendments that are just part of a political agenda" (*Congressional Record,* April 28, 1999, S4329). Democrats, like Republicans in 1993, insisted that the tactic was unnecessarily partisan and made them more likely to be obstructionist. Daschle exclaimed, "I am exasperated, frustrated, mystified that here in the Senate we are not allowed an opportunity to have a free and open debate."[12]

In fact, 1999 set a pattern for more recent Congresses. Minority party senators pursue a strategy of delay, which includes lengthy debate and offering numerous amendments, many of which are nongermane. The majority leader, trying to manage a tight schedule and exercise some control over floor proceedings, files a cloture petition at the start of the process and fills the amendment tree. When cloture is possible, the majority leader has a path for completing action on the bill. Otherwise, the Senate moves into a period of procedural stalemate in which nothing is accomplished until some unanimous consent agreement is made, if at all.

As the 106th Congress came to an end in 2000, with even fellow Republicans griping about losing opportunities to offer and get votes on their amendments, Lott announced his intention to "take up bills in regular order, subject to amendment" in the next Congress (Taylor 2000a, 2000b, 2000d; Beth et al. 2009). The 2000 elections produced a Senate split 50–50 between Democrats and Republicans, which eventually resulted in a power-sharing agreement between the parties that included a provision that neither party leader would fill the amendment tree (Taylor 2001a). Lott's successor, Democrat Tom Daschle, disavowed the practice but used it once near the end of the Congress for the purpose of freezing amendments while a time agreement on the consideration of amendments was negotiated (*Congressional Record,* September 25, 2002, S9205). The truce on use of the amendment tree would not last.

## UNORTHODOX APPROPRIATING, PART 2

Appropriations bills, the dozen or so bills that authorize spending by federal agencies, are central features of the congressional agenda and are often the subject of battles between the parties. Because most agencies need spending authority renewed each year, there is considerable pressure on legislators to pass these bills, but legislators also use them as a natural tool to gain bargaining leverage over a president. During this period, appropriations politics was transformed by partisan strategies that had a large impact on the Senate's floor proceedings.

After the 1986 elections, the Democrats held majorities in both houses, as they would through the 1994 elections. In 1987, congressional Democrats and President Ronald Reagan agreed to a multiyear budget deal, which paved the way for passage and signing of the regular appropriations bills over the next few years. In fact, Reagan had made the practice of omnibus continuing resolutions an issue in his 1988 State of the Union Address, in which he brought a copy of the thousand-page 1987 measure and threatened to veto the next one. A new five-year deal was struck between President George H. W. Bush and the Democratic Congress in 1990. While Bush vetoed seven appropriations bills during his presidency, the Democratic Congress continued to pass the regular appropriations bills.

Appropriations strategies changed after the Republicans won House and Senate majorities in the 1994 elections. In 1995, Speaker Newt Gingrich and the House Republicans chose to hold the appropriations bills hostage to their demand that President Bill Clinton and the Democrats accept their budget plan. After an impasse caused a shutdown of many federal agencies, Republicans acceded in early 1996 to the White House demand that an omnibus bill be passed. Feeling deeply bruised by their showdown with Clinton, the Republicans readily passed the regular spending bills for the next fiscal year.

Over the course of the Clinton administration, presidential vetoes, troublesome minority amendments, and minority-orchestrated delay eventually led the majority party Republicans to slow or even discontinue action on many domestic spending bills. In their place, Republicans negotiated the omnibus measures with the White House to prevent government shutdowns. Time and political pressures on the Republican majorities gave the White House some leverage to gain significant concessions from them.

Matters came to a head in 2000 over both majority and minority tactics. In the spring, Minority Leader Tom Daschle announced that he would refuse consent to take up any appropriations bill until the House version was received, as was the longstanding tradition that had been observed in the breach in the previous few years. This forced delays in Senate action on the spending bills. At about the same time, Democrats insisted on a vote on their "sense of the Senate" amendment to a military construction appropriations bill that would recommend background checks for sales at gun shows. The amendment was a difficult one for several Republicans mounting reelection campaigns that year. Lott asked to have the amendment ruled nongermane, but Daschle threatened to filibuster the bill if the Democrats did not get a vote on the amendment.[13]

The Democrats would get their vote, but Lott first moved to establish a precedent that future sense-of-the-Senate amendments are nongermane under Senate Rule XVI, the rule governing appropriations bills, and therefore not in order. To do this, he offered his own sense-of-the-Senate amendment, raised a point of order that it violated Rule XVI, and explained that sense-of-the-Senate amendments were causing long delays in acting on appropriations bills. Following the parliamentarian's expected advice, the presiding officer ruled against Lott's point of order, and Lott then appealed the ruling to the Senate. As Lott planned, the Senate Republican majority voted to overturn the ruling and support his point of order, the effect of which was to establish the precedent that would govern rulings in the future and spare the Republicans from facing more sense-of-the-Senate amendments. Democrats objected to this "power play." Senator Chuck Schumer (D-NY) observed, "I simply say, with all due respect to the majority leader, a man I respect and admire, the feelings on this side, and our inability to debate issues we think are important—whether they be gun control or education—are reaching the boiling point. I fear if we are throttled any further, the whole order and comity of this body will break down" (*Congressional Record,* May 17, 2000, S4065). Lott's appeal was successful on a party-line vote, the ruling was overturned, his amendment was killed, and a new precedent was set. No one outside of the Senate paid attention to the episode.

The 2000 precedent again illustrates how a frustrated Senate majority can reform the Senate rules—in this case limit the range of eligible amendments for appropriations bills—through use of a point of order backed by a simple majority. The method is similar to the Byrd precedents of the late 1970s (see chapter 4), which were also successful efforts to streamline Senate business by adding limits to senators' ability to debate or amend in limited circumstances. The majority again expressed a preference for new limits, the minority objected, few outsiders noticed, and, given the narrowness of the precedent, the minority did not resort to extraordinary tactics in retaliation. The episode contributed to heightened partisan tensions and probably encouraged both sides to further exploit the rules to full partisan advantage.

In the first decade of the new century, omnibus bills were standard features of the appropriations process. The exception was 2001, when the 9/11 events led to quick agreement on higher spending caps and the rapid enactment of the regular bills. Otherwise, both houses found it difficult to muster majorities for appropriations bills, but the Senate, much more often than the House, found it difficult to complete action on appropriations bills before continuing resolutions and omnibus bills were required to finish the job (for a count, see chapter 6).

After 2001, majority party Republicans found omnibus bills to be convenient vehicles to manage two strategic challenges. The first challenge was limiting spending to their chosen levels. This was easier to accomplish in a last-minute, omnibus measure than it would have been with bill-by-bill fights on the House and, especially, the Senate floors. The second challenge was facing a wide range of troublesome amendments and, in some cases, lengthy or unending floor debate in the Senate on the regular bills. An omnibus bill minimized the commitment of Senate floor time to appropriations bills.

The appropriations process seemed to reach its nadir in 2004, an election year in which the president and congressional Republicans wanted to avoid choices that might be unpopular. Only the defense appropriations bill was enacted by the start of Fiscal Year 2005 on October 1, three continuing resolutions kept agencies funded during the fall, and not until December did Congress pass a consolidated measure that incorporated the provisions of nine appropriations bills for the fiscal year that had started two and a half months earlier. In 2005, Senator Bryan Dorgan (D-ND) objected to what had transpired:

> [In late November] the Senate received an omnibus appropriations conference report that totaled 3,646 pages. It included nine different appropriations bills, seven of which had never been

> debated, amended or voted on by the Senate. It spent more than $388 billion. And it also included a miscellaneous title with several extraneous provisions that had nothing to do with appropriations. Like the appropriations titles, many of these non-appropriations items had never been considered in the Senate.
>
> Even though the vast majority of the Senate had never had a chance to review these provisions, the conference report was rushed to the Senate floor just hours after a handful of members and their staff had finished their work putting it together behind closed doors.
>
> Throughout the day, I and several members of my staff read and analyzed the provisions of this bill. During the examination, we discovered a particularly egregious provision. It would have allowed an agent of the Chairman of the House or Senate Appropriations Committee to look at the tax return of anyone in America. And, further, it would have allowed them to release the private information contained in those returns without any civil or criminal penalty. That would have created the opportunity for an abuse of power almost unprecedented in our history.
>
> Thankfully, my staff and I were able to catch this, and after strenuous debate the provision was nullified. But this is an indication of how completely flawed this process has become. None of us could know when the time came to vote, just a few hours after the bill was released, what other inappropriate provisions it contained. There simply had not been enough time to thoroughly scour the more than 3,600 pages in this bill. (*Congressional Record,* July 25, 2005, S8832)

## LOTT AND HOLDS

By 2000, senators' frustrations with holds had spread to the politically attentive public. At least some senators continued to abuse the process. Abuses cited by senators included holds placed on one bill to gain favorable action on an unrelated matter, rolling holds (senators taking turns placing holds on a bill to frustrate the effort to clear a bill for floor action), and retaliatory holds (placing a hold in response to another hold).[14] They had come to be particularly troublesome for a floor leader seeking unanimous consent to act on bills at the end of a session when time constraints made it difficult to process legislation without time agreements. Holds were, and still are, often used for innocent purposes, such as getting notice in order to offer an amendment in a timely way, but Majority Leader Lott and others believed that the leaders' efforts to limit abuses, extending over three decades, had failed.[15]

By this time, holds had gained an importance far beyond the idiosyncratic purposes of individual senators. The minority leader, it was claimed, sometimes used the excuse of the anonymous hold of a party colleague as a way to obscure partisan purposes for objecting to the majority leader's plans. Factions or groups of senators were coordinating holds to obstruct action. The practice of keeping confidential the identity of senators placing holds kept the cost of obstruction to a minimum. For matters of modest importance, the majority leader would observe the hold rather than risk objections to unanimous consent requests and waste floor time.

When Lott resigned as majority leader in late 2002, he remained frustrated with the practice of holds and, after taking over as chairman of the Committee on Rules and Administration in 2003, conducted a hearing on a reform proposal. The proposal, offered by Senators Charles Grassley (R-IA) and Ron Wyden (D-OR), would mention holds in the standing rules for the first time, something that some observers believed might legitimize the practice. Plainly, Grassley, Wyden, and Lott deemed a rule to be necessary to deal with a troublesome practice that complaints, leaders' proclamations, and pleas for good behavior had not changed. Grassley and Wyden proposed, after discussions with Lott, Byrd, and others, that a senator must provide written notice of a hold to his or her leader and submit a notice to the *Congressional Record* (S. Res. 216). The reformers hoped that eliminating the "secret" hold by forcing senators placing holds to disclose their identity would limit the use of holds and facilitate removing them.

To ease senators' concerns about giving away a longstanding practice, Lott suggested making the terms of the reform a standing order, which would have expired at the end of that Congress, rather than adopting the reform as a new standing rule. No action was taken, Wyden claimed, because an anonymous Republican objected to taking up the resolution on the Senate floor (*Congressional Record,* November 20, 2003, S15252). The Lott-Frist era ended with no formal response to senators' concerns about the abuse of holds.

## RECONCILIATION AND THE CIRCUMVENTION OF CLOTURE

In the face of deepened partisan polarization and intensified minority obstruction from the 1990s into the twenty-first century, it is not too surprising that Senate majority parties looked to avoid the supermajority requirements of cloture by pursuing legislative strategies that exploited the debate limits for budget measures, budget resolutions, and reconciliation bills. As the vehicles for enacting large parts of the parties' legislative agendas, these budget measures became a central focus of legislative battles. They were often the subject of intensely emotional and partisan debates and produced some of the greatest political drama of the period.

For a majority party seeking to avoid filibusters of its priority legislation, the Budget Act's debate limits for reconciliation bills protect the bills from filibusters and make the reconciliation process a natural place to package legislation. The primary obstacle to loading budget measures with nonbudgetary provisions is the Byrd rule, which bans the inclusion of extraneous matter in budget measures. The Byrd rule was first adopted in 1985 and then formally incorporated into the Budget Act in 1990. The rule is complicated and ambiguous.[16] It explicitly bars any provision that does not change outlays or revenues within the years covered by the bill, that causes a committee to fail to meet its deficit target, or that increases outlays or decreases revenues in years beyond the instructions in the budget resolution. There are exceptions and ambiguities that leave interpretation to the presiding officer, who must rule on points of order with the advice of the parliamentarian. In turn, the parliamentarian must consult, among other things, technical estimates of outlays and revenues by the Congressional Budget

Office. The Senate can waive the Byrd rule, but a waiver requires a three-fifths majority of all senators. The budget process and the Byrd rule would prove pivotal to Senate action on the most important health and tax measures of the 1990s and the early twenty-first century.

The Senate's parliamentarian has been critical to this process because of the presiding officer's strong inclination to follow the parliamentarian's advice on how to interpret the rules. If, following that advice, the presiding officer rules against a provision or an amendment for violating the Byrd rule, a three-fifths majority to set aside the ruling or waive the rule must be mustered. This may be an insurmountable obstacle to the majority. If the presiding officer finds no violation of the rule, the ruling can be appealed, but only a simple majority is required to support it. The result is that considerable attention has been given to the parliamentarian's views of the rule.

The stage for changing the use of reconciliation was set in 1993, when minority party Republicans opposed the House and Senate versions of that year's reconciliation bill. The parliamentarian, Alan Frumin, was asked to evaluate the provisions of a reconciliation bill that Democrats wanted to use to enact significant policies in order to avoid Republican obstruction in the Senate. The issues at stake included food stamps, low-tax zones for business, antifraud provisions for Medicare and Medicaid, changes in Social Security payroll tax, the earned-income tax credit for low-income taxpayers, and, perhaps most important, provisions to offset the impact of energy tax increases on low-income taxpayers. During initial Senate consideration of the bill and even more during conference deliberations on House-passed provisions, senators consulted with the parliamentarian about provisions that might violate the Byrd rule. While in conference, Democrats dropped dozens of provisions in response to what many of them thought were Frumin's very strict interpretations of the rule (*Congressional Record*, August 5, 1993, S10662, H6124–26).[17]

After the Republicans regained a Senate majority in the 1994 elections, they knew that they would want a more forgiving interpretation of the Byrd rule than Frumin had recommended two years earlier. They simply changed parliamentarians. Robert Dove, who was removed as parliamentarian by Byrd in 1987 and then moved to Republican leader Bob Dole's staff, was made parliamentarian again in 1995, and Frumin was relegated to associate parliamentarian. The revolving parliamentarians symbolized how politicized the procedural affairs of the Senate had become.

In 1996, Republicans passed a budget resolution that authorized three separate reconciliation bills. This allowed them to separate a welfare reform bill, another spending cut bill, and a tax cut bill, the latter expected to be vetoed, and protect them all from filibusters in the Senate. Democrats objected that this multiple-bill approach undermined the purpose of the reconciliation process, which, in their view, was to reconcile the various parts of an overall budget in a single comprehensive measure. The approach also allowed for treatment of a bill to cut taxes as a reconciliation tax cut bill that, by itself, would have the effect of increasing the deficit, also contrary to the intended purpose of the reconciliation process. With Dove as parliamentarian, the Democrats' point of order failed to get a favorable ruling and they lost an appeal on a party-line vote.

It turned out that only the welfare reform bill was enacted, but the precedent opened the path of special-purpose reconciliation bills that would serve the majority's interest of avoiding filibusters on controversial measures. Daschle asserted that the Republicans' strategy "is an absolutely unacceptable distortion of the reconciliation process; expanded use threatens all senators' rights to debate and amend" (*Congressional Record,* May 23, 1996, 12355). "If this precedent is pushed to its logical conclusion," he predicted," I suspect there will come a day when all legislation will be done through reconciliation" ("Republicans Spar" 1996).

In 1999 and again in 2000, with budget surpluses projected, the Republicans' budget resolution included instructions to the tax-writing committees to write reconciliation bills that cut taxes but, for the first time, did not offset any changes in spending. Democrats, of course, objected that the process undermined their right to conduct extended debate (i.e., filibuster and require cloture) on tax bills. But Democrats, knowing that President Clinton could successfully veto the bills, did not raise points of order against them.[18]

In 2001, however, with Republican president George W. Bush in the White House and a 50–50 division between the parties in the Senate, Republicans successfully enacted tax cut measures as reconciliation bills.[19] The strategy was not without procedural complications. Early in the process, Dove was fired after he frustrated Republicans with his view that only one tax measure per year could be considered under reconciliation and with his interpretation of the application of the Byrd rule to a provision for additional spending on disaster relief (Taylor 2001a; Rosenbaum 2001). At Byrd's urging, the Democrats did not raise a point of order against the use of reconciliation so as to avoid reinforcing the 1996 precedent. The budget resolution passed with the key vote going in favor of the Republicans, 51–49, with the help of one Democrat, Georgia's Zell Miller. The vote was on an amendment to instruct the Committee on Finance to report tax cut bills. Ultimately, after negotiations with the House, a tax cut reconciliation bill was created and eventually passed. The ultimate tax reconciliation bill included a sunset provision to gain compliance with the Byrd rule.

Republicans used the same general strategy again in 2003 to pass another tax cut measure. An important feature of the 2003 episode was a Senate Republican effort to authorize oil drilling in the Arctic National Wildlife Refuge (ANWR) through budget measures. It was widely believed that separate legislation to authorize drilling in ANWR would have been blocked by a filibuster, as it was in 2002. In 2003, Senate Republicans crafted the budget resolution so that it assumed future revenue from oil and gas leases from ANWR. If approved, the budget resolution would have allowed ANWR drilling provisions to be included in a subsequent reconciliation bill, which would be protected by a limitation on debate. An amendment to strip the provision from the resolution was approved with the support of Democrats and a handful Republicans, avoiding a precedent for wider use of reconciliation (Goldreich 2003).[20]

Senate Republicans' use of reconciliation to avoid filibusters on stand-alone tax measures extended the precedent set in 1996. A Senate majority party proved willing to circumvent the constraints of Rule XXII by using a budget resolution and follow-up reconciliation bills to allow a simple majority to enact a wide range of legislation, including measures that increased the federal deficit. Moreover, the majority party was willing to replace the parliamentarian to align the parliamentarian's interpretation of the Budget Act with the party's legislative interests. Minority party Democrats, predictably, considered this a thorough politicization of Senate procedure.

## BUDGET MEASURES AND FLOOR AMENDMENTS

The Budget Act governs the floor amending process for budget resolutions and the reconciliation bills they authorize. Budget measures became a central target of floor amending activity in the 1980s and have attracted a significant number of amendments whenever there has been no overarching bipartisan budget plan. Because the Budget Act limits debate but does not limit "consideration" on budget measures, all submitted germane amendments may receive a vote, even when the time for debate has expired. In fact, budget resolutions and reconciliation bills are the only types of legislation with a guaranteed right for any senator to offer and get a vote on a germane amendment. This often produces a "vote-a-rama" after time for debate has expired, in which each remaining amendment may receive a roll-call vote, a process that can take many hours.[21]

While the majority leader cannot avoid votes on eligible amendments to budget measures, he has other advantages for disposing of unfriendly amendments. The Budget Act requires amendments to be germane and prohibits amendments to reconciliation bills that cause the deficit to rise beyond targeted levels. Specifically, it bars amendments that reduce outlays by less than the amount instructed, or that cause it to increase revenues by less than the amount instructed, unless the resulting deficit increase is offset in the amendment. Amendments may not violate the Byrd rule on extraneous matters not related to outlays or revenues. Amendments to budget measures may be challenged on a point of order that they violate germaneness, deficit, or Byrd rule restrictions.

Once it has crafted its reconciliation bill to be consistent with the budget rules, a majority can use those rules to avoid unfriendly amendments. An amendment that violates the Byrd rule is likely to attract a point of order and a usually insurmountable three-fifths majority threshold to waive the rule or to successfully appeal a ruling of the presiding officer. The Budget Act also limits debate on any amendment to a budget resolution or reconciliation bill to two hours. Debate on amendments to amendments and other debatable motions and appeals is limited to one hour. With a total of fifty hours allowed for debate on a budget resolution and twenty hours on reconciliation measures, time can be exhausted before many amendments are subject to debate and a vote.[22] After time for debate has expired, eligible amendments may be called up and voted on without debate.

With debate limits and tight rules on amendments giving the majority party leader reasonably firm control over floor action on budget measures, the number of amendments became a major source of uncertainty. The number of floor amendments offered to budget resolutions and reconciliation bills waxed and waned in the 1970s and 1980s, but it has been high since the mid-1990s (figure 5.4), when conflict between the parties on budget measures intensified and vote-a-ramas became the norm.[23]

In 1997, the Senate responded to the surge in amending activity on budget measures and the associated vote-a-ramas by adopting a Byrd proposal that would bring all consideration of a reconciliation bill, including action on amendments, to an end when time expired. The provision was dropped in conference for lack of bipartisan support during negotiations over a large package of spending and tax cuts. In the years since then,

**Figure 5.4.** Number of Amendments to Budget Resolutions, by Disposition, 1982–2010

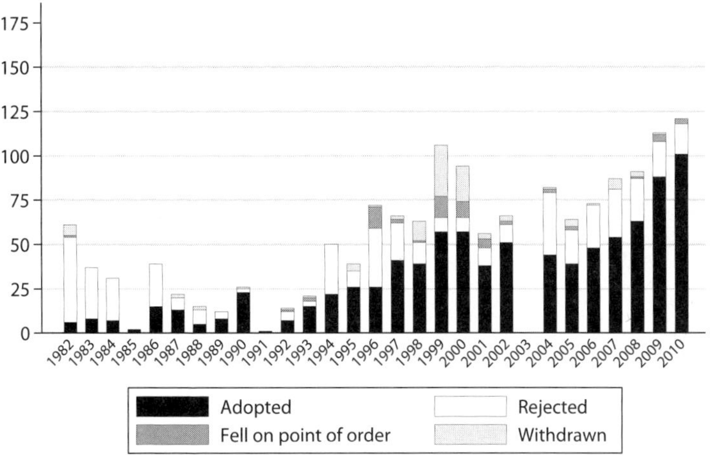


*Source:* Heniff and Murray (2011).

senators have proposed, but have failed to get adopted, reforms to limit consideration, limit the number of amendments any senator may offer, and set filing deadlines for amendments so that senators have time to study them.[24]

The Byrd rule, of course, is used in the context of a debate limit for budget measures. On most legislation and nominations, the minority often has leverage with the majority from the possibility of denying cloture or unanimous consent for a debate limit for other measures. It does not have similar bargaining power on budget measures. The minority can hope to craft amendments to crack the majority coalition or to at least make a political statement and put the other side on the record. The majority, lacking the ability to prevent votes on eligible amendments by filling the amendment tree, must suffer the consequences, unless, of course, the amendments can be killed on a point of order.

In fact, as figure 5.4 shows, points of order have long played a role in the disposal of amendments to budget measures. Reconciliation bills, which provide changes in law, are particularly prone to attract amendments that can be defeated on a point of order. The Byrd rule has proven to be reasonably effective. Between 1985 and 2010, the rule was used to bar consideration of thirty-four amendments to reconciliation bills on points of order. In the same period, there was only one successful waiver motion for an amendment. In most cases, the procedural issue was the failure of the amendment to address outlays or revenues (Keith 2010).

## JUDICIAL NOMINATIONS, THE SENATE CONFIRMATION PROCESS, AND THE NUCLEAR OPTION

Tension and partisanship about judicial nominations intensified through this period. Observers often cite the 1987 fight over President George H. W. Bush's nomination of Robert Bork to the Supreme Court as the turning point, but, as we have seen, the Bork fight is just one of many episodes of obstructionism, including obstructionism on nominations to executive branch positions, that were becoming more common during the 1980s. The 1990s were different. The percentage of nominees to appeals courts who were successfully confirmed dipped below 60 percent (and lower for some of the most important appeals courts). Successful confirmation of district court nominees dropped from over 90 percent in the 1970s to under 80 percent in the 1990s, and lower in the next decade. For confirmed nominees, Senate action took far longer (figure 5.5). The average time of Senate consideration of an appeals court nomination exceeded nine months by the end of the decade, while the average length of time to confirm a district court nominee nearly tripled between the 1970s and 1990s and has remained high since (Binder and Maltzman 2009, 2–6; Binder and Maltzman 2012).

Plainly, in parallel with other developments, judicial nomination politics changed radically during this era. Some observers of judicial confirmation episodes associate these developments

**Figure 5.5.** Mean Number of Days between Nomination and Confirmation, Federal Court Nominees, 1947–2010

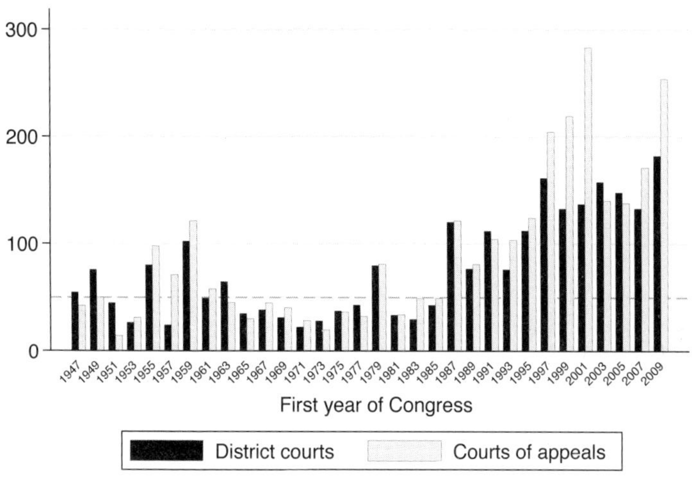


*Source:* Binder (2012). Updates from Sarah Binder.

with key events unique to the politics of judicial nominations, such as the mobilization of interest groups in the 1987 Bork case. As we have seen, the pattern of delay and obstruction is hardly unique to judicial nominations. Developments in the Senate's political environment, ideological alignments among senators, and the centrality of federal policy and its interpretation and implementation have changed senators' behavior across a wide range of issues, including judicial nominations. This became apparent in the late 1990s, when President Bill Clinton struggled with a Republican Senate majority. Senate action on nominees slowed considerably, and less than half of the appellate court nominees were confirmed. The pattern extended into the new century as vacancies were expected on an aging Supreme Court.[25]

Interparty conflict intensified in 2003, late in the first term of President George W. Bush and just after the 2002 elections had created a new Republican majority in the Senate. Openly adopting the delaying tactics they had witnessed a few years earlier from Republicans, Democrats blocked cloture on six judicial nominees to courts of appeals in 2003 (and four more in 2004). To highlight the Democratic obstructionism, Republicans staged a nearly forty-hour marathon session in November 2003, during which they charged that the Democrats, by forcing cloture votes, had effectively set a supermajority threshold for judicial confirmation, which, some of them argued, violated the simple-majority requirement implied in the Constitution. Democrats insisted that the president brought on their obstruction by systematically pushing to stack the judiciary with strongly ideological, conservative judges.

In 2002, President Bush proposed that the Senate adopt rules to require a floor vote on all nominees, but the two-thirds majority required to invoke cloture on a change in the rules made it pointless for the Republicans to push such a proposal. The president's frustrations in 2003 led him to fill two of the judicial vacancies by using his constitutional authority to make appointments while the Senate was in recess between the 2003 and 2004 sessions. Recess appointments are temporary—they expire at the end of the next session of Congress. Nevertheless, this circumvention of the Senate seemed to intensify partisan animosities. Minority Leader Daschle responded by insisting that the Democrats would block all nominees until the president forswore future recess appointments, a threat that led to a seven-week impasse on confirmations and a concession from the president to make no recess appointments through the November 2004 elections.[26]

In the meantime, Majority Leader Bill Frist (R-TN), who replaced Trent Lott as Republican leader in 2003, proposed a change in Senate Rule XXII to reduce the threshold for cloture on presidential nominations for executive and judicial branch posts. Specifically, Frist borrowed a long-standing proposal of Senator Tom Harkin (D-IA), which provided that the cloture threshold be ratcheted down by three votes in three steps (from 60 to 57 to 54 to 51) as the Senate cast repeated cloture votes. The Frist proposal would apply this process just to nominations.[27]

The Republicans on the Committee on Rules and Administration reported the reform resolution by voice vote, but, with a Democratic filibuster guaranteed, no further action was taken on the proposal.

Frist did not leave it there. He and other Republicans began to insist that the Senate had an affirmative obligation for an up-or-down vote, by a simple majority, on nominations. Moreover, Frist began to advocate a "constitutional option," a plan to have the presiding officer (presumably, Republican vice president Dick Cheney) rule on a point of order intended to allow a simple majority to invoke cloture on a judicial nomination. He asserted that the Senate was obligated to vote on judicial nominations under Article II, Section 2, Clause 2. The clause provides that the president "shall have Power, by and with the Advice and Consent of the Senate, to make Treaties, provided two thirds of the Senators present concur; and he shall nominate, and by and with the Advice and Consent of the Senate, shall appoint Ambassadors, other public Ministers and Consuls, Judges of the Supreme Court, and all other Officers of the United States." Because the Constitution does not stipulate a supermajority vote for confirmation, Republicans contended that requiring any threshold greater than a majority to get a vote on a judicial nomination was unconstitutional. Filibusters of judicial nominations, Frist declared, "can't be tolerated by the American people."[28]

As justification for pursuing the new constitutional option, Republicans argued that the Senate, at least until the very recent past, had observed the practice of bringing judicial nominations to a vote. They argued that no judicial nomination had been killed by a filibuster before the Republicans regained a Senate majority in the 2002 elections. They were required to go to extraordinary means to get votes on judicial nominations, they insisted, because Democrats had gone to extraordinary means to obstruct action on those nominations.

The extraordinary means would work like this: A Republican would make a point of order that the Constitution's "advice and consent" clauses imply an obligation on the Senate to vote on judicial nominations, which implies that a simple majority may invoke cloture on a nomination. The presiding officer, probably the Republican vice president Cheney, would rule in favor of the point of order. Democrats would appeal the ruling, but a Republican would be recognized to offer a motion to table the appeal. Because it takes just a simple-majority vote to adopt the nondebatable motion to table, the appeal would be tabled and the presiding officer's ruling on the point of order would stand. Thus, simple-majority cloture for nominations would be instituted by a ruling of the chair backed by a simple majority of senators.

This strategy has the effect of changing the rules, or at least the application of the rules, by a ruling of the presiding officer rather than by changing the standing rules. It is designed to avoid a filibuster on a resolution to change the rules, which would be difficult to circumvent under the Rule XXII requirement of a two-thirds majority for cloture on a measure that changes the standing rules. Once he started giving the constitutional option emphasis in 2004, Frist said little about his resolution to reform the Senate's standing rules.

The constitutional option was swiftly deemed the "nuclear option." The term reflects the expected minority response to the reform-by-ruling maneuver. The minority might counter the move by all-out obstructionism. No routine unanimous consent request would be approved, which would force innumerable roll-call votes and many more cloture votes. The time consumed would bring Senate action to a crawl and threaten the majority party's larger agenda.

The earliest reference to the term "nuclear option" that I have found is in a press report about Republican discussions of possible strategies to deal with the Democratic majority's delays in acting on the judicial nominations of President George W. Bush in 2002 (Kane 2002). The term was attributed to then-Minority Leader Trent Lott. In 2003 senators were using the term to describe a possible reform-by-ruling procedural move by the Republican majority and the likely Democratic response.

Lott later associated the term "nuclear option" with an exchange he had with a reporter (Lott 2005, 289). The term was first mentioned on the floor as the name for a procedural strategy in May 2003 by a senator who noted Senator Arlen Specter's use of the term in a committee hearing about obstructionism on judicial nominations (*Congressional Record,* May 7, 2003, S5839). It was in common use by senators by then (see Specter's comments, *Congressional Record,* June 9, 2003, S7529), at a time when Republicans, then in the majority, were looking for ways to overcome or circumvent Democratic obstruction to action on appeals court nominations of President George W. Bush. A law review article written by a former Senate Republican leadership aide used the term "constitutional option," which surely was intended to give the strategy greater legitimacy (Gold and Gupta 2004).

With some Republicans dubious about the precedent that the nuclear option would create and, perhaps more important, the presidential election of 2004 looming and Bush's popularity suffering, Frist chose not to highlight the issue of confirming conservative judicial nominees in 2004. That would change after the 2004 elections, which gave President Bush a second term and increased the Republican majority from 51 to 55 in the Senate.

## AVOIDING CONFERENCE, PART 1

It was inevitable that polarized parties and, in the Senate, the possibility, or even the likelihood, of minority obstruction would influence how majority leaders and bill managers choose to resolve differences between House and Senate versions of legislation. When compromise across party lines is unlikely, majority party leaders and bill managers often eschew formal meetings and discussions involving legislators of both parties. Instead, they may opt for informal negotiations between majority party members from the House and Senate. The question of how to gain House and Senate passage of their handiwork becomes a very practical one that often involves introducing a new bill. Minority obstruction in the Senate further complicates matters. A brief review of the mechanics of the legislative process is required to see why.

Bills, joint resolutions (such as appropriations continuing resolutions), and concurrent resolutions (such as budget resolutions) must be approved in identical form by both houses. Minor legislation is often accepted without change by the second-acting house, but major and complex legislation often emerges in different forms from the two houses and requires negotiations between them. For many decades, the most common way to resolve differences on major legislation has been to send the measure to a conference committee, with conferees appointed by each house. Typically, the delegation from each house consists of leading members of the standing committees in which the legislation originated and is divided between the parties in proportions roughly similar to those in which the parties are represented on those committees.

Until 2013, the Senate had to adopt three motions to get to conference: a motion that the Senate insist on its amendments to a House bill (or disagree with the House amendments to the Senate bill), a motion to request a conference with the House, and a motion to authorize the presiding officer to appoint conferees.[29] In most cases, these motions were wrapped into one unanimous consent request. If a senator objected to such a request, he or she could force a cloture vote on each of the three motions. If cloture was invoked, senators could force the full post-cloture debate on each motion and compel their colleagues to endure a lengthy delay in sending a bill to conference.

Conference committees make decisions by approving the content of a "conference report," which lists the modifications to be made in the legislation. The conference report must be approved by a majority of each chamber's conferees. The parent houses then must approve the report. In most circumstances, House and Senate rules prevent amendments to conference reports, so the conference is the last location at which the details of the legislation are changed. The conference report is debatable and can be filibustered. Bills that have made it to and through conference generally would be expected to attract enough support for cloture, but there have been many occasions when a filibuster of a conference report has proven to be a problem for the majority.

The House and Senate have other methods for reconciling differences. Informal negotiations can produce new legislation that is adopted by both houses or is incorporated into other legislation that is making progress to enactment (incorporating compromises into other legislation is facilitated by the lack of a germaneness rule in the Senate). Alternatively, one chamber can simply accept the other chamber's version. Or, one chamber can return the other chamber's bill with an amendment, which, in turn, might lead the other chamber to send it back with an amendment to the amendment.

In recent decades, this latter process, an exchange of amendments between the chambers, has been called the "ping pong" method. The process can extend to multiple stages—the first chamber passes a bill, the second chamber returns the bill with an amendment, the first chamber returns the amendment with an amendment, and the second chamber returns the amendment with an amendment with another amendment, and the first chamber approves the result. At any stage, a chamber can refuse to continue the process by insisting on its amendment, or it can accept the other chamber's amendment, or it can request a conference. Moreover, informal negotiations can be conducted in parallel to the formal actions and can lead to a new bill or to legislation that is tucked into another measure.

The alternatives to conferences—usually one chamber accepting the other chamber's bill at first or after just one exchange of amendments—have long been used more frequently than conferences. For legislation that is not too complex and generates little interest, the alternatives to conference involve few legislators and speed action. Even for complex matters, informal negotiations and the construction of an amendment to the version approved by one chamber may take far less time than convening a conference committee. And there are no "layover" requirements for the exchange of amendments process, unlike for conference reports, which must be available to senators for forty-eight hours before a vote (Senate Rule XXVIII).

Over the Congresses of the 1963–2010 period, 17.6 percent of enacted public laws were the product of a conference committee report (figure 5.6). The number of public laws shows a long-term downward trend, which reflects other related developments—changes in the congressional agenda, an increase in the number of omnibus bills, and more frequent divided party control of the House, Senate, and White House. Nevertheless, the proportion of enacted measures that were subject to a conference report fell to new lows during this period.

While seeking a conference opens the possibility of obstruction on the motions to go to conference, a conference offers a distinct benefit for a majority leader or bill manager. A conference report, unlike a House amendment, may not be amended. This can be important to resolving differences with the House and paving the way for Senate approval of the conference report. It also allows bill managers to accept a variety of provisions during initial Senate floor consideration of a bill and later strip them from the bill in conference without concern that the conference report will face amendments to restore them (Van Houweling 2006). Because filibusters of conference motions

**Figure 5.6.** Number of Public Laws Enacted and Measures in Conference, 1963–2010

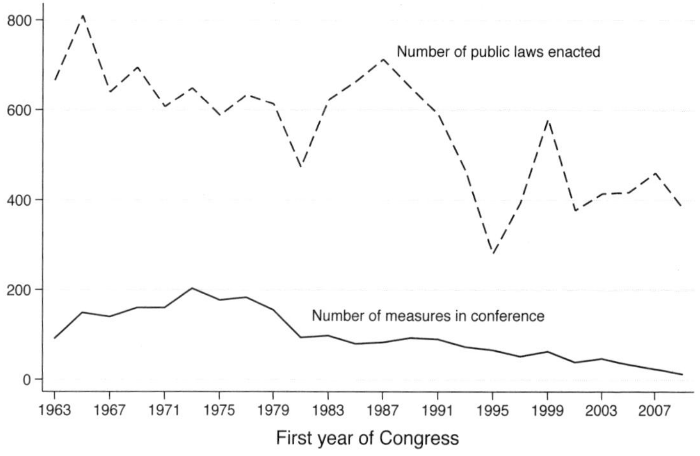


*Source:* Congressional calendars and *Daily Digest.*

and conference reports were not a problem until the 1990s, going to conference was the preferred option for majority leaders and bill managers for complex, controversial bills.

The first instance of a successful effort to block conference motions occurred in 1994, as the 103rd Congress was coming to an end and Republicans anticipated favorable outcomes in the upcoming elections (Oleszek 2008). Late in the summer of 1994, Democrats were prepared to move a campaign finance reform bill to conference but discovered that there would be objection to any unanimous consent request to do so. A credible journalist reported that Republicans intended to obstruct action on the bill to slow or prevent action on other measures "that might boost Democratic prospects in November" (Donovan 1994a, 1994b). In late September, bill opponents forced cloture on a motion to request a conference and were able to prevent cloture on a 52–46 vote, which killed the bill. Mitchell and other Democrats complained that it was the first time a filibuster had blocked an effort to take a bill to conference.

The 1994 episode gave a hint of what was to come in the process of reconciling House-Senate differences. The minority Republicans made the majority party's incompetence in running Congress a major theme in their campaign and backed it up by pointing to the dearth of legislation passed. Democrats repeatedly blamed the Senate Republicans for the legislative gridlock—Speaker Tom Foley (D-WA) called Republican strategy on the campaign finance bill "the worst case of obstruction by filibuster by any party that I've ever seen in my 30 years in Congress"—but the complaint did not register with the public. Republican majorities were elected to both houses.

The lessons of 1994 registered with legislators. As the partisan divisions continued to deepen in subsequent years, party leaders were expected to play a more central role in the process of reconciling House-Senate differences. A natural corollary of more leadership involvement was less exclusive reliance on the committee leaders and the formal conference process for critical negotiations. At the same time, deep party divisions led majority party legislators to conclude that giving minority party conferees a meaningful role in the negotiations slowed the process and encouraged gamesmanship. Private discussions among majority party negotiators from the two chambers did not need to include minority members and could just as easily take place without formal conferences. Added to this mix in the 1990s was the demonstrated willingness of the Senate minority to obstruct conference motions and reports. The consequence was that majority party leaders in both chambers were encouraged to be more assertive and creative in finding ways to acquire the approval of both chambers for controversial bills.

The House Republicans, after gaining a majority in their chamber in the 1994 elections, proved quite exclusionary in their approach to conducting conference negotiations. Republicans, Democrats frequently complained, allowed their top leaders to conduct all discussions with senators and happily prepared conference reports without Democratic participation or support. Minority party legislators had complained about not having a meaningful role in conference from time to time for decades, but the exclusion that Democrats experienced in the late 1990s was systematic and nearly universal.

The Senate was spared this kind of partisan exclusion in the 1990s, but such exclusion surfaced after the turn of the century. After Republicans regained a slim Senate majority in the 2002 elections, they excluded Democrats from meaningful participation on several conferences, which, Democrats said, motivated them to become more obstructionist on conference motions and reports. This came to a head in late 2003, when Democrats blocked motions to go to conference on prominent bills to protest their treatment in previous conferences. Minority Leader Tom Daschle announced that "we're going to insist that we be full partners or we're not going to have a conference at all" (Allen and Cochran 2003; Preston 2004).

Later in that Congress, while complaining about continuing mistreatment, Democrats refused to cooperate. In one instance, they refused to help form a quorum for the conference to meet. In another, they refused consent to have conferees appointed to a conference. In both cases, Democrats insisted on bipartisan agreement among senators before sending the bills to conference that certain provisions in the Senate versions would not be modified in conference without their participation. In the first case, Majority Whip Mitch McConnell declared: "What [the Democrats] are doing is saying that 41 of us will deny you the ability to go to conference unless we get to write the final bill. . . . It is simply unacceptable and will not be allowed" (Preston 2004). In the other case, after a nearly two-month delay, Majority Leader Frist promised that the Democrats would have a meaningful voice in the conference and conferees were appointed (Poole 2004).

The Senate minority's opportunities to block legislation do not end with the motions to go to conference. A motion to proceed to the consideration of a conference report or House amendment is privileged and not debatable—and therefore cannot be filibustered. But the conference report or House amendment can be filibustered. Very few conference reports or House amendments have been filibustered historically, but the number of instances in which cloture was sought on conference reports and House amendments has increased since the 1980s. In the last days of the 102nd Congress in 1992, for example, Mitchell confronted a series of obstructive moves by the Republican minority, which used delay to block legislation as time was running out at the end of the Congress. Mitchell filed five cloture motions on conference reports on a variety of bills in less than two weeks. Overall, the toll from minority obstruction of conference motions and conference reports during this period was at least a half dozen bills (Rybicki 2003; Sinclair 2012) blocked and killed. It also contributed to a systematic shift away from conferencing as the standard means for resolving House-Senate differences on major legislation. I return to this subject in the next chapter.

## CONCLUSION

By the turn of the twenty-first century, the individualistic Senate had been transformed into a thoroughly partisan institution.

The Senate began to exhibit most of the key features of the syndrome that would intensify in the next decade, including

- more frequent minority party obstruction by denying unanimous consent to motions to proceed and to requests for votes on legislation and nominations;
- more frequent minority party sponsorship of (often irrelevant) amendments to raise issues on the minority's agenda and force majority party members to cast difficult votes;
- greater majority party impatience in using cloture motions;
- majority party packaging of legislation to limit the number of measures subject to minority obstruction; and
- use of the amendment tree to avoid unfriendly and dilatory amendments and gain leverage with the minority.

It is tempting to say that both the majority and minority parties are to blame for the early signs of the Senate syndrome in the 1990s. That would not be the full story. The fact is that the minority party—first the Republicans at the start of the decade and then the Democrats at the end of the decade and stretching into the next—initiated more dilatory and obstructive action before the majority party responded with more aggressive use of cloture and related strategies. This process would continue into the second decade of the new century and is the subject of the next chapter.

CHAPTER 6

# THE EMERGENCE OF THE SENATE SYNDROME, 2005–2012

SINCE 2005, THE SENATE HAS MOVED deeper into a syndrome of partisan procedural entanglement. The Senate syndrome involves frequent minority delay and obstruction, usually taking the form of refusing to agree to unanimous consent requests to bring a major bill to the floor, resisting pleas from the majority leader to limit debate and amendments so that the Senate can complete its work on a measure, and blaming the majority party for its intransigence on finding bipartisan legislation to pass. It also involves the majority party's response, which often takes the form of quickly filing cloture petitions to close debate and avoid nongermane amendments, filling the amendment tree to stall the amendment process while trying to work with the minority, avoiding conferences that create more opportunities for minority gamesmanship, exploiting budget processes to sidestep the cloture process, and, of course, harping about minority obstructionism.

The syndrome created the "60-Vote Senate," a term that senators have applied to their own institution in recent years. The term reflects the assumption that the cloture threshold of a three-fifths majority of elected senators must be reached to pass any legislation of significance or controversy. The minority claims it should be that way; the majority claims that it has only recently come to be the standard. The Senate syndrome has so reshaped expectations about the Senate that outsiders, most notably the media, no longer explicitly state that the minority is obstructing and forcing the majority to muster 60 votes to move legislation through the process. Majority-party complaints appear to fall on deaf ears as the disincentives for obstructionism wither.

## DEEPENED POLARIZATION AND THE 60-VOTE SENATE

At the time Trent Lott and Tom Daschle were leading the Senate, it was hard to imagine that the partisan divide could deepen, but it did. The voting record gives us important clues about what happened, and we will take a look at it. The partisan vitriol that surfaced from time to time is more difficult to demonstrate.

New political elements—most important, on the right side of the political spectrum—deepened the partisan polarization. We cannot avoid associating much of this change with Majority Leader Bill Frist, who became leader in early 2003. In 2004, with majority control of the Senate on the line, Frist became the first floor leader to campaign in the state of his counterpart, Minority Leader Tom Daschle, in support of Daschle's opponent and against Daschle's reelection (Simon 2004). Daschle lost his seat, 49 percent to 51 percent, making him the first sitting Senate party leader to lose his seat in fifty-two years. It appeared to many Democrats that the personal politics of the House, associated with Newt Gingrich's rise to power, had arrived in the Senate.

While the new Democratic leader, Harry Reid, did not campaign in his counterpart's home state, he did the next best thing by authorizing a large campaign effort by the Senate Democrats' campaign committee to unseat Mitch McConnell, Frist's successor, in 2008. McConnell survived but apparently did not appreciate the Democrats' efforts and took many days to return Reid's congratulatory phone call for his reelection. Finding a strong challenger to Reid in 2010 became a high priority for McConnell and the Republicans (Stanton 2008).

On the floor of the Senate, a turning point appeared to be Frist's response to Democratic obstructionism on judicial nominations during the Bush administration. The Democrats tested Frist's patience. Frist, by most accounts, failed the test and threatened to alter the long-accepted interpretation of the cloture rule through a ruling of the presiding officer. This episode is discussed below. It appeared to represent a significant escalation in the parliamentary moves that the majority party leadership was willing to pursue in response to minority obstructionism.

Inside and outside of Congress, conservatives grew frustrated with the Bush administration and Republican track record on the federal deficit, military commitments, and other issues. The emergence of the Tea Party movement in 2009 produced organized conservative groups in most states and congressional districts that were instrumental in endorsing and promoting more conservative Republican candidates in 2010. About seventy Tea Party sympathizers among House Republicans formed a caucus in mid-2010. A few Senate Republicans, led by Jim DeMint (R-SC), associated themselves with the movement, and four of them formed a caucus of their own in 2011. Tea Party forces in the states continued to pressure Republican senators and, by supporting challengers, played a role in the endorsement defeat of Bob Bennett (R-UT) in 2010 and the primary defeat of Richard Lugar (R-IN) in 2012.

The sharpened partisanship was the subject of commentary by several senators, each known for his or her moderate style of governing, at the time of their exits from the Senate. In his retirement announcement in 2010, Evan Bayh (D-IN) complained about "too much narrow ideology and not enough practical problem-solving" (Schatz 2010). After losing a party endorsement battle to a Tea Party–supported opponent, Bennett explained that he was the victim of a "toxic" political atmosphere that did not tolerate a senator who was willing to work with the other side on "practical solutions" to the nation's problems (Vergakis 2010). Olympia Snow (R-ME), in announcing her retirement in early 2012, said, "I do not realistically expect the partisanship of recent years in the Senate to change over the short term" (S. Davis 2012). Lugar, who lost to a Tea Party–backed opponent, complained that his opponent embraced "an unrelenting partisan mindset" (Zapler 2012). Plainly, over recent decades senators' expectations about the behavior of their colleagues have changed in a fundamental way.

Blaming the other side for cynical, political, or partisan moves is commonplace in politics, of course, but the unspoken targets of these senators' commentaries included fellow partisans. Moreover, the comments came from senators who were known as team players for their parties. The intensity of the partisanship, the depth of the ideological divisions, and the parliamentary gamesmanship ratcheted up a few notches after Frist became leader.

These conditions, political scientist Sarah Binder explains, produced a wave of "strategic disagreement." She argues persuasively that polarized congressional parties, which do not expect to devise legislation that is acceptable to both parties on many important issues, "maneuver to push the other party off the cliff and to be the last one standing" (Binder 2013). For at least some Republicans during the Obama administration, the disagreement seemed to be more than merely strategic. It appeared that strongly conservative policy commitments produced a disdain for compromise, which contributed powerfully to leaders' inability to address even must-pass legislation in a timely way.

In the Senate, polarized parties and a small majority party are the ingredients for stalemate. Congressional parties are always seeking to balance competing electoral and policy interests, but, with stalemate as the expected outcome on important legislation, winning the next election can become a higher priority than maximizing the quality of legislative outcomes. Senators' expectations change: obstruction from the minority party becomes so common that everyone assumes that 60 votes are required to pass legislation. That changes the Senate. It reduces the incentive for investing in the legislative process and turns the floor into an arena for rhetorical battles. These have been the typical conditions of the Senate in recent Congresses—with Republican majorities in 2005–2006 and Democratic majorities in 2007–2008 and 2011–2014.

Enlarge the majority party and the Senate becomes a very different place. In the 111th Congress (2009–2010), following the 2008 elections that brought Barack Obama to the presidency and enlarged Democratic majorities in both houses of Congress, Senate Democrats eventually enjoyed having 60 senators in their party conference. The contested election in Minnesota delayed the certification of Al Franken's election until July 2009, but once in office, Franken gave the Democrats just enough votes to invoke cloture on health care reform legislation and pass a variety of other legislation. After the death of Edward Kennedy (D-MA) and his replacement with Republican Scott Brown, Democrats could no longer acquire cloture on health care reform and used the reconciliation process to avoid a filibuster.

While the Senate parties were quite polarized in their record of roll-call voting at the turn of the twenty-first century, they showed even more polarized behavior in this period (figure 6.1). The Republicans moved more rapidly to the right than the Democrats did to the left, but both parties became more homogeneous. These developments, of course, represented the floor behavior of senators and so were the product of both the general policy positions of senators and the floor strategies that they and their leaders chose to pursue. Those strategies are the subject of this chapter.

## THE 2005 JUDICIAL NOMINATIONS CRISIS AND THE NUCLEAR OPTION

As I observe in the previous chapter, by the spring of 2003, Republicans had become deeply frustrated with Democrats' obstruction on several judicial nominations and anticipated having the same problem with a Supreme Court nomination in the near future. At the time, Majority Leader Bill Frist proposed that Republicans pursue a reform-by-ruling strategy (see chapter 5), which he labeled the "constitutional option," though it was already popularly known as the "nuclear option" (see chapter 5). His threats stimulated a very sharp exchange of

**Figure 6.1.** Liberal-Conservative Scores, by Party, 1951–2010

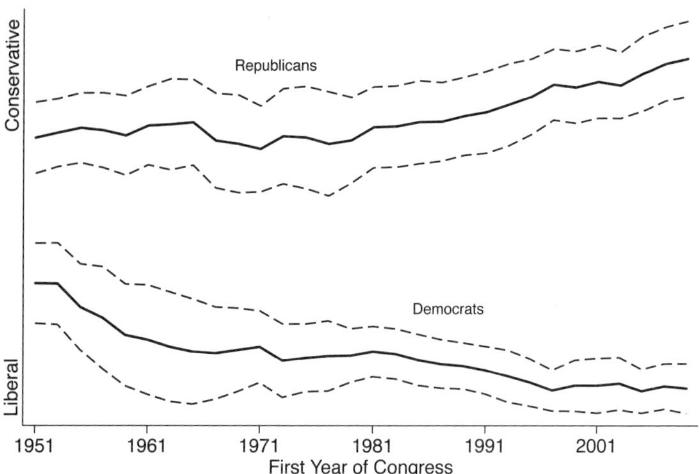


DW-NOMINATE scores. Party means (solid lines); standard deviations (distance between dashed lines).

words between the parties, with senators of both parties indicating a willingness to set new precedents to get their way, but the 108th Congress (2003–2004) ended with no action on the issue.

The Republican position was strengthened a little by the outcome of the 2004 elections. President George W. Bush was elected to a second term, House Republicans gained three additional seats, and Senate Republicans increased their Senate majority from 51 to 55. Senate Republicans knew that Democratic obstruction would still be the primary obstacle to their legislative agenda and the confirmation of court nominees. With more Republicans improving the chances of cloture, and the next elections (Bush's second midterm) likely to weaken their ranks, Republicans were anxious to make progress on their agenda. More determined to gain floor action on the confirmation of several appeals court nominees, Frist again threatened the reform-by-ruling option. In a speech following the elections before the conservative Federalist Society, he warned that if Democrats' obstruction on nominations continued, they "will have effectively seized from the president the power to appoint judges. Never mind the Constitution. Never mind the separation of powers. Never mind the most recent election, in which the American people agreed that obstruction must end. The Senate cannot allow the filibuster of circuit court nominees to continue. Nor can we allow the filibuster to extend to potential Supreme Court nominees" (Cochran 2005b).

This was a call for action against a Senate practice that, in Frist's view, undermined a constitutional process. Two considerations seemed to raise political tensions. First, talk surfaced in the winter of 2005 that Frist was interested in running for president in 2008 and needed support from conservatives. He would need to prove his commitment to getting conservative judicial nominees confirmed. Indeed, Frist took the step of setting an end-of-May deadline for action on court nominations to add credibility to the threat of pursuing the constitutional option. Second, and even more important to Republicans generally, many observers expected that one or two Supreme Court vacancies would occur during Bush's second term and would create the opportunity to add conservative justices. Clearing the procedural obstacle of a filibuster to judicial nominations could prove essential to doing so.

In the meantime, Frist gave new focus to his argument about the Senate's obligation under the "advice and consent" clause of the Constitution's Article II, Section 2. While the clause relates to executive and judicial branch nominations and to treaties, Frist promised to limit the threatened point of order on judicial nominations, which may have helped him with party colleagues who were concerned about the long-term implications of a new precedent. Frist's floor assistant pulled together a record of precedents, mainly those for which the Democrats were responsible, for the reform-by-ruling strategy, and these precedents found a place in a prestigious law journal (Gold and Gupta 2004).

Democrats were prepared to make a substantive argument in response to the Frist plan and rationale. Senator Carl Levin made the most direct attack on the reform-by-ruling strategy by citing the 1949 argument of Republican Arthur Vandenberg (*Congressional Record,* May 23, 2005, 10844–45). Levin started by incorrectly asserting that "whenever an effort was made to change the rule by fiat, it has been rejected by this body." As I describe in chapters 4 and 5, majority leaders have managed to narrow the application of Rule XXII and other rules through rulings backed by a Senate majority on more minor procedures on which, at least arguably, there was some ambiguity in the rules (Binder, Madonna, and Smith 2007). But Levin accurately cited a 1949 episode in which a ruling of the presiding officer reversed precedent but was overturned by the Senate after Vandenberg argued that

> the rules of the Senate as they exist at any given time and as they clinched [*sic*] by precedents should not be changed substantively by the interpretive action of the Senate's presiding officer, even with the transient sanction of an equally transient Senate majority. The rules can be safely changed only by the direct and conscious action of the Senate itself, acting in the fashion prescribed by the rules. Otherwise, no rule in the Senate is worth the paper that it is written on, and this so-called "greatest deliberative body in the world" is at the mercy of every change in parliamentary authority. (*Congressional Record,* March 11, 1949, 2227)

Levin and the Democrats were echoing the sentiments of not only the Vandenberg-era Republicans but also the Republicans of the late 1970s, when Byrd requested and received rulings to limit debate on some motions. The difference between 2005 and Byrd's actions in the 1970s, at least as some Democrats saw it, was the importance, directness, and explicitness of the encroachment on Rule XXII and long-established applications of the rule. In their view, the Republicans were threatening a more revolutionary change of the kind that the Republican Vandenberg had warned about.

There was an important feature of the procedural path that Frist appeared to be willing to pursue. Although we cannot be certain how he would have proceeded, the strong suggestion from Frist and his aides is that he would have asked the vice president, as the presiding officer, to rule on his point of order that the Constitution implies that a simple majority can get a vote on a judicial nomination. The Democratic leader would have been expected to appeal the ruling to the Senate, at which point a motion to table the appeal, which is not debatable, would have been approved and the ruling left standing. As noted in chapter 5, such an approach had been used before on several occasions.

Senate watchers properly observed that a point of order based on a constitutional argument should be, under precedent, submitted to the Senate to decide without a ruling from the chair (Riddick and Frumin 1992, 102; Palmer 2005). A submitted point of order is debatable and therefore subject to a filibuster. As a result, Frist would still be in a position of having to invoke cloture on the submitted point of order. To avoid this, at least in the simplest scenario, he would ask the presiding officer to ignore precedent on submitting a constitutional point of order and assume authority to rule on a constitutional question to trigger an appeal that could be tabled. Alternatively, the presiding officer could rule that the submitted question is not debatable. In the view of knowledgeable Democrats who were thinking through the possibilities, either of these steps to avoid a filibuster would be a radical one that would warrant a strong response.

As Frist's deadline for breaking the impasse approached, senators scrambled for a way to avoid the nuclear option. Robert Byrd (D-WV) and John Warner (R-VA) proposed the creation of a commission of academics and judges that would identify a pool of qualified candidates for federal judgeships. They argued that a nominee selected from the pool would face a relatively easy confirmation process. The proposal attracted favorable commentary, but neither the White House nor conservative Republicans offered any support for the idea.

Before the end of May, fourteen senators—seven Democrats and seven Republicans—announced their intention to oppose a constitutional option (thereby creating a majority in favor of an appeal), support Senate action on some of the nominations in dispute (thereby creating more than 60 votes for cloture), and obstruct judicial nominees only under "extraordinary circumstances." The "Gang of 14" announcement defused the situation. The refusal of the seven Republicans to support the constitutional option left Frist with at most 48 votes, fewer than the majority required to table an appeal of a ruling on his point of order. The seven Democrats' commitment to support cloture on a few judicial nominations guaranteed that cloture could be invoked on them. The technical feasibility of the reform-by-ruling strategy did not seem to be in doubt, but Frist was left without a majority to implement it (Binder, Madonna, and Smith 2007).

Notably, Democrat Ben Nelson (D-NE) and Republican John McCain (R-AZ) led the Gang of 14, which included Byrd and Warner. McCain's role was conspicuous because he was widely viewed as a Frist competitor for the 2008 Republican presidential nomination.

Frist was disheartened with the way the Gang of 14 pulled him away from triggering the nuclear option. The compromise prevented him from following through on his threat and meant that some of the Bush judicial nominees would remain blocked. A precedent that might prove important for Supreme Court nominations was not established. The episode also soured his reputation among conservatives, many of whom questioned his leadership skills, and gave McCain favorable publicity as a leader who could get things done (Cochran 2005a). In time, conservatives would question McCain's role (Hulse 2008), but for the time being Frist looked like the clear loser of the episode.

## FILLING THE AMENDMENT TREE

After the nuclear option episode ended in May 2005, Frist returned to the more aggressive parliamentary tactics employed by his predecessor, Trent Lott. The most conspicuous was the dual use of cloture and filling the amendment tree to control the amendment process (see chapter 5). Frist's first application of the technique was during the consideration in July of a measure to limit the liability of gun manufacturers to lawsuits. Similar bills had failed in the previous Congress after Democrats had attached amendments that were opposed by most Republicans, including an extension of the ban on assault weapons. This time Frist filed for cloture on the motion to proceed. Once cloture was invoked, he filed for cloture on the bill and filled the amendment tree. The move prevented consideration of amendments without unanimous consent to temporarily set aside the Frist amendments. With the votes to invoke cloture, Frist could limit the number of Democratic amendments and allow only those amendments that were damaging to the bill (Sandler and Stern 2005).

Democrats complained bitterly about this turn in the majority leader's procedural moves. Minority Leader Harry Reid observed:

> Mr. President, I am concerned about what is going on in the Senate procedurally. This is the first time I can remember, during the tenure of Senator Frist, we have had a bill where the so-called "tree" has been filled, allowing no amendments to be offered.
>
> Senator Frist, I have stated, has been very fair in allowing bills to go forward, with rare exception.
>
> I am concerned about what has gone on very recently: filing cloture on the Defense bill after 1 day of debate. . . .
>
> I participated in a conversation I am confident the manager of the bill was in on this morning where the distinguished majority leader said he wanted to take a little bit of time, after having filled the tree, which is very unusual, and he would look at the amendments offered by the Senator [Jack Reed] from Rhode Island and make a decision as to which of those he would allow to be debated. He did say he had no problem with him offering amendments and we would be able to debate—and I do not recall him saying "vote on them"—but at least debate specific amendments that were up. But I assumed in the tenor of the conversation there would be votes on the amendments.
>
> We have been on this bill now for 3 hours, after proceeding to it, and my friend from Rhode Island has been unable to offer

> any amendments. So I say to the manager of the bill, through the Chair, how much longer is it going to take before the majority makes a decision on something that should be fairly routine, as to when the Senator from Rhode Island can have some of his amendments heard before the body? (*Congressional Record,* July 27, 2005, S9103–S9104)

Frist's first effort to fill the amendment tree worked so well that he returned to the tactic at least six more times in the 109th Congress (2005–2006) (Beth et al. 2009). In five of the six cases, the technique was paired with the use of cloture as it was for the gun manufacturers' bill. In two cases, cloture failed and the bill was not considered further. In three cases, successful cloture and filling the tree allowed the majority leader to determine which of the minority amendments would receive a vote. The sixth case involved a reconciliation bill, for which all eligible amendments could receive a vote in the vote-a-rama following the expiration of time for debate (see chapter 5). In that case, filling the tree allowed the majority leader to negotiate an agreement on the order and time devoted to amendments during the time allowed for debate.

After the Democrats won a Senate majority in the 2006 elections, Majority Leader Harry Reid filled the amendment tree more frequently than Frist. Counting instances of filling the amendment tree is a little tricky. The majority leader sometimes fills the tree and quickly removes his amendments upon receiving unanimous consent for some other arrangement for considering amendments or disposing of the bill. Moreover, filling the tree may occur during either pre-cloture or post-cloture debate, and technically, the majority leader can refill the tree at any time. By any reasonable count, Reid filled the tree more than fifteen times in each of the next two Congresses—the 110th (2007–2008) and 111th (2009–2010).

In 2007, frustration with filling amendment trees motivated Senators Arlen Specter (R-PA), then still a Republican, and Tom Coburn (R-OK) to introduce a resolution to prohibit a senator from offering a second-degree amendment to his or her own first-degree amendment. Specter complained about "abusive procedural actions taken by both Republican and Democratic majority leaders" (*Congressional Record*, September 24, 2008, S9378). Nothing came of the resolution, and the complaints appeared to do little to change the majority leader's behavior.

Reid's more frequent use of the amendment tree served a variety of purposes. In many cases, filling the tree was intended to pause amending activity while negotiations were conducted between the majority and minority over the amendments to be allowed. In other cases, it appeared that the majority leader was seeking to avoid consideration of amendments that would force his party colleagues to cast difficult or embarrassing votes. And in some cases the majority leader clearly wanted to pass a "clean" measure without any amendments.

It bears repeating that the majority leader's ability to avoid amendments depends on the ability to gain cloture on a bill. Often, cloture is not possible. In 2008, for example, Reid filled the tree on an economic stimulus bill but was unable to acquire either agreement on a limited set of amendments or cloture on a broad committee bill. In order to pass a bill, he was forced to accept the minority leader's approach of considering a more limited House-passed version of it, along with a few amendments.[1]

## 60-VOTE THRESHOLDS AND THE ELABORATION OF UNANIMOUS CONSENT AGREEMENTS

For Senate insiders, a surprising procedural development in the Senate since the nuclear option episode of 2005 is the inclusion of 60-vote thresholds for votes on motions under many unanimous consent agreements.[2] The approach, essentially new to recent Congresses, provides that a motion or an amendment is considered adopted if supported by at least 60 senators; in most cases, the subject of the provision is an amendment, which is considered withdrawn if the 60-vote threshold is not reached. Most of the amendments to which the threshold is applied fail to achieve the required 60 votes. The 60-vote threshold is not arbitrary, of course. It reflects the supermajority threshold required for cloture that one of the contending sides can use to force delay on the matter at hand.

The origin of the 60-vote threshold in unanimous consent agreements is not known with confidence. In 1995, Majority Leader Bob Dole sought to abbreviate the process of invoking cloture on a motion to proceed to the consideration of an appropriations bill by successfully gaining unanimous consent for a 60-vote threshold on two such motions (along with a limit on debate and withdrawal of the motion if it was defeated). Dole explained that the arrangement "saves a couple of days going through the cloture route, intervening days and all these things. . . . But it also seems to me if we are not going to have any movement on the bill, we at least ought to make the effort and then withdraw the motion to proceed and lay the bill aside" (*Congressional Record,* September 27, 1995, S14407). It appears that no similar time agreement was proposed or approved again until Frist used it in 2005 (Beth, Heitshusen, Heniff, and Rybicki 2009).

In 2005, Frist turned to the 60-vote threshold for nine votes to manage a variety of problems on several bills. In the spring of that year, Frist struggled to pass a bankruptcy bill without a minimum wage amendment sponsored by Senator Ted Kennedy (D-MA) and favored by most Democrats, while giving Senator Rick Santorum (R-PA), who was facing a difficult election the next year, an opportunity for a vote on a different minimum wage amendment. Neither amendment was expected to win majority support in the Republican Senate, but the issue threatened to delay action on the bankruptcy bill, a legislative priority for Republicans. Frist's fix was to arrange, by unanimous consent, for limited debate on the amendments as side-by-side first-degree amendments (see chapter 5 for more discussion of side-by-side amendments) and to provide "that if either amendment does not receive 60 votes in the affirmative, then Senate action on the amendment be vitiated and the amendment be immediately withdrawn" (*Congressional Record,* March 3, 2005, S2050). Both amendments failed to reach the 60-vote threshold and were withdrawn, leaving Frist happy with the outcome. Minimum wage amendments to a defense authorization bill were handled the same way in 2006.

In late 2005, Frist was confronted with another politically sensitive problem, the efforts by Senator Tom Coburn (R-OK) to fight earmarks in spending bills written by the Republican-controlled Committee on Appropriations. Coburn proposed an amendment to take out funds for bridges in Alaska to pay for a bridge in Louisiana, a state devastated by Hurricane Katrina. Ted Stevens, Alaska's senior Republican senator and a long-term member of Appropriations, went ballistic, threatening to resign if the Senate backed Coburn. Stevens offered a compromise amendment, but Coburn wanted his amendment to receive a vote. Stevens accepted a side-by-side arrangement but only if the 60-vote threshold was applied in order to guarantee that the Coburn amendment would not pass (*Congressional Record*, October 20, 2005, S11636; Wolfe 2005).

The strategy was used again in 2006 to manage alternative approaches to stem cell research, a hotly debated issue that divided Republicans. Under an arrangement negotiated by Frist, each of three bills on the issue was subject to a 60-vote threshold, and no other measures relating to stem cell research would be in order for the remainder of the Congress (*Congressional Record*, June 29, 2006, S7169–70). As in the case of minimum wage amendments, Frist justified the approach as a time-saving move: "People ask why. We all agree to that because we can spend weeks and weeks on the floor of the Senate and with all the filibuster and cloture and the like, that is what you end up with, is you have to have a 60-vote threshold. That is why we have agreed with that" (*Congressional Record*, June 29, 2006, S7565). In this case, Frist also realized that there was no hope that either side would accept a simple-majority vote on the other side's legislation, so he arranged for both sides to get votes on their versions and then to set aside the troublesome issue so that he could move to other business.

Majority Leader Frist's use of a 60-vote threshold proved quite modest. In the next Congress, Democratic majority leader Reid worked with a 51-seat majority and struggled with a Republican minority that was quite willing to obstruct the Democratic agenda. The Congress started with Republicans' refusal to allow a simple-majority vote on a proposal critical of President Bush's Iraq policy and insistence that their own alternative receive a vote. After the Democrats failed to invoke cloture on their proposal, Minority Leader Mitch McConnell (R-KY) suggested that the Senate proceed under an agreement that allowed the proposals to be considered side by side with 60-vote thresholds. Reid turned down the offer and proved unable to overcome Republican obstruction to votes on the issue.

A few months later, Reid faced Republican opposition to voting on an amendment to a defense authorization bill offered by Democrat Jim Webb (D-VA) concerning redeployment of National Guard and Reserve troops to Iraq. After thinking that he had arranged a side-by-side agreement for the amendment and a Republican alternative, he discovered that the Republicans insisted on a 60-vote threshold, presumably because they were concerned that the Webb amendment would be adopted. McConnell explained:

> What we have frequently done is simply negotiated an agreement to have the 60 votes we know we are going to have anyway, and the reason for that is—well, there are several reasons. No. 1, if a cloture vote were invoked, it would further delay consideration of the bill because potentially 30 more hours could be used post cloture on an amendment. So what we have done, in a rational response to the nature of the Senate in this era, is to negotiate 60-vote votes. . . . We are perfectly happy to enter into an agreement, as I suggested yesterday, for a vote on the Webb amendment and the alternative that we would have, the Graham amendment, by consent, two 60-vote requirements. That is not unusual in the Senate; it is just common practice in the Senate, certainly for as long as I have been here. (*Congressional Record,* July 10, 2007, S8918)

McConnell was exaggerating how customary 60-vote thresholds had become in unanimous consent agreements by that time, as Reid was quick to observe: "It appears to me we are arriving at a point where, even on the Defense authorization bill, amendments leading up to a final vote on the Defense authorization bill, which is so important, are going to be filibustered. It is really wrong. It is too bad. We don't have to have this 60-vote margin on everything we do. That is some recent rule that has just come up in the minds of the minority" (*Congressional Record*, July 10, 2007, S8918).

McConnell was signaling, and Reid was receiving the message, that the Republicans were willing to continue their obstruction to voting on the Democratic amendment until they could be sure it would be rejected. Genuine debate was not the minority's objective, of course, as the Republicans were quite willing to accept very limited debate along with the 60-vote threshold. In fact, McConnell wanted the 60-vote threshold made easy—the minority could block legislation without any responsibility for delaying other Senate business.

Predictably, Reid again refused McConnell's offer, but nothing changed. Reid could muster only 56 votes for cloture on the Webb amendment. Three months later, with the Democrats still anxious to pass the bill, Democrats succumbed and agreed to a side-by-side arrangement for the Webb amendment and a Republican "sense of the Senate" amendment, both with 60-vote thresholds. Both amendments were rejected, with the Webb amendment garnering 56 votes.

Since 2007, the 60-vote threshold has become a common feature of the procedural repertoire of senators. More than 50 votes were cast in each of the 110th and 111th Congresses (2007–2008 and 2009–2010) under unanimous consent agreements providing for 60-vote thresholds. More than two-thirds of the votes subject to the special threshold were associated with amendments.[3] Most amendments were rejected this way (about 82 percent and 63 percent were rejected in the two Congresses, respectively). In the 111th Congress, 9 amendments, about 24 percent of amendments subject to a 60-vote threshold under unanimous consent agreements, were rejected after receiving more than a simple majority but fewer than 60 votes.

Majority Leader Reid complained about the frequency with which the minority insisted on the higher threshold for amendments and resisted the demand at times. For example, in January 2008, on a bill Republicans wanted at least as much as Democrats (the Foreign Surveillance Act, or FISA), Reid announced that "if there are Senators who do not like these amendments and think they should be subjected to 60-vote thresholds, these Senators are going to have to engage in an old-fashioned filibuster. We are not going to automatically have these 60-vote margins. These amendments are by and large germane. They should be adopted if a majority of the Senate supports them" (*Congressional Record,* January 24, 2008, S226). Reid's commitment did not last. After becoming frustrated with slow progress on the FISA bill, Reid relented and asked for 60-vote thresholds on some amendments.[4]

Circumstances changed in the 111th Congress after the seating of Senator Al Franken (D-MN), the 60th Democrat, in mid-2009. This altered the tactics in using the 60-vote threshold. For example, in the fall of 2009, when the Senate took up the health care bill, Reid acquired the cloture votes for key motions (a motion to proceed, a motion on a substitute plan, and a motion on the bill) and filled the amendment tree both before and after cloture. With the tree filled and cloture in the works, Republicans accepted 60-vote thresholds to get votes on at least a few amendments, some on a side-by-side basis, during the weeks of debate on the measure that took place while Democratic leaders were negotiating a final deal to muster 60 votes for cloture on the bill.

The same year, a deadline for raising the federal debt limit and avoiding government default motivated both parties to find a way to bring the matter to a timely resolution. Likely obstruction from at least many minority party senators motivated Reid to propose a 60-vote threshold for a set of amendments and for the bill. Republicans, who did not want to be blamed for failing to act by the deadline, accepted the arrangement.

Plainly, unanimous consent is required to impose 60-vote thresholds beyond those specified in the rules and so must serve at least the short-term interest of both majority and minority senators. Moreover, as just noted, the special threshold is used in variety of circumstances. When the majority lacks the votes to invoke cloture, the threshold sometimes helps placate a minority that threatens to delay or block action on a bill unless it receives votes on its amendments. When the majority can, or is likely to, invoke cloture on a bill, the majority leader can fill the amendment tree and control the amendment process. In that case, as for the health care bill, the minority may accept the high threshold as a condition for getting votes on its amendments and motions. In yet other circumstances, the threshold is used as a solution to a standoff among majority party members that threatens long delay and embarrassment for the party.

So far, the use of the 60-vote threshold in unanimous consent agreements has been concentrated in a few bills. In the 111th Congress (2009–2010), two bills, the health care reform and debt limit bills, accounted for a majority of the votes cast with the special threshold. For action on all other measures in the 111th Congress, votes related to thirteen other measures were subject to 60-vote thresholds under unanimous consent agreements.

The short history of 60-vote thresholds in unanimous consent agreements reflects both individualistic and partisan exploitation of the rules to force the acceptance of a supermajority decision rule and the challenges the majority leader confronts in managing the Senate agenda. At times, Majority Leader Reid has revealed his sensitivity to the potential harm of creating an expectation that unanimous consent agreements will be negotiated on every measure to establish a supermajority threshold. The fear, of course, is that ready acceptance of 60-vote thresholds in time agreements by the majority leader will reduce the burden on the minority of conducting extended debate and suffering whatever public disapprobation might follow. And yet at times, a majority leader who deems a threat to filibuster to be credible must look to cut his losses, find a way to bring 60 votes together to pass a measure, get to the inevitable backlog of legislation awaiting floor consideration, and risk that he is encouraging the minority to demand similar treatment in the future.

## 2007 AND 2011 RULES ON HOLDS

After Trent Lott's efforts in 2003 produced no action to limit the use of holds, senators continued to complain about the frequency with which holds were used to block or delay action on bills and nominations. "Secret" holds, those for which the source was kept anonymous by the floor leader, were particularly irksome. Secrecy made it difficult for a bill's sponsors to work to remove the hold and to gain floor consideration. Secrecy certainly made it difficult to hold the offending senator accountable for blocking action on a bill, and it certainly undermined accountability for something that had become so regularized that it seemed to be an official act. Some observers hypothesized that minority leaders used the holds of their colleagues as cover for their own efforts at strategic delay, but there was little doubt that individual senators were using holds for a wide variety of purposes (see chapter 5).

In 2007, a modified version of proposals discussed in 2003 was incorporated into an ethics reform bill.[5] The rule did not ban holds but rather was intended to make public the identity of senators placing holds under certain circumstances. It provided direction to majority and minority floor leaders that they recognize a "notice of intent" to object only if a senator, "following the objection to a unanimous consent to proceeding to, or passage of, a measure or matter on their behalf, submits the notice of intent in writing to the appropriate leader or their designee," and then, not later than six session days, "submits [a notice] for inclusion in the *Congressional Record* and in the applicable calendar."

The 2007 rule established a convoluted process full of ambiguity, reflecting the difficulty of regulating what had been, and remains, an informal, intraparty process. Disclosure is not required until after objection to taking up a bill is made publicly on the floor. The identity of the senator placing the hold need not be publicly disclosed for a minimum of six days (the rule does not specify how quickly the leader must be notified in writing or when the six-day clock starts). Until actual objection is made to a unanimous consent request, the hold remains secret and a private matter between a senator and the leader, as it had always been.

Just a few days after the 2007 bill was signed into law, a Republican senator objected to a motion to proceed on a bill on which a hold was known to exist. The senator's staff insisted that he was not the senator who placed the hold, and that was the end of the matter, at least for that bill (Pierce 2007). Some senators have long had a policy of disclosing their holds, but it is clear that confidential communications with leaders have not been forced to be disclosed. The new rule appeared to be of limited value. In the 110th Congress (2007–2008) and first session of the 111th Congress (2009), four notices of intent to object to proceeding were printed in the *Record*. No one believed that formal notices reflected the actual number of holds placed on bills.[6] When President Barack Obama called for an end to holds on executive nominations in his 2010 State of the Union Address, many senators' responses were quite negative and cynical (Shanton 2010).

By early 2011, however, senators had experienced more holds, including an episode in early 2010 that senators of both parties found embarrassing. Richard Shelby (R-AL) objected to Senate action on nearly seventy executive branch appointments because of his interest in acquiring an Air Force tanker project and an antiterrorism center for his state. Shelby's move brought White House criticism and national media attention. In a few days, surely under pressure from his own leadership, Shelby lifted his holds (Shiner 2010).

As a part of a 2011 agreement (see below), the Senate's party leaders agreed to tighten the rule governing holds.[7] The rule addresses "secret" holds, but it does not deal with a situation like the one created by Shelby in which a senator is quite willing to publicly object to the consideration of a measure. The rule gives senators two days to place a notice of intent in the *Record*, allows the requirement to be set aside if the senator who objects to a unanimous consent request mentions the senator for whom the objection is made, and, if the two-day requirement is not met, provides that the *Record* list the senator who made the objection. The rule is intended to apply to the "hotline" process within each party: when a leader seeks permission to take up a matter on the Senate floor through the party's internal notice system and a senator objects, the two-day notification requirement applies.

Even this disclosure rule is limited in effect and difficult to enforce. It does not ban holds. It is too early to tell whether the disclosure requirement will reduce the number of holds, as some reformers have predicted, and more recent reforms may have reduced the importance of holds (see chapter 11). The attitudes of the floor leaders are critical to the process. A floor leader can object to a unanimous consent request to consider a bill or nomination on his or her own even when another senator has placed a hold. Moreover, senators can place and remove holds in rapid sequence (a "rolling hold") so that no senator must submit a notice of intent. The penalty for failing to comply is that the objecting senator, most commonly the minority leader, will have his or her name placed in the *Record,* which is not a problem for a minority leader and rank-and-file senators in most circumstances.

## UNORTHODOX APPROPRIATING, PART 3

In February 2012, a bipartisan group of senators took the floor to praise the leadership of the Committee on Appropriations and the parties for committing to moving all twelve appropriations bills through the Senate on time—with time to negotiate with the House before Fiscal Year 2013 began on October 1, 2012. The problem, Senator Mark Pryor (D-AR) emphasized, was floor politics: "Last year the Senate Appropriations Committee dutifully passed all 12 individual appropriations bills. Yet, when they came to the floor, gridlock struck and the Senate was not able to pass these one by one as we should have. In fact, the last time we passed them one by one was in the year 2006, and even in that year the Congress did not get them done on time" (*Congressional Record,* February 27, 2012, S1043).

Senator Lamar Alexander (R-TN) added:

> The idea that we have not taken these 12 appropriations bills and brought them to the floor but 2 times since the year 2000 is a bad commentary on this body. It means it doesn't function the way it should function. I do think it functioned better in the 1970s and 1980s. When Senator Byrd and Senator Baker were the Democratic and Republican leaders, they would get unanimous consent agreements to bring bills to the floor. The minority would allow that, and the majority would allow a lot of amendments until people got tired of voting. But they could not have done that just by themselves. Senator Byrd and Senator Baker were very good leaders, but they could not have gotten that done if the Senators themselves didn't make it possible for the leaders to succeed. (*Congressional Record,* February 27, 2012, S1044)

Senators went on to describe their constitutional responsibilities to give adequate and timely consideration to appropriations bills. They also emphasized how opportunities for rank-and-file senators to contribute to appropriations bills had been badly undermined over the years. Senator Susan Collins (R-ME) acknowledged a frequently expressed sentiment:

> As the Presiding Officer is well aware, that means we would bring up each of the individual bills, they would be open to full and fair debate, they would be amended, they would be voted on, and we would avoid having some colossal bill at the end of the year that combines all the appropriations bills. Those bills are often thousands of pages in length. A lot of times some of the provisions have not had the opportunity to be thoroughly vetted. They really are not very transparent. They contribute to the public's concern about the way we do business here in Washington. (*Congressional Record,* February 27, 2012, S1042)

Senator Lindsey Graham added:

> I came here to do things. I think everybody who has spoken here tonight is telling the public and telling each other: Enough is enough. This is a lousy way—to appropriate a couple three trillion dollars at the end of the year in a big bill nobody reads.

> If you think that is a broken system, we agree. We don't like the idea of passing a bill in the last week of the fiscal year—3,000, 4,000 pages, whatever it is—and nobody knows what is in it, but that is the only way we can run the government if we didn't go back to the normal course of business. (*Congressional Record*, February 27, 2012, S104)

Senators were describing a pattern that is evident in figure 6.2. The Reagan presidency produced appropriations battles between the Democratic House and the administration (and Senate) that slowed or prevented the enactment of regular appropriations bills. The record has been very ragged since then, but the period since the turn of the twenty-first century has witnessed a repeated breakdown of the regular appropriations process. When the regular appropriations bills (which have varied in number from thirteen to ten to twelve) fail to pass, Congress eventually includes spending authority in continuing resolutions or omnibus bills that are enacted after the October 1 start of the fiscal year.

**Figure 6.2.** Number of Appropriations Bills, by Disposition, 1961–2009

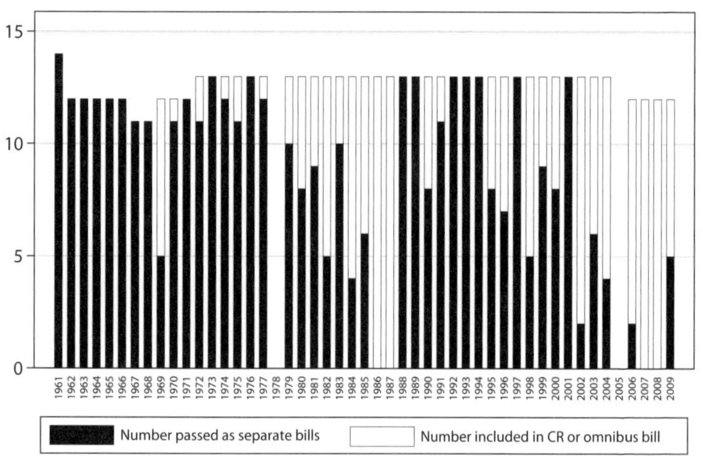


*Source:* thomas.loc.gov. Calendar years; CR = continuing resolution.

The forces underlying the demise of the appropriations process are not simple. Deep policy divisions associated with divided party control of the House, Senate, and presidency have been central to this breakdown in several years, particularly election years. In 2002, President Bush's veto threats for domestic spending bills discouraged the Senate Democratic majority from putting in the work to pass the thirteen regular appropriations bills that were reported from committee. Again in 2008, with Democrats in the majority in both houses but Bush still in the White House, Democrats chose to avoid the veto fights they experienced in 2007. The Senate passed no regular appropriations bills that year; the House passed one.

At other times, the Senate majority party leader has chosen to keep appropriations bills off the floor to avoid the exposure of intraparty divisions. This was a serious problem for Republicans in 2004 and 2006, both election years, when leaders chose not to push appropriations bills that would have exposed differences within party ranks on domestic spending and would have forced partisans to cast politically difficult votes. In 2006, when the Republicans feared losing their congressional majorities, they chose to spend the early fall on defense issues and left office with only a short-term continuing resolution in place.

The Senate bears disproportionate responsibility for the breakdown of the appropriations process. Figure 6.3 illustrates House and Senate action on regular appropriations bills since 2001 and the preparation of the Fiscal Year 2002 appropriations. During that period, the House passed 94 of 136 regular appropriations bills by October 1, while the Senate managed to pass just 64. To be sure, the Senate often failed to act when it was obvious that negotiations with the House or White House over individual bills would fail, but, as the senators commenting in 2012 recognized, much responsibility fell to the Senate for its inability to consider appropriations bills in a timely way. The problem has been most severe in recent years. The Senate did not pass any regular appropriations bills in 2008, 2010, 2011, or 2012.

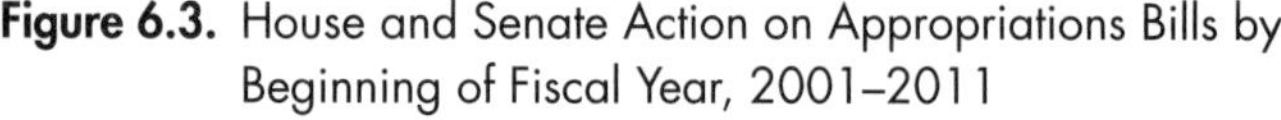

**Figure 6.3.** House and Senate Action on Appropriations Bills by Beginning of Fiscal Year, 2001–2011

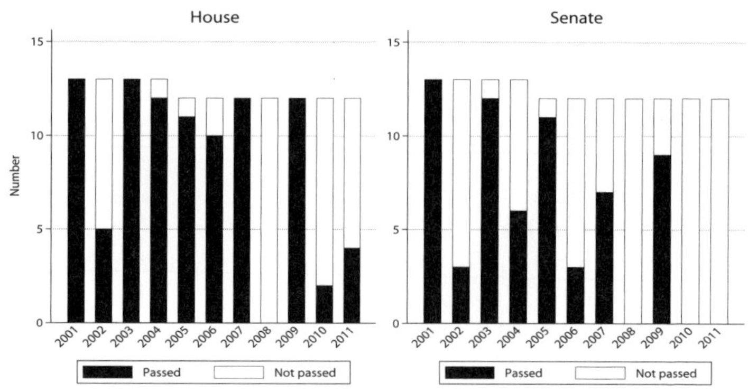


*Source:* www.thomas.gov.

What has happened in the Senate? Three ingredients—time constraints, the majority party agenda, and minority obstruction—blend in a unique way in the Senate. When the House Speaker and appropriations committee leaders decide to bring a bill to the floor, they know that they can gain action on the bill in a day or, at most, two days. A Senate majority leader, confronting great uncertainties about the time required to dispose of amendments and deal with minority delays, knows that bringing controversial appropriations bills to the floor risks that other legislative priorities will not receive timely action. Particularly troublesome are the large appropriations bills for domestic programs, which generate dozens of amendments and pitched partisan battles. The option of having the bills wrapped together in omnibus measures looks convenient as the October 1 start of the fiscal year approaches. Avoiding twelve separate appropriations fights is particularly attractive in election years, when many senators are eager to get home to campaign and want to avoid controversial floor votes.

As we have seen, at least some senators recognize that the demise of the regular appropriations process imposes a large cost on them and their institution. While the majority party muddles through difficult circumstances, senators lose their opportunities to shape policy through the details of appropriations bills. The text of many of the bills is added to a conference report for a bill already in conference, thereby avoiding initial floor consideration altogether. As in the 1980s, the conference reports are the only opportunities for senators to consider and vote on the appropriations bills folded into the omnibus appropriations measures (*CQ Almanac* 2004, 2006). But, with unified party control during the 2003–2006 period, the Democratic minority complained that Republicans were deliberately exploiting the conference process to avoid debate and floor amendments. Key decisions are left to majority party and appropriations committee leaders who structure the omnibus bills that are passed on an emergency basis just before and then after the October 1 start of the government's fiscal year.

In 2012, the Senate passed none of the regular appropriations bills, and all appropriations were included in a continuing resolution that extended spending authority through March 2013. All but one of the measures were reported from committee but none were brought to the floor. The House passed six of the twelve bills, but the bipartisan commitment among Senate appropriators to return to the regular process was abandoned by midyear, even for House-passed bills. The Democratic majority leader knew that gaining cloture on spending bills would be difficult and that avoiding amendments on a wide range of sensitive subjects would be impossible if he brought the bills to the floor. Republicans in both houses chose to avoid a showdown over spending and a government shutdown before the elections of that year.

## THE DEMISE OF THE BUDGET PROCESS

The majority party's interest in exploiting the debate limits imposed by the Budget Act on budget resolutions and reconciliation bills intensified during this period. Over the years, the debate limits that enable a simple majority to pass budget measures have proven important. Since 2001, only one budget resolution or reconciliation bill has received more than 60 votes and only two have received more than 54 votes. Plainly, the budget process created the possibility that a Senate majority party could enact legislative provisions through budget measures that it could not pass otherwise.

In 2005, Frist and Senate Republicans looked to a reconciliation bill to provide authorization for drilling for oil and gas in the Arctic National Wildlife Refuge (ANWR). On a separate energy bill, subject to a filibuster, an ANWR authorization had to be dropped because the bill's conference report would have been filibustered in the Senate. Proponents of ANWR drilling then looked to the budget process as a viable alternative path to enacting the provision.

ANWR drilling proponents crafted a provision for the budget resolution that complied with the Byrd rule. The provision received a budget estimate that the government would receive $2 billion in new revenue from leases in ANWR, making it a deficit-reducing provision that was in order under the Byrd rule. A bare majority supported the provision; the Senate rejected an anti-drilling amendment 49–51. The provision was included in the Senate version of the subsequent reconciliation bill, but when moderate House Republicans threatened to vote against the conference report on the bill if it included the ANWR provision, the provision was dropped at the urging of House Republican leadership.[8]

After the 2006 elections created Democratic majorities in both houses of Congress, Democrats moved to correct what they considered to be misuse of the budget process to protect tax-cut reconciliation bills and other measures. In 2007, they reinstated the pay-as-you-go (PAYGO) rule that Republicans had dropped in 2001 in order to pass separate tax-cut bills and added a point of order against reconciliation instructions that increased the deficit or reduced a surplus. This had the effect of requiring tax-cut measures, treated as separate reconciliation bills, to be subject to a 60-vote threshold to waive the rule (Heniff 2010b).

The 2007 rule did not prevent the Democrats from looking for ways to use reconciliation to protect important legislation from filibusters. In 2007, Democrats designed the budget resolution to provide for consideration of a reconciliation bill to achieve savings in education programs that they intended to use for expanding college student financial aid. Unpopular with many Republicans, the Democrats' plan was to reduce subsidies to private lenders and use the savings for federal programs. As long as the bill saved money overall, it would be in order. It was enacted. In 2009, the Democrats provided for a reconciliation bill on health care reform. They ultimately passed a regular bill with 60 votes to impose cloture, but they used a reconciliation bill in early 2010 to address House-Senate differences and avoid a standard conference report that could be filibustered. In 2010, Democrats again looked to provide reconciliation measures for jobs, energy, and tax legislation, but, for unrelated reasons, a budget resolution was not adopted.

In 2009, Republicans, who were willing to accept reconciliation as a means for enacting tax-cut measures and ANWR drilling authorization just a few years earlier, complained bitterly about the Democrats' use of reconciliation for health care reform. Senator Kit Bond (R-MO) referred to "little Chicago politics," while Judd Gregg (R-NH) called the move "an act of violence" against the minority (Welna 2009). Other Republicans warned that they would go "nuclear" by making it impossible for Democrats to conduct business in a normal way (Ruju and Martin 2009). At least some Democrats expressed a desire to pass a bill by "regular" means, and, with the prospect of finding 60 votes for a bill, Majority Leader Reid avoided the use of reconciliation, except for the purpose of avoiding a conference.

During most recent years, Democrats have struggled to gain support for budget measures and have given up much of the time, caught up in the same politics of fiscal policy that upset the appropriations process. A simple-majority threshold does not mean that it is easy or desirable to pass budget measures, particularly when there is divided party control of the House, Senate, and White House. Budget resolutions were adopted in 2007–2009 for the following fiscal years, but resolutions were not considered in 2010–2012. Between 2007 and 2012, the House and Senate managed to enact only two reconciliation bills—the specialized 2007 bill on college financial aid and the 2010 measure on health care reform. Divided party control of Congress and the White House in 2007–2008 and between the House and Senate in 2011–2012 contributed to the demise of the regular features of the budget process.

## JUDICIAL NOMINATIONS AND THE THURMOND RULE

The 2005 nuclear option episode did not end controversy about judicial nominations. With a Democratic majority in place in 2007–2008, President George W. Bush had considerable difficulty getting action on a handful of his nominees. Democrats reminded the Republicans of the difficulties President Clinton had experienced in getting Senate action under Republican majorities in the 1990s. The issue came to a head late in the Congress, when Democrats were explicit about their intention to refuse confirmation of judicial nominees in the last few months before the presidential election.

A little background is helpful: In 2004, a few senators described the practice of refusing to act on presidential court nominees in the months before a presidential election as adhering to the "Thurmond Rule," referring to an informal norm. The first use of the term in the *Congressional Record* is in 1997 by Patrick Leahy (D-VT), who used it in the context of complaining about the behavior of majority Republicans early in Clinton's second term in the White House: "We have followed, in the past, the so-called Thurmond rule of stalling a President's appointments to the judiciary in about the last few months of their term in office. I have never seen the stall start in the first few hours of a President's 4-year term" (*Congressional Record*, April 22, 1997, 5954). There is no agreement about the origin of the term and certainly nothing precise about the date after which confirmation is hopeless. The term is sometimes attributed to Senator Strom Thurmond's obstructive tactics on the confirmation of

Abe Fortas, President Lyndon Johnson's nominee to the Supreme Court in the months before the 1968 elections. Another version is that the term stuck after Thurmond, then the Judiciary Committee's ranking minority member, suggested to presidential candidate Ronald Reagan at the 1980 Republican National Convention that Reagan urge Senate Republicans to withhold support for moving President Jimmy Carter's judicial nominations until after the election. Thurmond insisted that a president about to face election should not be making life-tenure appointments to the courts (Gramlich 2011).

In 2004, in the months before the presidential election, minority Democrats were citing the rule to add legitimacy to their plans to obstruct Bush's judicial nominees (Rutkus and Scott 2008). In fact, Republicans had already established a pattern in the 1996 and 2000 presidential election years of making it difficult for Clinton's nomination to gain floor consideration. The Democrats continued the pattern in 2004 with Bush nominations. In 1996, no appeals court nominees were confirmed and 9 were left pending at the end of the Congress; in 2000, only 8 of 26 nominees were confirmed and none were confirmed after July 21. In 2004, only 5 of 20 were confirmed, the last on June 24. All of these rates of confirmation were far lower than in previous presidential election years (Wheeler 2012). Plainly, conditions had changed in a significant way.

In the period after the 2005 nuclear option episode, the battle over judicial nominations intensified. In the last Bush Congress (2007–2008), Republicans who feared that a Democrat would replace the unpopular Bush felt a sense of urgency to fill judicial vacancies. Claims about the Thurmond Rule were no longer new to most senators, and Judiciary Committee senators were thinking about the Thurmond Rule at the start of the Congress. On the first day of the Congress, the ranking Judiciary Committee Republican, Arlen Specter (R-PA), anticipated the Democrats' argument by citing the frequency with which district and appeals court nominees had been confirmed by the Senate after July 1 in a presidential election year in recent decades (*Congressional Record*, January 4, 2007, S27–28).

In April 2008, Majority Leader Reid observed on the floor that "you know, there is a Thurmond doctrine that says: After June, we will have to take a real close look at judges in a presidential election year" (*Congressional Record*, April 15, 2008, S3012). In July, Leahy, then chairman of the Judiciary Committee, indicated that the Senate was "now way past the time of the Thurmond rule . . . and I'm trying to respect that. We are still putting judges through. But I must note this point—further judges will be moved only by a consent of the two leaders of the Senate and the two leaders of the committee" (Rutkus and Scott 2008; Kady and Grim 2008). In fact, no appeals court nominees were confirmed after June 24.

In 2012, the tables were turned on the Democrats. Senate Democrats still had a small majority, but this time Democrat Barack Obama was in the White House and Senate Republicans asserted the Thurmond Rule. By the spring, conservative groups were urging Senate Republicans to refer to the "Leahy Rule" to emphasize the point that Leahy had invoked the Thurmond Rule in 2004 and 2008 (Gramlich 2011). In mid-June, Minority Leader McConnell announced that members of his caucus would refuse consent to consider and vote against cloture on all appeals court nominees (Stanton 2012). With only 53 Democrats, Reid and Obama could do little to gain floor votes on the 33 nominations to appeals courts that were pending at the time. More nominations than ever before were blocked by the Thurmond Rule.

## AVOIDING CONFERENCE, PART 2

The avoidance of conference committees to resolve House-Senate differences, even for the most complex, important measures, became the norm in this period. Bills taken to conference fell from 13 percent of enacted bills in the 103rd Congress (1993–94) to 9 percent in the 106th (1999–2000), 2 percent in the 110th (2007–2008), and 3 percent in the 111th (2009–2010).[9] For "major" measures, the percentage of enacted legislation going through conference fell from 75 in the 1961–90 period to 56 in the 1993–2008 period (Sinclair 2011). In the 111th Congress, thirteen measures made it through conference and to the president's desk, eleven of which were in the first session and nearly all of which involved appropriations measures. In that Congress, an additional five conferences were appointed but the conferencing process was aborted and amendments between the chambers were used to complete the resolution of House-Senate differences.

I note in chapter 5 that there are several ways by which a majority party leader and bill managers might avoid conference. The House might adopt the Senate-passed bill; bill sponsors might negotiate a clean bill and introduce and pass it in the House, leaving the Senate to approve the House-passed bill; or the House and Senate might exchange amendments. None of these strategies avoids filibusters altogether, but they can limit or eliminate meaningful minority party participation in House-Senate negotiations, reduce the number of opportunities for delay, limit or eliminate opportunities for the consideration of minority amendments, and speed action, all of which may be of political importance to the majority party.

Frist pursued nonconference strategies frequently. Informal discussions among majority party committee and party leaders produced an exchange of amendments between the chambers, the incorporation of new legislative language in other bills already in conference, and the introduction and passage of clean bills in order to avoid conference. Predictably, Democrats complained about being excluded in the process and, whenever the few conferences were appointed, having no meaningful role.

After gaining a majority in the House and Senate in the 2006 elections, Democrats made some efforts to correct the situation. Harry Reid wrote the new Republican leader, Mitch McConnell, that he intended to convene "real" conference committees with minority participation (Kady 2006).[10] The Democratic leaders' commitment to reinvigorating the conference process proved shallow (Hulse 2007). Of course, this is not something a Senate leader can really promise, because intercameral processes have to be arranged with House leadership. Reid, like Frist, found that efficiency and working around the minority served the interests of his party (Wolfensberger 2008).

Frist and Reid went a step further than merely avoiding conference. When the majority leader fills the amendment tree in conjunction with invoking cloture on a House amendment to a Senate bill or amendment, he eliminates opportunity for the opposition to offer amendments and delay a vote on the House amendment. Thus, in combination with cloture, a majority leader's use of an exchange of amendments between the houses and filling the amendment tree can streamline the process of resolving House-Senate differences and minimize the opportunities for votes on unfriendly or politically sensitive amendments.

Contingent on having 60 votes for cloture at each stage, these tactics tighten a majority leader's grip on floor action. If a majority leader can invoke cloture, he can pave a path through the legislative process that allows him to get a vote on his preferred version of a bill. The leader can fill the amendment tree before and after cloture and then get an up-or-down vote on his version of the bill. He can then invoke cloture either on a conference report or on a House amendment, followed by filling the amendment tree, to acquire an up-or-down vote on a House-Senate compromise he favors. This process makes House amendments effectively nonamendable, like conference reports, which encourages the exchange of amendments and avoids the creation of a conference committee.[11]

Frist appears to have been the first to fill the tree on a House amendment, doing so twice (Beth, Heitshusen, Heniff, and Rybicki 2009). Reid did so more frequently—at least eight times in his first three years as majority leader. The net result: less minority participation, less transparent deliberations, and fewer conference committees.

## ABORTED REFORM AND THE ABANDONED REID-MCCONNELL AGREEMENT, 2011

In 2010, Democratic frustrations with Republican obstruction motivated a set of hearings by the Senate Committee on Rules and Administration, chaired by Charles Schumer (D-NY).

The hearings stimulated new thinking about reform proposals, particularly among junior Democrats who were frustrated that their majority status was not producing legislative success. Some reformers hoped that proposals would be considered and adopted at the start of the next Congress, but their hopes for significant reform were dashed when their party lost six seats in the 2010 elections. With only 53 Democrats, and a few of them not supportive of simple-majority cloture, reformers had to pare back their plans.

In January 2011, several Democrats—led by Tom Udall (NM), Jeff Merkley (OR), and an old hand on the subject, Tom Harkin (IA)—attempted to negotiate a package of modest reforms that would attract at least majority support.[12] Their proposal would have limited debate on the motion to proceed to two hours, tightened the rule on holds by requiring disclosure of the name of the senator placing a hold, and cut the time for post-cloture debate on nominations to two hours. The proposal would have dealt with complaints about filling the amendment tree by guaranteeing each party's floor leader at least three amendments before a vote on a cloture motion on a bill.

Also in the package was a new proposal intended to require opponents of cloture to conduct continuous debate—that is, to conduct a "talking filibuster." Democrats had observed that Republican success in blocking legislation did not require that they actively debate legislation on the floor. Instead, a minority could succeed merely by defeating cloture motions and then leaving it to the majority-side senators to conduct debate if they chose to do so. The new proposal would require that the Senate enter a period of continuous debate after a cloture motion was rejected but was supported by a majority. No motion or quorum call would be allowed, so senators would have to keep speaking, and if at any point no senator sought recognition to speak, cloture could be invoked by a simple majority.

Democrats, some consulting with reformers outside of Congress, proposed a variety of alternatives to the Udall plan. Frank Lautenberg (D-NJ) proposed a stronger version that simply allowed the Senate to vote on a matter on which cloture failed if no senator was on the floor to debate it. Al Franken (D-MN) favored a requirement that more than two-fifths of elected senators (41, when all seats are filled) must vote against cloture for a cloture motion to fail. This would force cloture opponents, who sometimes did not bother to vote, to actually cast votes to prevent cloture from being invoked.[13] In order to appeal to as many Democrats as possible, the Udall team did not incorporate these ideas in their proposal.

Reid endorsed the Udall plan in general terms but did not favor using a reform-by-ruling strategy to gain simple-majority cloture on the resolution, as Udall and other reformers advocated. Instead, Reid turned to negotiations with Minority Leader Mitch McConnell (R-KY) over a "gentlemen's agreement" that was intended to smooth relations between the parties and avert a confrontation over formal changes in Senate rules. The negotiations, led by Rules Committee leaders Schumer and Lamar Alexander (R-TN), produced commitments from both leaders. McConnell promised to only rarely filibuster a motion to proceed and to endorse a change in the rules banning secret holds. Reid promised to protect minority-party opportunities to offer amendments. Both leaders agreed to refuse to pursue the "constitutional" option to reform in the 112th or 113th Congresses. Both leaders agreed to support legislation to reduce the number of executive branch positions subject to Senate confirmation (and, therefore, to minority obstruction) (Bolton 2011; Kucinich and Brady 2011; Kane 2011; Friel 2011).

The 60-vote threshold for cloture was not touched by the Reid-McConnell agreement. Instead, both leaders promised to exercise self-restraint. Reid said: "Our ability to debate and deliberate without restraints of time limits is central and unique to the Senate. It is supposed to be that way. It is in our DNA. It is one of the many traits intentionally designed to distinguish this body from the House of Representatives and from every other legislative body in the world. It has always been central to the Senate, and it always should be" (*Congressional Record*, January 27, 2011, S297). Reid twisted Senate history, as Byrd often did, to justify the agreement. Without Reid's support, stronger reform measures did not succeed and reformers gave up their efforts for the remainder of the Congress.

The Senate adopted the standing order on holds the same day as the Reid-McConnell agreement was announced. It later passed legislation to provide for a modest cut in the number of positions that required Senate confirmation. The requirement was dropped for about four hundred minor positions in departments, commissions, and boards. The House did not act on the measure.

By the fall of 2011, the gentlemen's agreement had disintegrated. From the Democrats' point of view, Republicans began to violate the terms of the agreement by the spring, when Reid was required to acquire cloture on motions to proceed and had to do so on several occasions during the summer and early fall. Over the summer, Reid and the Democrats complained of a Republican delay-and-obstruct strategy on the Economic Development Administration and a bill on enhancing grants for small businesses. Republicans offered dozens of amendments over several weeks of consideration, refused to agree to limits on debate and amendments, and blocked cloture. Reid eventually pulled the bills off the floor.

Tension reached the breaking point over two bills in the fall, the president's jobs bill and a bill on China's currency practices. With two Democrats joining with all Republicans, cloture on the jobs bill failed. The Democrats then sought consideration of two parts of the president's proposal as separate bills but failed to get cloture on the motion to proceed for each bill. After the first of the two bills died, Reid declared that the agreement with McConnell had "broken down big-time" because of Republican objections to the request to take up numerous measures, a flood of Republican dilatory amendments, and a general strategy to delay Senate action on Democrats' legislative priorities.

Particularly irksome for many Democrats was the need to invoke cloture on the motion to proceed and on the bill concerning China's currency practices. The bill had the support of at least 16 Republicans, who voted for the bill on passage.

Reid learned that Republicans demanded votes on a variety of unrelated amendments and filled the amendment tree before and after cloture on the bill was invoked. Among the amendments on which Republicans insisted on votes was the text of the president's original jobs bill, which was being offered to show that Democrats had rejected their own president's proposal. In filling the tree, Reid sought to avoid voting on that amendment and others but agreed to votes on several Republican amendments.

During post-cloture debate, Republicans took matters into their own hands by filing several motions to suspend the rule against considering nongermane amendments after cloture. Although a motion to suspend the rules required a two-thirds majority, Republicans intended to put Democrats on the record against their amendments, or at least on the motion to suspend to take up their amendments. Minority Leader McConnell observed that the "price for being in the majority is, you have to take bad votes; you have to take votes you don't like in order to get legislation across the floor and finished" (*Congressional Record*, October 6, 2011, S6285). The problem for McConnell was that the Democrats had invoked cloture, could allow nongermane amendments to be killed on points of order, and could fill the amendment tree to allow post-cloture debate to expire without consideration of the Republican amendments.

Using a motion to suspend to circumvent the ban on nongermane amendments in the post-cloture period was rare before 2010. In July 2010, Republicans sought to suspend the post-cloture rule five times when an unemployment benefits bill was considered. Two motions to suspend Rule XXII were offered again to a small business lending bill in September. None of the motions were approved, but Democrats were alerted to how little protection cloture could provide from confronting nongermane amendments if a two-thirds majority could be mustered for the amendments (Lesniewski 2010).

In October 2011, Reid argued that while there had been a few motions to suspend the rules for that purpose in recent years, a precedent should be set against the practice. He observed that successful motions to suspend the rules could enable an unlimited number of nongermane amendments, which created the possibility of "filibuster by amendment" (*Congressional Record*, October 6, 2011, S6314). He made the point of order that a motion to suspend was a dilatory motion, which the 1979 reform of Rule XXII prohibited. As expected, the presiding officer did not sustain the point of order, and Reid appealed the ruling to the Senate. The Senate voted 48–51 against allowing the ruling to stand, which sustained the point of order and set a new precedent.

Republicans immediately and loudly objected to Reid's reform-by-ruling move as a use of the nuclear option. Several Republicans promised retaliation—at a minimum, they would be more likely to obstruct and oppose cloture. They soon seemed to back up that threat by casting disciplined votes on the jobs legislation.

Senators Schumer and Alexander tried to cool the partisan passions of their colleagues, but it was clear that the self-restraint demanded by the Reid-McConnell agreement had given way to even deeper distrust. It was apparent to insiders that McConnell did not control the parliamentary tactics that his party colleagues might pursue. If rank-and-file Republicans insisted on consideration of their amendments or obstruction, McConnell seemed willing to let them proceed and then complain about Reid's efforts to set limits. Reid felt obliged to respond. Neither party wanted to allow the other party to use the Senate floor to score political points. On key issues, this created stalemate, and within nine months, the Reid-McConnell agreement was dead.

In the following months, the two leaders expressed predictable views about the Senate. Minority Leader McConnell promised a different Senate if his party won a majority in the 2012 elections. He would make filling the tree "the exception, not the rule" and give the minority an opportunity to offer its amendments. "The downside of being the majority," he said, "is that you have to take tough votes to get a measure across the floor" (Drucker 2012). He was willing to accept this burden.

Reminiscent of Robert Byrd's change of heart in 1978 and 1979 (see chapter 4), Majority Leader Reid's attitudes about filibuster reform continued to evolve in 2011 and 2012. Reid had opposed the reform-by-ruling approach advocated by Tom Udall (D-NM) and Jeff Merkley (D-OR) and had given only the most token support for the general idea of reform. But in May 2012, in the midst of work around Republican obstruction of a bill to limit interest rates on college student loans, Reid said, "These two young, fine senators said it was time to change the rules of the Senate, and we didn't. They were right. The rest of us were wrong—or most of us, anyway—what a shame" (Lesniewski 2012).

## INTERVENTION BY THE COURTS

Some outsiders, frustrated with the Senate and pessimistic about the chances of reform from within the Senate, sought a remedy in the federal courts. A recent case, *Common Cause, et al., v. Joseph R. Biden, et al.,* filed by Common Cause and other plaintiffs against the Senate in late 2012, illustrates the arguments that some senators and legal scholars have made. The basic arguments warrant brief consideration.

The plaintiffs asked the district court to find that the supermajority requirement of Rule XXII was unconstitutional. The plaintiffs' arguments were similar to those made in the past:

- the three-fifths requirement conflicts with the intent of the Framers of the Constitution, who sought to correct the supermajority requirement of the Articles of Confederation and, in the *Federalist Papers,* expressly rejected supermajority thresholds for Congress;
- the supermajority threshold for cloture conflicts with the Quorum Clause (Article I, Section 5), which provides that "a majority of each [house] shall constitute a quorum to do business";
- the Constitution does not specify a different process for the House and Senate and implies that a simple majority is mandatory in both;

- the Senate may not add to the exclusive set of exceptions to the majority standard (expelling a member, veto override, constitutional amendments, treaties, and conviction after impeachment) that are provided in the Constitution;
- the two-thirds requirement for cloture on a measure that amends the rules and the Rule V provision that Senate rules continue from one Congress to the next violate the implicit principle of Article I, Section 5, that a simple majority may determine the rules of the Senate;
- the federal courts have an obligation to review a rule that violates the constitutionally defined process for passing legislation.

The Senate counsel's brief in support of a motion to dismiss the case was limited to the standing of the plaintiffs and the power of the courts to intervene. It borrowed heavily from a brief prepared in response to a suit brought by a conservative group in 2005 in the aftermath of the nuclear option episode (*Judicial Watch, Inc., v. United States Senate et al.*). Standing, which usually requires a demonstration of direct harm, also requires good political science that is difficult for legal specialists to demonstrate. The brief argued, as expected, that the Senate, under Article I, Section 5, was empowered to determine the rules of its proceedings and so the matter was not judiciable and the federal courts could not intervene. This is the view that many senators share, including senators who advocate reform and reform-by-ruling strategies. As in the 2005 case, the district court dismissed the plaintiffs' motion on grounds of standing and therefore avoided the more difficult constitutional issues. At this writing, the appeal by Common Cause to the D.C. Court of Appeals is pending.

It is notable that the Senate counsel avoided a subject on which there is serious disagreement among senators: the substantive arguments about the constitutionality of supermajority cloture. By dismissing the cases on grounds of standing and judiciability, the courts have also avoided the most difficult issues. For now, the Senate is left to interpret the Constitution on its own.

## THE SENATE SYNDROME

During the period 2007–2012, a pattern of obstruction and restriction pervaded the Senate. Obstruction became so common that senators began to advocate and name norms to justify their behavior—the 60-Vote Senate, the Thurmond Rule. Efforts to circumvent, limit, and control obstruction became commonplace, too. Majority leaders always had an interest in sparing their party colleagues the burden of casting embarrassing votes, but in this era of frequent obstruction, majority leaders moved to seek more leverage with minority senators by restricting opportunities for debate and amendments.

The deep partisan divide of the past two decades intensified and broadened minority obstruction and majority reaction. Senators began to assume that the other party would fully exploit its procedural options and prepared to do the same. Moreover, senators expected their floor leaders to plan and implement party strategies, and they did. Trust between the leaders and the parties deteriorated as leaders experienced increased pressure to manipulate procedure for partisan advantage. Senators' appeals to their colleagues to exhibit better behavior failed. Even the semiformal Reid-McConnell agreement of early 2011 failed miserably, collapsing with even more exploitative steps taken by rank-and-file minority party senators and generating a strong response from the majority leader.

These conditions created a syndrome—multiple procedural manifestations of senators' aggressive pursuit of their political interests—that changed the character of the Senate. The majority cannot assume that a few days or even weeks of debate will lead to a vote on a bill or nomination. The minority cannot assume that opportunities to offer amendments will be preserved.

CHAPTER 7

# REFORM BY RULING, 2013

THE NUCLEAR OPTION—reform by ruling—was used for a direct attack on Rule XXII in November 2013. Appeals to senators of both parties to collaborate had produced little change in the Senate in 2013. A budget and appropriations bills were left unpassed by the start of the fiscal year on October 1, several major bills passed by one house or the other were ignored when sent to the other house, and important presidential nominations to executive and judicial posts were blocked by the Senate minority. The division between the parties was as deep as ever.

In November 2013, after years of frustration, Majority Leader Harry Reid acquired enough support from fellow Democrats to support his point of order that a simple majority may invoke cloture on a presidential nomination to executive and judicial branch positions, with the exception of the Supreme Court. After decades of parliamentary warfare, as the Senate syndrome seemed to have a vice grip on the institution, Democrats moved to change the rules by extraordinary means. The successful move surprised most senators and outside observers.

Reid's move rocked the Senate. For the first time, simple-majority cloture became the effective rule of the Senate for an important class of business. The Senate had limited debate for certain classes of legislation before, but it had never combined the cloture process with a simple-majority threshold until it accepted Reid's point of order. Moreover, for the first time, the reform-by-ruling approach was used to modify or qualify the provisions of Rule XXII in a major way. The self-perpetuating nature of the filibuster was undercut, at least for the moment.

At this writing, in late 2013, many questions about what led to the failure to negotiate a path to avoid the Reid point of order remain unanswered. We can start here by reviewing the events of 2013. Some of the implications of Reid's move are obvious, but many will take years to play out. I review the possibilities in this chapter.

## MODEST REFORM, JANUARY 2013

The breakdown of the 2011 Reid-McConnell agreement (see chapter 6) kept reform alive in the minds of many Democrats as the 112th Congress (2011–2012) ended and the 113th Congress (2013–2014) approached. In fact, conditions seemed riper for filibuster reform than they had in several decades. The 2012 elections increased the number of Senate Democrats from 53 to 55, and Harry Reid seemed to be converted to the cause of reform. The reformers knew that the minority would filibuster any change in the rules, so they plotted to use the nuclear option—what the Republicans first called the constitutional option—and believed that they had the support of Majority Leader Reid. The lead reformers, Senators Tom Udall and Jeff Merkley, made numerous media appearances to generate public support, and outside liberal groups organized lobbying efforts to pressure Democrats to pursue the strategy. In writing a new reform resolution, they were joined by Senator Tom Harkin, who had championed filibuster reform since the early 1990s.

Reformers focused their public appeals on the "silent filibuster," the term for the common practice of moving to other legislative business while a bill or nomination was being blocked by a minority that refused to grant unanimous consent or could prevent cloture. The new Udall-Merkley-Harkin resolution softened the procedure to force debate after cloture failed. Two years earlier, the reformers had proposed that, after the defeat of a cloture motion, the presiding officer must invoke cloture if no senator sought recognition to address the Senate. The 2013 version provided that, when no senator sought recognition after a cloture motion was defeated by a minority of senators voting, the presiding officer would put a new cloture motion to be decided by a simple majority of voting senators (Lesniewski 2013, Kane and Weiner 2013, Klein 2013a).

Besides the Republicans, a handful of Democrats stood in the way of the reformers. Carl Levin (D-MI), who had led the charge against Republican leader Bill Frist in 2005, made clear that he did not approve of the constitutional option. A few Democrats seemed to share his concerns. At the start of the new Congress in 2013, Levin started negotiations with John McCain (R-AZ) and a bipartisan group to avoid the nuclear option, and produced a set of proposals that were circulated as Reid began to discuss the issues with Minority Leader Mitch McConnell. Reid said he had the votes to pursue the nuclear option, but it appeared that his claims were intended to convince McConnell to accept a compromise package of reforms. In the end, Reid backed away from the nuclear option, declared a commitment to the Senate tradition of supermajority cloture, dropped the idea of forcing a "talking filibuster," and came to agreement with McConnell on two reform resolutions.

The provisions of one resolution (S. Res. 15, 113th Congress), cosponsored by Reid, Levin, and McCain, would expire at the end of the 113th Congress. The resolution created an alternative cloture procedure that limited debate to four hours on the motion to proceed and guaranteed each party two amendments on a bill. It also limited post-cloture debate to eight hours on lower-level executive branch positions and two hours on district court nominations. The resolution was adopted 78–16, with opposition from conservative Republicans and Vermont's socialist Bernie Sanders. In effect, this resolution created a second cloture process that could be used by the majority leader, but its use would depend on the majority leader's willingness to entertain minority amendments. Reid did not use this alternative cloture process in 2013.

The second resolution (S. Res. 16, 113th Congress) changed the standing rules, which would remain in place until changed, and was cosponsored by Levin, McCain, and McConnell. The resolution barred debate on a motion to proceed if the associated cloture motion was signed by the two floor leaders and seven senators of each party. The cloture motion still had to be adopted by a supermajority, as under the previous rule, but now a bipartisan group could force immediate action on the motion to proceed once a cloture motion was adopted.

The second resolution also combined the three motions to go to conference with the House (that is, to disagree or insist, to request a conference, and to authorize the appointment of conferees) into one motion. Debate on a cloture motion related to a conference motion was limited to two hours, and if the cloture motion was adopted, no further debate on the conference motion was allowed. The second resolution was adopted 86–9, with conservative Republicans and Sanders opposed.

For the majority Democrats, the reforms promised a streamlined process for bringing up a bill in the 113th Congress and facilitated quick action on a motion to proceed when there was bipartisan support for cloture. In exchange, the resolutions guaranteed the minority the opportunity to offer amendments. The reforms temporarily reduced post-cloture debate for most nominations, but not for the most important ones. They reduced filibuster targets from three to one at the stage of sending a bill to conference. Filibusters could still occur on bills, nominations, amendments, conference reports, and House amendments.

The early 2013 episode fit a pattern dating back to the 2005 episode. At least some members of the likely majority for reform were not willing to endorse a reform-by-ruling approach. The majority leader looked for a way to improve efficiency on the floor without alienating those of his fellow partisans who were opposed to the procedural strategy. Minority party senators opposed the reforms and threatened radical steps if the nuclear option was pursued, and a handful of senators successfully negotiated an outcome that few found ideal.

## THE NUCLEAR OPTION THREATENED AGAIN, JULY 2013

Reid immediately came under criticism from outside liberals for failing to pursue more substantial filibuster reform at the start of the 113th Congress in 2013. The critics crowed louder when Republicans obstructed an initial vote on President Obama's nominee for secretary of defense, former senator

Chuck Hagel, a Republican. Frustration among Democrats intensified during the first half of 2013 as Republicans stood in the way of votes on other nominees and legislation. By May, Reid was under considerable pressure from party colleagues to accept the idea of a new rule or precedent. He responded by announcing that he would act in July if Republicans continued their opposition to acting on a set of nominations to executive branch positions. The clear implication was that he was prepared to use the reform-by-ruling technique to get the Senate to adopt simple-majority cloture for nominations.

By focusing on executive branch nominations, Reid probably maximized Democratic support for taking action against obstruction. Democrats and the administration argued that good government required that senior positions in departments, agencies, and commissions be filled within a reasonable time. Republicans were holding up action on judicial nominations, too, but the Democrats may not have wanted to be associated with the Republicans' 2005 nuclear option threat. After a party conference meeting in early July, Reid observed that only two Democrats opposed taking steps against filibusters of executive branch nominations.

The crisis came to a head in mid-July, when Reid scheduled cloture votes on the nominations that had been blocked by Republicans (Sanchez 2013a; Lesniewski and Sanchez 2013). Negotiations led for the Republicans by McCain, who had been a central figure since 2005 in trying to avoid the nuclear option, and by Charles Schumer (D-NY) for the Democrats, averted the crisis. Following a closed-door session of all senators, Republicans agreed to allow votes on all but two of the nominations at issue and agreed to permit votes on replacement nominations for the other two (to the National Labor Relations Board). In turn, Reid merely agreed to withhold his procedural move. No "gang" was involved, but Reid's willingness to set aside a reform-by-ruling move for the time being ended the episode.

The July truce on executive branch nominations did not last. On October 31, the Republicans successfully opposed cloture on the nomination of Representative Melvin Watt (D-NC) to head the Federal Housing Finance Agency. Later the same day, they defeated cloture on a nomination to the U.S. Court of Appeals for the District of Columbia circuit (discussed below). The day's events led Reid to warn, "I hope my Republican colleagues will reconsider their continued run of unprecedented obstructionism. Something has to change, and I hope we can make the changes necessary through cooperation" (Sanchez 2013). Despite Republican speculation to the contrary, Reid was already planning to act.

## THE BATTLE OVER D.C. CIRCUIT JUDGES, NOVEMBER 2013

Given the record of intense ideological conflict over judicial nominations in the previous two decades (see chapter 5), it was no surprise that nominations to federal courts were a major problem for President Barak Obama after he took office in 2009. For the lower courts, the practice known as senatorial courtesy and the blue-slip process delayed many nominations and Senate action on them. Senatorial courtesy is the practice of consulting with senators from the state for which a nomination to a district or circuit court is made. A "blue slip" is the letter on blue stationery sent to senators from the state involved in a nomination. The letter solicits the home-state senators' opinion of a district or circuit court nominee. The Obama administration found that nominations involving states with two Republican senators proved difficult to clear, and many nominations faced delay and obstruction in the Senate, either through negative blue slips or obstruction on the floor.

The U.S. Court of Appeals for the District of Columbia circuit (D.C. circuit) is a special case. The court handles most litigation arising in the regulatory and rulemaking processes of federal agencies and attracts a large share of the cases involving the powers of the three branches of government, making it the second most important court in the federal system after the Supreme Court. The D.C. circuit court also is not associated with a state, so that senatorial courtesy and blue slips are not relevant. Without the state-based constraint, the president may appear to have greater freedom to nominate judges of his choosing, but the importance of the court motivates the president's ideological opponents to give nominations to the court close scrutiny.

In the spring of 2013, three of the eleven full-time judgeships on the D.C. circuit court were vacant, and President Obama made nominations in June to fill the positions. The nominees were Patricia Millett, Cornelia Pillard, and district court judge Robert Wilkins. By the end of October, the Committee on the Judiciary had reported all three nominations to the full Senate.

Even before the three nominations were announced, some Republicans charged that Obama intended to pack the court with liberals. They also argued that the court's workload did not require more judges. Nevertheless, most observers, and certainly the Democrats, insisted that Republicans were primarily concerned about the ideological balance on the court. Of the eight full-time judges left on the court, four had been nominated by Democratic presidents and four by Republican presidents. Moreover, five of the six part-time, semi-retired senior judges on the court had been nominated by Republican presidents, so Democrats had reason to be eager to get Obama's nominees confirmed.

With the three nominations ready for floor consideration and filibusters expected, Reid began to discuss the nuclear option with party colleagues. Over a period of three weeks, cloture motions to take up the nominations failed—with 55 votes for cloture on Millett, 56 on Pillard, and 53 on Wilkins, all short of the 60 votes required. By mid-November, Reid had a good head count of support for the nuclear option. Some senators, most notably Diane Feinstein and Barbara Boxer, both of California, changed from opposing to supporting the nuclear option. Others, including reformers Jeff Merkley (D-OR), Tom Udall (D-NM), and Tom Harkin (D-IA), were easily persuaded to give up their argument that simple-majority cloture on rules changes should occur at the start of a Congress (Everett and Kim 2013). President Obama called a handful of holdouts over the last couple of days preceding the key votes.

A few Republicans scrambled to see if they could find a way to avert Reid's move, but nothing came of their efforts. Reid was committed to his course. With his votes lined up, he went to the floor on November 21, three days after the last of the three nominations failed on a cloture motion. He chose to ask the Senate to reconsider the Millett nomination, the first of the three to fail on cloture three weeks earlier, as the basis for his challenge to the requirement for a three-fifths majority on a nomination. Reid briefly reviewed his efforts to gain action on executive and judicial nominations during the year and insisted that he had an obligation to make the Senate work. His comments included no reference to any of the long-standing arguments about the constitutional basis for simple-majority cloture or the right of a majority to get a vote on the rules.

Reid stated his point of order: "I raise a point of order that the vote on cloture under rule XXII for all nominations other than for the Supreme Court of the United States is by majority vote." The president pro tempore, Patrick Leahy (D-VT), followed the advice of the parliamentarian by ruling, "Under the rules, the point of order is not sustained." Reid appealed the ruling, which led the president pro tempore to pose the question for the Senate, "Shall the decision of the Chair stand as the judgment of the Senate?" By a 48–52 vote, the Senate did not sustain the ruling of the chair, and a new precedent was established. All Republicans voted to sustain the ruling, and all but three Democrats voted against the ruling. Democrats Carl Levin (D-MI), Joe Manchin (D-WV), and David Pryor (D-AR) voted to sustain (*Congressional Record*, November 21, 2013, S8417–18).

Along with several Republicans, Levin and Pryor took the floor after the votes to express their disappointment with both the new precedent and the use of the nuclear option. Levin insisted that he wanted to see the standing rule changed to guarantee floor votes on nominations, but he opposed use of the nuclear option and defended supermajority cloture for legislation. Pryor urged senators of the two parties to work with each other. Republicans criticized the Democrats for a "power grab" and for having violated their own previous positions on the nuclear option. On the other side, Leahy argued that unprecedented obstructionism on judicial nominations had pushed him to favor Reid's move. Tom Udall surely represented the majority of Democrats when he emphasized that the new precedent restored a balance between majority rule and minority rights that had been lost in recent years (*Congressional Record,* November 21, 2013, S8418–37).

Reid's strategy was simple and direct and, perhaps most important, was implemented quickly once he had the votes. Among the decisions Reid made was to exclude nominations to the Supreme Court from the point of order. Over the years, even reform-oriented Democrats had expressed some doubt about the wisdom of reducing the threshold for cloture for judicial nominations, because federal judges serve life terms. Setting aside Supreme Court nominations surely made it easier to attract the support of some party colleagues who held this view.

Reid also chose a "brute force" approach in offering a point of order concerning the threshold for cloture on nominations rather than introducing a reform resolution. A reform resolution could have been filibustered, but the Democrats could have made the argument, practiced for many years by reformers, that the Constitution implies that, contrary to the text of Rule XXII, a simple majority may invoke cloture on a measure related to the rules. Reid also paid no attention to the argument that a simple majority should be allowed to consider changes in the rules at the start of a Congress. Reid ignored the constitutional arguments, made the simple argument about making the Senate work, and took the quickest and most direct procedural path to establishing a new precedent.

## LINGERING QUESTIONS ABOUT REID'S MOVE

There is no simple answer to the question, Why was the nuclear option used successfully in November 2013? Several developments synchronized to produce the outcome, and some essential details about the thinking of key players are unknown. Plainly, the episode occurred after years of frustration among majority party Democrats with obstruction on executive and judicial nominations. Over the previous three years, several attempts at informal truces and modest new rules had failed to change minority party behavior for long. Still, it is not obvious why yet another negotiated settlement did not allow senators to muddle through the crisis. Several reasonable speculations about the behavior of the minority and the majority, most of them offered by senators, deserve consideration.

The thinking of Majority Leader Reid is a place to start. Reid had previously backed away from endorsing significant reforms of Rule XXII, but, after accepting commitments for less obstruction on several occasions over three years, he witnessed no real change in minority behavior. In 2013, he faced drawn-out action on a sizable set of important executive branch nominations (including one for a cabinet post), on the D.C. circuit nominations, and on other judicial nominations. Pressure from his own partisans continued build, and yet, even in October, Reid declared that he would prefer to avoid the nuclear option by gaining more cooperation from the minority.

By October, Reid appeared to gauge Republican intentions differently than he had in July. Earlier in the year, on the set of executive branch nominations, several Republicans were actively seeking to avert the nuclear option. In October, as he prepared to bring the D.C. circuit nominations to the floor, very little movement on the Republican side was visible. When the first of the three nominations was defeated on a cloture vote on October 31, he began discussing the procedural options, shaping the point of order he would make, and rounding up the necessary votes. Last-minute negotiations might begin anytime, of course, but no Republicans pursued serious negotiations until the very end. Reid appeared to face a choice between accepting defeat on the judicial nominations or following through on his threat to use the nuclear option.

Reid also appeared to make a lower estimate of the relative costs of "going nuclear" than he had in previous rounds (Raju 2013). A large part of the cost of pursuing the nuclear option had long been attributed to the prospect of minority retaliation. The retaliation would take the form of objecting to routine unanimous consent requests, requiring votes on every motion, and forcing cloture on every debatable motion, thereby slowing Senate business to a crawl. In November, Reid was giving plenty of notice that he was discounting the threat of retaliation. It would be difficult, he insisted, for Republicans to become even more obstructionist than they already were. The sheer frequency of Republican obstruction seemed to undermine the relative cost of retaliatory obstructionism.

Outsiders noted other considerations that may have reduced the estimated cost of going nuclear:

- Republicans would not want to weaken their party's reputation, which already was harmed by the failed tactics of House Republicans a few weeks earlier over government funding and the debt limit;
- more vigorous obstruction would distract from other themes that Republicans would want to emphasize in preparation for the 2014 elections;
- Republicans' calculations would continue to be case by case, as they picked issues to filibuster that were important to their electoral base and avoided obstruction on popular measures; and
- with the House of Representatives in Republican hands, there was no need for Senate Republicans to be any more obstructionist on legislation than they already were.

Thus, considerations associated with the particular political context appeared to reduce the additional costs that the minority could impose on the majority.

Much of the explanation for the timing of Reid's move rests with the Republicans, who made little effort to avoid the nuclear option. With many battles over the reach of federal statutes and regulations occurring in the courts, and with federal judges holding lifetime appointments, the composition of the federal judiciary appeared to be more important to conservatives and Republicans than the executive nominations that had brought on the averted crisis in the summer. In fact, it is very likely that external pressures from organized conservative groups, Republican activists, and materialized and potential primary challengers were considerably greater on judgeships than on executive posts. If so, some Republicans may have chosen to sacrifice the filibuster rather than placing their own political futures at greater risk.

Of course, Republicans, especially Minority Leader McConnell, may have miscalculated. Reporters observed that most Republicans were stunned by the outcome. In the weeks preceding Reid's move, Republicans said repeatedly that Reid's threat to pursue the nuclear option was not credible. From their public statements, it was clear that at least some Republicans believed that, with a significant chance that the Democrats would lose their majority in the 2014 election, they would not dare weaken minority rights in the Senate. Some believed that Reid would be deterred by his own views of the nuclear option and simple-majority cloture, which he had articulated on many occasions. Some, noting that a majority for significant reforms probably had not existed earlier in the year, simply estimated that Reid did not have the votes. Reid surprised most Republicans.

In the short term, the Reid move did not greatly affect the behavior of the minority Republicans on legislation. The polarized environment in which the minority operated continued to generate strong incentives to exploit their procedural tools. Even on nominations, now subject to simple-majority cloture, the minority showed an immediate willingness to force the majority to use the time-consuming cloture process. It is difficult to argue that partisanship intensified, but there was no immediate sign that partisanship would be tempered by the majority's ability to gain action on nominations.

## IMPLICATIONS OF REID'S MOVE FOR THE SENATE

Senators instantly and predictably drew a variety of conclusions about how their institution had changed. Everyone agreed that the Senate had just adopted one of the most important procedural changes in the institution's history. At this writing, within two weeks of the November reform-by-ruling event, it is far too early to know how the minority party Republicans would retaliate; whether the Democratic majority or future majorities would use the reform-by-ruling technique to reduce the threshold for cloture on legislation or resolutions on the rules; or even whether the new precedent would undermine traditional practices such as senatorial courtesy and blue slips in the treatment of judicial nominations. A few speculations are in order, however (Binder 2013; Koger 2013).

Most immediately, the new precedent, combined with the rules changes adopted in January 2013, created a streamlined process for Senate action on most nominations. The rule adopted in January for only the 113th Congress limited post-cloture debate to eight hours on lower-level executive branch positions and two hours on district court nominations. For nominations in those categories with majority support, simply-majority cloture means expeditious consideration. There still may be a two-day delay for a cloture petition to ripen, but, at least for the remainder of that Congress, a simple majority supporting a nomination could acquire a vote on the second day after the filing of a cloture petition.

The Reid precedent did not directly affect the senatorial courtesy and blue-slip practices for district and circuit court nominations. Senators may want to continue their power to veto court appointments affecting their states and may agree to continue to defer to one another on such nominations. However, the fact that a Senate majority that insists on confirming a judicial nominee can do so surely alters the bite of threatened opposition from home-state senators. A reasonable prediction is that consultations with home-state senators, particularly for senators in the minority party when their party does not control the White House, will become merely advisory.

Most senators and observers agree that the new precedent will make it somewhat easier for a majority to use the reform-by-ruling approach to acquire additional changes in the operation of Rule XXII and other standing rules. The reform-by-ruling technique had been used before but never for such a direct attack on the explicit provisions of Rule XXII. In this sense, a precedent of major significance has been established and could serve as the basis for an assault on the cloture threshold for legislation and resolutions on the rules. Harkin and Merkley, in fact, were quick to urge broader filibuster reform.

For 2013, however, a good guess is that there was no majority for even broader filibuster reform. At least Senators Boxer and Feinstein, and probably two or three others, had been holdouts on filibuster reform in the past, but now agreed that the extraordinary obstruction of nominations justified Reid's move. With Senate Democrats already unable to get much agreement with the Republican-controlled House, there was little incentive for the time being to think about changing the cloture threshold for legislation. The exception for Supreme Court nominations suggests that at least some of the 52 Democrats who supported Reid's point of order were not willing to include the highest court.

Nevertheless, the events of 2013 proved that senators' views of reform and the nuclear option can evolve, even within a single Congress, in response to the changing behavior of their colleagues and parties. The most likely situation to generate more support for extending simple-majority cloture to legislation occurs when supermajority cloture is the one obstacle to enacting a program. This is most likely when both houses of Congress and the presidency are controlled by the same party. I consider sources of support and opposition to filibuster reform more thoroughly in chapter 10.

As expected, critics of Reid's move warned that the Senate had taken a big step in transforming the institution into another House of Representatives. They meant that the ability of the simple majority to freely change the rules would eventually lead majorities to change the rules in ways that limit minority and individual rights and empower a majority to gain action on legislation at will. It might take decades to happen, but, step-by-step, interparty conflict would lead majority parties to seek greater control over Senate proceedings. Reformers do not fear this outcome, but there were at least a few senators, including Reid, who were sitting on the fence on filibuster reform and found this argument persuasive.

Even if the Senate moved to simple-majority cloture for all matters, the the chamber would remain a distinctive body. Six-year, staggered terms, state-based representation of two senators per state, the vice president designated as the presiding officer, and the Senate's much smaller size make it highly likely that the Senate will continue to be very different from the House. The mix of policy preferences in the Senate will not be identical to those of the House, and the Senate will continue to operate more informally and tolerate more debate than the House. Perhaps most important, the Senate's presiding officer is not a majority party leader granted strong parliamentary powers, as in the House.

The long-term effects of Reid's move are uncertain, though there was no shortage of speculation in the immediate aftermath of Reid's move (Klein 2013b). On the one hand, reformers may be emboldened, and majorities may be less strongly handicapped by arguments about Senate tradition. There may be effort to codify the new precedent in Rule XXII, which now hangs limply with the burden of a precedent that undercuts its explicit provisions for an important class of Senate business. A codification may produce additional change. On the other hand, minorities may be more selective in their efforts to block or delay majority action. If so, the Senate syndrome will become less acute and the incentive for further reform will be diminished.

## CONCLUSION

The Reid move is among the three or four most important events in the procedural history of the Senate. Ignoring the plain text of a standing rule, a majority of senators changed the effective rule by merely declaring it to be something else. The move was radical by Senate standards, but it was not precipitous. It followed years of minority obstruction and only modestly effective majority party responses—years of the intensifying Senate syndrome.

As far as I know, no senator or outside observer predicted that Reid would move successfully by the means he did. The institution's long history proved an inadequate basis for predicting what would happen in 2013. Senators surely expected that the nuclear option would be averted once again in November over judicial nominations, as it had been in July over executive nominations. Among scholars, as I discuss in chapter 9, one school of thought held that the threat of the nuclear option was enough to keep minority obstructionism in check. That proved wrong. Another school of thought insisted that the costs a minority could impose on the majority in the form of retaliatory obstruction were enough to keep the nuclear option from being exercised. That, too, proved wrong. Senators changed their institution.

# PART II

# IMPLICATIONS OF THE SENATE SYNDROME

CHAPTER 8

# CONTROVERSIES ABOUT SENATE PRACTICE

A LONG-TERM PATTERN RUNS THROUGH the Senate's variegated history. While eras of intensive minority obstruction have come and gone, senators have, step-by-step, invented and exploited new parliamentary strategies to obstruct the majority and counter minority obstruction. Senators, and the outsiders who find ways to motivate senators to act in their interest, observe how to play the game and insist that effective strategies be used in pursuit of their causes. Parliamentary strategies, once learned and used, tend to be imitated and remain a part of the political arsenal.

Over the course of the last quarter century, more-polarized parties have accelerated procedural innovation. The minority party leadership has come to play a more central role in orchestrating obstruction to majority party plans. Even when the minority leader does not initially take the lead to obstruct, other minority party senators sometimes act on their own and push the leader into a more obstructionist mode. The majority leader, long expected to manage floor strategy for his party, has responded with moves to limit or circumvent obstruction, control the amendment process, and manage time.

This process of minority moves and majority countermoves has escalated in the last decade into a full-blown syndrome. The elements of the Senate syndrome are detailed in previous chapters, but certain aspects of the causes and consequences of the syndrome warrant a closer look. I address them in this chapter in answering a set of questions about Senate practice:

- Are senators, rather than the rules and the larger political environment, the root cause of the Senate syndrome?

- Does the cloture threshold affect legislative outcomes?
- Does the filibuster kill legislation?
- Are Republicans to blame?

## ARE SENATORS THE PROBLEM?

I have noted many observations by senators, political scientists, and others about the causes of the Senate syndrome. I have emphasized the polarization of senators' policy positions and the alignment of their policy preferences with their party affiliations, the time constraints that the Senate's workload and obstruction create, variation in the size of the Senate parties, and, of course, the Senate's rules and accumulating precedents. As Senate majorities have operated with smaller numbers, greater partisan polarization, and more severe time constraints, the ability and willingness of the minority to obstruct have increased and the aggressiveness of the majority party has intensified. These are the common observations, which, quite properly, focus on the immediate fundamentals of congressional policy making.

There is a larger story that I have mentioned but have said too little about. The partisan polarization and the intensity of partisan behavior that goes with it are the product of a number of changes in the larger American polity. Several forces have been at work over recent decades that have influenced the policy preferences legislators have brought to Congress and have shaped incentives for their behavior once elected:

- the partisan realignment of the South;
- the sorting of the electorate into more ideologically homogeneous party coalitions;
- the development of new, organized, well-financed, and strongly ideological groups within the parties; and
- changes in the primary electorates, the electronic media, and information technology.

The most immediate effects of these forces were to make majority control of the Senate more competitive after decades of

Democratic domination and to drive apart the policy preferences of senators in the two parties. These developments created incentives for senators and their party leaders to be less compromising, to appeal to the well-organized and sometimes extreme elements of their parties, to gear legislative tactics to public relations and the next election, and to behave in ways that appear purely partisan. In the Senate, the minority party responded to these incentives with obstructionist strategies that often made the majority party appear incompetent at governing. The majority party tried to limit the damage by restricting the opportunities for the minority to block legislation and score public relations victories. The Senate syndrome emerged when these strategies became the norm in the early twenty-first century.

There is another argument worth noting, which has two parts. The first part is that senators are the problem. Senator Lamar Alexander's (R-TN) observation that "what we need is a change in behavior more than a change of the rules" is typical of anti-reform commentary in recent years. The conservative Alexander's comments are matched by liberal John Kerry's (D-MA): "We wouldn't even be where we are if you had the old bulls in both parties who wouldn't have stood for gamesmanship because they were caretakers of the institution first and foremost" (Arsenault 2010). The problem is not bad rules but rather bad senators. After all, the argument goes, Rule XXII has not been changed for decades, and yet the Senate is struggling with far more turmoil than ever. Personal character and will power, not the Senate rules, political alignment, or environment, are the problems.

Related arguments were made in the 1970s and 1980s, when conservatives opposed reform and argued that senators needed to restrain themselves. Senators, of course, did not exhibit renewed restraint after the revised rule was adopted in 1975. They continued on a path of frequent filibustering, became more aggressive in protecting their individual rights under time limitation agreements, placed more holds on bills, and created a way of doing business that many of them found intolerable (chapter 5).

The second part of the argument, which is made by many but not all who make the first part of the argument, is that the Senate would be a different place if it had more effective leadership. The claim is that the Senate needs leaders who are less tolerant of their colleagues' selfish behavior, who are willing to call the bluffs of senators who threaten to filibuster, and who demand that filibustering senators pay a high price in the commitment of time and effort to floor debate. With such a leader—the argument is really about the majority leader—the Senate could operate under "regular order," and stronger incentives for good behavior would be in place.

Evaluating this argument about senators' character and leadership is not easy. We have no way to measure senators' will power or personalities at any one moment, let alone over the last half century. Even if we did, there are serious challenges to drawing inferences about their effects.

First, the same forces that produce the divergence in the parties' policy positions (see figure 8.1)—the groups influencing nominations, the primary electorates, and so on—may select for candidates who are less willing to compromise and less attentive to the institutional interests of the Senate. If so, policy views and uncompromising demeanors are correlated, and their independent effects on the obstruct and restrict syndrome are not easily estimated.

Second, the claim that senators' political personalities contribute to the functioning of the Senate is reasonable, but the appeal to senators and leaders to change their behavior probably understates the strength of the incentives that have emerged for obstructive and partisan behavior and overstates the potential for leaders to resist demands for action. The demands for senators to fully exploit their parliamentary rights are real, frequent, intense, and often unforgiving. They originated in the 1960s and thus predate the period of polarized parties that we have experienced since the early 1990s. They will survive long beyond our time.

The claim that today's leaders could effectively rein in the resulting partisanship and individualism of senators is no better

**Figure 8.1.** Party and Senate Means, Liberal-Conservative Dimension, 1961–2010

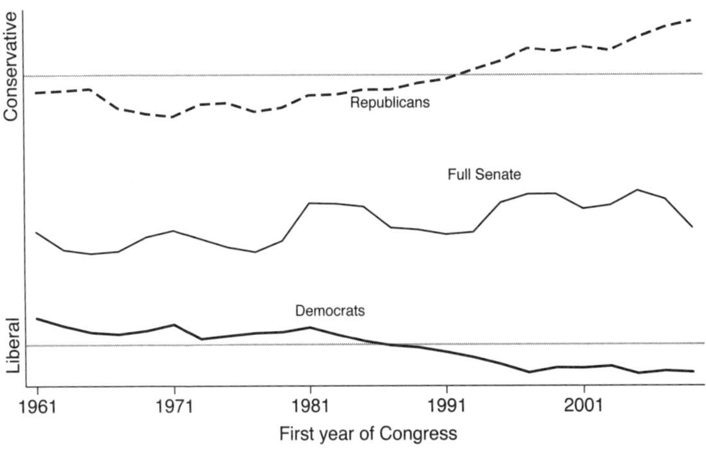


DW-NOMINATE scores (voteview.com). Reference lines are party means for entire period.

than a hunch. Indeed, Senate leaders cannot retain their positions without the support of their colleagues, and they have few resources they can use to motivate compliant behavior. And, as a procedural matter, the majority leader needs unanimous consent to conduct the normal business of the Senate and cannot afford to seriously alienate any of his colleagues. Beyond the short term, we would expect leaders to be elected who are willing to adapt to the powerful incentives outside the Senate that structure their colleagues' behavior.

The Senate syndrome is a long-term problem. It has been intensifying for half a century and pushed to extremes by interparty warfare, but it was becoming a serious problem long before the last few Congresses, when journalistic attention brought the Senate into somewhat better focus for Americans. Individual senators and well-organized factions were exploiting the opportunities for delay and obstruction in a way that produced deep frustration and demands for reform long before the nuclear option graced the lips of senators.

## DOES THE CLOTURE THRESHOLD MATTER?

An open question is whether the change in the cloture threshold matters. Reformers certainly insist that the threshold affects outcomes, but, in fact, opponents to reform have argued both sides of the question. On one side, reform opponents have argued that a determined majority backed by the public will eventually win (Binder and Smith 1997, 127–59). Arguing the other side, reform opponents have observed that the high threshold is essential to protecting minority rights and preserves the Senate's special role in American government. Either the cloture rule does not matter much or the quality of American democracy turns on its details, but it is hard to square these common arguments with each other.

The logical consistency of arguments for and against reform is worth notice, but it is more important to ask whether the threshold makes any difference in Senate legislative activity. Reformers expected that cloture would be easier to invoke with a lower threshold. With cloture made easier, they further hypothesized, the incentive to filibuster would weaken and the number of filibusters would fall.

Unfortunately, we cannot be sure what the volume of filibustering or cloture would have been if the 1975 reform had not been adopted. By virtue of senators' reports and the evidence reviewed in previous chapters, it is clear that obstructionism continued apace and eventually reached new levels. The frequency of obstruction might have been even greater without the lower threshold for cloture.

Still, the numbers bear a close look, and a good place to begin is the relationship between the cloture threshold and the size of the majority party. At the time the threshold was reduced to three-fifths of all senators, the majority party Democrats had enjoyed large majorities for many Congresses (see figure 8.2), but on many issues they could expect to lose the support of many conservative Democrats. Reducing the threshold to 60 put cloture within reach far more often. Starting with the 1980 elections, Republicans challenged for majority control and the

**Figure 8.2.** Decision Thresholds and Party Size, 1961–2009

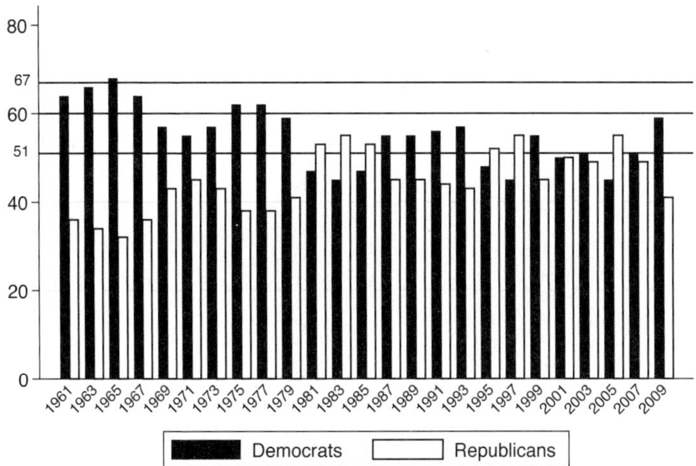


Reference lines indicate alternative decision thresholds.

typical majority party size fell well below the average of the 1960s and 1970s. In fact, only for a few months in the 111th Congress (2009–2010) did the majority party (the Democrats) have as many as 70, or three-fifths, of Senate seats.

Plainly, Senate Democratic liberals, the force behind the 1975 reform, managed to gain a reduction in the cloture threshold just a few years before their party would lose its grip on majority status. The Senate was about to enter a long period of small majorities during which reaching the three-fifths threshold for cloture would require votes from minority party senators. These conditions made at least a few minority senators pivotal players on many important issues, increased intraparty pressures for party loyalty, and contributed to frustration in the majority party.

Lowering the cloture threshold was associated with an increase in the number of cloture motions as well as their higher success rate. This is demonstrated in table 8.1, which reports the disposition of filed cloture petitions. The yearly number

**Table 8.1.** Disposition of Cloture Petitions, 1961–2010 (in percentages)

| | Pre-1975 reform | Post-1975 reform |
|---|---|---|
| Vote: failed | 63.2 | 37.5 |
| Vote: invoked | 17.9 | 32.8 |
| No action | 9.5 | 8.4 |
| Vitiated | 4.2 | 8.1 |
| Withdrawn | 5.3 | 13.2 |
| Total | 100.0 | 100.0 |
| Number | (95) | (1,156) |
| Number per year | (6.7) | (32.1) |

*Source:* www.senate.gov.
*Note:* Based on final action on cloture petitions.

of cloture petitions in the postreform period was nearly five times the number in the prereform period. The lowering of the cloture threshold was associated with a nearly doubled rate of success for cloture motions. Obstructionism, as noted in previous chapters, increased rather than decreased in the postreform period, contrary to the hopes of reformers in 1975.

It is noteworthy that after the reform, more cloture petitions were vitiated by unanimous consent or withdrawn by the sponsor. In major part, this reflects the majority leader's tendency in recent Congresses to file for cloture early in the process and then set aside a cloture petition after acquiring agreement on how to proceed with a bill. Both obstruction and the filing of cloture motions became the norm for major legislation.

We can better define the effect of the change in cloture threshold if we take into account the support and opposition to cloture motions that received a roll-call vote (table 8.2). A few cloture petitions did not attract majority support, but over 90 percent were supported by a majority of senators. In the prereform period, nearly two-thirds of cloture votes acquired the support of a majority that was too small to invoke cloture. In the postreform period, there was about a fifty-fifty chance of

**Table 8.2.** Vote Outcomes on Cloture Petitions, 1961–2010 (in percentages)

| Support for cloture | Pre-1975 reform | Post-1975 reform |
|---|---|---|
| Less than a majority | 9.7 | 7.0 |
| Majority, less than cloture threshold | 64.5 | 45.1 |
| Majority, greater than cloture threshold | 25.8 | 47.9 |
| Total | 100.0 | 100.0 |
| Number | (62) | (760) |

*Source:* www.senate.gov.
*Note:* Based on final action on cloture petitions coming to a vote.

cloture being invoked. Again, as reformers expected, the rule appeared to make a difference in the ease of gaining cloture (all of these differences are statistically significant).

Other factors—such as the size of the two parties, their cohesiveness, and the distance between them—may influence cloture vote outcomes, so a more complete model of cloture motion outcomes is required to satisfy the inference that reform mattered. Table 8.3 shows that the estimates of the effects of reform, majority party size, and the distance between the parties on the adoption or defeat of cloture motions (petitions that received action and were not vitiated or withdrawn) are statistically significant in the predicted direction. The change in the rule mattered.

We must exercise caution in interpreting the effect of interparty distance and intraparty cohesiveness on cloture success. The distance between parties is correlated with party cohesiveness. Both are measured on the first dimension of DW-NOMINATE, a scale derived from roll-call votes, and both depend on the mean values for each party. As the party means diverge, the parties' standard deviations shrink. If distance is removed from the estimated model, majority party cohesiveness becomes significant. We can infer that both senators' policy positions and the cloture threshold are related to cloture success.

**Table 8.3.** Estimates of the Effects of Reform, Majority Party Size, and Majority Party Cohesiveness on Cloture Motion Adoption, 1961–2010

| | |
|---|---|
| Reform | .93* (.44) |
| Majority-party size | 0.07* (.03) |
| Majority-party cohesiveness | –.28 (4.76) |
| Minority-party cohesiveness | 4.17 (4.13) |
| Distance between the parties | 4.17* (1.13) |
| Constant | –8.50* (1.95) |

Logit estimates; standard error in parentheses; $N$ = 828; pseudo $R^2$ = .044; log likelihood = –542.4;
$*p < .05$.
Dependent variable: adopted/failed (other petitions excluded). Independent variables: reform (pre-/post-1975 reform); majority party size (number of senators in majority); majority/minority party cohesiveness (standard deviation, first dimension DW-NOMINATE); distance between the parties (difference in means, first dimension DW-NOMINATE).

## DOES THE FILIBUSTER KILL LEGISLATION?

With the many filibuster episodes described in previous chapters and the measurable effects of the threshold on cloture outcomes that we just observed, it may not appear necessary to ask whether the filibuster forces majorities to modify or drop legislation. Yet, over the history of the Senate, defenders of Senate tradition have argued for decades that the filibuster does little harm (Binder and Smith 1997, 127–29). In recent decades, Senator Robert Byrd articulated this point of view the most frequently. In 1995, Byrd observed:

> The filibuster will not eternally kill something, kill legislation that the American people really want. It may slow it down for a while. It may stop it for a while. But in the process of education

> of the American people through unlimited debate, the American people often become more aware of what they are being asked to buy. . . . I have maintained that if the American people really understand a question, if they really understand it and they really want it, they will get it regardless of the filibuster. (*Congressional Record,* January 13, 1995, S933)

Given how frequently this "little harm" argument is made, we must take it seriously. We will start by making some observations about the nature of the argument. First, in 1995 there was no guarantee of unlimited debate. A three-fifths majority could limit debate. If the argument applied to a three-fifths threshold, it should apply to any threshold. It is hard to believe that Byrd, of all senators, really believed that the threshold did not matter.

Second, neither Byrd nor others have an explanation for the real change in cloture outcomes that is associated with the 1975 change in Rule XXII. I guess Byrd might make an argument that proponents of legislation have become more persuasive since 1975. That is not likely.

Third, timing matters in policy and politics, and delay is not without potentially serious consequences. Byrd seems to heavily discount the effects of delay (one decade to the next, one president to the next, one Congress to the next, and so on) in public policy on American society, on political developments, and even on the nature of the legislation enacted. The effects of delay on time-sensitive matters, like appropriations or debt limit measures, are worthy of special attention, but they hardly exhaust the important effects of delay. Byrd might argue that there are real benefits to delay, such as improving the public acceptance of the eventual policy, as was argued during the mid-twentieth century for civil rights legislation, but his arguments would largely ignore the importance of timing.

Fourth, the focus on killing legislation obscures the many ways that legislation is modified, sometimes substantially, in order to acquire the votes necessary for cloture. A case can be made, as defenders of Senate tradition often argue, that writing legislation or nominating candidates for office that acquire supermajority support is good for the American polity. But that argument cannot be made while arguing that the cloture rule makes little difference in the long run.

The empirical accuracy of the Byrd thesis bears careful consideration. The public's threshold for "really" understanding and wanting legislation is not clear, of course, and its ambiguity has given Byrd and others a great deal of rhetorical wiggle room. To give the thesis a serious test, we would have to clearly define the threshold and operationalize public "understanding" with measures of public knowledge and attitudes. A high level of public understanding is particularly difficult to define and test but, however operationalized, surely would be difficult to meet and thus would allow defenders of Senate practice to excuse Senate inaction for most policy questions. I will focus on "really wanting legislation."

We might translate the "really want" part of the thesis into this proposition: a large, intense, and lasting majority of Americans will eventually get Senate action on legislation when initially blocked by a large Senate minority. Some combination of size, commitment, and longevity of a supporting policy coalition in the general public produces a smaller obstructionist minority in the Senate. This seems to be a reasonable hypothesis and may be supported by the facts. In this translation, a large, intense, and lasting majority is a *sufficient* condition for Senate approval of legislation. The thesis does not imply that such a majority is a *necessary* condition—the Senate acts on many measures that attract little public attention. The proviso "when initially blocked by a large Senate minority" is added to narrow the population of relevant cases to which the filibuster applies.

The translated Byrd thesis is not easy to test. Indeed, no one has tested it with systematic evidence. We can imagine collecting data over a long period of time on public attitudes toward a wide range of measures, initially blocked by Senate minorities, and determining whether large, intense, and lasting majorities produce Senate action. Such data do not exist. Moreover, we would have difficulty identifying legislation successfully blocked by a minority. When a threatened filibuster leads the majority to make no formal attempt to gain Senate consideration of a measure, we cannot observe the effect of the obstructionism and would be unable to count the case as involving initial minority obstruction.

When a large majority of Americans supports a measure, it is likely that a large majority of senators will initially support the measure and no minority obstruction will occur. This makes it important to limit the test of the little-harm thesis to measures that were initially blocked by a minority. As a general rule, this proviso is ignored in studies that show that important new policies often attract the support of large congressional majorities (Mayhew 2005), and in studies that focus on the margin at final passage of all or important legislation (Wawro and Schickler 2006). These studies give us little relevant evidence on the impact of Senate rules and party governance.

A list of cases in which minority obstruction killed or delayed legislation is easy to construct. Binder and Smith (1997, 135) created a list of measures killed by filibuster for the period through 1994—twenty-four in the last thirty-four years of the period. Some issues on the Binder-Smith list, including several civil rights measures, were associated with legislation that was passed in a later Congress. But it would be easy to multiply the number of measures by a factor of two or three in the period since 1994. I have not done so.

It is useful to review some evidence compiled by political scientist Barbara Sinclair, mentioned in previous chapters (Sinclair 2012, 153, 262, 265). Limiting her focus to "major" legislation (primarily legislation subject to what Congressional Quarterly classified as "key" votes), Sinclair counted the number of measures subject to some form of floor obstruction. In the 1960s, less than 10 percent of major measures faced such a problem, a figure that rose to 27 percent in the 1970s and 1980s, to 51 percent in the 1990s through 2006, and to over 70 percent for the 2007–2010 period. During that period, 88 percent of major measures were adopted by the House within a Congress, but only 72 percent passed the Senate. Thus, for a class of measures most likely to matter to the public, at least the short-term effect of the Senate rule is to significantly, although not radically, reduce the probability of enactment.

Sinclair's evidence, of course, does not address what happened over the long term of legislation that was initially obstructed by a minority or the nature of public attitudes that might have changed as an issue lingered in the Senate, so her study cannot be taken as direct disconfirming evidence for Byrd's little-harm thesis. It is, however, reasonably persuasive circumstantial evidence. The data show a persistent and growing incidence of minority obstruction in the Senate, consistent with what is reported in previous chapters and with what is widely recognized by senators and close observers. The pervasiveness of minority obstruction in recent Congresses surely casts more serious doubt on the thesis than Binder and Smith did in the mid-1990s.

## ARE REPUBLICANS TO BLAME?

I do not like how the question is formulated in popular discourse as a matter of blame. Much of what senators and their party leaders do is not readily attributed to a grand scheme or malicious intent. The polarization of the parties is real, not contrived, and largely a product of the policy preferences that elected senators bring with them to Capitol Hill. Elected leaders have little influence over which candidates win primary elections and represent the party in general elections. Senators' legislative strategies, including their use of parliamentary procedure, follow from their policy objectives, the expectations of opinion leaders and voters in their electoral coalitions, and the parliamentary rules they inherit. In the larger picture, circumstances and rules, more than personal or political character, are driving the process.

Still, it is reasonable to ask, which party has contributed most to the emergence of the Senate syndrome? Answer: Republicans more than the Democrats. There are at least three distinguishable issues in attributing responsibility to the two Senate parties for the emergence of the Senate syndrome.

1. The first is the relative contributions of the two parties to the polarization that plays a major role in today's Senate. There is a considerable body of evidence, worth reviewing here, that Republicans have moved right more than the Democrats have moved left in recent decades.
2. The second issue is the question of innovation: Republicans have initiated new minority obstructionist tactics and new majority countermoves more frequently than Democrats have. The evidence, summarized here, comes from the accumulation of accounts in previous chapters.
3. The third issue is the all-out parliamentary warfare of recent Congresses: a fair reading of recent Congresses must conclude that minority Republicans have taken obstruction to a new level by trying to redefine the Senate's "regular order" as including a 60-vote requirement for action on most important measures.

These three features have propelled Republicans into new strategies for a Senate minority party, some of which the Democrats mimicked when they were in the minority and many of which they have sought to counter when in the majority.

## THE PARTIES AND POLARIZATION

I start with the partisan polarization of senators' policy positions. Figure 8.1 shows the mean liberal-conservative scores for the two parties and for the Senate as a whole.[1] On average, both parties have become less moderate since the early 1960s. The reference lines at the party averages for the period add some substantive interpretation. Senator Richard Lugar (R-IN), who lost his seat in a primary in 2012, had a common space score at almost precisely the mean for Senate Republicans during this era. In the 1980s, Lugar was more conservative than the average Republican, but he was more moderate than average in the 1990s and into the twenty-first century. On the Democratic side, Kent Conrad (D-ND), who retired at the end of 2012, was at his party's long-term mean for the period and in recent Congresses found his party becoming more liberal than he was.

Figure 8.1 also demonstrates that Republicans moved farther to the right (moving up in the figure) than Democrats moved to the left. The Republican shift appears to have occurred in two steps. The 1980 elections, in which Ronald Reagan won the presidency and the Republicans took a Senate majority for the first time since 1954, brought four southern Republicans and other conservatives into the Senate. Then, in the 1990s, a significant number of conservative House Republicans moved to the Senate. Many of them were "Gingrich senators," the label used by political scientists Sean Theriault and David Rohde to describe Republicans who served with former Speaker Newt Gingrich in the 1980s and moved to the Senate in the 1990s. Theriault and Rohde calculated a "polarization score"—the absolute value of a senator's DW-NOMINATE score (distance from a score of zero)—and found that the Gingrich senators accounted for three-fourths of the overall polarization of the 1990s (Theriault and Rohde 2011).[2]

## THE PARTIES AND PARLIAMENTARY TACTICS

Both parties, and both as minorities and majorities, have been responsible for innovations and expanded use of old techniques. In the 1970s, conservative Democrats, often joined by Republicans, expanded the use of the filibuster, and both conservative and liberal Democrats conducted the long post-cloture filibusters in that decade. It was Democratic majority leader Robert Byrd who used parliamentary rulings to limit obstructionist tactics on several occasions in the 1970s. And both Democrats and Republicans have exploited holds throughout the period since the 1970s.

Nevertheless, something changed in the 1990s. A common and accurate observation is that former House Republicans brought Gingrich-style political tactics with them to the Senate (Evans and Oleszek 2001; Lee 2009; Rae and Campbell 1999; Roberts and Smith 2003; Sinclair 2006). The key elements of the Gingrich strategy were adherence to strong conservative policy positions, party discipline, and procedural warfare. When House Republicans were in the minority, Gingrich advised them to sharpen their differences with Democrats, oppose Democratic legislation, exploit the rules to throw obstacles in the way of the Democratic majority, force Democrats from conservative districts to vote with their party in a liberal direction, and focus on winning elections and majority control of the House. Gingrich was given much credit for the 1994 House election outcomes, which produced the first Republican majority since 1954 and led to his election as speaker of the House.

The minority Republicans of the early 1990s proved more aggressive and obstructionist than previous minority parties. The early 1990s witnessed expanded use of the filibuster on the motion to proceed, a record number of filibusters on nominations, a surge in the number of holds, and the first instance of a successful effort to block votes on the motions to go to conference. Rank-and-file Republicans, such as Trent Lott, who had been elected to the Senate from Mississippi in 1988, initiated much of this obstruction.

Notably, Lott was elected Senate majority whip under Bob Dole, the Republican leader, when the Republicans gained majority control of the Senate after the 1994 elections. Before his election to the Senate, Lott served as the House Republican whip and associated himself with Gingrich strategies. In running for the Senate whip post against Alan Simpson (R-WY) after the 1994 elections, Lott found his relationship with the new speaker and his own combative style being frequently mentioned by journalistic observers and his support coming heavily from junior Republicans, many of whom came to the Senate from the House (Langdon 1994; Koszczukand 1994; Koszczuk 1996).

Nevertheless, at least at the start, the relationship between Lott and the new Democratic leader, Tom Daschle (D-SD), was usually civil, reflecting the even-tempered personalities of the two leaders and their long legislative careers. Lott, in practice, proved to be a good managerial technician and kept a low profile in the media. His reputation even benefited from the contrast with the leadership style of Speaker Gingrich. The public impression of the Senate of the late 1990s was that it was less partisan and more civil than the House.

In practice, the new Republican majority, now measurably more conservative than it had been a decade before, faced problems in overcoming Democratic obstructionism. Daschle and the minority Democrats were about as frequently obstructionist as the Republicans had become in the early 1990s. Daschle, in fact, coordinated a strategy to block action on Contract with America legislation, preventing Republicans from setting the agenda in coordination with the Dole presidential campaign. In some cases, Democrats used their ability to block legislation as a source of leverage to gain action on Clinton administration legislation. This represented a longer, more concerted effort by a minority leader to lead obstructionist efforts than ever before.

Lott responded in new ways. He more frequently filled the amendment tree, resorted to omnibus measures, and tucked more legislation into unamendable conference reports (see chapter 5). He coordinated conference negotiations that excluded minority-party Democrats, which was followed by Democratic obstruction on conference motions. And, to deal with certain Democratic filibusters on Bush administration tax cut bills, Republicans under Lott and Bill Frist (R-TN), who became leader in 2003, pressed forward by successfully using reconciliation to get the measures considered under debate limits.

An important turning point appears to have occurred under Frist during the 2003–2005 struggle over judicial nominations. Frist responded to Democratic obstruction with a threat to impose a new interpretation of Rule XXII by a ruling of the chair, and once the crisis passed in May 2005, he returned to filling the amendment tree. And he more frequently employed 60-vote thresholds in time agreements to speed action on a variety of measures. By the time he left office at the end of 2006, the Senate had become a different place.

## ALL-OUT PARLIAMENTARY WARFARE

A fair assessment is that both parties were responsible for the high frequency of obstructionism between the late 1980s and the first few years of the new century. Republicans showed the way in the early 1990s, but Democrats were their equal for the next decade. As is detailed in chapter 6, the last few Congresses have witnessed even more obstructionism, this time primarily by minority Republicans. The Republicans have made obstruction the norm and have begun to articulate the thesis that a supermajority is the proper threshold for passing legislation of even modest importance in the Senate.

Republicans have been explicit about making the 60-vote threshold the standard for the Senate. In early 2007, soon after becoming his party's floor leader, Minority Leader Mitch McConnell told CNN's Wolf Blitzer, "You know that every measure, virtually every measure with any degree of controversy about it in the United States Senate requires 60 votes. That's the ordinary procedure, not the unusual" ("CNN Late Edition" 2007; "The Hillbilly Watches" 2007). We can discount any one extemporaneous comment, but McConnell and other Republicans have repeated that theme many times in recent years (see chapter 6).[3] As a matter of historical accuracy, McConnell was wrong.

McConnell's comments presaged Republican behavior over the next few years. Since the 2006 elections, when Republicans fell back into minority status, minority obstruction has reached all-time highs. As we have seen, cloture efforts reached record heights. To be sure, cloture petitions are filed for a variety of reasons, but a large majority of the petitions are a response to actual or, most commonly, to threatened obstruction, as when objections to taking up bills or time agreements are signaled by the minority. The record level of obstruction is real.

Through this experience, Democrats have come to assume that a significant bill will be obstructed. Their response to heavy doses of minority obstruction has been heavy use of cloture and the amendment tree, circumvention of filibuster opportunities whenever possible, and the invention of techniques, such as 60-vote thresholds in unanimous consent agreements, to manage legislation on the floor (see chapter 6). If the 60-vote threshold is regular order, as McConnell claims, then the majority party response has become regular order, too.

## CONCLUSION

Most senators, it seems safe to say, do not see the combination of minority-spurred obstruction and majority-imposed restrictions as the Senate's regular order. In a long-term perspective, the behavior we have witnessed in recent Congresses is not the common pattern, even for controversial legislation. In fact, in recent Congresses, minority and majority tactics seem to have fed on each other as grievances have accumulated between the parties, and in recent Congresses they have created nearly standard strategies that I have called the Senate syndrome.

As a general rule, leading Republicans have taken the view that the long-term interest of conservatives is to retain supermajority cloture in the Senate. As Republicans have become more conservative over recent decades, this theme seems to have resonated more widely within the party. To be sure, *majority party* Republicans have exploited procedural devices to tame Democratic obstruction, and Bill Frist championed the "constitutional option" for judicial nominations. It is important to observe that Frist awkwardly limited his proposal to judicial nominations, and otherwise the Republican majorities of the 1995–2006 period did not entertain serious filibuster reform as the Democrats have done at other times.

The evidence in this chapter reinforces the theme of partisan differences. Republicans have moved farther right than Democrats have moved left in the last two decades. Moreover, on balance, Republicans in recent Congresses have practiced a more aggressive form of obstructionism than the Democrats did when they were in the minority. Democrats have been more selective in their obstructionism and have shown far greater support for filibuster reform.

Although defenders of Senate tradition often endorse the little-harm thesis, senators of both parties express the belief that Rule XXII matters. Indeed, the vehemence with which they have made their arguments indicates how important Rule XXII is to them as individual senators and partisans. They realize that stakes are high today, as they have proven to be in the past.

CHAPTER 9

# THE MEDIA, THE PUBLIC, AND ACCOUNTABILITY

ON MARCH 29, 2012, *The Hill,* one of a few high-quality publications that cover Capitol Hill, reported the outcome of Senate action on a controversial tax bill. The headline was "Senate defeats Democrats' measure to kill off 'Big Oil' tax breaks, 51–47." The story continued: "The Senate on Thursday thwarted Democratic plans to strip billions of dollars in tax breaks from the largest oil companies, just an hour or so after President Obama urged the chamber to kill off the deductions. Lawmakers voted 51–47 to move forward with Sen. Robert Menendez's (D-NJ) bill. Sixty votes were needed to advance the measure" (German and Ryan 2012).

The average reader might infer that there was a special 60-vote requirement for bills on tax breaks and the majority party Democrats failed to reach that threshold. A not-so-careful reader might even conclude that there were only 47 votes for the bill. Actually, 60 votes were required to invoke cloture, because Republicans refused to allow a vote or agree to a unanimous consent request to provide for a final vote on the bill. Fifty-one senators voted to invoke cloture, presumably because they favored the bill. Minority obstruction, not the regular procedure or the lack of a majority for the bill, killed the bill that day. Essential detail did not make it into the story.

If you were an average member of the general public, favored the bill, and sought to hold someone accountable on the basis of that story, you might conclude that the Democrats had failed you. The *Washington Post* did better with the headline "GOP blocks Obama's effort to end tax breaks for Big Oil," but not until the sixteenth paragraph did the *Post* report that "the measure ultimately failed—as expected—when 51 senators voted for cloture but 60 votes were needed to move to final passage." Even then, the *Post* did not state clearly why a cloture vote was required. Neither publication noted the partisan composition of the coalitions for and against the bill, and it was not a straight party-line vote.[1] This, we will see, is far too common.

As recent experience has shown, media reports on the Senate often lack the detail required to understand what transpired and which senators acted to support or oppose the legislation. Reporting on the "minutiae" of parliamentary procedure is not easy and may not appeal to the general news audience, but, as the piece in *The Hill* illustrates, reporting is often inadequate even for the most sophisticated publications and audiences. The public knows little about most of these parliamentary maneuvers and cannot possibly understand the "who did what" of Senate floor action.

The news media, general public, and interest groups are the subjects of this chapter. First, I examine the content of news coverage of the Senate and filibusters in sophisticated news outlets, both print and television. Second, I evaluate the public's attitudes toward the filibuster, majority rule, and minority rights in the Senate and consider the ways that partisan preferences and political knowledge structure those attitudes. Third, because interest groups work hard to hold senators accountable for their behavior, I examine the role of cloture votes in the voting ratings constructed by interest groups. I conclude with observations about the filibuster and Senate accountability.

## MEDIA COVERAGE

To avoid the potentially serious error of relying on a few stray cases to characterize media treatment of Senate procedural developments, I have examined the content of the coverage of all cloture votes during the 2009–2011 period in six prominent print publications that provide the most extensive coverage (*Boston Globe, New York Times, Washington Post, Roll Call,*

*The Hill,* and *Politico*). If conservative critics are to be believed, these news outlets have a liberal bias. In the period examined, this means that the media bias, if any, should favor the majority party Democrats' view of Senate developments. Even these news outlets are replete with softened language about minority party tactics.

The most obvious limitation of media coverage is that the cloture "hurdle" is not explained as a product of minority obstruction. Cloture itself may or may not be mentioned, but the critical feature is that the invocation of a 60-vote threshold is treated as if it is a standard element of Senate procedure with no need for further explanation. Indeed, the most common treatment of filibusters, obstruction, and cloture does not mention filibusters, obstruction, or cloture. Instead, journalistic accounts frequently use euphemisms—"procedural hurdle," "preliminary vote," "procedural vote," and so on. Mentions of a minority of senators that block, delay, or filibuster represent a minority of stories.

Even C-SPAN often sanitizes its on-screen description of cloture votes. In recent years, the cable network has placed this sentence at the bottom of the screen while a cloture vote on a motion to proceed is occurring: "This is a procedural vote to move forward with the [name] bill." The statement, of course, does not allow the viewer to distinguish between a cloture vote, usually required by the minority, and the motion to proceed, usually offered by the majority leader. Both are "procedural" motions, but knowing who is responsible for the motion and what the effects are of defeating the motion are essential to understanding what is transpiring.

Some coverage treats minority obstruction to Senate action on legislation as equivalent to a mere logjam or stalemate associated with a partisan divide on issues. The outcome is more than a natural consequence of polarized parties. It is the result of deliberate (and frequent) blocking actions taken by one side. It represents a false neutralism about the political actions taken and fails to report in sufficient detail the behavior of senators and their leaders.

This "false equivalence," journalist James Fallows emphasizes, places the media in a position of offering rhetorical camouflage for the Senate minority.[2] This kind of reporting, Fallows argues, reduces the public relations costs that obstructionists pay and may actually shift the costs to the majority. He points out that one filibuster in October 2011 led the *Washington Post* to publish a story with the "even-handed" headline, "Senate has become a chamber of failure." While the minority Republicans surely were responsible for obstruction, the Democrats were drawn into a discussion of polarized parties and dysfunction as if the two parties were playing equivalent roles at the time.

This is not the place to explain media behavior, but I can make a few purely speculative observations. Plainly, the media value brevity, avoid repetition, and believe that the audience has little interest in procedural details. "Cloture" and "filibuster" surely are terms that may need explanation for many readers. The sheer frequency with which the Senate gets tied up in procedural knots, with each side blaming the other for abusing parliamentary rights and for excessive partisanship, must leave reporters and editors tortured, too, eager to brush over procedural details and focus on outcomes.

Moreover, journalists and editors certainly try to avoid the appearance of bias. Using the terms "cloture," "block a vote," or "filibuster," even when they are technically correct, may appear to represent an anti-minority bias. There is less risk of being charged with bias in mentioning a mere "procedural vote" on which the parties take opposite sides. Unfortunately, this practice of studied neutrality yields a less informative description and often plays into the hands of the minority.

For the most part, news organizations, even the best ones, are populated with reporters and editorial staff with little congressional experience. My own experience is that, with a few important exceptions, reporters know little more than rudimentary Senate history, and few have taken as much as an undergraduate course on congressional politics. They often pick up a little history from congressional sources, many of whom have their own interests and little background themselves. Of course, there is a substantial body of political science literature on aspects of developments in the Senate. But for reporters, most of whom have arrived in Washington over the past two decades, filibusters, long delays, and the 60-vote threshold must appear normal and hardly newsworthy.

There are exceptions to the general pattern. The *Boston Globe,* for example, stands out for exceptional clarity in its headlines and leads about Senate cloture votes. Typically, this clarity requires the addition of a sentence that explains that the vote involved a motion to overcome a minority objection to considering a motion or bill.

Whatever the cause, a narrow conception of "balanced" reporting appears to have produced little coverage of the emergence of the Senate syndrome. To be sure, it has been a creeping phenomenon over the last two decades that few reporters are likely to have digested. In the media, at least, the state of the Senate has been left to online bloggers and commentators to discuss for very small audiences.

## PUBLIC ATTITUDES

What does the public think of the Senate's procedure? Pollsters and scholarly researchers seldom ask the question. It is certainly reasonable to hypothesize that the public is not likely to have meaningful attitudes about the subject, and when it does, Senate procedure is likely to be poorly understood. As we have seen, the media contribute less to public understanding of the Senate than it might. Moreover, much of the information distributed about the Senate comes from partisans who have their own interpretations and often target narrow audiences.

### *Knowledge*

Two national surveys that I have conducted with collaborators have asked questions to gauge public familiarity with the Senate filibuster. In one survey, conducted in July 2009, the respondents were given multiple responses to the question, "In

**Table 9.1.** Public Knowledge of Senate Procedure, 2009 (percentages)

| In your opinion, can you say which of the following is the best definition of the term "filibuster"? | |
|---|---|
| Extended debate intended to prevent a vote on an issue in the Senate | 63.8 |
| A presidential veto of legislation passed by the Senate | 10.2 |
| Banning all amendments during the consideration of a bill in the Senate | 10.2 |
| Don't know | 15.4 |
| Refused to answer | 0.2 |
| Total | 100.0 |
| (*N*) | (3000) |
| **There are procedures by which a filibuster in the Senate can be stopped. Which of the following statements best describes how a filibuster in the Senate can be stopped?** | |
| By a simple majority—51 senators if all 100 are voting | 23.7 |
| By a 3/5 majority—60 or more senators | 47.9 |
| All senators must agree to stop the filibuster | 14.5 |
| Don't know | 13.8 |
| Refused to answer | 0.2 |
| Total | 100.0 |
| (*N*) | (3000) |

*Source:* July 2009 national telephone survey.
*Note:* Response sets were randomly ordered. Weighted by Current Population Survey.

your opinion, can you say which of the following is the best definition of the term 'filibuster'?" A second question asked, "There are procedures by which a filibuster in the Senate can be stopped. Which of the following statements best describes how a filibuster in the Senate can be stopped?" The findings are reported in table 9.1.

At the time of the 2009 survey, the Democratic majority of the Senate was still working on a draft of health care reform, but floor action on the measure was months away. The filibuster was receiving some, but relatively little, attention in the media at the time. The findings: 63.8 percent of respondents could identify the correct definition of a filibuster among three alternatives, and 47.9 percent could correctly identify how many votes are required to "stop" a filibuster. Only 36.5 percent could choose the correct answer to both questions. Because we would expect one-third of the answers to be correct if respondents were guessing, and we know that multiple-choice questions like these give respondents a chance to guess or figure out the correct response, the level of public knowledge appears to be quite modest.

The other survey, conducted in January 2012, occurred after the Senate syndrome had a firmer grip on the Senate. The sample was asked to choose a response to this incomplete sentence: "The ability of a minority of senators to prevent a vote on a bill is known as . . . " Thus, in the 2009 version, the term "filibuster" is mentioned and a definition is selected; in the 2012 version, the definition is given and a term is selected. The 2012 results (table 9.2) are quite similar to the 2009 findings. Nearly 56 percent of respondents chose the correct response out of a lineup of four choices. It is reasonable to surmise that over half of Americans connect the filibuster to the correct definition in a multiple-choice test, but fewer are familiar with the procedural details.

In 2012, no question about the number of votes required to invoke cloture was asked, but respondents were asked to identify the length of a senator's term of office. Only 41 percent could correctly identify six years as the correct answer out of a set of four alternatives (two, four, six, and eight years). Only 32 percent of respondents could answer both questions about the Senate correctly.

It appears that accurate basic knowledge of the Senate is held by about one-third of the public. This puts knowledge of the Senate at a level substantially below knowledge of the basic general structure of American politics. In the 2012 survey, 89 percent correctly identified the maximum number of terms a president may serve, 70 percent correctly identified the term of

**Table 9.2.** Public Knowledge of Senate Procedure, 2012 (percentages)

| The ability of a minority of senators to prevent a vote on a bill is known as . . . | |
|---|---|
| a filibuster | 55.7 |
| a veto | 12.7 |
| enrollment | 0.8 |
| suspension of the rules | 0.9 |
| Don't know | 27.7 |
| Total | 100.0 |
| (N) | (1,609) |

*Source:* January 2012 online survey: The American Panel Survey (taps.wustl.edu).
*Note:* Response sets were randomly ordered. Weighted by Current Population Survey.

office for members of the Supreme Court, and 89 percent could identify the name of the vice president, all with a set of four possible answers plus "don't know."

### *Attitudes about the Filibuster*

The surveys also measured attitudes about the filibuster. Any inferences about filibuster attitudes must be qualified by the observation that most attitudes are not backed by substantial knowledge of Senate procedure. Nevertheless, senators put considerable effort into persuading the public of the procedural abuses perpetrated by the other side. We can ask whether these efforts make any difference.

*Panel Study.* The July 2009 survey was followed by the Senate debate on health care reform. During the fall of that year, the Senate considered and finally passed the health care reform bill on Christmas Eve. The minority Republicans required the majority Democrats to muster 60 votes for cloture on several motions. Compromises arranged by Majority Leader Harry Reid with a few senators whose votes were required to get to 60 were widely covered in the media. Both sides engaged in considerable discussion of the fairness of Senate rules during the process. The minority Republicans complained that the public interest was not served by Democrats; Democrats complained that the minority was obstructionist and forced the creation of a supermajority to pass the bill.

The July 2009 survey asked, "In general, what's your opinion of allowing the minority to block a vote on a piece of legislation?" and offered a four-point scale ("strongly approve," "approve," "disapprove," "strongly disapprove").[3] The question was asked again in January 2010, just weeks after the Senate initially passed the bill, of a random sample of the July 2009 respondents. This yielded a before-and-after look at public attitudes, with one of the most salient and partisan filibuster episodes occurring in the intervening months.

At the start of the 2009 episode, 50 percent of respondents approved of the filibuster, but there were significant partisan differences: 44 percent of self-identified Democrats approved or strongly approved of the filibuster practice, and 58 percent of Republicans did so. This balance may have reflected the majority- and minority-party status of the parties in that period (Democrats had been in the majority since 2007). Unfortunately, we have no comparable data on public attitudes about the filibuster for the previous period with Republican majorities.

By the following January, 60 percent of respondents approved of the filibuster—46 percent for Democrats and 76 percent for Republicans. Democratic views did not change much in the aggregate, but Republicans became substantially more supportive of the proposition that a minority of senators should be able to block a vote. In January, 44 percent of health care bill supporters approved of the filibuster, while 75 percent of respondents who opposed the bill because it went too far did so. Remarkably, a majority of the 13 percent of respondents who opposed the bill because it was not sufficiently liberal (mostly Democrats) approved of the filibuster.[4]

Another way to view these data is to compare respondents' "approval rating" in July with their rating in the following January. For Democrats, 61 percent reduced their support for the filibuster to some degree (many from "disapprove" to "strongly disapprove"), while only 29 percent of Republicans did so. For Democrats, 36 percent raised their rating, but 50 percent of Republicans did so. Parallel patterns occurred for bill supporters and opponents. Overall, 40 percent of respondents (about the same for both parties) chose the same rating on the four-point scale in both surveys. Attitudes are not very stable, but the partisan influence is obvious.

Public attitudes appear to be weak and pliable. During the 2009 health care episode, a small majority of Americans expressed approval of the filibuster. During the course of the episode, short-term forces—the way in which the filibuster benefits the contending forces in a prominent legislative battle—appear to have had a substantial influence on those attitudes.

Senators may recognize that the balance of attitudes, particularly within partisan electorates, is not fixed, and, for at least a majority, filibuster attitudes are not strongly held. One implication of this political reality is that senators need not feel constrained by the public's procedural attitudes and can reshape the balance of opinion, particularly within their own constituency groups. Going to battle for the right policy cause, more than carefully observing regular order in the Senate, is the more effective strategy for winning and maintaining public support.

*A Survey Experiment.* We also want to know what the public thinks about majority rule and minority rights in legislative bodies, whether the distinction between the U.S. House of Representatives and Senate matters, and whether partisan preferences color these attitudes. To explore this, I conducted a survey experiment in May 2012, well into the period of the Senate syndrome, to see if mentioning the party in the majority and minority influenced attitudes about the procedural principles involving majority rule and minority rights.

A national sample of Americans was asked whether they agreed or disagreed with each of these statements about majority rule and minority rights in a legislature:

- The majority party should be able to pass legislation that is supported by a majority of legislators.
- The majority party should be able to limit or prohibit amendments to its legislation.
- The minority party should be able to delay or block action on legislation supported by the majority party.
- The minority party should be able to get a vote on its amendments to legislation.

Thus, two questions address getting a vote on legislation and two questions address the right to offer amendments, with one question in each set emphasizing the majority party and one question emphasizing the minority party. In the survey, the minority party variations were asked about ten minutes after the majority party variations. The respondents were given a five-point scale on which to locate their views ("strongly agree," "agree," "neither agree nor disagree," "disagree," "strongly disagree").

The respondents were randomly assigned to three groups. Each group received a different treatment in the form of a preface to the questions, as outlined in table 9.3. For Group 1, a single set of questions about legislatures in general was asked. For Groups 2 and 3, in which the House and Senate were mentioned, the four questions were asked for each house. Groups 2 and 3 differed: in Group 3, but not in Group 2, the identity of the majority and minorities parties was included.

*Majority Rule and Minority Rights.* The public clearly favors both (a) the right of the majority to gain a vote on its legislation and (b) the right of the minority to have its amendments considered. This is plain in table 9.4, in which the mean response for the three groups is provided on a five-point scale (1 is "strongly agree," 5 is "strongly disagree"). In each case, there is a statistically significant difference in mean responses for the majority right to pass over the minority right to block and for the minority right to offer amendments over the majority right to limit amendments.

**Table 9.3.** Group Treatments in Survey Experiment, 2012

| | | |
|---|---|---|
| Group 1 | Generic legislature | We would like to know your views on how a legislature, such as a city council, state legislature, or Congress, should operate when it is making law. We are not interested in how legislatures actually operate; rather, we want your views about how they *should* operate. |
| Group 2 | Congress, House and Senate mentioned | We would like to know your views on how the U.S. Congress in Washington, D.C., should operate when it is making law. We are not interested in how Congress actually operates; rather, we want your views about how Congress *should* operate.<br><br>We will ask you first about the U.S. House of Representatives, and then about the U.S. Senate. |
| Group 3 | Congress, House and Senate, and majority/minority parties mentioned | We would like to know your views on how the U.S. Congress in Washington, D.C., should operate when it is making law. We are not interested in how Congress actually operates; rather, we want your views about how Congress *should* operate.<br><br>We will ask you first about the U.S. House of Representatives, and then about the U.S. Senate.<br><br>[For House:] As you probably know, in today's House of Representatives, the Republicans are the majority party and the Democrats are the minority party.<br>[For Senate:] As you probably know, in today's Senate, the Democrats are the majority party and the Republicans are the minority party. |

**Table 9.4.** Mean Responses to Majority Rule and Minority Rights Questions, by Treatment Group (5-point scale)

| | Majority emphasis (first question) | Minority emphasis (second question) | *t*-value | *n* |
|---|---|---|---|---|
| Group 1. Generic institution (no chamber, no party mentioned) | | | | |
| (1) majority right to pass *vs.* (2) minority right to block | 2.49 | 3.18 | −10.170 | 451 |
| (1) majority right to limit amendments *vs.* (2) minority right to offer amendments | 3.08 | 2.40 | 10.218 | 442 |
| Group 2. Chamber mentioned (party *not* mentioned): House | | | | |
| (1) majority right to pass *vs.* (2) minority right to block | 2.23 | 3.18 | −13.635* | 383 |
| (1) majority right to limit amendments *vs.* (2) minority right to offer amendments | 2.72 | 2.37 | 5.344* | 372 |
| Group 2. Chamber mentioned (party *not* mentioned): Senate | | | | |
| (1) majority right to pass *vs.* (2) minority right to block | 2.23 | 3.14 | −13.432* | 389 |
| (1) majority right to limit amendments *vs.* (2) minority right to offer amendments | 2.71 | 2.41 | 4.425* | 379 |
| Group 3. Chamber and party mentioned: House | | | | |
| (1) majority right to pass *vs.* (2) minority right to block | 2.57 | 3.06 | −6.132* | 410 |
| (1) majority right to limit amendments *vs.* (2) minority right to offer amendments | 2.87 | 2.47 | 5.646* | 404 |
| Group 3. Chamber and party mentioned: Senate | | | | |
| (1) majority right to pass *vs.* (2) minority right to block | 2.50 | 3.09 | −8.904* | 429 |
| (1) majority right to limit amendments *vs.* (2) minority right to offer amendments | 2.83 | 2.57 | 4.128* | 426 |

*$p < 0.05$ for paired samples *t*-test. Weighted by Current Population Survey. Scale: 1 (strongly agree) to 5 (strongly disagree).

The pattern is clearest in the distinction between allowing the majority to get a vote on its legislation and allowing the minority to delay or block legislation. Whatever the treatment, whether the chambers are mentioned and whether or not parties are mentioned, the mean response leans in the direction of favoring a majority party right to pass legislation favored by a majority of legislators. Moreover, the mean response is opposed to allowing the minority to delay or block a vote on legislation.

On the rights to limit or offer amendments, the differences always favor the minority right to offer amendments over the majority right to limit or prohibit amendments. The differences are not as large as they are for passing or blocking legislation, but the differences consistently favor the minority's right to offer amendments, whatever the treatment. However, when primed to associate the questions with the House and Senate, respondents indicate mean support (a mean less than 3.0) slightly in favor of the majority's right to limit or prohibit amendments as well as the minority's right to offer amendments.

Of the four propositions, the proposition that a minority can delay or block action on legislation supported by a majority party is the least popular. Whatever the treatment, the mean response leans to the "disagree" side of the five-point scale. Moreover, the proposition that a majority should get a vote produces responses concentrated on "agree," while the proposition that a minority should be able to delay or block produces a rather even distribution over the "agree" to "disagree" range of the scale (figure 9.1).[5] Perhaps reflecting greater ambivalence about minority rights, the percentage responding "neither agree nor disagree" for minority blocking is nearly twice the percentage responding "neither agree nor disagree" for the majority's right to pass. The consensus in favor of the majority's right to vote is far stronger than the opposition to the minority's right to block.

*House versus Senate.* We must conclude that the public, on balance, favors two general principles—the right of the majority to get a vote on its legislation and the right of the minority to

**Figure 9.1.** Responses to Majority Pass and Minority Block Questions (Group 1), in Percentages

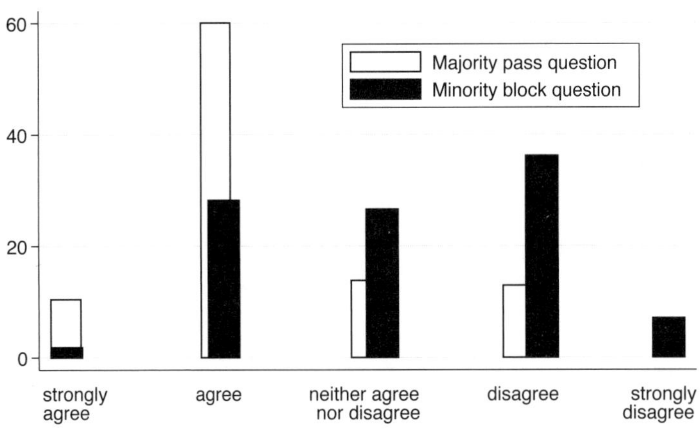


*Source:* The American Panel Survey, May 2012.

offer amendments. The public adheres to these principles even when prompted to think about the House and Senate and the current majority and minority parties in those chambers. In practice, of course, the Senate fails the first test and the House fails the second test. Does the American public recognize a normative distinction between the two houses of Congress?

The responses of Groups 2 and 3 (table 9.5), for whom the treatment mentioned the two houses of Congress, allow us to infer that the public makes little distinction between the House and Senate when expressing a view about majority rule and minority rights. With no mention of the identity of the majority and minority parties, there is no statistically significant difference in the mean response for any of the four propositions. Only when the identity of the majority and minority parties is incorporated is there a statistically significant difference for two propositions. For the majority right to get a vote, there is actually more agreement for the Senate than for the House, the opposite of expectation. For the minority right to offer amendments, there is more agreement for the House than for

**Table 9.5.** Mean Responses to Majority Rule and Minority Rights Questions, by House-Senate Treatment Groups (5-point scale)

| | House version mean | Senate version mean | *t*-value | *n* |
|---|---|---|---|---|
| Group 2. Chamber mentioned | | | | |
| majority right to pass | 2.25 | 2.28 | –0.937 | 423 |
| majority right to limit amendments | 2.72 | 2.73 | –0.204 | 403 |
| minority right to block | 3.18 | 3.13 | 1.632 | 387 |
| minority right to offer amendments | 2.37 | 2.40 | –1.116 | 387 |
| Group 3. Chamber and party mentioned | | | | |
| majority right to pass | 2.58 | 2.50 | 2.067* | 445 |
| majority right to limit amendments | 2.86 | 2.82 | 1.084 | 436 |
| minority right to block | 3.03 | 3.09 | –1.332 | 430 |
| minority right to offer amendments | 2.49 | 2.58 | –2.517* | 432 |

*$p < 0.05$ for paired samples t-test. Weighted by Current Population Survey. Scale: 1 (strongly agree) to 5 (strongly disagree).

the Senate, as expected. In both cases, the balance of opinion is substantively similar—there is a small substantive difference on the same side of the scale.

These findings do not allow us to determine why the public does not distinguish between the two houses of Congress. Two possibilities come to mind. First, typical Americans may be insufficiently familiar with the procedures and "elite" normative arguments about the two houses to make normative distinctions themselves. Second, the procedural principles (the majority right to a vote, the minority right to amendments) may be sufficiently important that typical Americans believe that they should apply to both houses. In either case, it is obvious that members of Congress cannot reference public attitudes for defending the core procedural differences between the two houses.

*Partisanship and Other Factors Shaping Attitudes about Congressional Procedure.* The survey experiment conducted in May 2012 occurred more than five years after the Democrats assumed majority control of the Senate and more than a year into the Republicans' return as the House majority party. This context may have shaped Americans' attitudes about proper procedure for the House and Senate. In particular, the respondents' partisan preferences and knowledge of Congress may have conditioned and interacted with their attitudes about the exercise of majority and minority parliamentary rights. To test this, Park and Smith (2013) estimated multivariate equations that accounted for the treatment effect and the respondents' party identification, controlling for the political knowledge of the subject (based on a battery of knowledge questions). They found that party identification influences attitudes about the filibuster, majority rule, and minority rights, but it does so only for the more knowledgeable individuals.

## ACCOUNTABILITY

Senate procedure creates a special problem for holding senators and their parties accountable for Senate outcomes. A long-standing problem is how to hold senators and their parties accountable when a minority prevents a majority from acting. The Senate majority will blame an obstructionist minority, but the minority is sure to blame the majority for being unwilling to compromise enough to attract more votes. This problem has become more severe in the last two decades.

The Senate syndrome generates a more general problem. By preventing the majority party from proceeding to the consideration of many measures, at least in a reasonably timely way, the minority creates doubt about the competence of the majority party to govern. The majority party responds in a predictable way—saying that minority obstructionism has tied up the Senate—but the minority party surely scores political points by allowing the public to become frustrated with the lack of legislative progress that the Senate's majority party is able to demonstrate. A typical American, paying minimal attention to the inner workings of the Senate, must become terribly confused but may have only one viable option—to blame the majority party.

As we have seen, the media often fail to adequately clarify who is doing what in the Senate, and the public's views of the Senate's procedural workings are malleable. In this concluding section, I consider additional aspects of the accountability problems generated by the Senate's practices, starting with individual senators and moving to Senate parties.

### *Individual Senators*

Political science offers several persuasive perspectives on the accountability of members of Congress. Most voting and much of senators' other public behavior can be viewed as "position taking," creating a record of policy stances that influence voters' choices (Mayhew 1974). Senators seek to develop a record over the long series of issues and votes they confront that appeals to a majority of voters at home. Just which issues will prove important at election time is a little difficult to predict, but legislators try to do so by considering the organized groups that might raise certain issues and mobilize voters in the next campaign (Arnold 1992). In any case, legislators anticipate the need to explain their votes to both general and specialized constituencies and are always looking for ways to explain that they demonstrate fealty to, and certainly empathy with, the interests of important constituencies (Fenno 1978).

Legislators and political scientists have long observed that direct votes on bills and amendments create a somewhat different position-taking, record-building, and explanatory challenge than votes on procedural motions (Froman and Ripley 1965; Rohde 1991). In the House of Representatives, it is often observed, voting on special rules yields more perfect party-line voting than the bills for which the special rules enable floor consideration and facilitate passage (Sinclair 1994). There are two related reasons for the difference between procedural and substantive votes.

The first reason is that a procedural vote does not constitute direct endorsement or opposition to a substantive policy position for which legislators might be held accountable at home. A procedural motion may directly affect the fate of a legislative proposal, but legislators are given the opportunity to explain a procedural vote on some procedural grounds—they preferred to continue the debate, they wanted an opportunity to offer an amendment, the chamber needed to move to higher-priority matters, and so on. Legislators and other close observers testify to the importance of this distinction.

The second reason is that legislators view their parties as procedural cartels (Cox and McCubbins 2007). That is, members of each majority party conference often articulate the need for unity in procedural matters so that the party can effectively control the agenda—get votes on legislation it seeks to pass and block votes on legislation it wants to avoid. Consequently, expectations of loyal behavior from party members are particularly explicit for procedural votes.

The distinction between procedural and substantive votes is made for the Senate, too (Den Hartog and Monroe 2011; King, Orlando, and Rohde 2010; Lee 2009). The motion to table, for example, is cited for its frequency of use by the majority party to dispose of unfriendly amendments. By loosening senators' accountability by moving to table an amendment rather than having a direct vote on it, the majority leader may gain pivotal votes. Motions to table are used with great frequency.

Cloture motions, of course, are procedural motions that provide for a limitation on debate. They do not constitute a direct vote on the underlying bill, amendment, or nomination, although rejection of a cloture motion may kill the legislation. Senators often argue that a vote against cloture merely indicates an interest in having a full debate and time for consideration of numerous amendments and is not necessarily a vote against the substance of the bill at issue.

It is notable that political scientists who make a case for a majority party advantage in the use of motions to table have little to say about cloture motions. Perhaps this is because the political logic of cloture votes may cut both ways. While a motion to table is most often a procedural tool of the majority, the filibuster and the cloture threshold are procedural tools of the minority that may allow a few senators who otherwise would find it costly to oppose a bill, amendment, or nomination to vote against cloture. Majority senators complain about this from time to time. The other side is that party pressure may be more effective on cloture votes than on the comparable substantive votes, which naturally benefits the majority party.

The general argument about procedural votes has a great deal of merit. At a minimum, legislators have more rhetorical room to maneuver in devising explanations for procedural votes than for direct substantive votes. Rhetorical leeway can be particularly helpful in live appearances before groups, in debates, or on radio and television, when a credible response is more important than a complete one.

In practice, the accountability of legislators is a more complicated matter. There are sophisticated intermediaries who observe and interpret legislators' behavior and then inform both the general public and specialized constituencies. The news media are filled with news outlets for specialized audiences in the various segments of economic, social, and political life. Organized interest groups pay close attention to congressional activity, inform their membership of developments on Capitol Hill, and applaud and condemn legislators for their voting records. Political parties and campaign organizations do so, too. Consequently, a procedural vote that might confuse an average voter may not be a costless vote at all for senators. Knowledgeable observers are plentiful and their reports can be consequential.

With the mix of forces at work inside and outside the Senate, it is not too surprising that there are statistically significant differences in party support between procedural and substantive votes. To be sure, on average, procedural votes show deeper party divisions than substantive votes, but the challenge is to find comparable sets of votes when so many procedural votes are not followed by a substantive vote on the same matter. A successful motion to table kills the associated amendment or motion; a failed cloture vote often kills or forces changes in the associated measure, amendment, nomination, or motion.

When we have comparable votes, or can otherwise account for differences in circumstances through statistical techniques, we still are looking for small differences. In a pinch, a party leader can be expected to press for only the votes he or she needs to win. One or two additional votes from the 55 or more fellow partisans may be all that is required to win a vote. Moreover, the senators approached are likely to be those who are somewhat undecided about the underlying issue. Determining whether their votes would have been different on the two types of votes is a task that even the best statistical analysis probably cannot manage.

Available evidence confirms these concerns (Smith, Ostrander, and Pope 2013). Analysis of senators' voting indicates that there is no significant difference between motions to table votes and amendment votes in the probability of supporting the majority leader among majority party senators. Furthermore, campaigns and prominent interest groups have used motions to table to characterize senators' policy positions. Thus, while senators' testimony should be taken seriously, it appears that motions to table are used most often for reasons of convenience and efficiency (motions to table are not debatable and expedite disposal of amendments).

Cloture votes may be different. On the surface, they seem to be (Smith, Ostrander, and Pope 2013). Controlling for the distance of a senator's ideological location from the majority leader, cloture votes tend to produce more support for the majority leader's position among majority party senators than do direct votes on amendments. However, cloture votes are similar to final passage votes in this respect, so again it appears that procedural votes do not give the majority leader much advantage.

Even more than motions to table, cloture motions have received considerable attention from interest groups engaged in evaluating senators' voting records and advertising their

**Table 9.6** Percentage of Votes in Interest Group Scales That Are Cloture Votes, 2007–2009

| | |
|---|---|
| Americans for Democratic Action | 35.0 |
| American Constitutional Union | 25.3 |
| U.S. Chamber of Commerce | 23.1 |
| AFL-CIO | 42.6 |

*Source:* Group websites.

analyses. A wide range of groups select votes that represent their policy interests and report ratings that reflect the frequency with which individual senators support their positions.

For our purposes, it is enough to demonstrate the recent practice of four major groups. Americans for Democratic Action (ADA) and the American Constitutional Union represent liberal and conservative forces, respectively. The U.S. Chamber of Commerce and the AFL-CIO represent business and labor interests, respectively. As table 9.6 illustrates, these four groups have used cloture votes with great frequency in recent years. The ADA and AFL-CIO, the two liberal groups, were negatively affected by Republican obstruction during the 2007–2009 period used here and were more likely than the two conservative groups to include cloture votes in their studies.

### *Senate Parties*

Are Senate parties held accountable for filibusters? This is a difficult question to answer, but a reasonable working hypothesis is that they are not. The argument would be that the public cares much more about the policies that Senate parties pursue than the procedural strategies that they employ, knows little about the Senate, and has quite unformed and pliable attitudes about the filibuster practice itself. And, when filibustering might result in a measurable cost at election time, the minority party and its leader do a good job of resisting the temptation to filibuster.

The little evidence that we have on filibuster attitudes and voting is consistent with this view of party accountability. A sample of the 2009 respondents were interviewed again in the weeks following the 2010 elections and asked whether they approved or disapproved of the filibuster, just as they had been earlier. While respondents' filibuster attitudes are weakly correlated with their vote in 2010 Senate races, there is no relationship once their party identification, ideological self-identification, or general policy views are taken into account (data not shown).[6] In 2010, filibuster attitudes had no relationship to voting for Senate candidates, independent of other considerations.

## CONCLUSION

The world of Senate politics does not allow for clean inferences about the Senate syndrome and accountability. But we have made some progress in confirming and disconfirming a few propositions about accountability.

- Media coverage contributes to public confusion about what transpires in the Senate. Public knowledge of Senate procedure is limited, and attitudes about the filibuster are malleable and subject to partisan influence.
- For individual senators, cloture voting may provide some but not much insulation from public scrutiny.
- We can be certain that senators do not successfully hide from interest groups and political opponents by voting on procedural rather than substantive votes.
- The minority party suffers no measurable disadvantage at election time by its use of the filibuster on prominent legislation beyond what it might on policy grounds.

CHAPTER 10

# THE IMPLICATIONS OF REFORM-BY-RULING

THE CONFLICTED NATURE OF senators' procedural attitudes has been brought into focus in recent years by threats of reform-by-ruling and the arguments that those threats have generated. Even senators who defend the supermajority threshold for cloture usually articulate the view that the vast majority of the Senate's legislative and executive business should be conducted without filibusters and cloture motions. Only in recent years has the minority party argued that the 60-vote threshold is and should be the norm for any important issue.

The resort to reform-by-ruling represents the weakness of a majority party operating in such a supermajority environment. With Rule XXII's two-thirds majority threshold for measures that change the rules, using the inherited standing rules to change the rules proves difficult and often impossible. A Senate majority looks for a way to circumvent the provisions of Rule XXII, turns to the reform-by-ruling approach, and finds a rationale for doing so in the Constitution. In 1975, the successful use of a parliamentary ruling motivated the minority to accept a change in Rule XXII. On two occasions since then, rulings have altered Senate precedents related to post-cloture debate. Some senators, even a few who favor a change in Rule XXII, dislike a move to set aside the express language of Rule XXII to get a vote on reform, which has handicapped reformers' efforts over the past half century.

In this chapter, I review key controversies about the reform-by-ruling strategy. I begin with a quick review of the essential procedural arguments and then turn to the argument that the limited deployment of the reform-by-ruling strategy is evidence of senators' preferences about their rules. This is more than a theoretical argument about how to interpret the Senate's history, although the theoretical argument about how the Senate rules evolve is important. Senators often turn to their institution's history for guidance and certainly to justify their own positions on the question of reform. I then describe and provide additional commentary on today's reformers' arguments about Senate precedent and the procedural paths to reform. I conclude with a discussion of the contested lessons from the 2005 and 2013 "nuclear option" episodes, in which a bipartisan group of senators defused a serious threat to use the reform-by-ruling strategy.

## A REVIEW OF THE ESSENTIALS

Reforming the Senate's formal rules is not easy—or is it? The nuclear option episode of 2005 exposed senators and outsiders to the real possibility that the Senate could make a significant change in Rule XXII, or at least its application, by a simple-majority vote to table an appeal of a ruling of the chair. This possibility made a change in the rules a simple matter. It required just a majority willing to support the strategy and could be facilitated by a friendly presiding officer with a favorable parliamentary ruling.

This possibility, which I call "reform-by-ruling" in previous chapters, creates challenges for both defenders of Senate practice seeking to use the rules to preserve the rules and for senators and scholars seeking an accurate interpretation of the history of Senate reform. Defenders of Senate practice argue that the ability of a transient majority to change the rules through a point of order runs counter to Senate tradition and, worst of all, makes the Senate like the House. Scholars ask whether the existence of the reform-by-ruling approach but its very limited use—it has never been used to rule that Rule XXII is unconstitutional—is evidence that Senate majorities favor supermajority cloture and have always done so.

At least before 2005, most attentive outsiders assumed that the Senate's rules were extremely difficult to change. Senate Rule V provides that "the rules of the Senate shall continue from one Congress to the next Congress unless they are changed as provided in these rules," and Rule XXII provides that "the necessary affirmative vote shall be two-thirds of the Senators present and voting" for cloture on a "measure or motion to amend the Senate rules." Continuity of the standing rules, an explicit requirement that rules be changed by means provided in the standing rules, and a two-thirds threshold for cloture on a change in the rules seem to create a high barrier for change and help explain why the Senate's rules change infrequently, protect minority rights, and frustrate majorities.

The few senators and scholars who were paying attention knew of another route to reform, but most insiders and outsiders had lost sight of some basic facts. The possibility that rules can be reinterpreted or limited by simple-majority endorsement of a point of order casts doubt on the proposition that the standing rules govern a change in the rules. Reformers justify reform-by-ruling strategies on constitutional grounds. Because the standing rules must be consistent with the Constitution, a point of order that a rule is inconsistent with a provision of the Constitution legitimizes a majority's support for the procedural shortcut. Opponents will disagree with the interpretation of the Constitution and argue that long-standing rules and traditions deserve deference.

In the 2003–2005 battle over judicial nominations, Republican majority leader Bill Frist asserted that Article II, Section 2, of the Constitution—the advice-and-consent clause—obligated the Senate to cast a vote on each judicial nomination. The limitation of the argument to the advice-and-consent clause, and then even more narrowly to judicial nominations, surely reflected Republican interest in preserving supermajority cloture for other matters. As I noted in chapters 5 and 6, Frist cited precedents for the reform-by-ruling approach that were set by former majority leader Robert Byrd. Byrd and Democrats argued that the Byrd precedents did not involve constitutional matters and that Frist's interpretation of the advice-and-consent clause was unfounded.

Democrats later discussed pursuing Frist's constitutional option themselves but did not threaten its use until 2013. Instead,

Democratic reformers concentrated on amending Rule XXII rather than merely establishing precedent to limit the rule's application. Because the two-thirds majority threshold stands in their way of amending the rule, Democrats have focused on getting a ruling that the Constitution implies that a simple majority may invoke cloture on a reform proposal. There are additional features to their arguments that I consider below, but the key feature is reliance on the reform-by-ruling strategy to get to a direct vote on amending Rule XXII. Democratic leader Harry Reid seemed to resist that approach until 2012, when he indicated support for the efforts of Democratic reformers. Republicans insisted that this would be a radical move on the part of the Democrats and contrary to the explicit provision of Rule V that the rules are to be "changed as provided in these rules." Democrats, of course, asserted that even Rule V is subordinate to the Constitution.

As a matter of constitutional interpretation, we should not consider Article I and Article II constitutional arguments to be equally valid. They are not. Although the Democrats' argument about the right of a majority to get a vote on the rules is debatable, the substance of Republicans' advice-and-consent argument has no historic or legal foundation. Nevertheless, and I review the relevant issues below, a key feature of the Democrats' most common argument—that it applies to the start of a Congress—is not well founded either.

Plainly, senators of both parties have shown substantial interest in finding a method to circumvent or displace the standing rule with the help of an extraparliamentary, constitutional argument. In 1975, a Senate majority successfully adopted the strategy, which motivated a compromise on reform, but otherwise no significant amendment or interpretation of Rule XXII has been accomplished with a reform-by-ruling strategy. I argue in the next section that a reasonable interpretation of Senate history is that a majority of senators have always been cautious about changing the rules by pursuing a reform-by-ruling strategy. The 1975 reform episode has proven to be an important exception. This observation must be distinguished from the claim that a majority of senators have always favored supermajority cloture. Views on supermajority cloture do not perfectly parallel views on reform-by-ruling, a distinction that scholars and senators do not give sufficient attention.

## THE SCHOLARLY DEBATE OVER SENATE RULES

### *The Contending Arguments*

Scholars offer two alternative accounts of the Senate's reluctance to alter its rules of debate. Perhaps the most widely accepted view emphasizes the ability of the minority to block majority efforts to amend the rules (Binder and Smith 1997; Binder, Madonna, and Smith 2007). This happens in two ways. First, the minority uses Rule XXII to require a two-thirds majority for cloture on a measure that amends the rules. Second, the minority threatens to impose heavy costs on the majority, such as by bringing legislative activity to a crawl by objecting to all unanimous consent requests and demanding cloture on all matters. The threat of minority retaliation is sufficient to persuade some reform-oriented senators that reform is not worth the effort, which would derail efforts to significantly curtail the filibuster, even by some means other than amending Rule XXII. In this view, the modern Senate is what Senate majorities have been forced to accept, not what they have always preferred.

The other account argues that the Senate has always lacked majorities dedicated to filibuster reform (Koger 2002; Wawro and Schickler 2006). This interpretation rests on the observation that Senate majorities always have the reform-by-ruling path available but have not resorted to using it for significant reform. This available-but-not-exploited pattern is taken as evidence that Senate majorities have preferred to preserve supermajority cloture. Throughout the Senate's history, in this view, minorities have tempered their obstructionism so as not to prompt the majority to turn to a reform-by-ruling.

These accounts find parallels in senators' arguments about their institution. Senate reformers emphasize the ability of minorities to block reform, which makes Rule XXII self-perpetuating. They observe the need to find a procedural path to circumvent Rule XXII and to get a simple-majority vote on a reform proposal. Defenders of Senate practice claim that senators always wanted, and still want, to retain the traditional character of their institution that formed in the Senate's early decades.

Evaluating these arguments is a tricky business. Some basic historical facts are difficult to pin down. Most important, the Senate's documented history does not give us a measure of the support for reform of Rule XXII in most Congresses. This leaves room for the contending accounts to provide different interpretations of the historical record, which is filled with inaction and failed reform. Defenders of Senate tradition often insist that reform would have been forced by a majority committed to reform, if such a majority had existed, so there must never have been a committed majority for reform. Reformers respond that Rule XXII is self-perpetuating: either a minority blocks a vote on reform proposals that are likely to receive majority support, or the majority, recognizing that it can be blocked, does not bother to offer reform proposals.

Over the decades since the nineteenth century, the direction of change in the standing rules has been to make cloture easier and more effective, and nearly all precedents have been moves to narrow the range of obstruction by extended debate or motion. The Senate adopted significant reforms on several occasions—1917, 1959, 1975, 1979, 1986—to establish cloture, lower the cloture threshold, and tighten post-cloture debate—and to adopt majority-backed precedents on several occasions to limit loopholes or narrow the application of cloture. Moreover, as detailed in chapter 3, the 1975 rule, providing for a three-fifths majority threshold, had been supported by a simple majority of senators for years before its adoption. Since then, Senate majorities have adopted rules for budget measures and other special classes of measures that limit debate and have sought to expand the range of legislation that is covered by those rules. We can say, at a minimum, that Senate majorities have frequently exhibited a desire to further limit debate in important ways, have found ways to do so, and have not settled on some stable set of minority rights. Every step of the way, at least some senators have complained about violating Senate traditions.

It is more difficult to determine whether a Senate majority has favored *simple-majority* cloture or a motion of the previous question. In their review of the Senate record, Binder and Smith (1997, 169–82) provided these observations, among others:

- In 1873 and again in 1949, the Senate voted on a proposal to allow a simple majority to close debate. The proposal was defeated both times.
- In 1957 and 1959, a Senate majority rejected a motion to consider new rules.
- In 1963, 1967, 1969, and 1971, a majority (but not a two-thirds majority) voted to invoke cloture on reform proposals (for a three-fifths majority of senators present and voting).
- In 1967 and 1969, a majority voted against proposals to allow simple-majority cloture on a change in the rules at the start of a Congress.
- In 1975, a majority endorsed a ruling that a simple majority may close debate on a change in the rules at the start of a Congress and appeared ready to support a substantial reduction in the cloture threshold.

This simplified listing is enough to demonstrate that majority support for filibuster reform and for a reform-by-ruling approach has waxed and waned. Successfully obstructed majorities have materialized for the proposition that a simple majority may invoke cloture for a reform proposal at the start of a Congress and for a lower cloture threshold. Most important, except for the two instances mentioned (1873 and 1949), the Senate has not voted on simple-majority cloture. Consequently, we cannot confirm either the claim that a Senate majority has supported simple-majority cloture on occasion or the claim that a Senate majority has never supported simple-majority cloture.

### *The Comparison with the House of Representatives*

A bicameral legislature with a long history creates a natural experiment. Comparison of the House of Representatives with the

Senate may yield insights about the two houses (Koger 2002). In the nineteenth-century House, Speaker-driven reform-by-ruling precedents and additions to the standing rules limited minority obstruction by enhancing the powers of the Speaker. Clearly, at least temporary House majorities favored such moves, and over the decades since that time House majorities have limited minority rights in many ways. The Senate did not take steps like those of the House, which, the argument goes, should be taken as evidence that Senate majorities did not want to follow the House model.

This is not a persuasive argument. It assumes that the parliamentary context of the House at the time that critical House precedents were set was comparable to the context of the Senate, then and now. The contexts are not comparable in at least two ways.

First, the relationship between the majority party and presiding officer is different in the two houses. The House did not take steps to limit an obstructionist minority until the speaker was given the confidence of his party to take the lead on procedural matters (Jenkins and Stewart 2012). At the time that key precedents were set, the House majority party could reasonably expect the speaker to use the reform process (reform-by-ruling) and the new precedents in a manner that served its interests.

In contrast, the Constitution requires that the vice president serve as the Senate's presiding officer. The vice president, of course, may not share the same party affiliation as the majority party and, in the modern era, will almost certainly act in the interest of the sitting president. Senate majority parties are concerned about using a process that could be employed by the presiding officer, perhaps backed by a temporary majority coalition, to alter the interpretation of the Senate's rules in a manner that undermines the majority party's interests. For the majority party, the vice president is an untrustworthy partner in such a process.

Second, the status of the rules at the start of a new Congress is different in the two houses. The House has always adopted its rules and elected a speaker after its entire membership is sworn into office at the beginning of a new Congress. This is a new House of Representatives—not a returning one—and it must elect a speaker and approve rules before it conducts other business. This process of approving the rules every two years has created an opportunity for a House majority—really, the House majority party—to adopt revisions of the rules at the start of each new Congress. Over many decades, the result is a body of House standing rules that total over sixty-five thousand words and grant strong control over floor proceedings to a simple majority.

The context is much different in the Senate, for which the Constitution creates three classes of seats with staggered six-year terms of office. Because the term of office for only one class expires at the end of any one Congress and the terms of two-thirds of senators continue from one Congress to the next, the Senate's standing rules are considered to continue from one Congress to the next. There is no need to approve the rules at the start of a new Congress. Amendments to the rules may face minority obstruction and require cloture, so amendments that put the minority at a disadvantage are unlikely to gain ready approval. One result is that Senate rules, which are about thirty-seven thousand words, are less elaborate than House rules.

For at least some senators, even some who profess an interest in filibuster reform, the continuity of the Senate's rules has been an important principle and has led them to object to a reform process that circumvents the inherited standing rules (for the 1960s and 1970s, see Binder and Smith 1997, 176–82). In recent decades, most reformers have made a counterargument that Article I, Section 5, must imply that a simple majority can revisit the rules at the start of a Congress, but even some reform proponents have not found that argument persuasive. This process dimension has worked to the disadvantage of reformers. At times, at least some senators appear to have favored a lower cloture threshold but were wary of setting aside the principle of the continuity of the rules that was essential to getting a vote on amendments to the rules.

### *The Costs of Reform*

The 2005 judicial nominations episode (see chapter 5) demonstrates the role of the costs that the minority can impose on the majority in forcing the majority to back away from significant cloture reform. As I have emphasized in previous chapters, time and votes are a Senate majority leader's most prized resources, and minorities know how to exploit time to their advantage. A threat to delay action on any part of the leader's large legislative agenda, and certainly a threat to engage in all-out obstruction, must be taken seriously by a majority leader concerned with his party's reputation for governing. The minority's threat to go "nuclear," a term coined by a majority leader, is not an idle threat.

The minority response to what it considers an abuse of majority power forces us to take seriously the question of political costs (Binder, Madonna, and Smith 2007). The technical feasibility of reform-by-ruling is only part of the story. Political feasibility is another matter. The transaction and opportunity costs entailed in employing the technically feasible mechanism of reform-by-ruling may be judged to be too great by enough senators, even some who favor reform, to prevent a majority for a reform-by-ruling strategy to materialize. The threat of reform-by-ruling, particularly for a significant change in cloture practice, is seldom a viable threat. And if it is not a viable threat, the infrequency of its use cannot be taken as evidence of the majority's preference for supermajority rule. Instead, its very rare use for a direct attack on Rule XXII is equally consistent with the view that the costs that a minority can impose on the majority are too great for the majority.

## THE REFORMERS' ARGUMENTS FOR REFORM-BY-RULING

As I have mentioned, Democratic and Republican arguments about the need to change Senate practice have had different constitutional foundations. Since the 1950s, Democratic reformers have emphasized that Article I, Section 5, implies that a majority can get a vote on a reform proposal, at least at the beginning of a Congress (see chapters 1 and 2). Republicans, for the most part, have not adopted that view, even when in the majority. When in the majority during the 2003–2006 period, most Republicans appeared to be willing to accept Frist's view that Article II, Section 2, obligates the Senate to vote on judicial nominations. These perspectives reflect the differences in objectives between liberals and conservatives and continue to serve as the rationale for reformers of the two stripes.

### *Recent Liberal Arguments*

Liberal reformers have pursued two approaches over the last half century. Some of them, whom we will call "purists," argue that supermajority cloture is unconstitutional. The argument is that (a) the Constitution implicitly provides for majority rule by explicitly providing for supermajority thresholds only for a limited set of matters (veto overrides, treaty ratification, constitutional amendments, conviction after impeachment, and expulsion of a senator) and (b) the use of the words "passed," "determine," and "consent" in the Constitution imply that other acts are accomplished by simple majorities. If so, the Senate cannot establish a rule that prevents a simple majority from exercising the powers of passing legislation, determining the rules, or consenting to appointments and treaties.[1] The liberals' 1957 brief on cloture reform (see chapter 2) took this position, although most senatorial arguments for reform only implicitly endorse this view.

In recent years, most liberal reformers, who might be called the "compromisers," have taken a somewhat different view of Article I, Section 5. They ignore the purists' argument that the supermajority threshold of Rule XXII is simply unconstitutional. Instead, they focus their critique on the "continuing body theory" and the entrenchment of Senate rules, and they argue for the principle that one Senate cannot bind future Senates.[2] They cite Vice President Richard Nixon's 1957 advisory comments that endorsed the principle that a simple majority can revisit the rules at the start of a Congress, a view endorsed by Vice President Nelson Rockefeller in 1975.

Compromisers have not only taken a narrow view of Article I, Section 5, but they have also usually advocated something less than simple-majority cloture. They have often proposed to limit debate for motions to proceed or motions to go to conference. They have emphasized the need to make the sources of holds more transparent without limiting the ability of a single senator to object to unanimous consent requests and force cloture votes. Typically, they have insisted that they are seeking to restore the Senate tradition of occasional but infrequent filibusters and obstruction.

The dissimilarities between the purists and the compromisers may reflect genuine differences in interpretations of the Constitution and even differences in the kind of Senate envisioned, but they surely reflect differences in legislative tactics. All liberal reformers of the past few decades have agreed that Article I, Section 5, implies that a simple majority may get a vote on the rules. Purists insist that a simple majority may get a vote on the rules at any time. Section 5 does not, after all, set a time limit, and in practice, the Senate has addressed its rules throughout its sessions. Purists argue that Rule XXII has long violated the Constitution and must be reformed to allow for simple-majority cloture or the institution of a motion on the previous question.

Compromisers want to reduce minority obstructionism, but, perhaps in order to appeal to concerned colleagues, they do not want to create the impression that their proposals will radically change the character of the Senate. They want to counter the charge that their reform proposals will turn the Senate into another House of Representatives. They certainly claim that their beginning-of-a-Congress argument does not imply that the rules can be changed at any time at the whim of a temporary majority. Compromisers acknowledge the value of stable rules but argue that today's Senate has become dysfunctional and that a majority has the power to take modest corrective steps.

### *Recent Conservative Arguments*

The Frist argument, endorsed by President George W. Bush, has been reviewed in some detail (chapters 5 and 6) but deserves additional consideration. Frist insisted that the advice-and-consent clause obligated the Senate to vote on judicial nominations. Congressional and legal scholars have not come to Frist's defense. Instead, the predominant view is that the clause lacks any directive for the Senate to act, that mandatory actions are given a "shall" directive in the Constitution and there is none in this clause, and that the version used in states at the time the Constitution was written and that served as a model for the clause was not viewed as obligating the confirming body to act (A. White 2005).

As Republican frustration with Democrats' obstruction on judicial nominations and other matters was building in the early Bush administration, many Republicans began to offer constitutional arguments. They found themselves claiming the existence of an implied right for majorities to act, usually going beyond the advice-and-consent clause to an argument typical of liberal purists. One of many examples: John Cornyn (R-TX), who had served as Texas attorney general and would later be elected to Senate Republican leadership positions, argued in 2003: "If the Constitution provides that only a majority is necessary to confirm judges, any Senate rule that purports to prevent a majority of the Senate from exercising that confirmation function directly contradicts and offends our constitutional design" (Cornyn 2003).

Cornyn's comments fit a more general pattern. While he applied his observations to judicial nominations, the logic of his constitutional argument applies to any Senate "function" authorized under the Constitution that requires a majority, including action on legislation and nominations to judicial and executive branch positions. Indeed, the Frist argument that a ruling based on the advice-and-consent clause could be limited to judicial nominations is weak, and the Republicans often made a more general argument. It is an argument that they chose to ignore as soon as they became a minority party after the 2008 elections.

## REVISITING THE 2005 NUCLEAR OPTION EPISODE

The events surrounding Frist's efforts in May 2005 to gain Senate action on several judicial nominations have drawn considerable attention from legal and political science scholars (Binder, Madonna, and Smith 2007; Koger 2008; Wawro and Schickler 2010). One interpretation of those events, offered by legal scholar Charles Tiefer (2007), warrants special consideration.

According to Tiefer, the 2005 episode was at least a short-term victory for Majority Leader Frist. The outcome of the reform-by-ruling threat was a piece of a larger "Republican revolution" of "one-party rule" that included the use of reconciliation, the amendment tree, new uses of conference reports, and other procedural developments by the majority leader (Tiefer 2007). Although the Gang of 14 blocked the use of the reform-by-ruling strategy (see chapter 6), it allowed some pending nominations to receive votes and promised to refrain from filibustering future nominees except in "extraordinary circumstances." In this view, the threat and the Gang of 14 memorandum paved the way for votes on Supreme Court nominees Samuel Alito and John Roberts in the following months (Wawro and Schickler 2010).[3] In fact, the members of the Gang of 14 met to discuss the next three Supreme Court nominees and agreed to support cloture.

Evaluating a counterfactual argument—in this case, we want to know what would have happened if Frist either had not threatened the constitutional option or had successfully pursued it—is never easy. We can examine the short-term effects of the Gang of 14 statement on the contested nominations and on the rules. We can also examine the longer-term effects on efforts to limit obstructionism on judicial nominations. On balance, it is hard to view the outcome as a victory for Frist.

Some background: The Gang of 14's move did not occur until Frist and Reid had exchanged compromise proposals on how to proceed. Reid's last offer, made in late April, was to allow the Senate to act on four of the seven nominations to federal appeals courts, an offer that Frist rejected as inadequate (Perine 2005). The Gang of 14 statement provided for action on four of the seven, and in fact, five were confirmed within three weeks of the Gang of 14 agreement. Along with the Supreme Court nominations, which included promotion of Roberts to chief justice, this record represented progress for Bush nominees.

Frist was disappointed with the outcome. The Gang of 14 explicitly excluded two nominations from its commitment to allow votes, and by the end 2006, due to Democratic objections, three appeals court nominations were withdrawn and not renewed in the next Congress ("'Gang of 14'" 2006; Lewis 2007). In addition, the Gang of 14 promised to oppose any change in the standing rules or precedent that would obligate the Senate to vote on judicial nominations, Frist's central principle. The day after the agreement was announced, Frist observed: "I was not a party to that agreement, nor was our Republican leadership. It stops far short of guaranteeing up-or-down votes on all nominees. It stops far short of the principle on which this leadership stands" (*Congressional Record,* May 25, 2005, S5860).

Perhaps most frustrating for Frist was that Republican support for the constitutional option was in doubt. It appears that only two Republicans, Lindsey Graham (R-SC) and Mike DeWine (R-OH), would have supported the move "if we had to," as Graham explained on the Senate floor (*Congressional Record,* May 24, 2005, S5821). Congressional Quarterly reported that three of the seven Republican members of the Gang of 14 were openly opposed to the Frist plan, with the other three "publicly noncommittal" ("'Gang of 14'" 2006).

It is worth notice that many senators considered the Democratic threat to block all nonessential legislation if Frist followed through with his threat to be credible and costly. Even Graham made it clear that the outcome was better than the chaos that would have ensued if Frist had proceeded with his procedural move and the Democrats had responded as promised (*Congressional Record,* May 24, 2005, S5821). The minority party was able to make Frist's move appear to be so costly to the Republican members of the Gang of 14 that they were willing to undercut their leader's strategy and sign the agreement.

Over the longer term, obstructionism on judicial nominations continued apace. In the following Congresses, the rate of confirmation for district and appeals court nominees remained as low as it had been, and on average, delays in confirmation actually became more extended (see chapters 5 and 6). Moreover, the 2008 Democrats and 2012 Republicans invoked the informal "Thurmond Rule" that no judicial nominations make it to a vote in the last few months of a presidential term. All of this represented a continuation of previous practices and a failure of the Senate minority to accept the principle that the Senate is obligated to vote on judicial nominees, the principle that Frist so strongly advocated and professed to keep alive, even after the Gang of 14 agreement was announced (*Congressional Record,* May 24, 2005, S5816).

The events of May 2005 seemed to initiate an era in which the Senate syndrome blossomed. At the time of the Gang of 14 memorandum, the nomination of John Bolton for U.S. ambassador to the United Nations was pending. Democrats blocked the nomination and Bolton was given a recess appointment, but, lacking Senate confirmation, he was forced to resign the position at the end of the next session of Congress. More generally, minority obstruction, with partisan retribution expressed from time to time, widened. Minority party leadership came to play a central role in orchestrating that obstruction. The majority leader more reflexively pursued parliamentary paths that limited obstructive opportunities but, often lacking 60 votes to invoke cloture, found his legislative agenda blocked by the minority. If the threat of reform-by-ruling was ever serious enough to tame the minority, the events of 2005 appear to have undercut that threat, at least for the following three Congresses.

Reform-by-ruling did prove to be a serious threat, but the option was taken off the table by the Gang of 14 for a while.[4] It may have shaped senators' responses to judicial nominations for a time, but it failed over the longer term and no one can claim that it had serious influence on senators on other matters. By mid-2012, then–Majority Leader Reid began to discuss using reform-by-ruling to get a majority vote on rules reform at the start of the next Congress, but even Reid did not adopt the purist view that a point of order could or should settle the question of majority rule in the Senate.

## REVISITING THE 2013 NUCLEAR OPTION EPISODES

The most recent reform-by-ruling episodes involved the Democratic majority's struggle to get votes on several presidential nominations in 2013. As noted in chapter 7, in July 2013 Majority Leader Harry Reid threatened to establish a new precedent that a simple majority may invoke cloture on executive nominations. Republicans relented on executive nominations at issue and Reid backed off his threat saying that he would return to it if Republicans returned to filibustering executive branch nominations. Several elements of the 2013 episode bear special attention.

First, Democrats did not bother to justify their threat on the advice-and-consent clause. The primary justifications for Reid were that (a) excessive Republican obstructionism required an extraordinary response by the Senate majority party and (b) reform-by-ruling had been done before. The advice-and-consent rationale developed by Frist a decade earlier was mentioned but not emphasized by Reid and other Democrats. The emphasis was on the need to give President Obama his team so that government could function properly.

Second, Reid narrowed his procedural threat to executive nominations. Delays in acting on several prominent nominations were his central concern and appear to have been a serious concern for nearly all Democrats. The party consensus on the matter helped Reid make the credible claim that he had 51 votes for the procedural move he planned. Republicans had had a similar, although less complete, consensus on judicial nominations eight years earlier.

Third, Reid's claim of having 51 votes, a Senate majority, for his procedural move was credible and was not undermined by the efforts of the Republican leadership to find an easy way to end the crisis. The 51 votes, including Reid's own support for a reform-by-ruling move, were conditioned on the Republicans failing to allow votes on Obama's nominations. Reid indicated that he would not pursue a reform-by-ruling move if Republicans allowed votes on the executive nominations.

It is reasonable to suppose that Reid and at least a few of his Democratic colleagues were eager to force a change in the cloture threshold even for the limited purpose of executive nominations.

Fourth, while few close observers doubted that a Senate majority existed to implement Reid's reform-by-ruling strategy if required, the threat of Republican retaliation and further deterioration of interparty relations was real, too. This threat of retaliation surely conditioned support for the Reid move: for at least some Democrats, reform-by-ruling was worthwhile only if Republicans refused the Democrats' demands on executive nominations. The outcome allowed those Democrats to get votes on the executive nominations without risking the fallout from Republican retaliation.

Finally, the public record does not identify the Democrats who refused to support Reid's threat in July. Some Democrats —most notably, Carl Levin (D-MI) and David Pryor (D-AR)— who had opposed the Merkley-Udall plans in early 2013 did not openly oppose Reid's threatened move. They may have wanted to give Reid the leverage he needed to win concessions from the Republicans without committing to voting with Reid on the required procedural motions.

A few months later, in November 2013, when Reid successfully used the reform-by-ruling approach to impose simple-majority cloture for executive and judicial nominations, he similarly avoided making a constitutional argument of any kind (*Congressional Record*, November 21, 2013, S8414–15). Again, necessity, or at least practical politics, but not a constitutional principle, was Reid's focus. The differences between purists and compromisers in his party were not exposed. This may have been intentional. Reid may have realized that it was not necessary to build a consensus among his party colleagues for the constitutional basis for majority action on the rules at a time when nearly all of his party colleagues could agree on the need to change the threshold for cloture on nominations.

This time, roll-call votes were cast on Reid's point of order, so we learned which Democrats did not support his move. Only three Democrats—Levin, Pryor, and Joe Manchin (D-WV)—voted against Reid's position, which allowed it to win with 52 votes. Only Levin took the floor after the deed was done to warn that Reid's move set a precedent for making major rules changes in the future by circumventing the standing rules with a point of order (*Congressional Record,* November 21, 2013, S8421–23). Levin argued about more than just the procedural method for the rules change. He objected to the reform-by-ruling approach because it would eventually be used to adopt a simple-majority cloture threshold for legislation.

The events of 2013 settle two issues in the academic literature. First, a majority can change the rules by the reform-by-ruling approach. That was not in much doubt, though some scholars insist that this possibility forced us to rethink the reasons that Senate rules seem so difficult to change. Second, a majority favored simple-majority cloture for an important class of Senate business. It had been doubted that such a majority had ever existed (or would ever exist). Indeed, it was argued that senators see so much value in the high threshold that they would not want to change it. That view is wrong, at least at times.

We can add that at least a few senators held views about how rules should be changed that were separable from their views about the proper cloture threshold. The majority party Democrats who voted for Reid's point of order were persuaded that the harm done by minority obstruction under supermajority cloture on nominations was greater than the harm done by using the reform-by-ruling method. Democrats Diane Feinstein and Barbara Boxer, both Californians, were among those who openly balanced these competing considerations and, over the course of 2013, changed how they viewed that balance.

## CONCLUSION

Political scientists have struggled to evaluate the balance of opinion about simple-majority and supermajority rule among senators. The Senate has produced very few direct votes on the matter to assist with this evaluation. Even the 2005 nuclear option episode left ambiguous the attitudes of many senators. The episode involved an unusual constitutional argument, was limited to judicial nominations, generated a clear minority threat to make most legislating very difficult for the majority, and never produced a vote on the procedural principles. The variety of considerations that senators necessarily took into account was typical of filibuster reform episodes. Such episodes usually yield no clear expression of Senate opinion and leave considerable uncertainty about whether the threat of reform-by-ruling is viable. The 2013 episode proved different. The Senate changed.

CHAPTER 11

# THE SENATE SYNDROME AND REFORM

I HAVE LABELED THE SENATE'S TENDENCIES, taken now to greater extremes than at any time in the institution's history, the Senate syndrome. It is a syndrome because it involves the emergence of several behaviors that combine to make the Senate's decision-making process much different from what we have seen during most of its history. These behaviors include the greater frequency of minority obstruction, more concerted efforts by the majority to limit amending activity and circumvent the floor, the invention of new parliamentary strategies, quicker resort to last-resort tactics, and an enhanced role for party leaders in designing and implementing strategies. An obstruct-and-restrict pattern has dominated the Senate in recent Congresses—minority obstructive strategies are met by majority strategies to limit debate and amendment. "Regular order" evaporates, and the Senate, known historically for its informality, is tied up in procedural knots.

A more derogatory term that majority party members might use is "ransom politics." Deliberation, debate, and bargaining are, and should be, an everyday feature of legislative politics. Senators and knowledgeable outsiders know that the Senate of recent years has gone far beyond occasional obstruction and normal bargaining. The minority's goal has shifted from preventing enactment of the most undesirable legislation to creating political failure for the majority party. "Meet our demands or [politically] die" is not too far from the minority's stance. The majority party has responded by circumventing floor debate when it can and otherwise clamping down on the minority's opportunities to freely offer amendments. Both parties have legitimate complaints about the behavior of the other side, but there is no doubt that the minority encourages the worst behavior from the majority.

In this chapter, I return to senators' attitudes about their rules and reform proposals. I begin with a somewhat abstract consideration of the political motivations that may guide senators' evaluation of their institution's rules. This leads to expectations about who is likely to support and oppose reform. I then turn to a description of reform proposals and their sponsors, which confirms those broad expectations about senators' views of reform. I conclude with observations about the likely future of Senate procedure.

## LAYERS OF MOTIVATION

The United States Senate is similar to other legislative bodies in having acquired strong procedural tendencies. Most legislative bodies develop procedural tendencies that reflect the rules under which they operate, the party structure and other divisions among legislators that characterize their decision making, and, to some degree, the expectations of outsiders whose support and opposition is vital to legislators. At any moment, inherited rules and practices, which vary widely in their ambiguity and specificity, establish decision rules that shape legislators' strategies. The repetition of those strategies creates norms that are recognized and sometimes taken as evidence of how things should operate. Prescriptive norms may include even expectations or constraints on changing the rules (Binder and Smith 1995).

The lack of rules and precedents that would give the majority a strong hand in setting the agenda has shaped the historical path of the Senate's procedural practices. The high cloture threshold and cumbersome process for limiting debate and gaining a vote on legislation or nominations has produced heavy reliance on unanimous consent to arrange the agenda and the development of formal and informal practices associated with unanimous consent requests. The majority leader's right of first recognition came fairly late in the Senate's history (the 1930s) but has proven essential to the majority party's ability to direct floor activity in the modern Senate. Other tools, including a small set of nondebatable motions, have also proven helpful to the majority. Nevertheless, the weakness of the majority party's tools has been exposed in recent years as the minority party has engaged in frequent, well-organized, and effective obstruction.

In their battles over parliamentary rules, senators have expressed a variety of motivations for their evaluations of Rule XXII and cloture practices. No one has or probably ever will determine the relative importance of these motivations for senators, individually or in the aggregate. It is certainly reasonable to question the sincerity of public pronouncements about the rules. Senators, like all politicians, seek to translate personal, factional, or partisan interests into public interest and are skilled in crafting rhetorical camouflage for their motivations.

My working assumption is that senators vary in their motivations, both across individuals and over time (Smith 2007). They also likely vary in their assessment of the relative emphasis that their parties should give to collective policy and electoral goals. Electoral time horizons matter, too. Senators who are little concerned about anything but the next election may think differently about filibuster reform than senators who are worried about passing or blocking legislation over the next decade or generation. And hunches about the future strength of parties, factions, and even demographic groups in the Senate may condition views about majority rule and minority rights.

With so many uncertainties about matters of importance, it is not surprising to hear senators voice a variety of rationales in support of or in opposition to reform proposals and then change their emphasis over time. Nevertheless, there are several layers of motivation worth distinguishing. They reflect the multiple ways that senators may benefit from serving as a veto group that can delay or block Senate action. These layers serve as the basis for a reasonable hypothesis about the support of and opposition to filibuster reform.

### *Individual Senators*

Individual senators benefit from the ability to at least delay Senate action by refusing to consent to unanimous consent requests to limit debate or amendments and move to votes. Holds represent an informal practice that recognizes this possibility. This power gives senators the ability to impose costs in time and effort on their colleagues—particularly the majority leader and bill managers—and often yields at least modest bargaining leverage. That leverage can be used for a wide variety of purposes. Placing a hold or engaging in a filibuster is also a way to demonstrate commitment to a cause or to serve the interests of important constituencies. And threatening delay is a way to protect opportunities to debate and offer amendments.

It bears repeating that the Senate's heavy reliance on unanimous consent, which empowers the individual senator, is a by-product of Rule XXII and supermajority cloture. The difficulty of using Rule XXII—finding a three-fifths majority, waiting for a second day to get a vote on a cloture motion, and taking the time for post-cloture debate—leads the majority leader to rely on unanimous consent agreements whenever possible to expedite Senate business. With unanimous consent requests for so many everyday motions, the majority leader wants to remain on good terms with his colleagues. A rank-and-file senator has an incentive not to be so troublesome that his or her colleagues object to requests made to accommodate his or her legislative or scheduling needs. Nevertheless, the need for unanimous consent and the burden of cloture give the individual senator a source of leverage found in few other parliamentary bodies.

All things being equal, the preservation of supermajority cloture and the reliance on unanimous consent are in the interest of most individual senators. It is true that senators can both initiate and suffer obstruction, but their wide variety of local, parochial, and specialized interests is well-served by rules that empower them as individual senators. The burden of managing this individualistic process falls on the shoulders of party and committee leaders, who often take a more negative view of Senate practices.

### *Parties and Factions*

Only a little more needs to be said about party interests and majority party control of the Senate. Considerable attention has been given to the way majority and minority party status conditions leaders' views about filibuster reform. I have joked that immediately after a change in party control, Democrats and Republicans enter a dark room and exchange their speeches about filibusters and cloture. Plainly, from a purely partisan perspective, the majority party prefers simple-majority to supermajority decision rules.

A general preference for majoritarian rules does not mean that the majority party always seeks simple-majority cloture. Other considerations, such as disruption of the party's legislative agenda, divisions within the party, and the prospects of soon becoming a minority party, weigh heavily in the party's calculations. A reform effort that delays action on the party's program and exposes divisions within the party might be avoided.

Moreover, a party that controls the presidency may find supermajority cloture to be an advantage or disadvantage, depending on whether it wants to pass or block legislation. There are times when the filibuster serves to obstruct action on the president's program, as when Democrats sacrificed a public insurance plan as part of health care reform in 2009 in order to acquire 60 votes for cloture when confronting a filibuster. There are other times when the filibuster can be used to block legislation that the president opposes. In such cases, a successful filibuster may spare the president from paying the political consequences of vetoing a popular measure.

Factions within a party may have interests that are quite distinct from those of the rest of the party. Most obviously, southern Democrats in the mid-twentieth century were dedicated to preserving supermajority cloture in order to block civil rights measures, a position that put them at odds with liberal

Democrats. The factionalism led party leaders to avoid the issue of reform or to pursue compromise when the issue was forced upon them.

### *Ideological Coalitions*

In any Congress, the balance of conservatives and liberals in the Senate may color attitudes about filibuster reform. That balance, historically, is related to the size of the two parties and is driven by considerations similar to partisan and factional factors. Since Rule XXII was adopted in 1917, both conservatives and liberals have had large legislative agendas, if only to change the policies put in place by the other coalition. A reasonable hypothesis is that the stronger coalition favors filibuster reform more than the weaker coalition.

Time horizons are potentially significant. For the short term, one ideological perspective or the other may be seeking to preserve the policy status quo. Since 2010, liberals seeking to defend the 2010 health care law and entitlement programs have benefited from the supermajority threshold for cloture.

For the long term, liberals, who seek government policies to address the problems of American society, view obstacles to enacting legislation to authorize new programs as undesirable. It may be for this reason that Senator Tom Harkin, a liberal Iowan first elected to the Senate in 1984 and retiring in 2014, has advocated filibuster reform, although with varying degrees of vigor. Conservatives see another veto point to efforts to expand the role of government as desirable. This helps account for the very narrow and tortured interpretation of the Constitution that Majority Leader Bill Frist advocated in 2003–2005 on judicial nominations. Thus, it appears that senators' general view of the role of government, what we usually refer to as their ideology, disposes them for or against filibuster reform.

### *Institutional Interests*

Nearly all senators articulate their views about the filibuster in terms of the proper balance between majority rule and minority rights in the Senate. This, in turn, is wrapped in commentary about the proper role of the Senate in federal policy making. For defenders of Senate practice, this always means emphasizing the importance of deliberation, minority rights, and the representation of states. For reformers, this always means allowing a majority to address the pressing problems of American society. Thus, while the Senate's institutional interests almost always play a central role in discussion of Rule XXII, there is seldom a consensus among senators about how to define those interests.

Senators also express concerns about the effect of stalemate on the role of their institution in policy making. The demise of the appropriations process has drawn the most attention, but senators have complained about the absence of "regular order" more generally (see chapter 6). By "regular order" they mean the standard legislative process—committee action, floor amendments, floor passage, conference committee—that they consider important to full and fair deliberation on policy problems.

Moreover, senators occasionally associate the stalemate and demise of regular order with the low level of approval for congressional job performance. It is impossible to judge how much senators care about this, but it is reasonable to speculate that as a general rule, incumbents prefer to be working in an institution that enjoys popular approval to one that does not.

### *Support and Opposition to Filibuster Reform*

A reasonable hypothesis is that support for reducing the cloture threshold is most likely to come from majority, liberal Democrats. To accomplish reform, such Democrats must constitute a Senate majority, but this is not a common condition. When the Democratic conference grows large, it is likely that a significant number of Democrats come from moderate or conservative states and will not be eager to endorse a filibuster reform.

Conservatives and Republicans, when in the majority, may want to overcome obstruction but are more conflicted than liberals about the long-term implications of a reduction in the cloture threshold. Instead, they would be looking for alternatives to a general reduction in the threshold by focusing on means to overcome minority obstruction on their highest-priority issues.

Using the reconciliation process for tax cuts would allow the majority to avoid minority obstruction without directly changing Rule XXII. Narrowly targeted limitations on debate, such as those on judicial nominations or trade agreements, would minimize the harm to Rule XXII.

Individual senators may resist the strategies implied by their partisan and ideological interests. In the abstract, we cannot be sure how senators balance their personal interests with the strong partisan and ideological interests at stake in filibuster reform, but a reasonable guess is that only a few senators follow the path dictated by individual interests. The 2005 nuclear option episode provided some clues. The Gang of 14 consisted of a small set of senators who pursued a path somewhat independently of their party leaders (see chapter 10). A case can be made that the 7 Democrats found a compromise similar to what their own leader proposed, which leaves only the 7 Republicans who clearly bucked their party leader. Thus, somewhere between 7 and 14 senators out of 100 took their own path, with the lower number being a best guess.

Ten percent of the Senate is more than enough to tip the balance in a battle over reform of Rule XXII, as it was in 2005. Even for that 10 percent, evaluating motivations is not easy. In 2005, some members of the Gang of 14 expressed a clear preference for retaining a supermajority threshold for cloture; others expressed a fear of the effect of the nuclear option on conducting other business. But with at least a handful of senators taking their own path, clean predictions of when filibuster reform will occur and when it will be successfully resisted are not easy.

As a general rule, conditions that enhance partisan, ideological, and electoral pressures for reform will reduce the relative strength of incentives to individual power. Those conditions might include the president advocating reform when his or her popular policy proposals have passed the House and are subject to minority obstruction in the Senate. Even then, a Senate minority might, in a timely way, selectively allow action on some legislation or nominations to relieve the pressure for filibuster reform and allow individualism to resurface among majority senators. The majority party is always under pressure to move forward with its policy agenda, even if it means giving up filibuster reform for the time being.

Plainly, the conditions for direct reform of Rule XXII, and certainly reform pursued under the terms of Rule XXII, are seldom ripe.

## APPROACHES TO REFORM

Reformers have generated a wide variety of proposals, ranging from a reduction of the cloture threshold in Rule XXII to limitations on debate for specific motions or measures. Most reform proposals aim to limit debate for just some motions and measures, but a few proposals seek to address the minority's concern that majority tactics bar or limit opportunities to offer amendments. I have summarized in table 11.1 the proposals introduced as resolutions in the 112th Congress (2011–2012) that address Rule XXII in some way.

### *Thresholds, Motions, and Measures*

Remarkably, no proposal introduced at the start of the 112th Congress, even any introduced by liberal Democrats, replaced supermajority cloture with simple-majority cloture. Senator Tom Harkin returned to a proposal that he first designed in the early 1990s, which would have reduced the cloture threshold from the current level (three-fifths of senators duly chosen and sworn) by three votes in a series of steps until a simple majority was required. If all current Senate seats were filled, the threshold would be reduced from 60 to 57 to 54 to 51, so that simple-majority cloture would occur on the fourth attempt. Among the proposals formally introduced in recent Congresses, this is the closest to a purists' position, as defined in the previous chapter. It was sponsored by some of the most liberal Democrats—Majority Whip Dick Durbin (D-IL), Senator Barbara Mikulski (D-MD), Senator Jeanne Shaheen (D-NH), and Senator Brian Schatz (D-HI).

Most proposals represented the compromisers' view that more modest reform is feasible or perhaps even desirable. These proposals, in the view of their authors, would reduce the harm of obstructionism without eliminating the possibility of a filibuster. The proposals included a limit on debate on the motion to proceed so that a majority could bring a bill to the floor. A filibuster would be possible on bills, House amendments, and conference reports. In addition, reformers proposed limits on debate for motions to go into executive session, for motions to go to conference, and for post-cloture debate on nominations.

Democrats also included features that would appeal to the minority, a direct response to Republican complaints about abuses of the amendment tree and the post-cloture process. These included dividing post-cloture debate equally between the parties and guaranteeing each party's leader a number of post-cloture amendments. Moreover, to address complaints about abuses of filling the amendment tree, Harkin proposed the creation of a simple-majority, nondebatable motion to set aside pending amendments that could be used a limited number of times. To expand post-cloture amendment opportunities even more, one reform measure proposed a three-fifths majority, nondebatable motion to waive the germaneness requirement for amendments in post-cloture debate.

Democrats devised procedures to address what they considered to be abuses of the cloture process. Because Rule XXII requires a three-fifths majority of senators duly chosen and sworn to invoke cloture, the proponents of cloture must muster 60 votes even if no opponents of cloture bother to vote. In fact, on some cloture votes in the previous few years, less than a two-fifths minority voted. Two proposals have been offered to correct for this. Senator Tom Udall (D-NM) proposed changing the rule to three-fifths of senators present and voting, which effectively reduces the threshold for cloture when senators fail to vote. Senator Al Franken (D-MN) proposed that a filibuster can continue only when more than two-fifths of senators duly chosen and sworn cast negative votes on the cloture motion.

In addition, Democrats complained about the minority forcing cloture but refusing to conduct debate on the floor—the "silent filibuster." When minority senators do not seek

**Table 11.1.** Cloture Reform Proposals, 112th Congress (2011–2012)

| Chief sponsor, resolution | Reduce cloture threshold | Add debate limits | Post-cloture | Require debate | Nominations | Holds | Non–Rule XXII provisions |
|---|---|---|---|---|---|---|---|
| Harkin (D-IA), S. Res. 8 | Reduce threshold by 3 votes on succeeding cloture motions until a simple majority is required | | Guarantee each leader 3 amendments | | | | |
| Lautenberg (D-NJ), S. Res. 9 | | | | After cloture filed and before cloture vote, bar motions, and, if no senator seeks recognition, majority leader may put question on cloture | | | |
| Udall (D-NM), S. Res. 10 | | 2 hours of debate for motion to proceed | Guarantee each leader 3 amendments | After cloture vote fails, bar motions, and, if no senator seeks recognition, | Limit post-cloture debate to 2 hours | No senator may object on behalf of another senator without disclosing name | |

| | | | | | | | |
|---|---|---|---|---|---|---|---|
| | | | | require presiding officer to announce that cloture is considered invoked | | | |
| Wyden (D-OR), S. Res. 11 | | | | | | Require senator placing hold to submit notice of intent in *Cong Record* within one session day | |
| Udall (D-CO), S. Res. 12 | Change from 3/5 of senators "duly chosen and sworn" to "present and voting" | 4 hours of debate for motion to proceed; make motion to go into executive session nondebatable; bar debate after complete substitute is agreed to; 4 hours of debate for conference motions | Divide time equally between majority and minority | | No post-cloture debate | | Rule XV: create nondebatable motion to set aside a pending amendment (1 motion per senator, 5 total motions per calendar day); create a nondebatable motion to waive germaneness requirement (3/5 majority of senators duly chosen and sworn) |

*(continued)*

**Table 11.1.** Cloture Reform Proposals, 112th Congress (2011–2012), *continued*

| Chief sponsor, resolution | Reduce cloture threshold | Add debate limits | Post-cloture | Require debate | Nominations | Holds | Non–Rule XXII provisions |
|---|---|---|---|---|---|---|---|
| Franken (D-MN), S. Res. 13 | Decided in the affirmative by a majority if not more than 2/5 of senators duly chosen and sworn vote in the negative | | | | | | |
| Merkley (D-OR), S. Res. 21 | After cloture vote fails with majority support and no senator seeks recognition, majority leader may put the question on cloture, to be decided by a majority of senators chosen and sworn | | | After cloture vote fails with majority support, motions are barred, and, if no senator seeks recognition, majority leader may invoke cloture | | | |

recognition to speak, the majority must move to other business or adjourn the Senate, both of which allow the minority to obstruct by inaction. Reformers proposed ways to force real debate. Senator Frank Lautenberg (D-NJ) originally proposed that after a cloture motion has been filed but before a vote on the motion, senators must seek recognition to speak or the majority leader may have the cloture motion put to an immediate vote. In Senator Tom Udall's version, an unsuccessful cloture motion supported by a majority starts a period of "extended debate" in which a senator must seek recognition to speak or the presiding officer announces that cloture is invoked. A later Udall version provided for simple-majority cloture in the event that the original cloture motion received majority support and no senator sought recognition in the period of extended debate. Under these proposals, actions that would give filibustering senators a rest, such as a quorum call, would be barred during the specified debate periods.

In recent years, the purists' proposals for simple-majority cloture have not been given serious consideration. Compromisers' proposals were the basis for the modest reforms adopted in early 2013 (see chapter 6). Republicans questioned Democrats' true motives (such as setting the stage for simple-majority rule) and surely would have filibustered any effort to bring reform resolutions to the floor. Udall, Merkley, and others urged action by getting a ruling that a simple majority can invoke cloture on a change in the rules at the start of a Congress, but that effort was undercut by Majority Leader Harry Reid's willingness to accept a limited set of reforms negotiated with Minority Leader Mitch McConnell.

To further reduce opportunities for delay and obstruction, Congress enacted a proposal on nominations that had surfaced during the Senate's 2010 hearings on filibuster reform. The legislation (S 679) dropped the statutory requirement of Senate confirmation for 169 executive branch positions. This was a very modest step in light of the fact that more than 1,200 positions were subject to confirmation at the time. The measure attracted bipartisan support and was approved by the House and signed by the president in 2012. In addition, by standing order (a rule adopted without formal incorporation into the standing rules), the Senate put 270 positions of only modest importance—members of minor boards, most assistant secretaries, and others—in a new category labeled "privileged nominations." For that category, a streamlined process was created to allow the nominations to go directly to the floor without committee referral unless a senator requested referral.[1]

### *Reform Strategies*

The behavior of senators over the past decade confirms that partisan and ideological interests shape attitudes about the rules. The strongest reformers are liberal Democrats, who emerge when their party is in the majority. The strongest opponents of reform are conservative Republicans, but even they are willing to accept targeted "reforms" and tactical efforts to circumvent filibusters when their party is in the majority.

The primary methods for establishing authoritative procedures are amending the standing rules and establishing precedent (reform-by-ruling). The difficulty of amending Rule XXII has led senators to consider reform-by-ruling strategies, but reform-by-ruling is not the only alternative approach to limiting obstruction to majority-favored legislation. The Senate has accepted statutory provisions that set Senate procedure for a variety of measures. In fact, when the Senate has approved special rules for a particular policy arena, it has generally done so in statute rather than in its standing rules. This warrants a brief discussion.

The justification for statutory procedures is usually that there is a special need for prompt and predictable consideration of a certain type of legislation. In some cases, these procedures are considered to be a vital part of a larger process. Budget measures and trade agreement authority are the best-known types of legislation for which prominent fast-track procedures have been created. But there are many more for which statutory limits on debate have been set (Binder and Smith 1997). Indeed, when first established, the debate limits for many measures were given little attention and were supported without complaint by senators who had vehemently opposed reform of Rule XXII. The need to act has been given priority over minority rights many times.

The Budget Act, like most rulemaking statutes, includes a section called "exercise of rulemaking power" and contains the following provisions:

> (a) The provisions of this title . . . are enacted by the Congress—
>
> (1) as an exercise of the rulemaking power of the House of Representatives and the Senate, respectively, and as such they shall be considered as part of the rules of each House, respectively, or of that House to which they specifically apply, and such rules shall supersede other rules only to the extent that they are inconsistent therewith; and
>
> (2) with full recognition of the constitutional right of either House to change such rules (so far as relating to such House) at any time, in the same manner, and to the same extent as in the case of any other rule of such House.
>
> (b) Any provision of title III or IV [enacting sub-chapters I and II of this chapter] may be waived or suspended in the Senate by a majority vote of the Members voting, a quorum being present, or by the unanimous consent of the Senate. (Title 2, *U.S. Code,* section 621, 2011 edition)

Each house retains its rulemaking authority and can unilaterally modify the statutory provisions affecting it by resolution, but each house treats the provisions of the statute as regular rules until they are changed (Riddick and Frumin 1992).

Under long-standing precedent, procedural rules placed in statutes are not considered to be standing rules of the Senate. This is important. Because statutory rules are not standing rules, the cloture threshold for bills that include such procedural provisions is three-fifths of senators duly chosen and sworn, as it is for other bills. It is *not* two-thirds of senators voting, as it is for measures or motions that amend the standing rules. The barrier is still high, but under Rule XXII and its interpretation, it is easier to invoke cloture on debate limits to be placed in statute than it is on resolutions to change the standing rules. Of course, a bill must also be approved by the House of Representatives and is subject to presidential signature or veto.

For the most part, senators' attitudes about statutory limits on debate have not shown the partisan and ideological motivations that are more central to the consideration of reform of Rule XXII. Instead, institutional motivations have played a role that legislators have frequently expressed. Statutory rules are often associated with efforts to check the exercise of power by the executive branch, as may be delegated to the executive branch in the same statute. In the case of the Budget Act, Congress was responding to the challenges posed by the Nixon administration in managing the budget. The Senate had to be willing, in a fast-track process shared with the House, to allow a majority to pass legislation so that Congress could control annual budgeting.

The typical bill providing for "expedited consideration" involves a delegation of power to the president that is coupled with a review process in Congress (Binder and Smith 1997, 185–94). The model for many statutes has been the executive branch reorganization acts that give the president authority to restructure federal agencies, subject to a possible "resolution of disapproval" that would be privileged and subject to debate limits. The 1939 reorganization act was the first to do this and it incorporated, for the first time, the provision that preserves "the constitutional right of either House to change such rules (so far as relating to such House) at any time, in the same manner, and to the same extent as in the case of any other rule of such House." Numerous statutes that provide for resolutions of approval or disapproval provide for debate limits.

The delegation of power to the executive branch has often been controversial and has produced partisan and ideological divisions among senators. When controversy has arisen about the fast-track process for considering resolutions of approval or disapproval, the ban on floor amendments has been controversial far more frequently than the limitation on debate. In most cases, guaranteeing a vote has been viewed as essential to enabling the Senate to check the exercise of power delegated to the president.[2]

## THOUGHTS ABOUT THE REFORMS OF EARLY 2013

With bipartisan support, two resolutions were adopted in January 2013 to address majority and minority party concerns about Senate floor procedure. Even with the new precedent on nominations adopted in late 2013, these reforms remained in place. One resolution changed the Senate's rules in two ways:

1. The three motions to go to conference (to disagree with the House or insist on the Senate version, to request or agree to a request for a conference, and to appoint conferees) are combined into one motion. Cloture on the new motion is subject to a two-hour debate limit and no post-cloture debate on the new motion is allowed.
2. A cloture motion on a motion to proceed that is signed by the majority leader, minority leader, and at least seven members of each party comes to a vote on the following day (as opposed to the second day for other cloture motions), and, if such a cloture motion is adopted, a vote occurs on the motion to proceed without further debate.

Neither change to the standing rules significantly limits the ability of the minority to filibuster. The conference provision streamlines action when cloture can be invoked. Before the change, a minority could filibuster each of the three conference motions and force lengthy post-cloture debate on each one. The conference provision limits the ability to filibuster to the new conference motion and bars post-cloture debate. However, multiple cloture votes at the stage of going to conference have not been common. In the 112th Congress (2011–2012), no cloture votes were taken on one of the three conference motions. Far more common are cloture votes on House amendments to Senate bills and conference reports, which are not affected by the rule.

Cloture motions are very seldom signed by both floor leaders, so the effect of the second change depends on a change in behavior. Until the new rule was adopted, the majority leader could count on getting the requisite number of signatures for a cloture petition (sixteen) from members of his own party with little difficulty. The majority leader now has a new reason to request the signature of minority party members. At this writing, it is too early to determine whether this will change behavior so that expedited action on a motion to proceed can be realized from time to time.

A second reform resolution took the form of a standing order that expires at the end of the Congress (the 113th Congress), although it can be renewed in the next Congress. The resolution had three major provisions:

1. Debate on a motion to proceed is limited to four hours. This bars filibusters on the motion to proceed.
2. Four amendments are guaranteed for every measure following adoption of the motion to proceed, in order: a minority amendment, a majority amendment, a minority amendment, and a majority amendment. If an amendment is not offered, the opportunity is lost, but these four amendments are guaranteed even if cloture is invoked.
3. Executive branch nominations, except for the top positions, are subject to eight hours of post-cloture debate; district court nominations are subject to two hours of post-cloture debate. Other nominations, those for top executive and judicial posts, are subject to the standard limit of thirty hours of post-cloture debate.

These temporary reforms are potentially more important than the changes to the standing rules. The debate limits on motions to proceed and post-cloture consideration of nominations represent a minority concession to the majority, while the guarantee of amendments is a majority concession to the minority. The two sides, with the exception of the most conservative Republicans, viewed this as a fair compromise, although both sides realized that it was an experimental arrangement that might not be renewed in the next Congress.

Each of the three parts of the standing order deserves comment. Motions to proceed have become a frequent target of cloture petitions. It has been common in recent Congresses for 40 percent of all cloture motions to concern a motion to proceed. Majority leaders and reformers have made several related arguments about limiting debate on the motion to proceed. First, by getting debate on a measure underway without a filibuster, it has been argued, momentum for a measure will develop and make it more costly for senators to kill a measure by filibuster. Second, some reformers have argued that a filibuster of a bill or nomination is more visible and therefore subjects obstructionists to more public pressure than a filibuster of a motion to proceed. Finally, it is observed that holds, which target the motion to proceed, will be undermined by allowing majority votes and reducing the majority's reliance on unanimous consent to bring up legislation and nominations.

These hopes that limiting debate on the motion to proceed will have a leavening effect on Senate proceedings seem overly optimistic. Reformers would find it difficult to identify legislation killed by filibuster of motions to proceed in recent Congresses that would have survived if the motion to proceed had been readily adopted. They have cited none. Moreover, nominations have not required a motion to proceed and yet frequently generate holds and obstruction. It is hard to argue that obstruction has been caused by the ability of minority senators to hide behind a procedural motion. They have been quite willing to openly delay and block legislation.

The guarantee of amendments reduces the leverage that a majority leader gains from filling the amendment tree. Using this guarantee wisely, the minority can get a vote on its highest-priority amendments. The amendments are subject to a point of order, as any amendment would be, but in the absence of cloture, they guarantee the minority the right to raise nongermane and irrelevant matters as amendments and to get a vote on them. This may prove to be a more important concession to minority Republicans than some Democrats realized.

The most obvious feature of the 2013 reforms is that the minority can still filibuster. A filibuster can be conducted to block action on a bill or nomination, an amendment, a motion to go to conference, or a conference report or House amendment. Limiting post-cloture debate on motions to proceed, motions to go to conference, and minor nominations will speed floor action from time to time, but the net effect depends on the minority's behavior. If the minority chooses to filibuster more often or, in the case of minor nominations, to insist on post-cloture debate more frequently, the expected efficiencies may not be realized.

## THOUGHTS ABOUT 2013

As the Reid-McConnell-Levin rules were being adopted in early 2013, the leading reformers appeared to be skeptical that the reforms would be adequate. Reid's rationale held out hope that a new balance between majority rule and minority obstruction had been found that did not insist on the right of a simple majority to change the rules. For a time in 2012, Reid seemed to have concluded otherwise, but in early 2013 he returned to the theme of restoration—returning the Senate to its mid-twentieth-century form, when obstructionism was limited even with a high threshold for cloture. In the deeply polarized Senate of his time, many members of his party and outside liberals were not persuaded by Reid's view.

Reid's frustration with Republican obstruction of his legislation and nominations soon returned. By May 2013, he was convinced that the second Obama administration would be undermined by delays in Senate action on important executive branch nominations and threatened a reform-by-ruling move patterned after Frisk's threat on judicial nominations in 2005. In July, Reid's deadline for moving the nominations to a vote, the Republicans relented and Reid set aside his threat for the time being. The details are discussed in chapter 6. There are several issues lingering from the mid-2013 episode that warrant close attention.

Some observers were puzzled by the outcome. With the Democrats seemingly united behind Reid's threat, why did they fail to impose reform, at least for executive nominations, and accept the Republican offer to allow the controversial nominations to come to a vote? The most important part of the answer is that the Democrats who supported Reid's threat were doing so for a variety of reasons. Most Democrats may have favored reform, and many of them supported even more radical reform, but they probably did not constitute a majority of the Senate without the support of a few Democrats who wanted to use the threat of reform only for the purpose of gaining the Republican concessions that were obtained. This latter group, which included Reid, was essential to Reid's leverage but also pivotal to pursuing reforms in both early and mid-2013.

Perhaps Democrats were concerned by the retaliation that Republicans promised if Reid pulled the "nuclear option trigger." Again, Democrats did not seem to share a single view of the matter. Reformers long believed that the threat of retaliation, which would take the form of demanding more votes and more filibusters to slow Senate action even more, was either not credible or not worth the price. At least a few Democrats, most notably Levin, remained silent during the events of mid-2013 but had long expressed concerns about the damaging effects of the retaliatory moves that could be expected and the deepened partisanship that would result. Even if the Republican leadership would continue to be selective in obstructing the majority party, rank-and-file conservative firebrands would lose any remaining self-restraint and force the Senate to a standstill. These Democrats may have been pivotal.

Republicans, too, were not monolithic in their response. John McCain (R-AZ) and a few other Republicans conceded that their party had gone too far in blocking action on nominations, feared that their party's reputation was becoming too radically conservative, declared that they wanted to forestall Reid's reform-by-ruling move, took the lead away from McConnell in negotiating with Reid, and arranged for votes on the contested nominations. McCain needed only about a half dozen Republicans to back him up to make a credible claim that cloture would be possible on the nominations, and he appeared to have about that much support. McConnell soon reported that he could have cut a better deal for his party than the one negotiated by McCain, a view that appears to have been shared by many other Republicans.

Thus, while the Senate of early and mid-2013 was a remarkably polarized body, it is unwise to treat either party conference as homogeneous in its views of the best strategy. At least a handful of senators of both parties were critical to getting more radical elements to back away from a procedural showdown. A majority of senators, nearly all of them Democrats, were willing to impose reform, but a few of them seemed to do so only for tactical reasons. A small number of Republicans, all that were needed, promised votes on the nominations. The Senate returned to the status quo ante, with only executive nominations temporarily spared the consequences of the Senate syndrome.

As we have seen, attention quickly turned to judicial nominations. It is not clear why the peacemakers—McCain, Alexander, Schumer, and others—proved weak later in 2013 when the nuclear option was employed after obstructed votes on judicial nominations. Several factors may have been at work. On the side of the majority party Democrats, the patience of Reid and others seemed to be exhausted after several rounds of crisis management over blocked nominations. By moving within two days after the third of three circuit court nominations failed to gain cloture, they left little time for a negotiated settlement. They were not persuaded that Republican threats of retaliatory obstruction would be any worse than what they were already experiencing. And some of them were now persuaded that the Republicans would not hesitate to limit filibustering by a point of order if their party won a Senate majority in the 2014 elections.

On the side of the minority party Republicans, there may have been a stronger commitment to blocking judicial nominations than there had been to blocking executive nominations early in the year. Judicial appointments involve lifetime tenure. In this case, the appointments were to the D.C. circuit court, a court particularly important to Republicans because it oversees most cases that emerge from the regulatory and rulemaking activity of the federal government. Of course, Republicans may have miscalculated, thinking that Reid still did not have a majority to back a point of order. Miscalculation is likely when the leaders are plotting strategies against each other and sharing little information about the business of the Senate.

## REVERSIBILITY

I have emphasized a series of factors that have shaped senators' procedural strategies and contributed to the emergence of the Senate syndrome:

- inherited rules—supermajority cloture enables minority obstruction and facilitates limited majority responses;
- the distribution of senators' policy positions—polarized majority and minority coalitions are motivated to fully exploit their procedural prerogatives;
- the relationship between policy positions and party affiliation—polarized parties will have leaders who coordinate and maintain procedural strategies;
- the size of the two parties—a small majority party is readily obstructed by a large minority party;
- electoral competitiveness—the minority party has reason to believe that denying success to the majority will contribute to gaining majority party status;
- outside demands—organized interests will pressure senators to exploit their procedural prerogatives; and
- learning—senators continue to use procedural tactics once they are invented and prove successful.

Sharply polarized parties, with a broadened range of procedural tactics and pushed by outside groups, threaten majority rule and produce stalemate. Whenever a large minority considers passing no legislation to be better than the other party's legislation, stalemate is the outcome. Even on legislation that the minority party will let pass, the minority party is motivated to slow action in order to make the Senate consume time that might allow more of the majority party's agenda to reach the floor, to show that the majority party cannot govern by delaying action, and to embarrass majority party senators with difficult votes on amendments. The majority party responds when it can by avoiding floor debate and amendments. Mutual resentment builds as each side, with cause, assumes that the other side will fully exploit its parliamentary rights in the legislative fight. Move and countermove, the 60-vote threshold, and mutual partisan distrust become customary. It gets reported that way by the media and loses its newsworthiness, so the majority finds itself without a way to register blame and even suffers in public opinion for its lack of action on legislation.

Not everyone considers procedural entanglements and legislative stalemate to be dysfunctional. To the contrary, as I emphasize in chapter 8, the minority party has recently argued that its part in the entanglement is both the empirical and prescriptive norm. In its view, it is behaving as it *ought* to be and as the other party did when it was in the majority. More than a little inconsistently, minority party senators have also argued that the extraordinary steps taken by the majority necessitate an extraordinary response.

The ability of the senators to reverse course and reduce the severity of the Senate syndrome is an open question. Can senators overcome their circumstances and bring a new attitude to Senate proceedings? Will the conditions that generate powerful incentives for senators to behave as they do change in the foreseeable future?

In chapter 8, I address the question of whether senators and leaders are the problem. My conclusion is that it is unrealistic to expect the parties to call a truce unless they are forced to do so by internal factions. There is no neutral outcome for polarized parties, and neither party wants to unilaterally disarm. In any case, in recent decades, senators have expressed deep and genuine concern about the incentives for "abusing" the procedural prerogatives they enjoy, and they have managed only the most modest changes in rules or practice.

The hope that senators can save themselves continues. The Reid-McConnell agreements in 2011 and 2013 reflected this sentiment. As we have seen, Reid considered the 2011 agreement to be dead before the year ended. The next year, anticipating that his party would regain a Senate majority in the 2012 elections, McConnell is reported to have promised his party conference "to let the Senate operate in the way it was intended to operate" (Dennis 2012). The problem for any majority leader is that he cannot control the behavior of the opposition, and in the heat of battles over important legislation, fellow partisans will not allow him to unilaterally disarm.

Richard Fenno, perhaps the most prominent scholar of congressional politics in the late twentieth century, hypothesized that frequent changes in majority control of Congress would lessen partisanship (Fenno 1982). The experience of serving in the majority and then in the minority in rapid succession would keep each party anticipating a change in roles, moderate each party's parliamentary tactics, and civilize congressional proceedings. In the early 1980s, after more than a quarter century of one-party rule in both houses, that appeared to be a viable hypothesis.

The Senate (and the House, for that matter) has not behaved as Fenno predicted. To the contrary, since the early 1980s, majority control has changed hands more frequently, but, if anything, the civility of congressional policy making has declined. The competitiveness of the parties, which has been associated with a polarized Congress and a polarized electorate, may have generated party strategies that are less compromising. In fact, as I detail in chapter 5, much of the change in strategies is deliberate and tied to the goal of majority control of Congress.

Political scientists are more likely to place hope in the natural cycle of partisan politics to provide the necessary and only effective correction for the Senate syndrome. This is a reasonable hypothesis. If the coalitions of voters who nominate and elect senators evolve away from the quite polarized pattern we have witnessed in the last two decades, more moderates are likely to be elected and more heterogeneous and less polarized Senate parties will emerge. Minority obstructionism and majority restrictiveness will generate loud protests within the respective parties and temper the strategies that party leaders pursue. Appealing to pivotal senators to create the necessary majorities for cloture and passage will entail more cross-party bargaining and compromise.

This view of Senate politics may be too sanguine. The Senate's track record is that senators do not voluntarily give up use of procedural strategies once invented and deployed. Moreover, individual senators and factions, particularly on the minority side, have shown a willingness to exploit parliamentary procedure in ways that a floor leader has hesitated to do. The incentives for senators to show commitment to the causes of important constituencies will remain strong. The individualism that emerged in the 1960s and 1970s did not disappear and may become even stronger if party leaders assume a somewhat less central role in the process.

## CAN MAJORITY RULE AND SUPERMAJORITY CLOTURE COEXIST?

The genius of the Senate, in the view of many senators and outsiders, is the protection of minority rights with supermajority cloture. Even compromising reformers articulate a defense of the Senate as a special institution when they insist that they want to restore some balance between majority rule and minority rights. They want minority obstruction to be rare rather than common.

Most recent reformers, whom I label compromisers above, are not very specific about the place in history to which they would like to see the Senate practices restored. Many of them point to the mid-twentieth century, when filibusters were rare and seemed to be reserved for the most important issues. This wish reflects self-deception or ignorance. Most of the reformers are liberals who surely would not like to return to the Senate of the mid-twentieth century. After the New Deal, conservatives dominated the Senate and managed to keep a great deal of legislation bottled up in committee and off the floor—and therefore free of filibusters. Liberals of that era were at least as agitated as today's reformers about how parliamentary procedure was used to block action on their legislation.

The compromising reformers' search for a new balance between majority rule and supermajority cloture is likely to fail. As long as there are senators who are willing to exploit the fact that there is a higher threshold for cloture than for passing a bill, compromisers will continue to be frustrated with the rules. After all, the strong incentives for delay and obstruction that are generated in modern American politics are likely to remain even after the passing of our current period of deeply polarized parties.

The search for a new balance may have another motivation. Many senators, I suspect, also want to preserve the personal leverage that comes with the ability to threaten obstruction or delay. They do not like to make their personal privileges the focus of public debate about their institution and so defend their procedural preferences in terms of the public interest and institutional traditions. The influence of concerns about personal power on attitudes about Senate procedure is impossible to gauge. Concerns about personal power surely help motivate the search for compromise solutions to the Senate syndrome.

In the context of modern American politics, it is unrealistic to expect that majority rule and supermajority cloture can coexist in a way that satisfies a large majority of senators and avoids the Senate syndrome. Constituent pressure, organized interests, electoral pressures, media attention, and personal ambitions induce legislators to take advantage of their parliamentary prerogatives. Even top party leaders cannot stem the tide of individual and factional exploitation of Senate rules. Partisanship may subside, but unlearning how to use the process to the advantage of one interest or another is not going to happen.

At this writing, in late 2013, reformers seem to be edging toward the view that they have to make a choice between majority rule and supermajority cloture. For some of them, the modest reforms of January 2013 and the precedent of November 2013 already seem inadequate, as the 60-vote threshold appears to be assumed for just as many important measures as before. Agitation for additional action can be heard.

## CONCLUDING THOUGHTS

Writing in the late 1980s, I distinguished between debate and deliberation and argued that the House and Senate showed a rhetorical commitment to different rationales for legislative decision making (Smith 1989, 236–46). Debate is an argumentative oratorical contest between legislators with opposing and established views, while deliberation involves sharing and discovering ideas about how to define problems and solutions. Debate is intended to lead to a vote and a majority winner; deliberation involves mutual education with the goal of consensus. Members of the House hope for effective debate about defined alternatives in a structured, time-limited setting, but one that gives the minority meaningful opportunities to debate and offer amendments. Senators articulate the value of deliberation in a free-wheeling discussion that, most of the time, allows discussion and proposals on any subject from any senator without a standard limit on debate or the content of amendments.

In recent decades, each house has failed to live up to its ideals as the polarization of the parties has intensified its acquired procedural tendencies. In the House, the majority party wins a battle of wills. It uses restrictive standing and special rules to carefully limit debate and amendments and has become aggressive in its use of restrictive procedures in the last two decades. The House minority has had no effective response.

In the Senate, the minority party has become much more aggressive in its obstructionism and the majority has struggled to respond. The majority party has an effective response only when it has 60 votes for cloture. Nevertheless, whether it wins or not, the majority party seeks to limit the political inconveniences generated by a minority that stands in the way of pursuing the majority's agenda and offers numerous unfriendly and often dilatory amendments.

In both houses, highly partisan policy-making processes take key decisions out of committee rooms and place them in the hands of central leaders, who are expected to devise legislative and political strategies for their parties. Individual legislators find that their influence is reduced and must be channeled through party organs and factions. More decisions are wrapped into omnibus measures or guided by budget deals that are negotiated by party leaders.

The issue of accountability separates the two houses and remains a serious concern for the Senate. The responsibility of the House majority party for that chamber's agenda and most outcomes is plain. At times, divided party control of the House, Senate, and White House creates problems for assigning responsibility for policy outcomes, but for the House the responsibility is reasonably clear.

Attributing credit and blame is often difficult for the Senate. A common pattern is that the Senate majority party leadership complains about obstruction, delays, and undesirable compromises forced by the minority, while the minority complains about the majority's uncompromising stance and procedural unfairness. The public is left with partisan spin, news reports that provide an inadequate basis for determining what happened, and little basis for judging the responsibility of the two parties for outcomes. The Senate syndrome, which makes this pattern a weekly phenomenon, makes it even more challenging to hold Senate parties accountable for their behavior.

# NOTES

## CHAPTER 1

1. S. Res. 4, 113th Congress, with chief sponsors Tom Udall (D-NM), Jeff Merkley (D-OR), and Tom Harkin (D-IA), and fifteen additional cosponsors.

2. S. Res. 15 and 16, 113th Congress. The details of the 2013 reforms are provided in chapters 6 and 7.

3. I thank Gregory Koger for his data. See Koger (2010) for a description of the method by which filibusters were identified. The correlation between the number of filibusters in Koger's count and the number of cloture motions filed is 0.75.

4. Using the relative size of the parties yields results similar to those produced by the measure used here.

5. The literature on the polarization and partisanship in the American electorate and activist community is too vast to cite here. Good places to start are Abramowitz (2010), Sinclair (2006), and Theriault (2008).

## CHAPTER 2

1. The Vandenberg ruling was appealed to the Senate by Robert Taft (R-OH), the leading Republican of the Senate. Vandenberg and Taft led different factions among Senate Republicans.

2. In some quarters, Nixon's motives were suspect. He could anticipate facing Johnson in the 1960 presidential contest and might benefit from being perceived to be on the side of civil rights (*New York Times,* January 2, 1957, 20) while facing an opposing party divided on the issue. His opinion, as well reasoned as it was, might be viewed as exploiting an opportunity to deepen the divide between the liberal and conservative wings of the Democratic party.

3. "All around Robin Hood's barn" is a now-dated idiom that refers to moving by an indirect or circuitous route.

## CHAPTER 3

1. Southerners are senators from the former confederate states plus Kentucky, Tennessee, and Texas, consistent with the traditional measures of the conservative coalition by Congressional Quarterly.

2. We cannot rule out some strategic behavior among senators. It seems likely that some senators wanted to block reform, which could be accomplished by tabling the submitted constitutional question, but then appear to be supportive of reform on cloture.

3. Information about holds is available only in party and leader records. The records of only two floor leaders provide reasonably comprehensive accounts of holds, and both are Republicans—Howard Baker and Bob Dole. See Evans, Lipinski, and Larson (2003), Evans and Lipinski (2005), and Howard and Roberts (2012). The study shows that holds are more common in the minority party but more effective in the majority party.

4. Holds became a regular subject of complaints from majority leaders, bill managers, and other senators. For a sampling of floor discussion, see *Congressional Record,* April 17, 2002, S2850; *Congressional Record,* December 9, 1987, 34449; *Congressional Record,* February 20, 1986, S1465.

5. It also is noteworthy that unanimous consent agreements have often included a provision that provides for a vote "in relation to" an amendment. The Senate has used this language to allow an amendment to be subject to a motion to table. That many time agreements with this form gain unanimous consent suggests that amendment sponsors do not believe that the outcomes on their amendments are likely to be affected by the use of a motion to table. The "in relation to" clause is unnecessary in most unanimous consent agreements providing for a certain time for a vote on an amendment. Thus, in recent years, when a larger proportion of amendments has been accommodated in unanimous consent agreements, the motion to table has appeared less frequently (see chapter 6).

6. An amendment to a treaty, if approved by the Senate, changes the text of the treaty and requires that the treaty be renegotiated with the foreign country. A reservation, which is far more common than an amendment, is a recommendation to modify the treaty that takes the form of an amendment to the resolution of ratification. In practice, few reservations result in renegotiated treaty provisions.

7. Votes for which the minority is less than 10 percent are excluded. This excludes a considerable number of amendment votes that receive no opposition.

8. Titles I-IX of the Congressional Budget and Impoundment Control Act of 1974.

9. The process usually takes longer than twenty hours because motions and amendments may be voted on without debate at the end of the period, yielding what has been labeled a "vote-a-rama" as the last step in considering a budget measure.

10. For background on the Byrd rule, including a review of points of order and waivers considered under the rule, see Keith (2008). Also see chapter 5.

11. The enlarged liberal contingent targeted Senate committee practices for reform, which paralleled a more extensive effort in the House. Liberal Democrats also pushed Senate rules to open meetings to the public, a party conference rule to subject committee chairs to a secret ballot vote in the conference, and a rule to allow rank-and-file senators to appoint additional staff to assist them with committee work. Other developments contributed to the sense of a new era in the Senate. A special committee was appointed to investigate the Central Intelligence Agency, which was considered to reflect a lack of confidence in the standing committee chairman, John Stennis (D-MS), with jurisdiction over the matter. Liberals were named to the Democratic Steering Committee, which made committee assignments, to give them the opportunity to fill vacancies with friendly colleagues.

12. The motion was offered by Senator James Pearson (R-KS):

> I move that the Senate proceed to the consideration of Calendar item No. 1, Senate Resolution 4, amending rule XXII of the Standing Rules of the Senate with respect to limitation of debate; and that under article I, section 5, of the U.S. Constitution, I move that debate upon the pending motion to proceed to the consideration of Senate Resolution 4 be brought to a close by the Chair immediately putting this motion to end debate to the Senate for a year-and-nay [*sic*] vote; and, upon the adoption therefor by a majority of those Senators present and voting, a quorum being present, the Chair shall immediately thereafter put to the Senate, without further debate, the question on the adoption of the pending motion to proceed to the consideration of Senate Resolution 4. (*Congressional Record*, February 20, 1975, 3835)

13. Mansfield made similar comments a year earlier, also in response to Allen's tactics (*Congressional Record*, July 18, 1975, 23597).

14. Allen died of an apparent heart attack on June 1, 1978, at age sixty-five. See Farber (1978).

15. In the case of the House of Representatives, scholars have argued that resolving the most important procedural matters within

the majority party is the mark of a mature "cartel" (Jenkins and Stewart 2012). Plainly, a central feature of Senate parliamentary procedure, arguably its most distinctive and important feature, was not left to be decided internally by the majority party. Repeatedly, over a generation, an important division among Democrats spilled onto the Senate floor and was resolved again and again with clear winners and losers with the party. A complicating factor in the Senate is that the majority party does not control the identity of the presiding officer. The vice president and Senate majority may not share the same party label, so entrusting the presiding officer to execute the will of the party is unwise. The majority party must instead work through its floor leader to influence the agenda. The right of first recognition is a precedent vital to this potential influence, but even this right does not automatically produce a vote on most motions that a majority leader may make.

## CHAPTER 4

1. The 1970s carpet was replaced in the 1980s with another blue carpet with a more formal design that included red and white emblems and small gold crosslets. The same design was used in a new carpet installed in 2012.

2. Personal correspondence, Martin Paone, Democratic floor aide in the 1980s and 1990s.

3. See chapter 8 of Abourezk (1989) for his description of the events of 1977.

4. Rule XXII, Paragraph 2, provided (and still provides) that "no dilatory motion, or dilatory amendment, or amendment not germane shall be in order. Points of order, including questions of relevancy, and appeals from the decision of the Presiding Officer, shall be decided without debate."

5. A ruling a few days earlier provided that amendments to the bill, considered after cloture was invoked on the substitute to the bill, were considered under the post-cloture provisions of Rule XXII even when the cloture petition applied to the substitute to the bill. If the motion to adopt the substitute failed, cloture would end and further consideration of the bill for amendment would continue without cloture until an additional cloture motion was adopted.

6. These "reform-by-ruling" episodes set precedents relevant to the judicial nominations crisis of 2005 (Binder, Madonna, and Smith 2007; Gold and Gupta 2004; Wawro and Schickler 2006). See chapter 5.

7. This approach is implied in Rule XXII(1), which lists a motion to "proceed to the consideration of executive business" but does

not mention a motion to go directly to a particular treaty or nomination on the Executive Calendar.

8. The House began televising its floor proceedings in 1979. Fenno's (1989) account of the debate over Senate television deserves the attention of every serious student of congressional politics. I draw from Fenno's account, news accounts, and the floor debates.

9. A compromise version applied the two-thirds rule for overriding the presiding officer only when the germaneness requirement was imposed by itself (but not after cloture was invoked).

10. The debate is in the *Congressional Record,* February 26, 1986, 2832–43.

11. On holds, see Evans and Lipinski (2005), Hook (1993), Oleszek (2007), Sinclair (1989), and Smith (1989).

12. Ehrenhalt (1982). Also on Metzenbaum, see Calmes (1987).

13. Personal correspondence, August 23, 2012.

14. Byrd made these remarks, which are widely and imprecisely cited, at an orientation of new senators in 1996.

## CHAPTER 5

1. Quoted in Elving (1988). Partisanship also had sharpened in the House of Representatives in the short speakership of Jim Wright (D-TX), who left the speakership after Representative Newt Gingrich (R-GA) initiated ethics charges against him.

2. In addition, concern about Boren's weak support for his party on a number of budget and other issues was reported to have limited his persuasiveness with party colleagues on procedural reforms. See Hook (1993).

3. The practice is described by Martin Paone, former Democratic party secretary, in Paone (2009–2010).

4. Martin Paone, personal correspondence, March 14, 2012.

5. For background, see Rovner (1990).

6. See comments by Majority Leader Trent Lott, *Congressional Record,* April 12, 2000, 5369. Lott's party secretary, Elizabeth Letchworth, reported that "the practice of allowing alternative amendments on a specific subject actually began in the 80s and into the 90s and could be called alternative amendments. You are correct, the practice morphed into being called side-by-sides by Senator Lott for the reason you stated" (personal correspondence, March 15, 2012).

7. In this case, opponents to the amendment indicated their willingness to block a vote, resulting in a stalemate—Craig lacked 60 votes for cloture on his amendment and Democrats lacked 60 votes for cloture on the bill. The bill never passed and Interior

appropriations were incorporated in a series of continuing resolutions.

8. Billy Dale was the director of the White House Travel Office through the Reagan and Bush administrations and was acquitted on charges of embezzlement in 1995.

9. *Riddick's Senate Procedure* is the authoritative source for precedents. See Palmer (2007).

10. More complex trees are possible, depending on the nature of the first amendment. In some cases, up to five amendments may be pending, but seldom does the majority leader use more complex amendment trees.

11. Episodes of the amendment tree being filled are reported in C. Davis (2011).

12. *Congressional Record,* April 29, 1999, S4332. See Senator Arlen Specter's comments in 1993 (*Congressional Record,* April 3, 1993, S4244–45).

13. For background, see Taylor (2000c).

14. See Hook (1993), Doherty (1998), Eisele and Kelly (1998), Friel (2007), and Pierce (2007).

15. For a review of leaders' efforts and reform proposals, see Oleszek (2007). I am ignoring the practices of the Senate Committee on the Judiciary with respect to blue slips and holds on judicial nominations that are registered with the committee. See Binder and Maltzman (2009) and Palmer (2005).

16. A provision is considered to be extraneous if it falls under one or more of the following six definitions: (1) it does not produce a change in outlays or revenues; (2) it produces an outlay increase or revenue decrease when the instructed committee is not in compliance with its instructions; (3) it is outside the jurisdiction of the committee that submitted the title or provision for inclusion in the reconciliation measure; (4) it produces a change in outlays or revenues that is merely incidental to the nonbudgetary components of the provision; (5) it would increase the deficit for a fiscal year beyond the "budget window" covered by the reconciliation measure; or (6) it recommends changes in Social Security.

17. Cohen (1993), Hager (1993), Jacoby (1993). In 1994, House Democrats agitated for changes in the Byrd rule so that it would not apply to conference reports. Nothing came of their efforts (Jacoby 1994).

18. In both cases, the bills included sunset provisions to avoid violating the Byrd rule for reducing revenues in "out years" beyond the formal scope of the bills.

19. With a Republican vice president as the tie-breaking vote, the Republicans assumed majority status for purposes of organizing the Senate in early 2001.

20. Senate Republicans successfully included the provision for the use of reconciliation for ANWR in the 2005 budget resolution, and authorizing legislation was included in the Senate version of the reconciliation bill. The provision was dropped at the insistence of the House.

21. For a description of the budget reconciliation process, see Heniff (2010b). The term "vote-a-rama" appears to have been coined by Keith Hennessey, an aide to the Senate Budget Committee and later the Republican floor leader. See Hennessey (2012).

22. Time to vote and to read amendments is not counted against the time limits.

23. Some years did not have a budget resolution or reconciliation bill. The figure includes amendments subject to a voice vote, roll-call vote, or unanimous consent as the method of disposition.

24. For background on the 1997 reform effort, see the testimony of G. William Hoagland, a Budget Committee and majority leader (Hoagland 2011).

25. See Binder (2012) for a review of arguments about trends in judicial confirmation politics.

26. "Acrimony over Judges" (2005). Also see Koger (2008).

27. S. Res. 138, 108th Congress.

28. Frist made many such comments. See, for example, Babington (2005). For more background, see Binder, Madonna, and Smith (2007).

29. In 2013, the Senate combined the three motions to go to conference into one motion. The change in the standing rule was a part of a negotiated package of reforms that are discussed in chapter 6.

## CHAPTER 6

1. "Stimulus Bill" (2009). In a 2010 case, Reid filled the tree on a defense authorization bill that included a provision that repealed the "don't ask, don't tell" (DADT) policy on gays in the military. Republicans opposed the DADT language and several other provisions and prevented cloture from being invoked on the motion to proceed to consideration of the bill. In this case, the DADT language had the support of more than 60 senators—so at least a few Republicans supported it but still voted against cloture. Reid then substituted the DADT language for the text of an unrelated small business bill that the House had passed, gained cloture,

and gained House support for the amended bill. See "'Don't Ask, Don't Tell'" (2011).

2. A few, but very few, precedents have been found in previous Congresses. Beth et al. (2009) find nine votes under the terms of such a unanimous consent agreement in the 109th Congress and a surge to 51 such votes in the 110th Congress.

3. Of the 103 votes, 38 were on the adoption of amendments.

4. Senator Diane Feinstein (D-CA) complained:

> I want to briefly comment on procedure. I very much regret that this amendment faces a 60-vote threshold when the other two amendments relating to telecom immunity face majority votes. Clearly, someone was afraid this might get a majority vote and, therefore, they put on a 60-vote requirement. This, I believe, is prejudicial, and it places a higher burden on this amendment. And the irony is, this amendment could be an acceptable solution for the other House, which has passed a bill that doesn't contain any provisions for immunity and has said they would not provide any provision for immunity. This is the way to handle that particular issue. (*Congressional Record,* February 11, 2008, S831–32)

Feinstein's amendment was rejected. Several other amendments were subject to a 60-vote threshold the next day.

5. The Honest Leadership and Open Government Act of 2007 (P. L. 110-81), Section 512.

6. In late 2009, the watchdog group Citizens for Responsibility and Ethics in Washington wrote the leadership of the Senate Committee on Ethics to investigate the enforcement of Section 512. It is noteworthy that Section 512 is directed to the floor leaders. Section 512 becomes relevant only when an objection to a unanimous consent request is voiced on the floor, but that hardly exhausts the ways in which a hold can affect floor action. See Yachnin (2009). There is some evidence that Section 512 stigmatized holds and may have reduced their frequency, at least at first.

7. S. Res. 28, 112-1, January 27, 2011. The new rule is a standing order that continues from one Congress to the next.

8. "Energy Overhaul" (2006). In 2006, differences among Republicans, along with no plans for additional tax cuts, killed any hope of House and Senate approval of a budget resolution. The Senate's budget resolution again provided for ANWR drilling authorization, but the budget resolution died when House and Senate leaders did not name a conference. See "GOP Splits Sink Budget Resolution" (2007).

9. Jansen (2009), Rybicki (2010). 111th Congress counted by the author.

10. In January 2007, the House of Representatives adopted a new rule that required conference committees to be open to all conferees.

11. It also bears notice that the Senate rules limiting a conference report to the scope of the differences between the House and Senate versions of a bill and being available online for forty-eight hours before a floor vote do not apply to amendments between the houses (Beth et al. 2009). It also is noteworthy that Senate Republicans adopted a standing order as a part of a 1996 bill that provided that conference reports were not required to be read. House amendments were not exempt, so a reading of an amendment could consume considerable time.

## CHAPTER 8

1. Common space scores, which give each legislator a single score for his or her career, show very similar patterns.

2. The Gingrich senators were much more conservative than House Republicans who made a similar move in the 1970s or early 1980s, and they proved more conservative than Republicans entering the Senate from outside of Congress. Democrats from the House who made the move in the 1990s and thereafter were just slightly more liberal on average than their predecessors.

3. See "Sen. Reid" (2011).

## CHAPTER 9

1. Two Republicans, Maine's Susan Collins and Olympia Snowe, voted with most Democrats; Democrats Mark Begich of Alaska, Mary Landrieu of Louisiana, Ben Nelson of Nebraska, and Jim Webb of Virginia voted with the rest of the Republicans.

2. Fallows frequently blogged about the issue on *The Atlantic* website. See http://www.theatlantic.com/james-fallows.

3. The full question: "As it turns out, the filibuster is a means by which a minority of Senators can extend debate endlessly and thereby prevent a vote on an issue in the Senate. In general, what's your opinion of allowing the minority to block a vote on a piece of legislation?" Responses: strongly approve, approve, disapprove, strongly disapprove.

4. The number of respondents was 701 (a random sample of the July 2009 respondents). All figures were weighted by the Current Population Survey (CPS).

5. Figure 8.1 shows the distributions for the two questions for Group 1. The distributions for the other groups are very similar.

6. For example, logit estimates for the effects of filibuster attitude (F) and party identification (P) on the Senate vote (party of

candidate) are: Vote = .006(F) + .355(P), with t values of 0.28 for F and 19.12 for P (weighted by the CPS, $n = 433$). Source: 2009 telephone survey conducted by Abt/SRBI for the author.

## CHAPTER 10

1. For a recent exposition of this view, see Chafetz (2011). For the case for the constitutionality of the filibuster, see Gerhardt (2004).

2. Udall (2011). For a more complete legal argument, see P. Bruhl (2010).

3. It should be noted that Tiefer (2007) disapproved of the precedent that Frist advocated.

4. Reid said that the Gang of 14 memorandum "took the nuclear option off the table" (*Congressional Record,* May 24, 2005, S5817). Senator David Pryor (D-AR), a member of the Gang of 14, used Reid's phrase the next day: "Basically, we were able to take the nuclear option off the table." See Brand (2005).

## CHAPTER 11

1. S. Res. 116, 112th Congress. For background on the confirmation procedure, see Rybicki (2011).

2. The most recent proposal for an expedited process came from House Republicans, who were looking for ways to guarantee Senate action on a House-passed tax bill. In late 2012, as part of a tax bill that passed the Republican House but was not considered in the Democratic Senate, House Republicans proposed a fast-track process for considering tax legislation in 2013 (H. R. 6169, 212th Congress). The proposal allowed for debate (and therefore a filibuster) on the bill, but the bill provided for a nondebatable motion to proceed, debate limits and a germaneness requirement for amendments, and automatic approval of motions to go to conference.

# REFERENCES


Abourezk, James G. 1989. *Advice and Dissent: Memoirs of South Dakota and the U.S. Senate.* Chicago: Lawrence Hill Books.

Abramowitz, Alan. 2010. *The Disappearing Center: Engaged Citizens, Polarization, and American Democracy.* New Haven, CT: Yale University Press.

"Acrimony over Judges Continues." 2005. *CQ Almanac 2004,* 60th ed., 12–15–12–16. Washington, DC: Congressional Quarterly. http://library.cqpress.com.libproxy.wustl.edu/cqalmanac/cqa104–836–24354–1084686.

Albright, Robert C. 1949. "GOP-Dixie Coalition Takes Over Control of Senate, Ends 16-Day Rules Filibuster." *Washington Post,* March 16, 1.17.

Allen, Jonathan, and John Cochran. 2003. "The Might of the Right." *CQ Weekly Online* (November 8): 2761–62. http://library.cqpress.com/cqweekly/weeklyreport108-000000899550 (accessed August 27, 2012).

Andrews, Marshall. 1949. "Majority Vote Gag on Senate Debate Fails." *Washington Post,* March 6, 8M.

Arnold, Douglas R. 1992. *The Logic of Congressional Action.* New Haven, CT: Yale University Press.

Arsenault, Mark. 2010. "Democrats Seek to Curb Filibusters." *Boston Globe,* December 31. http://www.boston.com/news/nation/washington/articles/2010/12/31/senate_democrats_seeking _to _rein_in_use_of_filibusters.

Ayres, Drummond B., Jr. 1979. "Senate Votes to Cut Post-Cloture Debate." *New York Times,* February 23, A17.

Babington, C. 2005. "Frist Urges End to Nominee Filibusters." *Washington Post,* April 25.

Berman, William. 1970. *The Politics of Civil Rights in the Truman Administration.* Columbus: The Ohio State University Press.

Beth, Richard S., Valerie Heitshusen, Bill Heniff, Jr., and Elizabeth Rybicki. 2009. "Leadership Tools for Managing the U.S. Senate." Paper prepared for the Annual Meeting of the American Political Science Association, Toronto, Canada, September 3–6.

Binder, Sarah A. 1995. "Partisanship and Procedural Choice: Institutional Change in the Early Congresses, 1789–1823." *Journal of Politics* 57 (4): 1093–118.

———. 1997. *Minority Rights, Majority Rule: Partisanship and the Development of Congress.* New York: Cambridge University Press.

———. 2006. "Parties and Institutional Choice Revisited." *Legislative Studies Quarterly* 31 (4): 413–532.

———. 2013. "The Politics of Legislative Stalemate." In *The Principles and Practice of American Politics,* edited by Samuel Kernell and Steven Smith, 230. Washington, DC: CQ Press.

———. 2013. "Fate of the Filibuster in a Post-Nuclear Senate." *Washington Post* (November 24). http://www.washington post.com/blogs/monkey-cage/wp/2013/11/24/fate-of-the-filibuster-in-a-post-nuclear-senate/.

Binder, Sarah A., Eric D. Lawrence, and Steven S. Smith. 2002. "Tracking the Filibuster, 1917–1996." *American Politics Research* 30 (July): 407–23.

Binder, Sarah A., Anthony J. Madonna, and Steven S. Smith. 2007. "Going Nuclear, Senate Style." *Perspectives on Politics* 5 (4): 729–40.

Binder, Sarah A., and Forrest Maltzman. 2009. *Advice and Dissent: The Struggle to Shape the Federal Judiciary.* Washington, DC: Brookings Institution Press.

———. 2012. "Advice and Consent: The Politics of Selecting Federal Judges." In *Congress Reconsidered,* 10th ed., edited by Lawrence Dodd and Bruce Oppenheimer. Washington, DC: CQ Press.

Binder, Sarah A., and Steven S. Smith. 1995. "Acquired Procedural Tendencies and Congressional Reform." In *Remaking Congress: Change and Stability in the 1990s,* edited by James A. Thurber and Roger H. Davidson. Washington, DC: CQ Press.

———. 1997. *Politics or Principle: Filibustering in the Senate.* Washington, DC: Brookings Institution Press.

———. 1998. "Political Goals and Procedural Choice in the Senate." *Journal of Politics* 60 (2): 398–416.

Bolton, Alexander. 2011. "Reid, McConnell Reach Agreement on Speeding Pace of Senate Business." *The Hill,* January 27. http://thehill.com/homenews/senate/140745-reid-mcconnell-reach-agreement-on-speeding-senates-pace-of-business-.

Brand, Madeline. 2005. "Sen. Pryor on the 'Gang of 14' Filibuster Deal." National Public Radio, May 24. http://www.npr.org/templates/story/story.php?storyId=4664385.

Brinkley, Alan. 1995. *The End of Reform: New Deal Liberalism in Recession and War.* New York: Knopf.

Bruhl, P. 2010. "Burying the 'Continuing Body' Theory of the Senate." *Iowa Law Review* 95:1401.

Burdette, F. 1940. *Filibustering in the Senate.* Princeton, NJ: Princeton University Press.

"Byrd Seeking Changes in Rules to Speed Up Business in the Senate." 1979. *New York Times,* January 14, 19.

Calmes, Jacqueline. 1987. "Democratic Gatekeeper: Howard Metzenbaum." *CQ Weekly Report* (January 3): 16–17.

Caro, Robert A. 2002. *Master of the Senate: The Years of Lyndon B. Johnson.* New York: Knopf.

Carson, Jamie L., Anthony J. Madonna, and Mark E. Owens. 2011. "Defensive Agenda Control: The Evolution of Tabling Motions in the U.S. Senate, 1865–1947." Paper presented at the Annual Meeting of the Southern Political Science Association. New Orleans, LA.

Chafetz, Josh. 2011. "The Unconstitutionality of the Filibuster." *Connecticut Law Review* 43:1003.

Cloud, David S. 1992. "Senate Sends $27 Billion Bill Straight for a Veto." *CQ Weekly Online* (October 10): 3132–33. http://library.cqpress.com/cqweekly/WR102408626.

Cochran, John. 2005a. "Frist Down, Not Out." *CQ Weekly Online* (May 30): 1421. http://library.cqpress.com.libproxy.wustl.edu/cqweekly/weeklyreport109-000001700932 (accessed August 27, 2012).

Cochran, John. 2005b. "Frist Has No Room to Move." *CQ Weekly Online* (May 16): 1293–98. http://library.cqpress.com.libproxy.wustl.edu/cqweekly/weeklyreport109-000001675072 (accessed August 27, 2012).

Cohen, Richard E. 1990. "Teaming Up in a Chamberful of Egos." *National Journal,* June 23, 1553.

———. 1993. "Running Up against the 'Byrd Rule.'" *National Journal,* September 4, 2151.

Cohodas, Nadine. 1994. *Strom Thurmond and the Politics of Southern Change.* Macon, GA: Mercer University Press.

"Congress Clears Voting Rights Act Extension." 1976. In *CQ Almanac 1975,* 31st ed., 521–33. Washington, DC: Congressional Quarterly. http://library.cqpress.com/cqalmanac/cqa1751214971.

Cornyn, John. 2003. "Our Broken Judicial Confirmation Process and the Need for Filibuster Reform." *Harvard Journal of Law and Public Policy* 27 (1): 197–99.

Cox, Gary W., and Mathew D. McCubbins. 2007. *Legislative Leviathan: Party Government in the House.* New York: Cambridge University Press.

*CQ Almanac.* 1972–73, 1975, 1982–1984, 1986–87, 1996, 2004–2006, 2008, 2010. Washington, DC: CQ Press.

Dauster, William. 1993. *Budget Process Law Annotated.* 103rd Cong., 1st sess., S. Prt. 103–49, 229–46.

Davis, Christopher M. 2011. "Measures on Which Opportunities for Floor Amendment Were Limited by the Senate Majority Leader or His Designee Filling or Partially Filling the Amendment Tree: 1985–2011." Congressional Research Service memorandum, October 7.

Davis, Susan. 2012. "Maine GOP Sen. Snowe's Retirement Makes Way for the Democrats." *USA Today,* February 28. http://www.usatoday.com/news/politics/story/2012-02-28/snowe-retirement-Maine-politics/53292996/1 (accessed August 27, 2012).

Den Hartog, Chris, and Nathan W. Monroe. 2011. *Agenda Setting in the U.S. Senate: Costly Consideration and Majority Party Advantage.* Cambridge: Cambridge University Press.

Dennis, Steven T. 2012. "GOP Promises New, Improved Senate." *Roll Call,* July 24. http://www.rollcall.com/issues/58_10/GOP-Promises-New-Improved-Senate-216368-1.html.

Doherty, Carroll J. 1998. "Senate Caught in the Grip of Its Own 'Holds' System." *CQ Weekly Report* (August 15): 2242.

Donovan, Beth. 1993. "Mitchell's Complaint." *CQ Weekly Online,* May 22. http://library.cqpress.com/cqweekly/.

———. 1994a. "Democrats' Overhaul Bill Dies on Senate Procedural Votes." *CQ Weekly Report* (October 1): 2757.

———. 1994b. "Republican Plan Filibusters, Imperiling Senate Schedule." *CQ Weekly Report* (September 24): 2655.

"'Don't Ask, Don't Tell' Repeal Clears." 2011. In *CQ Almanac 2010,* 66th ed., edited by Jan Austin, 6-7-6-8. Washington, DC: CQ-Roll Call Group. http://library.cqpress.com.libproxy.wustl.edu/cqalmanac/cqa110-1278-70360-2371609.

Drucker, David M. 2012. "Mitch McConnell Promises More Open Process." *Roll Call,* March 26. http://www.rollcall.com/issues/57_115/Mitch_McConnell_Promises_More_Open_Process-213379-1.html.

Ehrenhalt, Alan. 1982. "Every Man Is an Island: In the Senate of the '80s, Team Spirit Has Given Way to the Rule of Individuals." *CQ Weekly Report,* September 4.

Eisele, Albert, and JoAnn Kelly. 1998. "Texas-Minnesota Senate Feud Blocks Measure Honoring LBJ Foe Former Sen. McCarthy." *The Hill,* October 7, 6.

Elving, Ronald. 1988. "Mitchell Will Try to Elevate Policy, Predictability." *CQ Weekly Report* (December 3): 3423.

"Energy Overhaul Includes Many Bush Priorities, but Not Arctic National Wildlife Refuge (ANWR)." 2006. In *CQ Almanac 2005*, 61st ed., 8–18–8-19. Washington, DC: Congressional Quarterly. http://library.cqpress.com.libproxy.wustl.edu/cqalmanac/cqa105–766–20110–1042577.

Evans, C. Lawrence, and Dan Lipinski. 2005. "Obstruction and Leadership in the US Senate." In *Congress Reconsidered*, edited by L. C. Dodd and B. I. Oppenheimer. Washington, DC: CQ Press.

Evans, C. Lawrence, Daniel Lipinski, and Keith J. Larson. 2003. "The Senate Hold: Preliminary Evidence from the Baker Years." Paper presented at the Annual Meeting of the Midwest Political Science Association, Chicago.

Evans, C. Lawrence, and Walter J. Oleszek. 2001. "Message Politics and Senate Procedure." In *The Contentious Senate: Partisanship, Ideology, and the Myth of Cool Judgment*, edited by Colton C. Campbell and Nicol C. Rae, 107–27. Lanham, MD: Rowman & Littlefield.

Evans, Rowland, and Robert D. Novak. 1966. *Lyndon B. Johnson: The Exercise of Power; A Political Biography*. New York: New American Library.

Everett, Burgess, and Seung Min Kim. 2013. "Tom Udall, Jeff Merkley Clock 'Nuclear' Win." *National Journal* (November 21). http://www.politico.com/story/2013/11/tom-udall-jeff-merkley-clock-nuclear-win-100239.html.

Farber, M. A. 1978. "Senator James B. Allen Dies; Alabamian Led Canal Pact Fight." *New York Times*, June 2, B2.

Fenno, Richard F. 1978. *Home Style: House Members in Their Districts*. Boston: Little, Brown.

———. 1982. *United States Senate: A Bicameral Perspective*. Washington, DC: American Enterprise Institute for Public Policy Research.

———. 1989. "The Senate through the Looking Glass: The Debate over Television." *Legislative Studies Quarterly* 14:313–48.

Finley, Keith, M. 2008. *Delaying the Dream: Southern Senators and the Fight against Civil Rights, 1938–1965*. Baton Rouge: Louisiana State University Press.

Foley, Michael. 1980. *The New Senate: Liberal Influence on a Conservative Institution, 1959–1972*. New Haven, CT: Yale University Press.

Frederickson, Kari. 2001. *The Dixiecrat Revolt and the End of the Solid South*. Chapel Hill: University of North Carolina Press.

Friedel, Frank. 1965. *FDR and the South*. Baton Rouge: Louisiana State University Press.

Friel, Brian. 2007. "Wrestling with Holds." *National Journal,* January 13.

———. 2011. "Senators Negotiate Proposed Rules Changes on Holds, Filibuster Power." *CQ Weekly Online* (January 10): 125. http://library.cqpress.com/cqweekly/.

Froman, Lewis A., Jr., and Randall B. Ripley. 1965. "Conditions for Party Leadership." *American Political Science Review* 59 (1): 52–63.

Gamm, Gerald, and Steven S. Smith. 2000. "Last among Equals: The Senate's Presiding Officer." In *Esteemed Colleagues: Civility and Deliberation in the U.S. Senate,* edited by Burdett A. Loomis. Washington, DC: Brookings Institution Press.

———. 2009. "The Dynamics of Party Government in Congress." In *Congress Reconsidered,* edited by Lawrence C. Dodd and Bruce I. Oppenheimer. Washington, DC: CQ Press.

"'Gang of 14' Averts Judicial Showdown." 2006. In *CQ Almanac 2005,* 61st ed., 14-8-14-9. Washington, DC: Congressional Quarterly. http://library.cqpress.com.libproxy.wustl.edu/cqalmanac/cqa105-766-20099-1042151.

Garson, Robert A. 1974. *The Democratic Party and the Politics of Sectionalism, 1941–1948.* Baton Rouge: Louisiana State University Press.

Gerhardt, Michael J. 2004. "The Constitutionality of the Filibuster." *Constitutional Commentary* 21 (2): 445.

German, Ben, and Josiah Ryan. 2012. "Senate Turns Back Sweeping Oil-Drilling Amendment." *The Hill,* March 13. http://thehill.com/blogs/floor-action/senate/215787-senate-turns-back-sweeping-oil-drilling-amendment.

Gold, Martin, and Dimple Gupta. 2004. "The Constitutional Option to Change Senate Rules and Procedures: A Majoritarian Means to Overcome the Filibuster." *Harvard Journal of Law and Public Policy* 28:205–72.

Goldreich, Samuel. 2003. "Vote against ANWR Drilling Hits Core of Bush Energy Plan." *CQ Weekly Online* (March 22): 698–701. http://library.cqpress.com/cqweekly/weeklyreport108-000000638270 (accessed August 24, 2012).

"GOP Splits Sink Budget Resolution." 2007. In *CQ Almanac 2006,* 62nd ed., edited by Jan Austin, 3-8-3-13. Washington, DC: Congressional Quarterly. http://library.cqpress.com/cqalmanac/cqa106-1421530.

Gramlich, John. 2011. "If Judiciary Confirmations Slow This Election Year, It's the 'Leahy Rule.'" *CQ Today Online News,* May 22.

http://public.cq.com/docs/news/news-000004092436.html?ref=corg.

Hager, George. 1993. "The Byrd Rule: Not an Easy Call." *CQ Weekly Report* (July 31): 2027.

Hanson, Peter. 2009. "Taming the Floor: Vote Skipping and Omnibus Spending Bills in the U.S. Congress." Paper prepared for the Annual Meeting of the American Political Science Association, Toronto, September 3–6.

Heniff, Bill, Jr. 2010a. "Budget Enforcement Procedures: Senate Pay-As-You-Go (PAYGO) Rule." Congressional Research Service Report RL31943, January 12.

———. 2010b. "The Budget Reconciliation Process: A Majoritarian Tool in the Senate, with Limitations." Newsletter, Legislative Studies Section, American Political Science Association. http://www.apsanet.org/~lss/Newsletter/jan2010/Heniff.pdf (accessed March 1, 2012).

Heniff, Bill, Jr., and Justin Murray. 2011. "Congressional Budget Resolutions: Historical Information." Congressional Research Service Report RL30297, April 4.

Hennessey, Keith. 2012. "What Is a Vote-a-rama?" Keith Hennessey: Your Guide to American Economic Policy. http://keithhennessey.com/2010/03/25/vote-a-rama/ (accessed March 1, 2012).

Hess, David. 2009. "Orszag Pushes Reconciliation as Option for Upcoming Fight." *National Journal Daily,* March 11. http://www.nationaljournal.com.libproxy.wustl.edu/member/daily/orszag-pushes-reconciliation-as-option-for-upcoming-fight-20090311.

Hightower, Jim. 1989. Forward to *Advice and Dissent: Memoirs of South Dakota and the U.S. Senate,* by James G. Abourezk. Chicago: Lawrence Hill Books.

"The Hillbilly Watches Mitch McConnell." July 17, 2007. YouTube video, accessed February 2012. http://www.youtube.com/watch?v=Fj3ui5f9-N8&feature=player_embedded.

Hinckley, Barbara. 1971. *Seniority System in Congress.* Bloomington: Indiana University Press.

Hoagland, William G. 2011. "Senate Procedures for Consideration of the Budget Resolution/Reconciliation 'Vote-A-Rama': Testimony before the Committee on the Budget, U.S. Senate." Octber 4. http://budget.senate.gov/democratic/index.cfm/files/serve?File_id=f2e40d72–7694–4f72–9d47–1546027a20e0 (accessed February 10, 2012).

Hook, Janet. 1987. "Parliamentary War Erupts over Defense Bill." *CQ Weekly Online* (May 16): 1977. http://library.cqpress.com/cqweekly/.
———. 1989. "Mitchell Learns Inside Game." *CQ Weekly Online* (September 9): 2293–96. http://library.cqpress.com/cqweekly/.
———. 1992. "Extensive Reform Proposals Cook on the Front Burner." *CQ Weekly Online* (June 6): 1579. http://library.cqpress.com/cqweekly/.
———. 1993. "Bad Blood Clouds Efforts to Reform Congress." *CQ Weekly Online* (September 18): 2514. http://library.cqpress.com.libproxy.wustl.edu/cqweekly/WR103402370.
Howard, Nicholas O., and Jason M. Roberts. 2012. "Holding Up the Senate: Bob Dole and the Politics of Holds in the U.S. Senate." Paper presented at the 2012 Congress and History Conference, University of Georgia, Athens, GA, May 22.
Huitt, Ralph K. 1961. "The Outsider in the Senate: An Alternative Role." *American Political Science Review* 55 (September): 566–75.
Hulse, Carl. 2007. "Congressional Memo: In Conference, Process Undone by Partisanship." *New York Times*, September 26, A1.
———. 2008. "Distrust of McCain Lingers Over '05 Deal on Judges." *New York Times*, February 25, A1.
Jacoby, Mary. 1993. "Senate Parliamentarian Purges Budget Bill of Measures That Could Violate Byrd Rule." *Roll Call*, August 5, 9.
———. 1994. "Sabo Bill Would Kill Byrd Rule for Good." *Roll Call*, July 25, 12.
Jansen, Bart. 2009. "Capitol Hill's Conferences: Can They Be Revived?" *CQ Weekly Online* (January 5): 18. http://library.cqpress.com/cqweekly/.
"Javits Sees No Filibuster Contingency Forcing Him to Join Senate Before Jan. 9." 1957. *New York Times*, January 2, 20.
Jenkins, Jeffrey A., and Charles Stewart, III. 2012. *Fighting for the Speakership*. Princeton, NJ: Princeton University Press.
Kady, Martin. 2006. "Get Along or Get Nowhere." *CQ Weekly Report* (November 13): 3010–13.
Kady, Martin, and Ryan Grim. 2008. "Nominations Stare Down in the Senate." *Politico*, March 5. http://dyn.politico.com/printstory.cfm?uuid=7C757E4A-3048–5C12–0036366D276FCED8.
Kane, Paul. 2002. "GOP Mounts Judges Offensive." *Roll Call*, May 6.
———. 2011. "Senate Leaders Agree on Changes in Filibuster, Confirmation Process." *Washington Post*, January 28.
Kane, Paul, and Rachel Weiner. 2013. "Senate Filibuster Deal Disappoints Reformers." *Washington Post* (January 24). http://www

.washingtonpost.com/blogs/post-politics/wp/2013/01/24/senate-filibuster-deal-disappoints-reformers/

Keith, Robert. 2008. "The Budget Reconciliation Process: The Senate's 'Byrd Rule.'" Congressional Research Service Report RL30862.

———. 2010. "The Budget Reconciliation Process: The Senate's 'Byrd Rule.'" Congressional Research Service Report RL30862.

King, Aaron S., Frank J. Orlando, and David W. Rohde. 2010. "Beyond Motions to Table: Exploring the Procedural Toolkit of the Majority Party in the United States Senate." Prepared for the Annual Meeting of the Midwest Political Science Association, Chicago.

Klein, Ezra. 2013a. "Harry Reid: 'I'm Not Personally, at This Stage, Ready to Get Rid of the 60-Vote Threshold." *Washington Post* (January 24). http://www.washingtonpost.com/blogs/wonkblog/wp/2013/01/24/harry-reid-explains-why-he-killed-filibuster-reform/

———. 2013b. "Nine Reasons the Filibuster Change Is a Huge Deal." *Washington Post* (November 21). http://www.washingtonpost.com/blogs/wonkblog/wp/2013/11/21/9-reasons-the-filibuster-change-is-a-huge-deal/?hpid=z1.

Koger, Gregory. 2002. "Obstruction in the House and Senate: A Comparative Analysis of Institutional Choice." PhD diss., University of California, Los Angeles.

———. 2008. "Filibustering and Majority Rule in the Senate: The Contest over Judicial Nomination, 2003–2005." In *Why Not Parties? Party Effects in the United States Senate*, edited by Nathan W. Monroe, Jason M. Roberts, and David W. Rohde, 159–81. Chicago: University of Chicago Press.

———. 2010. *Filibustering: A Political History of Obstruction in the House and Senate.* Chicago: University of Chicago Press.

———. 2013. "Reid's Tactical Nuke and the Future of the Senate." *Washington Post* (November 21). http://www.washingtonpost.com/blogs/monkey-cage/wp/2013/11/21/reids-tactical-nuke-and-the-future-of-the-senate/.

Koszczuk, Jackie.1996. "GOP Firebrands Set to Fortify Their Hold on Congress." *CQ Weekly* (June 8): 1571–76. http://library.cqpress.com.libproxy.wustl.edu/cqweekly/WR401941.

Koszczukand, Rubin. 1994. "With Lott Victory, Senate GOP Chooses a Bolder Approach." *CQ Weekly* (December 3): 3437. http://library.cqpress.com.libproxy.wustl.edu/cqweekly/WR103406474.

Krutz, Glen S. 2001. "Tactical Maneuvering on Omnibus Measures in Congress." *American Journal of Political Science* 45 (1): 210–23.

Kucinich, Jackie, and Jessica Brady. 2011. "Changes to Senate Rules Fall Short of Drastic Proposals." *Roll Call*, January 27. http://www.rollcall.com/news/-202907-1.html.

Langdon, Steve. 1994. "GOP Leadership Fight Opens as Lott Takes On Simpson." *CQ Weekly* (November 19): 3327. http://library.cqpress.com.libproxy.wustl.edu/cqweekly/WR103406403m.

Lee, Frances E. 2009. *Beyond Ideology: Politics, Principles and Partisanship in the U.S. Senate*. Chicago: University of Chicago Press.

Lee, Frances E., and Bruce I. Oppenheimer. 1999. *Sizing Up the Senate: The Unequal Consequences of Equal Representation*. Chicago: University of Chicago Press.

LeLoup, L. 2005. *Parties, Rules and the Evolution of Congressional Budgeting*. Columbus: Ohio State University Press.

Lesniewski, Niels. 2010. "Senate Republicans Revive an Old Maneuver." *CQ Weekly* (July 26): 1785. http://library.cqpress.com.libproxy.wustl.edu/cqweekly/weeklyreport111-000003709289.

———. 2012. "Harry Reid Raises Prospect of Filibuster Curb." *Roll Call*, May 10. http://www.rollcall.com/news/Harry-Reid-Raises-Prospect-of-Filibuster-Curb-214446-1.html.

———. 2013. "Senate Opens with Filibuster Changes." *CQ Weekly* (January 28): 216. http://library.cqpress.com/cqweekly/weeklyreport113-000004210865.

Lesniewski, Niels, and Humberto Sanchez. 2013. "'Nuclear Option' Averted Again." *CQ Weekly* (July 22): 1276–77. http://library.cqpress.com/cqweekly/weeklyreport 113-000004318753.

Lewis, Neil. 2007. "Bush Drops Plans to Renominate 3 Judges." *New York Times*, January 10. http://www.nytimes.com/2007/01/10/washington/10judges.html?_r=1&hp&ex=1168491600&en=5c108b792ee44a94&ei=5094&partner=homepage.

Lott, Trent. 2005. *Herding Cats: A Life in Politics*. New York: Regan Books.

Manley, John F. 1973. "The Conservative Coalition in Congress." *American Behavioral Scientist* 17:223–46.

Margolis, Joel Paul. 1973. "The Conservative Coalition in the United States Senate, 1933–1968." PhD diss., University of Wisconsin–Madison.

Matthews, Donald R. 1960. *U.S. Senators and Their World*. New York: Vintage Books.

Mayhew, David R. 1974. *Congress: The Electoral Connection*. New Haven, CT: Yale University Press.

———. 2005. *Divided We Govern: Party Control, Lawmaking, and Investigations 1946–2002.* 2nd ed. New Haven, CT: Yale University Press.

Oleszek, Walter. 2007. *Congressional Procedures and the Policy Process,* 7th ed. Washington, DC: CQ Press.

———. 2008. "Whither the Role of Conference Committees: An Analysis." Congressional Research Service Report 7–5700, August 12.

Oppenheimer, Bruce I. 1985. "Changing Time Constraints on Congress: Historical Perspectives on the Use of Cloture." In *Congress Reconsidered,* 3rd ed., edited by Lawrence C. Dodd and Bruce Oppenheimer, 393–413. Washington, DC: CQ Press.

Orfield, G. 1975. *Congressional Power: Congress and Social Change.* New York: Harcourt, Brace & Jovanovich.

Ornstein, Norman, Robert Peabody, and David W. Rohde. 1977. "The Changing Senate: From the 1950s to the 1970s." In *Congress Reconsidered,* edited by Lawrence C. Dodd and Bruce Oppenheimer, 3–20. New York: Praeger Publishers.

Ostrom, Elinor. 2000. "Collective Action and the Evolution of Social Norms." *Journal of Economic Perspectives* 14 (Summer): 137–58.

Palmer, Betsy. 2005. "Changing Senate Rules: The 'Constitutional' or 'Nuclear' Option." Congressional Research Service Report RL32684.

———. 2007. "The Amending Process in the Senate." Congressional Research Service Report 98–853, November 26.

Paone, Martin. 2009–2010. "Martin P. Paone: Senate Democratic Cloakroom Staff to Majority Secretary, 1979–2008." Oral History Interviews, Senate Historical Office, Washington, DC. http://www.senate.gov/artandhistory/history/resources/pdf/Paone_4.pdf.

Park, Hong Min, and Steven S. Smith. 2013. "Public Attitudes about Majority Rule and Minority Rights in Legislatures: A Survey Experiment." Paper presented at the Annual Meeting of the Midwest Political Science Association, Chicago, April 11–14.

Patterson, James T. 1967. *Congressional Conservatism and the New Deal.* Lexington: University of Kentucky Press.

Peabody, Robert, Norman Ornstein, and David W. Rohde. 1976. "The United States Senate as a Presidential Incubator: Many Are Called but Few Are Chosen." *Political Science Quarterly* 91 (Summer): 237–58.

Perine, Keith. 2005. "Senate Inches Ever Closer to Filibuster Show down." *CQ Weekly Online* (May 2): 1146. http://library.cqpress

.com.libproxy.wustl.edu/cqweekly/weeklyreport109-000001650753.

Pierce, Emily. 2007. "Mystery Still Surrounds Filing Hold." *Roll Call*, September 26, 1.

Polsby, Nelson W. 1989. "Tracking Changes in the U.S. Senate." *PS: Political Science and Politics* 22 (4): 789–93.

Poole, Isaiah. 2004. "Senate Clears 60-Day Extension of Surface Transportation Bill, but Partisan Standoff Simmers." *CQ Weekly Online* (May 1): 1026. http://library.cqpress.com/cqweekly/weeklyreport108-000001131891.

"Presiding: Hazardous Duty." 1988. In *CQ Almanac 1987*, 43rd ed., 44. Washington, DC: CQ Press. http://library.cqpress.com.libproxy.wustl.edu/cqalmanac/cqa187–1143786.

Preston, Mark. 2004. "Conference Battle Escalates." *Roll Call*, February 2. http://www.rollcall.com/issues/49_71/-4172–1.html.

Rae, Nicol C., and Colton C. Campbell. 1999. *New Majority or Old Minority: The Impact of Republicans on Congress.* Lanham, MD: Rowman & Littlefield.

Raju, Manu. 2013. "Harry Reid's Gambit." *Politico* (November 21). http://www.politico.com/story/2013/11/harry-reid-senate-fillibuster-100243.html.

"Republicans Spar over Budget Plan." 1997. *CQ Almanac 1996*, 52nd ed. Washington, DC: CQ Press. http://library.cqpress.com/cqalmanac/cqa196–841–24598–1091823.

Riddick, Floyd, and Alan Frumin. 1992. "Riddick's Senate Procedure: Precedents and Practices." Washington, DC: US Government Printing Office. http://www.gpo.gov/fdsys/pkg/GPO-RIDDICK-1992/pdf/GPO-RIDDICK-1992–102.pdf.

Ripley, Randall. 1969. *Power in the Senate.* New York: St. Martin's Press.

Ritchie, Donald A. 2000. "Charles Lee Watkins." In *Arkansas Biography*, edited by Nancy A. Williams. Fayetteville: University of Arkansas Press.

Roberts, Jason M., and Steven S. Smith. 2003. "Procedural Contexts, Party Strategy, and Conditional Party Voting in the U.S. House of Representatives, 1971–2000." *American Journal of Political Science* 47 (April): 305–17.

———. 2007. "The Evolution of Agenda-Setting Institutions in Congress: Path Dependency in House and Senate Institutional Development." In *Party, Process, and Political Change in Congress*, Vol. 2, edited by David Brady and Mathew McCubbins, 165–81. Stanford, CA: Stanford University Press.

Rohde, David W. 1991. *Parties and Leaders in the Post Reform House.* Chicago: University of Chicago Press.

Rosenbaum, David. 2001. "Rules Keeper Is Dismissed by Senate, Official Says." *New York Times,* May 8. http://www.nytimes.com/2001/05/08/us/rules-keeper-is-dismissed-by-senate-official-says.html.

Rovner, Julie. 1990. "Emergency AIDS Relief Bills Advancing Quickly on Hill." *CQ Weekly* (May 19): 1561.

Ruju, Manu, and Jonathan Martin. 2009. "GOP Warns about Budget Hardball." *Politico,* March 24. http://www.politico.com/news/stories/0309/20400.html.

Rutkus, Denis Steven, and Kevin M. Scott. 2008. "Nomination and Confirmation of Lower Court Judges in Presidential Election Years." Congressional Research Service Report RL34615, August 13, 9–11.

Rybicki, Elizabeth. 2003. "The History of Bicameral Resolution Practices in the U.S. Congress." PhD diss., University of Minnesota.

———. 2010. "Amendments between the Houses: Procedural Options and Effects." Congressional Research Service Report RL41003, January 4.

———. 2011. "Senate Consideration of Presidential Nominations: Committee and Floor Procedure." Congressional Research Service Report RL31980, July 14.

Sanchez, Humberto. 2013. "Senate Democrats Set Showdown over Filibusters of Nominees." *CQ Weekly* (July 15): 1212. http://library.cqpress.com/cqweekly/weeklyreport113-000004314380.

Sandler, Michael, and Seth Stern. 2005. "Frist Orchestrates Passage of Gun Bill." *CQ Weekly Online* (August 1): 2118–19. http://library.cqpress.com.libproxy.wustl.edu/cqweekly/weeklyreport109-000001805532.

Schatz, Joseph J. 2010. "No Winners in a 'Broken' Congress." *CQ Weekly* (February 22): 434.

Schick, Allen. 2000. *The Federal Budget: Politics, Policy Process,* rev. ed. Washington, DC: Brookings Institution Press.

Schickler, Eric. 2000. "Institutional Change in the House of Representatives, 1867–1998: A Test of Partisan and Ideological Power Balance Models." *American Political Science Review* 94:269–88.

"Sen. Reid: 'It's Always Been the Case You Need 60 Votes.'" 2011. Republican. Senate.Gov. http://www.republican.senate.gov/public/index.cfm/2011/7/sen-reid-it-s-always-been-the-case-you-need-60-votes (accessed July 2012).

Shanton, John. 2010. "Senators Won't Fold on the Hold." *Roll Call,* February 1. http://www.rollcall.com/issues/55_84/news/b42806-1.html.

Shelley, Mack. 1983. *The Permanent Majority: The Conservative Coalition in the United States Congress.* Tuscaloosa, AL: University of Alabama Press.

"Shifting Power: 1981–1993." 2008. In *Guide to Congress,* 6th ed., Vol. 1. Washington, DC: CQ Press. http://library.cqpress.com/congressguide/g2c6e1-972-36391-1839660.

Shiner, Meredith. 2010. "Richard Shelby Lifts Hold on Obama Nominees." *Politico,* February 8. http://www.politico.com/news/stories/0210/32718.html.

Simon, Richard. 2004. "Senate Leader Frist to Campaign against Daschle." *Los Angeles Times,* May 21. http://articles.latimes.com/2004/may/21/nation/na-decorum21.

Sinclair, Barbara. 1989. *The Transformation of the U.S. Senate.* Baltimore: Johns Hopkins University Press.

———. 1994. "House Special Rules and the Institutional Design Controversy." *Legislative Studies Quarterly* 19, no. 4 (November): 477–94.

———. 2000. *Unorthodox Lawmaking: New Legislative Processes in the U.S. Congress,* 2nd ed. Washington, DC: CQ Press.

———. 2006. *Party Wars: Polarization and the Politics of the Policy Process.* Julian Rothbaum Lecture Series. Norman: University of Oklahoma Press.

———. 2011. "Ping Pong and Other Congressional Pursuits: Party Leaders and Post-Passage Procedural Choice." Paper presented at the 2011 Annual Meeting of the American Political Science Association, Seattle, WA, September 1–4.

———. 2012. *Unorthodox Lawmaking: New Legislative Processes in the U.S. Congress,* 4th ed. Washington, DC: CQ Press.

Sitkoff, Harvard. 1978. *A New Deal for Blacks: The Emergence of Civil Rights as a National Issue; The Depression Decade.* New York: Oxford University Press.

Smith, Steven S. 1989. *Call to Order: Floor Politics in the House and Senate.* Washington, DC: Brookings Institution Press.

———. 2007. *Party Influence in Congress.* New York: Cambridge University Press.

Smith, Steven S., and Marcus Flathman. 1989. "Managing the Senate Floor: Complex Unanimous Consent Agreements since the 1950s." *Legislative Studies Quarterly* 14, no. 3 (August): 349–74.

Smith, Steven S., and Gerald Gamm. 2013. "The Dynamics of Party Government in Congress." In *Congress Reconsidered,* edited by Lawrence C. Dodd and Bruce I. Oppenheimer. Washington, DC: CQ Press.

Smith, Steven S., Ian Ostrander, and Christopher Pope. 2011. "Senate Parties and Procedural Motions." Paper presented at the Congress and History Conference, Brown University, Providence, RI, June 9–10.

Smith, Steven S., Ian Ostrander, and Christopher Pope. 2013. "Weak and Strong Party Theories of the U.S. Senate: Procedural Motions and Majority Party Power." *Legislative Studies Quarterly* 38 (May): 205–36.

Stanton, John. 2008. "Senate Leaders' Rapport in Tatters." *Roll Call,* November 20. http://www.rollcall.com/issues/54_59/-30337-1.html.

———. 2012. "GOP Begins Judge Blockade." *Roll Call,* June 14. http://www.rollcall.com/issues/57_151/GOP-Begins-Judge-Blockade-215369-1.html?pos=hftxt.

"Stimulus Bill Provides Tax Rebates." 2009. In *CQ Almanac 2008,* 64th ed., edited by Jan Austin, ed., 7-17-7-19. Washington, DC: CQ Press. http://library.cqpress.com.libproxy.wustl.edu/cqalmanac/cqa108–1090–52026–2174946.

Taylor, Andrew. 2000a. "Congressional Affairs: Senate Leaders' Parliamentary Ploys." *CQ Weekly Online* (February 26): 394–99. http://library.cqpress.com/cqweekly/weeklyreport106-000000039618 (accessed August 24, 2012).

———. 2000b. "A Different Sense of Urgency." *CQ Weekly Online* (September 30): 2255–56. http://library.cqpress.com/cq weekly/weeklyreport106-000000145680 (accessed August 24, 2012).

———. 2000c. "Gun Control Vote Provokes Clash between Lott, Daschle over Management of the Senate." *CQ Weekly Online* (May 20): 1181. http://library.cqpress.com/cqweekly/weekly report106-000000087477.

———. 2000d. "Republicans Expected to Welcome Back Floor Votes." *CQ Weekly Online* (October 21): 2449 http://library.cq press .com/cqweekly/weeklyreport106-000000157215 (accessed August 24, 2012).

———. 2001a. "Law Designed for Curbing Deficits Becomes GOP Tool for Cutting Taxes." *CQ Weekly Online* (April 7): 770. http://library.cqpress.com/cqweekly/weeklyreport107-000000235233 (accessed August 24, 2012).

———. 2001b. "Senate GOP to Share Power." *CQ Weekly Online* (January 6): 21–22. http://library.cqpress.com/cqweekly/weekly report107-000000193017 (accessed August 24, 2012).

Theriault, Sean M. 2008. *Party Polarization in Congress.* New York: Cambridge University Press.

Theriault, Sean M., and David Rohde. 2011. "The Gingrich Senators and Party Polarization in the U.S. Senate." *Journal of Politics* 73 (4): 1011–24.

Tiefer, Charles. 2007. "Congress's Transformative 'Republican Revolution' in 2001–2006 and the Future of One-Party Rule." *Journal of Law & Politics* 23:233.

Todd, Chuck, Mark Murray, Domenico Montanaro, and Ali Weinberg. 2010. "First Thoughts: Good/Bad Jobs News." First Read on NBCNews.com, February 5. http://firstread.msnbc.msn.com/archive/2010/02/05/2195404.aspx.

Tolchin, Martin. 1977. "Senators Open Partisan Debate on Antifilibuster Rule." *New York Times,* May 10, 13.

Towell, Pat. 1987. "Sen. Nunn at the Center: Critical Showdown over SDI Under Way on Capitol Hill." *CQ Weekly Online* (May 16): 973–81. http://library.cqpress.com.libproxy.wustl.edu/cqweekly/WR100401001.

"'Trivialized' Filibuster Is Still a Potent Tool." 1988. In *CQ Almanac 1987,* 43rd ed., 47–51. Washington, DC: CQ Press. http://library.cqpress.com/cqalmanac/cqa187-1143802.

Udall, Tom. 2011. "The Constitutional Option." *Harvard Law & Policy Review,* January 9. http://hlpronline.com/2011/01/the-constitutional-option-reforming-the-rules-of-the-senate-to-restore-accountability-and-reduce-gridlock.

Van Houweling, Robert. 2006. "An Evolving End Game: The Partisan Use of Conference Committees, 1953–2003." In *Process, Party and Policy Making: Further New Perspectives on the History of Congress,* edited by David Brady and Mathew McCubbins. Stanford, CA: Stanford University Press.

Vergakis, Brock. 2010. "Senator Bob Bennett Ousted at Utah GOP Convention." *Huffington Post,* May 8. http://www.huffingtonpost.com/2010/05/08/bob-bennett-utah-gop-senate_n_568988.html.

Wawro, Gregory J., and Eric Schickler. 2006. *Filibuster: Obstruction and Lawmaking in the U.S. Senate.* Princeton, NJ: Princeton University Press.

———. 2010. "Legislative Obstructionism." *Annual Review of Political Science* 13:297–319.

Welna, David. 2009. "Will Democrats Seek GOP Votes or 'Reconciliation'?" National Public Radio, March 24. http://www.npr.org/templates/story/story.php?storyId=102280111.

Wheeler, Russell. 2012. "Judicial Confirmations: What Thurmond Rule?" *Issues in Governance Studies,* March. http://www.brook

ings.edu/~/media/research/files/papers/2012/3/judicial%20wheeler/03_judicial_wheeler.pdf.

White, Adam J. 2005. "Toward the Framers' Understanding of 'Advice and Consent': A Historical and Textual Inquiry." *Harvard Journal of Law and Public Policy* (Fall): 103.

White, William S. 1957. *Citadel.* New York: Harper and Brothers.

Wieck, Paul R. 1973. "The Efficiency Byrd: Keeping Senate Traffic Moving." *New Republic,* January 20, 13–14.

Wolfe, Kathryn A. 2005. "Coburn Sets Off Earmark Battle." *CQ Weekly Online* (October 24): 2854. http://library.cqpress.com.libproxy.wustl.edu/cqweekly/weeklyreport109-000001925495.

Wolfensberger, Don. 2008. "Have House-Senate Conferences Gone the Way of the Dodo?" *Roll Call,* April 28, 8.

Yachnin, Jennifer. 2009. "Watchdog Wants Investigation of Senate 'Holds.'" *Roll Call,* December 2. http://www.rollcall.com/news/41085-1.html.

Zapler, Mike. 2012. "Lugar Unloads on 'Unrelenting' Partisanship." *Politico,* May 9. http://www.politico.com/blogs/on-congress/2012/05/lugar-unloads-on-unrelenting-partisanship-122891.html.

# INDEX

*References to figures and tables appear in italic type.*


Abourezk, Jim, 86, 131–32, 134
Accountability for Senate outcomes, 305–306. *See also* Individual senators, accountability of; propositions about accountability
Advice-and-consent clause of U.S. Constitution: argument not used by Democrats, 346; Cornyn's comments in 2003, 342; Frist's justification for simple majority, 199, 215, 332, 342; and Rule XXII, 333
AFL-CIO, 310, *310*
Agnew, Spiro, 95, 109
Alexander, Lamar, 231, 244, 247
Alito, Samuel, 325, 343
Allen, James: death of, 365n14; delaying tactics of, 110, 113–15, 157; as first systematic obstructionist, 132; procedural tension inspired by, 117, 119; southern leader, 97; supports Byrd, 129; warning on changing Rule XXII, 120
Amendment tree, Senate: defined, 180; example of, *181*. *See also* Filling the amendment tree; Lott and filling the amendment tree
American Constitutional Union, *310*
Americans for Democratic Action (ADA), 310, *310*
Americans with Disabilities Act, 170
Anderson, Clinton, 56, 66, 70, 72–73, 93
ANWR. *See* Arctic National Wildlife Refuge
Appropriating, unorthodox, part 1 (1977–1988), 155–56
Appropriating, unorthodox, part 2 (1989–2004), 183–87; appropriations process in 2004, 186; Dorgan's objections to process, 186–87; and emergence of partisan strategies, 183; and government shutdown, 184; and omnibus bills, 186; and passage of appropriations under H. W. Bush, 184; and precedent set by Lott's power play, 185–86
Appropriating, unorthodox, part 3 (2005–2013), 230–35, *232*; and deep policy divisions, 233; number of appropriations bills (1961–2009), *232*; and Senate responsibility for

Appropriating (*continued*) breakdown, 233–35; and senators' objections to gridlock on appropriations, 230–32
Arctic National Wildlife Refuge (ANWR), 192–93, 236, 237, 369n20, 370n8
Armstrong, William, 138–39
Atomic Energy Commission (AEC), 57

Baker, Howard: and Byrd-Baker agreement (1977), 134–35; and debate on television in Senate, 144–45, 146, 367n8; and germaneness issue, 147–48; and holds problem, 150; minority leader (1977), 130; and post-cloture debate length, 148; and reconciliation bill, 134–35; Republican party leader (1981–86), 87, 101, 144
Baker years, 144–48
Barkley, Alben, 53
Bayh, Evan, 211
Bennett, Bob, 211
Binder, Sarah, 212
Blue-slip practices, 256, 263
Bolton, John, 327, 345
Bond, Kit, 237
Boren, David, 154, 173, 174–75, 367n2
Bork, Robert, 154–55, 196–97
Boxer, Barbara, 264, 330
Brown, Scott, 24, 213
Bryan, Richard, 179
Budget Act of 1974: Byrd rule incorporated into, 143, 189, 193; and complexity for parliamentary rulings, 157; enactment of, 107–108, 365nn8–9; and "exercise of rule-making power," 347; and floor amending process for budget resolutions, 193
Budget Enforcement Act (1985), 108
Budget measures and floor amendments, 193–96; and Budget Act requirements, 193–94; and Byrd rule, 195, 196; and debate limits, 194, 369n22; and role of points of order, 195; surge in amending activity, 194–95, 369n23; and vote-a-rama, 193, 369n21
Budget process, demise of: and ANWR bill in 2005, 236, 370n8; and debate limits, 235–36; and Democratic struggle, 237–38; and divided party control, 238; and House and Senate action on bills (2001–2011), *234*; and PAYGO rule (2007), 236; and reconciliation use, 237
Bush, George H. W., 163, 171, 184
Bush, George W.: and Democratic obstruction of judicial nominations, 200, 201, 238; elected to second term (2004), 214; fast-track procedures restarted for, 142; Frist argument endorsed by, 323–24; and judicial confirmations, 197–98; tax-cut measures as reconciliation bills under, 192; and Thurmond Rule, 238
Byrd, Robert: attainment of majority leader post (1977), 129; chair of Appropriations Committee, 174; and

commission to identify academics, 217; and concerns for quality of life of colleagues, 151; on the filibuster, 160–61, 278; and floor management role, 117, 120–21; and holds problem, 149, 150; on maintaining long hours in Senate, 169–70; Mansfield's whip in 1970s, 77, 91–92, 97–98; and Morning Hour strategy, 152–53; and 1979 reform, 135–37; in opposition to reform-by-ruling, 314; and Panama Canal treaty debate, 104–105; and parliamentary procedure usage, 160, 284, 292; and "real filibuster" approach, 153–55; response to abuse-of-leadership complaints, 134; response to Allen's tactics, 115–16; strategy on presidential nominations, 139–40; and tracking, 99; and use of unanimous consent, 123–24; views of Senate and cloture, 158–61, 367n14; warning to reform Democrats, 109–10. *See also* Debate, limiting (1977–88)
Byrd-Baker agreement (1977), 134–35
Byrd era in retrospect, 161–62
Byrd rule, 108, 189–190, 365n10, 368n16

Carpet replacement (1975), 120, 366n1
Carter, Jimmy, 239
Cheney, Dick, 199, 200
Church, Frank, 95, 133
*Citadel* (White), 49
Civil Rights Act of 1964, 92
Civil rights issues, 49, 54–55, 73–74
Clearance practices, 99–100, 161
Clinton, Bill: election of, 163; fast-track procedures not renewed by Republican Congress, 142; first midterm election, 164; and government shutdown, 184; obstructionism confronted by, 173; and Republican Senate majority, 197, 239; and Thurmond Rule, 197; veto power of, 192
Cloture motions, frequency of (1961–2010), *19*
Cloture motions filed, actual and predicted, *36*
Cloture petitions (1961–2010), *98*, 99
Cloture reform, proposals in 112th Congress (2011–2012), *341–43*
Cloture reform (1949), 51–54
Cloture reform (1953), 54–56
Cloture reform (1959), 71–73
Cloture threshold: adoption of in 1917, 32; arguments for and against, 274; changes in, 32–33; and cloture motion success, 122; decision thresholds and party size (1961–2009), 274–75; disposition of cloture petitions (1961–2010), 275, *276*; Does it matter? 274–77; and DWNOMINATE scale, 277; and effects of reform, *277–78*; and 1948–49 episode, 52–54; and 1954 episode, 56–59; and reform of 1975, 275; and size of majority

Cloture threshold (*continued*) party, 274–75; vote outcomes on cloture petitions, *277*

Clubby to individualistic Senate, 84–88, 121; and changing political environment, 84–85; and individualism's rise in 1970s and 1980s, 85–86, 121; leadership more reserved by late sixties, 85–86; and party cohesiveness lacking, 87; and sharp party polarization, 87–88

Coalitions, ideological, and reform, 337

Coburn, Tom, 220, 223

Cohen, Bill, 147

Collins, Susan, 231

*Common Cause et al. v. Joseph R. Biden et al.*, 248, 249

Common pool resource problem, 88–89

Composition of Senate, 78–*79*

Conditional party government thesis, 37

Conference avoidance (part 1) (1989–2004), 201–207; alternatives to conference, 203–204; change in conference motions in 2013, 202, 369n29; first motions blocked by filibuster in 1994, 205; and gamesmanship after 1994 episode, 205–206; informal negotiations opted for with polarized parties, 201; and partisan exclusion in 2003, 206–207; public laws enacted as result of conferences, 203–205, *204*; and systematic shift away from conferencing, 207

Conference avoidance (part 2) (2005–2013), 240–42; and filling the amendment tree before and after cloture, 242, 371n11; nonconference strategies used by Frist, 241; norm for this period, 240–41; and Reid's attempt to correct situation, 241, 371n10. *See also* Conference avoidance (part 1)

Congressional calendar, 31–32

Conrad, Kent, 283

Conservative coalition in Senate (1940s–1950s), 50–51

Conservative coalition voting (1925–2010), *51*

Conservative Democrats filibuster (1960), 73–75

Conservative Opportunity Society, 165

Constitutional guidelines for Senate: limited guidance provided, 21–22; simple-majority threshold implied for "each house," 55; and two-thirds majority for specific matters, 5; and two-thirds threshold for specific matters, 55. *See also* Nuclear option

Constitutional option. *See* Nuclear option

Contract with America, 177–78, 286

Controversies about Senate practice, 269–288; cloture threshold question, 274–77; conclusion, 288; filibuster as legislation killer, 278–82; overview, 269–270; parliamentary warfare, 286–87; parties and parliamentary

tactics, 284–86; parties and polarization, 283–84; Republicans responsible for syndrome, 282–83; senators as problem, 270–73
Cornyn, John, 342
Costs of reform, 314
Craig, Larry, 177, 367n7
Cranston, Alan, 111
C-SPAN, 291
Curtis, Carl, 104–105

D'Amato, Alfonse, 171
Daschle, Tom: and appropriations bill decision, 184; defeat of, 210; disavowal of amendment tree practice, 183; and Frist's active opposition, 210; on irony of Lott's complaints, 179; and Lott, 179, 285; multiple-bill approach opposed by, 191; and side-by-side amendments, 177
D.C. circuit court, 7–8
D.C. circuit judges battle of November 2013, 256–59; and delayed nominations for Obama administration, 256–57; nuclear option gained support, 257; Obama charged with packing the court, 257; and Reid's move for nuclear option, 258; simple strategy pursued by Reid, 259
Debate, limiting (1977–88), 138–41; on budget measures, 107–108; and Byrd's elimination of delays, 139–40; Byrd's points of order as model, 138, 141, 366n6; Byrd's strategy on presidential nominations, 139–40, 366n7; and germaneness of Armstrong amendment, 138–39; and post-cloture length, 148; strategy on presidential nominations, 366n7
DeMint, Jim, 211
DeWine, Mike, 326, 344
Dilatory motions: and Baker, 144; forbiddance of, 26; as issue in post-reform Senate, 112; Johnson's tactics and, 74; Pastore's point of order on, 115; and Reid, 247; and Rule XII on, 366n4. *See also* Germaneness requirement
Dirksen, Everett McKinley, 103; as assertive Republican leader, 87, 94, 97; death of, 97; and Dirksen-Hickenlooper amendment, 90; and Johnson, 72, 74–75, 103; and motions to table, 103
Dixiecrat Party, 71
Dole, Robert ("Bob"): aggressiveness pushed by "Gingrich senators," 166; and Dove as parliamentarian, 158; and hold requests received by (1985–96), 172; and holds problem, 150; Minority Leader Byrd allowed to take lead by, 146; and 60-vote threshold in 1995, 222; succeeds Baker as majority leader, 144
Domenici, Pete, 174
Dorgan, Bryan, 186–87
Douglas, Paul, 56
Dove, Robert, 158, 191, 192
Durbin, Dick, 340

DW-NOMINATE scale, 277
"Dysfunctional," as adjective to describe today's Senate, 2–3, 45, 292, 341, 355

Eastland, James, 65
Ehrenhalt, Alan, 150
Eisenhower, Dwight, 57, 70, 71–72, 73
Elections and party polarization (1989–2005), 164–67
Ellender, Allen, 95
Ervin, Sam, 71
Explanation of Senate syndrome, 30–31; limits of previous models, 36–40; previous studies, 31–36. *See also* Party size; Policy-making trend in recent decades

Factionalized to polarized Senate (1961–1988), 78–84; composition of, 78–*79*; and conservative coalition, 83–*84*; and factionalism within parties, 80–*81*; and partisan polarization established, 83–*84*; and rise of liberal Democrats, 82–83; and voting alignments by region, 81–*82*, 364n1
Factions and parties, 336
Fair Employment Practices Commission, 51–52
Fallows, James, 371n2
Feinstein, Diane, 264, 330; in support of reform, 257
Fenno, Richard, 356
Filibuster, attitudes about: overview, 296; House versus Senate, 302–305, *303*; mean responses to majority rule and minority rights questions, *304*; panel study, 296–98, 371n4; partisanship and other factors shaping attitudes about congressional procedure, 305; survey on majority rule and minority rights, 298–99, *300*, *301*, 302, 311; 2009 survey on, 297–98, 371nn3–4
Filibuster, silent, 344
Filibuster as legislation killer, 278–82; and "little harm" argument, 278–81, 288; Sinclair evidence on, 281–82
Filibustering: between 1917 and 1996, 32; Byrd's views on, 160–61; first use of, 4–5; incentives for, 32–33; liberal Democrats (1954), 56–59; limits of previous models, 36; new model for prediction of, 33–34, *35*, 363n3; origin of, 25–26; and "real filibuster" strategy (mid-1980s), 153–55; "talking" filibuster as uncommon, 39
Filibuster reform: and nuclear option opportunity (2012), 15–17, 18; observations by Binder and Smith, 336; proposals for, 15–16, 363n1; support and opposition to, 338–40; 2010 hearings on, 345–46. *See also entries beginning with* Reform
Filling the amendment tree: Daschle's disavowal of, 183; and Frist's aggressive parliamentary tactics, 218–19; objections made by Reid on Frist's, 219–21; by Reid, 219–21, 369n1; and Specter's resolution to curtail, 220–21.

*See also* Amendment tree, Senate; Lott and filling the amendment tree
Floor management issues, 88–89, 101, 122–23
Foley, Tom, 205
Ford, Wendell, 145
Fortas, Abe, 92, 239
Franken, Al, 24, 213, 226, 344
Frist, Bill: and active support of Daschle's opponent, 210; aggressive in pursuing party interests, 166; became leader in 2003, 286; on Democratic conference tactics, 214; and filling the amendment tree, 218–19, 220, 242; nuclear option proposed by, 198–99, 213–14, 288, 314–15, 325–26, 368n28; response to Democratic obstructionism, 210–11
Frumin, Alan, 158, 190, 191

Gang of 14, 218, 339, 343–44, 345
Gang of 14 memorandum, 325–27
Germaneness requirement, 147–48; and Armstrong's germaneness defense, 138–39; defined, 61; and Mansfield's insistence on, 91; resistance to inclusion of, 89–90. *See also* Dilatory motions
Gingrich, Newt: elected Speaker of the House, 285; as party whip in 1989, 87–88; political tactics of, 284–85; Republican whip (1983), 165–66
"Gingrich senators," 166–67, 284, 371n2
Goldwater, Barry, 92, 147
Gore, Albert, 95
Gorman, Arthur Pue, 27–29
Graham, Lindsey, 231–32, 326, 344
Grassley, Charles, 188
Great Society programs of the 1960s, 97, 107
Gregg, Judd, 237

Harkin, Tom, 198, 243, 337, 340; supported reform, 257
Harris, Fred, 86
Hart, Gary, 134
Hayden, Carl, 52, 72
Health care reform bill (2010): and fast-track provisions, 142; filibuster attitudes reflect partisan influence, 298; and Franken's election, 213, 226; passage on Christmas Eve (2009), 296; public insurance plan blocked by filibuster threat, 336; and reconciliation bill, 237, 238
Helms, Jesse, 145, 157, 172, 175–76
Hickenlooper, Bourke, 90
*Hill, The*, 289
Holds: abuses of, 187–88; anonymous, 188–89, 228, 370n5; common by late 1980s, 171–72, 172; emergence of, 100–101, 364nn3–4; and obstructionism, 148–51, 335; rolling, 230; rules in 2007 and 2011 on, 228–30, 370nn6–7. *See also* Reform, motivations for
Hollings, Ernest, 124
Howard, Nicholas, 171–72

Humphrey, Hubert, 59, 67, 94–95

Impoundment battle, 107
Individualism, rise of (1961–76), 77–119; overview, 31, 77–78; and amendments and use of motions to table, 101–107; clubby to individualistic Senate, 84–88; and common pool resource problem, 88–89; and debate limits in budget measures, 107–108; factionalized to polarized Senate (1961–88), 78–84; and failure of reformers (1961–73), 92–96; Mansfield era in retrospect, 118–19, 365n15; and 1975 reform, 108–12; and post-reform Senate, 112–18; and southern restraint ends, 96–99; and tracking and holds, 99–101; and unanimous consent agreements, 89–91
Individualism and obstructionism (1977–88), 120–62; overview, 120–21; and Baker years, 144–48; Byrd era in retrospect, 161–62; Byrd's views of Senate and cloture, 158–61, 367n14; elaboration of unanimous consent agreements, 123–29; and failed majority tactics (1987), 151–55; and holds problem, 148–51; individualism, obstructionism, and floor management, 121–23; new precedents limiting debate, 138–41; new statutory limits on debate, 141–43; 1979 reform, 135–37; parliamentary warfare (1980s), 156–58; and real filibuster strategy, 153–55; taming post-cloture filibuster, 129–34, 137; unorthodox appropriating (part 1), 155–56
Individual senators, accountability of, 306–10; and cloture motions, 307, 309; and difference between procedural and substantive votes, 306–7; and motions to table, 307, 308, 309; and percentage of votes in interest group scales that are cloture votes (2007–2009), *310*; and position taking, 306; and procedural votes, 308–309; and special-interest groups, 308–11
Inouye, Daniel, 162
Institutional interests in reform, 337–38
Intervention by the courts, 248–49
Introduction, 1–14. *See also* Explanation of Senate syndrome

Jackson, Henry ("Scoop"), 131
Javits, Jacob, 91, 95, 134
Jefferson, Thomas, 159
Jeffords, James, 164
Johnson, Lyndon, 363n3; as civil rights advocate, 73–74; and filibuster (1960), 74–75; Fortas nominated by, 239; heavy-handed leadership of, 86–87; and innovations in parliamentary tactics, 61, 64; and Johnson years in retrospect, 75–76; and motions to table, 103;

and new programs in administration of, 39; and perception of Johnson era, 66; preparing presidential campaign (1960), 73–74; and reaction to Nixon ruling (1957), 69–70, 363n3; and S. Res. 5, 72–73; and second year as Democratic leader, 58; use of time limitation agreements, 61, *62–63*
Johnson years in retrospect, 75–76
Johnston, J. Bennett, 162
Judicial nominations: Bork nomination as turning point, 196; under Clinton, 197; and Democratic obstructionism, 198; and Frist proposal to change Rule XXII, 198–99; and length of Senate action, 196–*97*; pattern extended to new century, 197; and recess appointments by Bush, 198. *See also* Thurmond Rule
Judicial nominations crisis (2005). *See* 2005 judicial nominations crisis and nuclear option

Keating, Kenneth, 90
Kennedy, Edward ("Ted"), 113, 148, 175–76, 213
Kennedy-Hatch amendment, 176
Kern, John, 60
Kerry, John, 271
Key features of syndrome, 208
Key-vote measures subject to cloture petitions (1962–2010), *20*
Knowland, William, 52–53, 57–58, 70
Koger, Gregory, 32–33

Lautenberg, Frank, 243–44, 344–45
Leahy, Patrick, 148, 238, 240, 259
Legislative strategy, 167–69
Levin, Carl: opposition to germaneness proposal, 147; opposition to reform-by-ruling strategy, 216; opposition to reform move, 1, 252, 253; opposition to Reid's threat, 329; Reid's nuclear option threat not openly opposed by, 347, 353; voted against Reid's move, 258, 330
Levin, McCain, McConnell resolution (S. Res. 16, 113th Congress), 253–54
Liberal-conservative scores, by party (1951–2010), 213–*14*
Long, Russell, 110, 133, 146, 147
Lott, Trent, 166; Dole replaced by as majority leader (1994), 178; and Gingrich-style strategies, 285; and holds problem, 188–89; tactics of, 182, 286; term "nuclear option" used by, 200–201
Lott and filling the amendment tree, 177–83; and Contract with America, 177–78; Daschle's response to Lott, 179; effectively stalling amendment process, 181–82; and Lott replaced Dole as majority leader (1996), 178; and Lott's aggressiveness, 180, 368n10; and Lott's complaints on minority tactics, 178–79, 368n8; and Lott's use of "first

Lott (*continued*)
recognition," 180–81; and pattern set in 1999, 182–83; previous uses of tactic, 182; and truce on use of amendment tree, 183. *See also* Filling the amendment tree
Lugar, Richard, 211, 283

Major developments in Senate procedure (1949–2013), *10–13*
Majority party: behavior prompting minority obstruction, 39–40; competition for control of, 43–44; strategies of, 168–69
Majority tactics, failure of (1987), 151–55; and filibuster threat, 151–52; and Morning Hour strategy, 152–53; and sharp polarization of parties, 151
Manchin, Joe, 258, 330
Mansfield, Mike: and common pool resource problem, 88; Democratic leader (1961–76), 77, 87; and difficulty in managing party, 83; era in retrospect, 118–19, 365n15; as Johnson's whip, 72; and the Long compromise on temporary cloture threshold, 110–11; position on rule changes, 94; remarks of disappointment with Senate behavior, 116–17, 119, 365n13; and stalemate on cloture reform until 1975, 78; and tracking, holds, and clearance under, 99; use of unanimous consent agreements by, 90–91
Mansfield era in retrospect, 118–19, 365n15
Matthews, Donald, 64
McCain, John, 218, 353; and negotiations with Levin, 253
McClure, James, 150
McConnell, Mitch: and blockage of appeals court nominees, 240; on Democratic conference tactics, 207; and filibuster negotiations with Reid, 16–17; on promises of different Senate if he were in majority, 247; reelection opposed by Democrats, 210; Reid's negotiations with, 6, 7; on 60-vote threshold as the norm, 224–25, 287. *See also* Reid-McConnell agreement (2011)
McGovern, George, 94
Media, public, and accountability, 289–311. *See also* Accountability for Senate outcomes; Filibuster, attitudes about; Media coverage; Public knowledge
Media coverage, 290–93; and avoidance of appearance of bias, 292, 293; detail lacking in, 290; minority obstruction neutralized in, 291–92, 371n2; and political science background lacking in reporters, 292–93; public confusion attributed to, 311; 60-vote threshold treated as standard, 291. *See also* Public knowledge
Merkley, Jeff: simple-majority rule urged by, 345; sponsor of resolution, *343*; in support of reform, 252, 259; and

Udall-Merkley-Harkin resolution, 243, 347
Merkley-Udall plans, 329
Metzenbaum, Howard: against germaneness amendment, 147; and delaying strategies with Abourezk, 131–32; and filibuster ended, 134; and holds ("Senator No"), 150; and individualism of era, 150; and 1978 debate on tuition tax credits, 124–28; and pride in delaying "foolish" legislation, 121
Mikulski, Barbara, 340
Miller, Zell, 192
Millett, Patricia, 257
Mitchell, George: Byrd replaced by as majority leader (1988), 162, 163; consultative leadership style of, 170; and growing polarization, 171–72; and holds problem, 150; reforms proposed by, 172–73; and return to Byrd's tactics, 174; and side-by-side amendments, 175–76
Modern Senate, emergence of: factors influencing, 24–25, 354; and floor leaders, 26–27, 101–102; and forces driving obstructive tactics, 31; and omission of previous-question motion, 25; and procedural strategies, 30–31; and unanimous consent agreements (1914), 27–29
Mondale, Walter, 132, 133, 158
Morning hour episode (1987), 152–53, 154, 158
Morse, Wayne, 57, 71
Motions to table an amendment, 101–107; advantages of motions to table, 102–103; and civil rights bill (1960), 103; increase in amendments since 1970s, 101, 104; and majority party's struggle to move Senate business, 104, 364n5; number of motions to table that received roll-call votes (1949–2010), *103*; outcomes for four Congresses (1969–76), *106*–107, 364n7; and Panama Canal treaty debate, 104–106, 364n6
Muskie, Edmund, 133

Nickles, Don, 158
1975 reform, 108–12; Byrd's warning to Democrats, 109–10; and intensification of floor management challenges, 121; liberals gain majority, 108–109; and Long compromise endorsed by leadership, 110–11; and Mansfield's point of order, 109, 110, 112; pro-reform majority (1975), 109, 365nn11–12; review of developments for, 112; and Rockefeller as vice president, 109
1979 reform, 135–37
Nixon, Richard: and advisory comments in 1957 on simple-majority rule, 340; and budget management, 348; Democratic majorities faced by administration, 82–83, 107; and increased workload during administration, 39; and renewal of fast-track procedures, 141–42;

Nixon, Richard (*continued*)
resignation of, 96. *See also* Nixon surprise (1957)
Nixon surprise (1957), 66–71; and Anderson's motion, 66, 70; and debate on rules, 66–67; and Johnson's reaction to, 69–70; Nixon to rule on Rule XXII, 66; and significance of Nixon ruling, 69, 363n2; and Thurmond's filibuster, 71
Nuclear option: as direct attack on Rule XXII, 251; earliest reference to, 200–201; procedural strategy of majority party, 15, 17, 18; proposed by Frist, 198–99, 213–14; threat of significance to leader, 339; and Trent Lott's use of, 200–201; used by Reid on November 21, 2013, 1–2, 7–9. *See also* Mid-2013 episode; Partisanship, deepening; 2005 judicial nominations crisis and nuclear option; 2005 nuclear option episode revisited; 2013 nuclear option episode revisited
Nuclear option episodes of 2013 revisited, 328; and limited purpose of executive nominations, 329; Reid's early threat of, 328; Reid's justifications for, 328; Senate changed by, 331; two issues settled by, 330
Nuclear option threat of July 2013, 254–56

Obama, Barack: and blockage of "big oil" bill, 289–90; election of (2008), 213; end to holds called for by (2010), 229; nominations blocked in Congress, 346–47; reelection of, 7; and Reid's frustration with Republican obstruction of legislation, 352; and Republican opposition, 212; and Thurmond Rule, 240
Observations in conclusion, 359–60
Obstruction, as standard feature of modern Senate, 3
Obstructionism: confronted by Bill Clinton, 173; eruption of in 1970s, 96, 121–23; and holds, 335; and Mitchell, 169–75; and parliamentary warfare, 156–58, 286–87; taken to new level by Republicans, 283; volume of, 33, 39, 41–42, 44. *See also* Individualism and obstructionism (1977–88); Judicial nominations; Obstructionism (1950s)
Obstructionism (1950s), 59–66; factors resulting in few filibusters in 1950s, 64–65; and frustration of liberal Democrats, 59–60; procedures of Johnson Senate, 60–61, 64; and right of first recognition, 23, 60; and unanimous consent agreements, 61
Oppenheimer, Bruce, 97
Organization of book, 9–14
Ornstein, Norman, 158

Packwood, Bob, 125
Panama Canal treaty debate, 104–106, 364n6
Paone, Martin, 153

Parliamentarians, role of, 156–58
Parliamentary warfare: and Democratic responses to minority obstruction, 287; and high frequency of obstructionism, 286–87; in 1980s, 156–58; Senate syndrome as result of, 288
Parties and factions, 336
Partisanship, deepening (2005–2013), 209–54; overview, 209–10; aborted reform and the abandoned Reid-McConnell agreement (2011), 242–48; avoiding conference (part 2), 240–42; deepened polarization and the 60-vote Senate, 210–13; and demise of budget process, 235–38; filling the amendment tree, 218–21; intervention by the courts, 248–49; judicial nominations and the Thurmond rule, 238–40; pattern of Senate syndrome, 250; 60-vote thresholds and the elaboration of unanimous consent agreements, 221–27; 2005 judicial nominations crisis and nuclear option, 213–18; 2007 and 2011 rules on holds, 228–30. *See also entries beginning with* Obstructionism; 2005 nuclear option episode revisited; 2013 nuclear option episode revisited
Partisanship, rising (1989–2004), 163–208; overview, 163–64; budget measures and floor amendments, 193–96; conference avoidance (part 1), 201–207; Dole, Lott, and holds, 187–89; elections and party polarization (1989–2005), 164–67; judicial nominations, the Senate confirmation process, and the nuclear option, 196–201; and key features of syndrome, 208; Lott and filling the amendment tree, 177–83; Mitchell and intensifying obstructionism, 169–75; polarization, individualism, and legislative strategy, 167–69; reconciliation and the circumvention of cloture, 189–93; and side-by-side amendments, 175–77; unorthodox appropriating (part 2), 183–87
Party alignment, *35*
Party polarization: after Byrd's leadership ended, 121; between early 1990s and present, 167–69; evidence that Republicans have moved right more than Democrats have moved left, 283; increase in since 1970s, 36–37, 42, 363n5; mean liberal-conservative scores (1961–2010), 273; and policy positions, 283–84, 371n1
Party size, 42–43, *79*
Party strength, 31
Pastore, John, 115
Pattern of Senate syndrome, 208; and balance between majority rule and minority rights, 24; and gamesmanship, 271; key features of, 208; as long-term problem, 273; obstruct and

Pattern of (*continued*)
restrict pattern of, 17–19, 332; and obstruction and restriction pervasive, 250
Pay-as-you-go (PAYGO) rule (2007), 236
Pearson, James, 145
Pearson-Ribicoff report, 145–46
Pillard, Cornelia, 257
Ping pong method of reconciliation, 203
Polarization and legislative strategy, 167–69
Polarization of parties. *See* Party polarization
Policy-making trend in recent decades, 19–20, *20*, 41–42
Post-cloture filibuster, taming of (1977–88), 125–29; Abourezk amendment in violation of Rule XXII, 132–33, 366nn4–5; Byrd as majority leader (1977), 129; and delaying tactics by Abourezk, 131–32; and resolution of Rules Committee revised, 129–30
Post-reform Senate after 1975 reform, 112–18; and new tactics, 112; and Pastore on dilatory motions, 115; and post-cloture obstructionism, 112–13, 137. *See also* Allen, James
President of Senate, 21
President pro tempore of Senate, 22
Presiding officer, 284–86
Previous question motion, 25
Procedural condition of Senate (1950s): overview, 49; cloture reform (1949), 51–54; cloture reform (1953), 54–56; cloture reform (1959), 71–73; conservative Democrats filibuster (1960), 73–75; Johnson years in retrospect, 75–76; liberal Democrats filibuster (1954), 56–59; Nixon surprise (1957), 66–71; obstructionism (1950s), 59–66; red carpet Senate, 49–51
Procedural innovation, 44–45
Propositions about accountability, 311
Pryor, David, 151–52, 230, 347; opposition to Reid's threat, 329; voted against Reid's move, 330; voted against ruling, 258
Public knowledge, 293–96; of Senate procedure (2009), *294*, 371n5; of Senate procedure (2012), *296*; survey on (2009), 293–95; survey on (2012), 295–96. *See also* Filibuster, attitudes about; Media coverage

"Quality of Life" task force, 162

Ransom politics, 332
Reagan, Ronald: and appropriations battles, 232; and Bork nomination, 154; election of (1980), 78, 284; and multiyear budget deal, 183–84; and Thurmond Rule, 239
"Real filibuster" strategy (mid-1980s), 153–55
Recess appointments, 198, 345
Reconciliation and circumvention of cloture, 189–93, 369n20; for ANWR, 192–93, 369n20; budget

measures focus of battles, 189; and Byrd rule, 189–90, 192, 368nn16–17; and informal negotiations, 203; multiple-bill approach opposed by Daschle, 191; and parliamentarian change, 191, 193–96; and use on tax bills, 191–92, 368n18; and use on tax bills under Bush, 192, 369n19; and use on tax bills under Clinton, 191–92. *See also* Nuclear option
"Red carpet" Senate, 49–51
Reform, 332–61; costs of, 339; early 2013 reforms, 348–52; layers of motivation for, 333–40, 335; majority rule and supermajority coexistence, 357–59; mid-2013 episode, 352–54; observations on the future, 359–60; reversibility, 354–57; support and opposition to filibuster reform, 338–40; thresholds, motions, and measures, 340–46. *See also* Reform, approaches to; Reform, motivations for
Reform, approaches to: cloture reform proposals, 112th Congress (2011–2012), 341–43; Franken's proposal, 344; Harkin's proposal, 340; reform strategies, 346–48; thresholds, motions, and measures, 340–46; Udall's proposals, 344–45
Reform, modest (2013): and motions to proceed, 350–51; and streamlining of process, 349
Reform, motivations for: ideological coalitions, 337; individual senators, 335; institutional interests, 337–38; parties and factions, 336
Reform by ruling (2013), 251–66; overview, 251–52; battle over D.C. circuit judges (November 2013), 256–59; implications of Reid's move for Senate, 262–65; lingering questions about Reid's move, 259–262; modest reform (January 2013), 252–54; nuclear option threatened again (July 2013), 254–56; significance of Reid move in history, 265–66
Reform-by-ruling, implications of, 312–31; overview, 312–13; and Bill Frist, 314; and comparison with House debate, 336–38; conclusion, 347–48; and contending arguments in scholarly debate on, 316–20; and costs of reform, 321; justifications for, 314; recent conservative arguments, 341–42; recent liberal arguments, 322–24; reformers' arguments for, 321–24; review of essentials, 313–16; scholarly debate over Senate rules, 316–21; 2005 nuclear option episode revisited, 313, 325; 2013 nuclear option episode revisited, 328–30; weakness of majority party, 312
Reformers, failure of (1961–73), 92–96; cloture reform unsuccessful, 92–93, 364n2; and filibusters, 92; and liberals support retaining filibuster, 96

Reform of January 2013, 252–54
Reform of Senate syndrome, overview, 332–33
Reforms of 2013, temporary nature of, 6
Regular order, absence of, 338
Reid, Harry: converted to cause of reform, 252; and evolving attitude toward reform, 6, 7; and filibuster negotiations with McConnell, 16; and filling the amendment tree, 219–21, 246, 369n1; and frustration with Republican obstruction, 352; and move for nuclear option, 1, 246–47, 258, 329; and negotiations with McConnell, 253; nuclear option procedure used by, 1–2; as obstructionist to Lott, 179; and opposition to McConnell's reelection, 210; and reform-by-ruling discussions in 2012, 327; on rejection of 60-vote threshold, 224–25; and reluctant acceptance of 60-vote threshold, 226; and Rule XXII reform, 333; self-restraint promised by, 244–45. *See also* Reid-McConnell agreement
Reid-Levin-McCain resolution (S. Res. 15, 113th Congress), 253
Reid-McConnell agreement (2011): breakdown of, 252; and commitments made by both sponsors, 244; and deepening distrust, 247; disintegration of, 245, 250, 356; and hearings on reform proposals, 242–43; reform package proposed by Democrats, 243; and Reid's reform-by-ruling move, 246–47
Reid-McConnell negotiations (2013), 16
Reid's move, implications of, 262–65; historic significance of, 265–66; precedent set for possible future reforms, 263–64; retaliation uncertain early on, 262–63; streamlined process for judicial nominations, 263; uncertainty of long-term effects, 265; and warnings that Senate had become the House, 264–65
Reid's move, questions about, 259–62; considerations noted by outsiders, 261; and little effect on behavior of minority, 262; and little opposition by Republicans, 261–62; and Reid's thinking, 260–61; and Republican surprise, 262; speculation on, 259–60
Reid's move in November 2013, 329
Republicans responsible for syndrome, 282–83
Reversibility of syndrome, 354–57; factors influencing emergence of syndrome, 354; hope of move away from polarization, 356–57; new strategies tied to goal of majority control, 356–57, 372n2; possibility of reversing course open question, 355–56; sharp polarization of parties, 354–55

Ribicoff, Abraham, 145
Riddick, Floyd, 157, 158
*Riddick's Senate Procedure: Precedents and Practices*, 23
Right of first recognition: advantages for majority leader, 27, 29–30, 43, 60; and Byrd, 133; defined, 23; as essential tool for majority party, 334; and filling the amendment tree, 180; and Johnson, 73; and Mansfield, 94; partisan use of, 182
Roberts, Jason, 171–72
Roberts, John, 325, 343, 344
*Robert's Rules of Order*, 25
Rockefeller, Nelson, 109
Rohde, David, 284
Roosevelt, Franklin D., 50
Rules, inherited, 40–41
Rules, standing. *See* Standing rules
Rule XXII: adoption of in 1917, 32, 337; and Anderson's motion, 73; under Byrd, 161; central to Senate syndrome, 23, 24; changing rules under, 55–56; constitutionality of, 248–49; direct attack on, November 2013, 251; effect of, 4; importance of to both parties, 288; and pro-reform majority (1975), 109, 365nn11–12; provision of, 314; and reform efforts, 51–52; revisions to, 54; and Senate efforts to circumvent, 333, 354; unanimous consent byproduct of, 335; and Vandenberg's ruling, 52–53, 363n1. *See also* 1975 reform; Reform-by-ruling, implications of
Russell, Richard, 144; and cloture opposition as fundamental principle, 58; death of, 97; leader of southern Democrats, 53, 92; and opposition to television, 144; point of order overruled by Nixon, 70–71; Rule XXII reform blocked by (1953), 54–55

Saltonstal, Leverett, 72
Sanders, Bernie, 253
Sanders, Newell, 28
Sarbanes, Paul, 105, 132, 133
Schatz, Brian, 211, 340
Schumer, Charles, 185, 242, 244, 247
Scott, Hugh, 87, 97
Senate, compared to the House, 336–38; continuity of rules important to Senate, 338; majority party and Senate presiding officer may differ, 337; Senate rejection of House model, 336–38; and status of rules at start of new Congress, 337–38; terms of office differ, 338
Senate parties, accountability of, 310–11
Senate Rule V, 313–14
Senate syndrome: overview, 15–17; choosing rules, 22–24; grappling with Senate syndrome, 5–9; modern Senate, emergence of, 24–29; organization of book, 9–14; defined, 17–19; veto players in American governance, 3–5
Senate syndrome and reform. *See entries beginning with* Reform

Senate workload. *See* Workload of Senate
Senatorial courtesy, 256, 263
Senators as problem, 39–40; and changes in American polity, 270–71; claim that stronger leadership would curtail partisanship, 272–73; and groups influencing nominations, 272–73; and senatorial behavior, 34, 39–40
Seniority system, 64–65
Shaheen, Jeanne, 340
Shelby, Richard, 229
Side-by-side amendments, 175–77, 367n3
Silent filibuster, 252, 344
Simple-majority cloture: and Frist strategy, 200; and Johnson, 76; mixed feelings among senators on, 93, 243, 341, 345; and Reid, 244; and Senate majority support for, 336, 340; and Truman, 52; and Udall amendment, 345; and use of points of order to achieve, 141. *See also* Supermajority cloture
Simpson, Alan, 285
Sinclair, Barbara, 281–82
"60-vote Senate," 5
60-vote thresholds, 221–27, 312; common procedure since 2007, 225, 370n3; and Franken's seating in mid-2009, 226; Frist's use of, 222–23; origin of uncertain, 222; and Reid's struggle with 51-seat majority, 223–24; and unanimous consent agreements, 221, 226–27, 370n2
Snow, Olympia, 211
Southern restraint, end of, 96–99
Southern senators, number of (1951–2010), 79
Specter, Arlen, 201, 220
Standing rules: choosing, 22–24; inherited, 40–41; and majority/minority rights, 23–24, 30; number of, 22; Rule V, 333, 355–56; Rule VIII, 152; Rule XII(4), 28–29; Rule XIV, 70–71; Rule XVI(4), 138; Rule XXII(2), 26; Rule XXV, 70–71. *See also* Rule XXII
Statutory procedures, justification for, 346–48
Stevens, Ted, 132–33, 223
Stevenson, Adlai I., 159
Supermajority cloture: and Byrd, 160; and caution on changing, 333–34; challenges to, 70; constitutionality of, 248, 340; and gridlock, 169; and Harkin proposal, 340; and leverage of individual senator, 335; minority obstruction enabled by, 40; and party of president, 336; and Republicans, 288, 332; and Senate majorities, 355. *See also* Simple-majority cloture

Taft, Robert, 54
Tea Party movement, emergence of (2009), 211
Television resolution, 144–46, 367nn8–9
Tennessee Valley Authority, 57
Theriault, Sean, 284

Thurmond, Strom, 71, 74, 238–40
Thurmond Rule, 238–40, 250, 327
Tiefer, Charles, 325, 343, 372n3
Time: as common pool resource, 88–89; as precious resource for Senate majority leader, 161, 339
Time constraints, 31, 32, 35, 38, 187
Time limitation agreements, 60, 61, *62–63*
Tracking, 32, 99
Tracking and holds, 99–101
Truman, Harry, 52–53
Tuition tax-credit debate (1978), 125–29, 150
2005 judicial nominations crisis and nuclear option: advice and consent clause of Constitution invoked by Frist, 199, 215, 332, 333, 342, 346; costs imposed by minority on majority shown in, 339; and Democratic obstruction of judicial nominations, 213; and Frist's nuclear option proposal, 213–14; and Frist's plan of action, 217; and Levin's response to Frist's plan, 216; proposals for pool of candidates rejected, 217; and situation diffused by Gang of 14, 218, 339. *See also* 2005 nuclear option episode revisited
2005 nuclear option episode revisited, 343–46; and Gang of 14, 343–44, 345–46, 372n4; as short-term victory for Frist, 343; and Thurmond Rule invoked, 343–44. *See also* Partisanship, deepening (2005–2013)
2013 nuclear option episode revisited, 346–47; and 51 votes for majority, 346; and Reid threatened nuclear option on executive nominations, 346; and threat of minority retaliation, 347

Udall, Tom, 252, 259; and reform package (2011), 243; reform package endorsed by Reid, 244; simple-majority proposals presented by, 344–45
Udall-Merkley-Harkin resolution, 243, 252, 347
Unanimous consent agreements: Byrd's use of, 123–24; customization of, 91; and germaneness requirement, 89–91; under Johnson's leadership, 60–61; as orders of Senate in 1914, 27–29; provisions of (1935–2000), *62–63*; Senate's heavy reliance on, 335; and 60-vote threshold, 221, 226–27, 370n2; and tuition tax credit debate (1978), 124–29; unlimited debate and, 4
U.S. Chamber of Commerce, *310*

Vandenberg, Arthur, 52–53, 216, 363n1
Veto player, defined, 3–4
Vietnam War, 96, 107
Vote-a-ramas, 193, 194, 220, 369n21
Voter registration issue, 96

Voting Rights Act of 1965, 49, 92, 157

Warner, John, 217
Washington, George, 159
Watkins, Charles, 156–57
Webb, Jim, 224
Weicker, Lowell, 147
White, William S., 49
Wilkins, Robert, 257
Wilson, Woodrow, 26
Workload of Senate: associated time constraints, 38–39, 270; expansion in late twentieth century, 88, 97, 123; indicators of (1961–2010), *38*
Wright, Jim, 87, 165
Wyden, Ron, 188